# Making Human Rights a Reality

# Making Human Rights a Reality

*Emilie M. Hafner-Burton*

PRINCETON UNIVERSITY PRESS

Princeton and Oxford

Copyright © 2013 by Princeton University Press
Requests for permission to reproduce material from this work should be
  sent to Permissions, Princeton University Press
Published by Princeton University Press, 41 William Street,
  Princeton, New Jersey 08540
In the United Kingdom: Princeton University Press, 6 Oxford Street,
  Woodstock, Oxfordshire OX20 1TW

press.princeton.edu

Library of Congress Cataloging-in-Publication Data

Hafner-Burton, Emilie.
  Making human rights a reality / Emilie M. Hafner-Burton.
    pages cm
  Includes index.
  ISBN 978-0-691-15535-7 (hardcover : alk. paper) — ISBN 978-0-691-15536-4
(pbk. : alk. paper)    1. Human rights.    I. Title.
  JC571.H25 2013
  323—dc23
                                                              2012041049

British Library Cataloging-in-Publication Data is available

This book has been composed in Sabon.

Printed on acid-free paper.

Printed in the United States of America

10 9 8 7 6 5 4 3 2 1

For Eero and Apple

# Contents

# Preface

Two decades ago, I worked in the blacksmithing industry. I had a college degree under my belt—with concentrations in political science, philosophy, and women's studies. And I was apprenticing with artists who taught me the trade of blacksmithing. Then I took a hiatus that changed my life.

I won a fellowship, moved to Geneva, Switzerland, and started working for an international nongovernmental organization dedicated to the promotion of human rights and disarmament. That job, and another that followed, put me inside the United Nations. There, I experienced first-hand how international laws are made and managed through a sprawling bureaucracy involving different—often-mismatched—interests, competences, and intentions. I witnessed the potential of international cooperation. I also witnessed the power of governments and individuals to stymie it. I saw the hair-pulling frustrations of paperwork, official procedures, red tape, and ceaseless committee meetings. And I saw the powerlessness of many advocacy organizations to have much direct impact on this system. I left. I am still grateful for this experience, which set me on the path I'm on today and motivated this book.

Now I am a political scientist, university professor, and codirector of the Laboratory on International Law and Regulation.[1] Our mission at this laboratory is social science research to explore when and why international laws actually work. We aim to craft more effective solutions to global problems, such as the persistence of human rights violations that contribute to the suffering of millions of people. I write and teach courses on international law, human rights, political economy, public policy, and other topics.

This book has been many years in the making. It's based on a great deal of research—some that I've conducted, and much more by other scholars in a lot of fields, including anthropology, criminology, history, law, political science, psychology, and sociology. It represents my thinking after nearly two decades of experience and investigation about the problem of human rights as well as the efficacy of the international legal and foreign policy systems created in response.

One reason it's taken so long to write this book is that I've come to realize that human rights scholarship can't fit neatly into any single field. Research (including my own) that concerns human rights tends to be specialized, focused on the debates and methods that are germane to a particular academic discipline. That's understandable because it's impossible to be an expert in all subjects. But it's also a hurdle to understanding the problem of human rights and crafting solutions, which don't fit neatly in our academic boxes.

I built my case in this book from the field I know best: political science. But each step in my argument led me to new fields of scholarship. I needed to learn more about the psychology and the behavior of perpetrators, the laws we've created to rein them in and how they actually work, and foreign policy and institutional reform. Those needs led me to discover entire literatures that I'd never encountered before. After years of search and discovery, I'm still an interloper in these other fields; no doubt experts in these other fields will see many gaps in my impressions. But that is the nature of interdisciplinary scholarship on real world problems. Along the way, I've learned a lot about human rights; each new discipline and literature has taught me something invaluable.

The other reason it's taken so long to publish this book is that my arguments do not sit comfortably with many people—especially people on the front lines of protecting human rights—and that's made me uncomfortable. My goal is to convey a vision for how to reduce human suffering. As I pursued that aim, I wanted to be as careful and courteous to my critics as I could. I've taken their concerns seriously while remaining steadfast to my own evolving convictions.

Some characterize me as too pessimistic, and believe that I'm mistaken in my depictions of how the international legal system is malfunctioning. Many of these critics are lawyers, and they see more effect of international law than I think the evidence merits. Others, though, portray me as too optimistic, and are critical of the argument I will make: that a few governments (what I call "stewards") have the power to advance human rights around the world. Those stewards, I suggest, can also play a pivotal role in making international human rights law more effective. I see myself walking a fine line between these impressions: I am both profoundly skeptical about the global reach of the law to protect human rights and optimistic about a future where law, in tandem with state power, could advance human rights. I surely won't convince all my critics, though I've made sincere efforts to deliberate over their apprehensions. Finding that balance has taken a long time and taught me a lot.

I wrote this book for a broad audience. It includes scholars (and their students) from many disciplines as well as policymakers, human rights promoters, and others who are interested in human rights, international law, or state power. For clarity and simplicity, I have relegated most of the details that are such an essential part of serious scholarship to the notes.

Of course, I did not create this book alone. It draws from over a dozen articles (and another book) that I've written over the past decade. I had a tremendous amount of help all along the way, from people involved years ago in my dissertation research, to my colleagues and mentors since, many commentators and critics in the scholarly and practitioner communities that have weighed in on my work, and an army of fabulous research assistants, contributors, and collaborators. I'm especially grateful to David Cingranelli, Wade Cole, Peter Cowhey, Christian Davenport, Dan Drezner, Lynn Eden, James Fearon, Martha Finnemore, Charles Franklin, Stephanie Giry, Oona Hathaway, Darren Hawkins, Stephan Haggard, Roger Hayden, Susan Hyde, Miles Kahler, Robert Keohane, David Lake, Edward Mansfield, Lisa Martin, Walter Mattli, John Meyer, Helen Milner, Cindy Milstein, Christine Min Wotipka, Alex Montgomery, Andrew Moravcsik, Eric Neumayer, Jon Pevehouse, Stephen Poe, Mark Pollack, Tonya Putnam, Francisco Ramirez, Kal Raustiala, James Ron, Peter Rosendorff, Kenneth Roth, Kathryn Sikkink, Beth Simmons, Anne-Marie Slaughter, Jeffrey Staton, Oskar N. T. Thoms, Kiyoteru Tsutsui, Leslie Vinjamuri, Erik Voeten, Jana von Stein, and James Vreeland for their input on my work at various stages. I appreciate all their support, including the criticisms I've received.

A lot of research support has made this book possible. I'm especially indebted to the Bobst Center for Peace and Justice at Princeton University, the Center for International Security and Cooperation at Stanford University, the Center on Democracy, Development, and the Rule of Law at Stanford University, the Dean of Faculty at Princeton University, the Laboratory on International Law and Regulation at the University of California, San Diego, the MacArthur Consortium, the National Science Foundation, the Niehaus Center for Globalization and Governance at Princeton University, and Nuffield College at Oxford University.

Finally, I give a special thanks to my colleagues Larry Helfer and Jack Snyder for their focused intellectual guidance on this manuscript, to my editor at Princeton, Chuck Myers, for his continued support and direction, and to some of my students, Jonathan Chu, Catherine Daly, Elaine Denny, Joseph Drapalski, Kristy Pathakis, Linda Wong, and most especially, Hallie Stohler, for their invaluable assistance, teamwork, and inspiration. Most of all, I offer gratitude to David G. Victor, my editor, collaborator, and supporter.

# Research

The following original research by the author has contributed to this book:

Hafner-Burton, Emilie M. "Right or Robust? The Sensitive Nature of Political Repression in an Era of Globalization." *Journal of Peace Research* 42, no. 6 (2005): 679–98.

———. "Trading Human Rights: How Preferential Trade Agreements Influence Government Repression." *International Organization* 59, no. 3 (2005): 593–629.

———. "Sticks and Stones: Naming and Shaming the Human Rights Enforcement Problem." *International Organization* 62, no. 4 (October 2008): 689–716.

———. *Forced to Be Good: Why Trade Agreements Boost Human Rights*. Ithaca, NY: Cornell University Press, 2009.

———. "The Power Politics of Regime Complexity: Human Rights Conditionality in Europe." *Perspectives on Politics* 7, no. 1 (March 2009): 33–38.

———. "International Human Rights Regimes." *Annual Review of Political Science* 15 (2012): 265–86.

Hafner-Burton, Emilie M., Laurence R. Helfer, and Christopher J. Farris. "Emergency and Escape: Explaining Derogations from Human Rights Treaties." *International Organization* 65, no. 4 (Fall 2011): 673–707.

Hafner-Burton, Emilie M., Miles Kahler, and Alexander H. Montgomery. "Network Analysis for International Relations." *International Organization* 63 (Spring 2009): 559–92.

Hafner-Burton, Emilie M., and Mark A. Pollack. "Mainstreaming Gender in Global Governance." *European Journal of International Relations* 8, no. 3 (September 2002): 339–73.

Hafner-Burton, Emilie M., and James Ron. "Preventing Human Rights Abuse." *Journal of Peace Research* 44, no. 4 (2007): 379–83.

———. "Seeing Double: Human Rights Impact through Qualitative and Quantitative Eyes." *World Politics* 61, no. 2 (2009): 360–401.

———. "The Latin Bias: Regions, the Western Media, and Human Rights Coverage, 1981–2000." *International Studies Quarterly* (2013).

Hafner-Burton, Emilie M., and Jacob Shapiro. "Tortured Relations: Human Rights Abuses and Counterterrorism Cooperation." *PS: Political Science and Policy* 43 (2010): 415–19.

Hafner-Burton, Emilie M., and Kiyoteru Tsutsui. "Human Rights Practices in a Globalizing World: The Paradox of Empty Promises." *American Journal of Sociology* 110, no. 5 (2005): 1373–411.

———. "Justice Lost! The Failure of International Human Rights Law to Matter Where Needed Most." *Journal of Peace Research* 44, no. 4 (2007): 407–25.

Hafner-Burton, Emilie M., Kiyoteru Tsutsui, and John Meyer. "International Human Rights Law and the Politics of Legitimacy: Repressive States and Human Rights Treaties." *International Sociology* 23, no. 1 (2008): 115–41.

Hafner-Burton, Emilie M., David Victor, and Yonatan Lupu. "International Relations for International Law." *American Journal of International Law* (2012).

Hafner-Burton, Emilie M., Susan D. Hyde, and Ryan S. Jablonski, "When Governments Use Election Violence to Stay in Power." *British Journal of Political Science* (2013).

———. "Surviving Elections: Election Violence and Leader Tenure," December 14, 2011, http://papers.ssrn.com/sol3/papers.cfm?abstract_id=1975026 (accessed May 10, 2012).

# Introduction

This book concerns the promotion and protection of human rights. Human rights are basic rights and freedoms to which all people are entitled regardless of nationality, sex, ethnic origin, race, religion, language, or other status.[1] They are moral assurances and prerequisites to human well-being. Many laws provide for them—from rights to life, liberty, and personal security, to education, peaceful assembly, opinion, and expression. Those assurances are for everyone: the principle of universality is the cornerstone of international human rights law. Human rights are indivisible: we aren't supposed to pick and choose among them.

Of course, universal assurances don't automatically translate into human rights protection for everyone. Governments and their envoys deprive millions of people of their rights. Many abusers get away with impunity. There are no easy ways to change these realities. Massive resources are spent on an international human rights legal system that has made great strides in articulating universal norms it alone can't implement. Some governments try to help by adopting supportive foreign policies, but their efforts can't stop abuse everywhere. These hard facts pose a challenge for protecting human rights in a world already dense with international legal norms, obligations, procedures, and advocates. Why do human rights violations endure despite the expansion of global efforts at human rights promotion?

I believe that human rights values are essential to all humanity. The rights enumerated in the Universal Declaration of Human Rights are fundamental—although to have more practical impact, international law must become more relevant in local practices. Like almost everyone who studies and works inside the international human rights legal system, I think reforms are needed to increase both the legitimacy and deterrence capacity of the system; both are essential if the system is to become more effective. Nonetheless, what's clear is that the legal system already articulates a wide array of rights. Articulation alone has value.

Yet human rights promotion can become more pragmatic. Rather than investing in the ever-expanding lists of members, obligations, and procedures of the international human rights legal system, what's needed is a more strategic effort to make the most important, existing aspirations a lot more effective in practice. That entails a turn away from universalism.

This book grapples with a fundamental tension in the international human rights legal system: it is both a successful articulator of global norms and yet also a gridlocked promoter, almost powerless to put its own aspirations into practice. Over more than six decades the architects of this system have made a series of decisions—to allow any country, regardless of performance, to participate in the development of an ever-growing list of rights that the system aims to promote and protect with a long list of procedures—that have led to gridlock. Today's system faces a crisis of legitimacy and relevance because it is packed with countries that have no intention (or ability) to honor its norms. The international legal system has an observable impact on only a slice of countries. For all the rest, bold international human rights norms don't appear to get traction. Moving beyond this stalemate—to an international human rights legal system that works better—requires choices that are difficult to discuss and implement.

This book is about the politics of implementing human rights laws and norms. At the center of my investigation are states—the motivations that drive abusing governments as well as those that inspire the "stewards" to use their power to advance human rights. What unfolds is a political strategy that puts consequences at the center of human rights steward-ship. This strategy values legal norms but hinges on evaluating actions according to what works. Law has a role to play alongside many other actions, such as threats of sanction, offers of reward, diplomacy, and many other forms of power that stewards use to promote human rights. Power plays a major role in the story that unfolds on these pages; so does legitimacy. And because power is a limited resource that can contravene legitimacy, it is crucial that governments and sympathetic nonstate actors make choices about where they can use their power with maximum effect—a process I call "triage." This strategic approach to promoting human rights will be easier to implement unilaterally and in small groups of stewards rather than in the hyperuniversal settings of the United Nations.

This is not a book "for" or "against" international law; this is a book for human rights. It's a vision of how to make law and power work in tandem: for how sober assessment of what works can lead to policies that are more effective. As a work of political science, it offers a strategy for human rights promotion that is hard nosed about what is politically sustainable and scalable.

Making Human Rights a Reality

# The Problem of Human Rights

On June 12, 2009, Iran held a presidential election whose outcome was preordained. The next day, authorities declared the incumbent president Mahmoud Ahmadinejad the winner. Protests erupted. Millions of people flooded the streets to dispute the results. The world watched while the government responded with sweeping human rights violations.

Plainclothes forces attacked a Tehran University dormitory and reportedly killed student protesters.[1] The government banned foreign journalists from the streets after arresting almost one hundred people, including former government ministers and senior political figures.[2] Among the casualties was Neda Agha, a young bystander killed by riot police who became an icon for the antigovernment movement. Protests continued and the government responded with more violence. Thousands would be arrested over the next few months as the death toll mounted.

Undeterred, President Ahmadinejad was sworn into office for a new term in August. Meanwhile, show trials began against detainees, many allegedly coerced into falsely confessing that they had participated in a foreign-backed attempt to overthrow the government. Security officials shut down the offices of a committee that collected information about torture and other abuses against protesters and detainees. Journalist Ali Reza Eshranghi was sent to prison, followed by scholar Kian Tajbakhsh and other prominent intellectuals, political figures, and journalists.[3] Many were sentenced to death; some have been executed.[4]

By law, none of this should have happened. International customary law prohibits extrajudicial killing and torture.[5] And since 1975, Iran has been a party to the UN International Covenant on Civil and Political Rights, a global treaty that prohibits torture as well as cruel, inhuman, or degrading treatment or punishment. The treaty requires fair public hearings by competent, independent, and impartial tribunals established by law. It also mandates that everyone have the right of peaceful assembly.

Iran is not alone, of course. Most governments swear to pursue, promote, and protect human rights. They make legally binding promises, which they break when convenient.

While the data aren't perfect, organizations have been building records of human rights abuses.[6] Figure 1 summarizes what they show worldwide since the 1970s for a wide array of abuses—murder, torture, political imprisonment, and forced disappearances along with other violations of political rights and civil liberties, including censorship and the suppression of political association as well as workers' rights. The dotted lines depict the total number of countries that have ratified the principal treaty outlawing these crimes, the International Covenant on Civil and Political Rights, thought to be one of the most effective international legal instruments for protecting human rights.[7] The striped boxes show every year that a number of those countries, despite belonging to this treaty, were alleged by credible sources to engage in these prohibited acts.

There is unabashedly good news in one category—disappearances are declining from their peak two decades ago. That effect stems mainly from democratization in Latin America, which removed from power military dictators who made a habit of disappearing their political opponents. On all the other rights shown in figure 1, the rise in global membership in this human rights treaty has run in parallel with a rise in measured abuse. Countries are good at joining treaties, but bad at honoring commitments. The same patterns are evident in other human rights treaties as well.[8] In spite of the expanding international legal system outlawing these acts, reports of human rights abuse endure.

Why do countries legally devoted to human rights on paper so often break the law? More important, what can be done to close the gap between paper and practice? This book aims to answer those questions. It looks at whether more international legal instruments and procedures would be helpful while probing the actions that states can take in tandem to the large and increasingly elaborate international human rights legal system.

Ever since the adoption of the Universal Declaration of Human Rights more than six decades ago, it has been clear that the world needs to do more to respect the human rights that are integral to life with dignity. That's not the issue. Instead, today the questions concern strategy. What's the best strategy for promoting respect for human rights?

Governments and NGOs have created a system of international law and procedures based on universal principles. Membership is growing across a wide array of international treaties and institutions.[9] That approach articulates a powerful vision for the promotion of human well-being everywhere. It already has made significant achievements. The approach has shifted the goalposts for what is acceptable and also motivated foreign policy on human rights. But for many victims of tyranny, brutality, discrimination, and deprivation, the results of that universal approach have been underwhelming. For some, the approach is alienating because the system of international norms and procedures is at odds with accepted local cultures and social practices.[10] A fresh look at how the system works—and its troubles—is overdue.

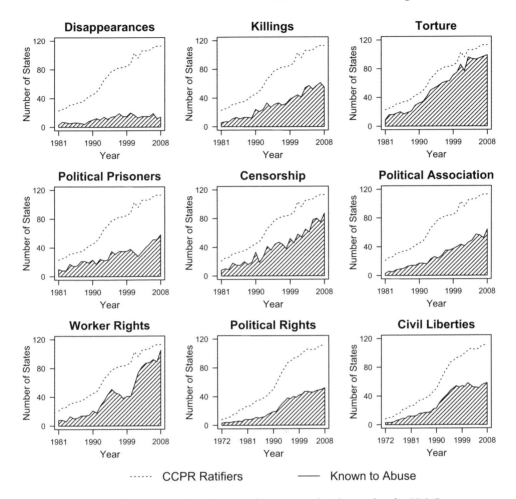

Figure 1. Ratifications and violations of 9 protected rights under the UN Covenant on Civil and Political Rights (CCPR).

Understandably, a sober appraisal of the human rights promotion system is not a popular activity. Legal scholar Makau Mutua ventures an explanation for why this is so. Until recently, he suggests, "human rights scholars and activists have been reluctant to ask uncomfortable questions about the philosophy and political purposes of the human rights movement. Such questions are often taken as a mark of disloyalty to the movement, or an attempt to provide cover and comfort to those states that would violate its norms. . . . The result is a paucity of good critiques about one of the most powerful ideologies of modern times."[11]

Given how much is at stake, critical evaluations of efforts to promote human rights are essential. Improving human rights requires a clinical assessment of why people commit human rights abuses. It demands assessments of when the international human rights system functions well and when it falls short. Analysis is also needed of the many ways, in addition to legal instruments, that states can promote human rights effectively. No single field has all the answers.[12] I look to research in anthropology, criminology, economics, history, law, political science, psychology, and sociology—along with a large dose of practical insight from the people in the field who work to promote human rights. Bringing all those insights to bear on the human rights challenge is the goal of this book. Along the way, I hope to help these different communities learn about work in other fields. I aim as well to offer a strategy for stewardship that could be influential in making human rights more of a reality.

## The Argument in Brief

While this is a large book that examines a wide array of human rights issues and examples, I make three central arguments.

First, the evidence and analysis I present here suggest that the current system of international human rights law corresponds well with protecting human rights only in special circumstances—generally in the settings where the worst human rights abuses are least likely to occur. Despite that evidence, much of today's policy efforts focus on creating more international treaties and implementation procedures as well as expanding the number of countries that sign and ratify those agreements. I will assert the opposite.

People obey laws when the rules coincide with how they would act without the laws in place (coincidence), when they fear punishment or other consequences for lawbreaking (coercion), or when they come to believe laws have legitimate authority and value (persuasion).[13] For all these reasons, international legal principles factor into the calculus of abuse in a number of settings that are ideally suited for international law to work; examples fill the pages of this book. But the biggest abuses arise in contexts where the incentives for protection are weak and the international legal system probably can't have much immediate impact.

My first contention is that the tendency to swell the list of countries that are members of international human rights agreements along with the list of rights themselves makes the bureaucratic challenge of promoting rights harder to solve. That is because it is difficult to enforce the law by threatening punishments alone—there isn't enough coercive capacity to deter every act of defiance. Authorities also need a lot of willing compliance—because laws coincide with what countries will do anyway or because societies have been persuaded that laws are legitimate.[14] More laws and members erode legitimacy if they lead to lower levels of compliance. Lower compliance makes it hard for abusing countries as well as the many different actors in the international human rights system to know which laws they should take seriously. Reforms to the international human rights legal system should dampen its tendency to swell in size and ambition while refocusing efforts on better protection of core rights. The system needs reform and legitimacy before expansion.

Second, solutions require relying heavily on the actors that can have the largest impact on patterns of abuse. States are at the center of this problem and the solution. I focus especially on the countries that have a strong national interest in advancing human rights abroad: the steward states.[15] Stewardship is not an entitlement; rather, it's a description of a foreign policy decision that any state can make to promote human rights in another country. Stewards tend to have pretty good human rights records at home and also face public pressure to advance human rights overseas. They are the government engines of international human rights promotion, and with the correct strategy they can do a lot more. Steward states can give perpetrators of abuse a reason to act differently even when legal procedures don't have much influence on their reasoning. The evidence presented in this book will show that the international human rights legal system is associated with significant improvements in human rights mainly in a narrow subset of countries. For the rest, including countries where the most severe abuses take place, laws need backing with power. That's where the steward states are so vital—by deploying their power and other resources to advance human rights in the settings where international law, on its own, won't have much impact. Over time, these efforts fail unless they build legitimacy and help persuade perpetrators that respecting human dignity is appropriate and not just cost-effective.[16]

To be successful, steward states must also be aware of the many limitations and risks as they wield power around the globe. Foreign pressures won't have much impact on human rights inside countries unless foreign policies are "localized," by which I mean vetted, translated, and supported by local "norm entrepreneurs."[17] Those entrepreneurs, intermediaries between locals and foreign actors, can tailor outside pressure so it is more legitimate and effective in the local setting. Successful stewardship requires working with NGOs and national human rights institutions (NHRIs) over sustained periods. Done well, which is not easy, this approach can lend power to the service of international law so that both law and power work in tandem.

Third, stewards can become more strategic in how they allocate their resources. Human rights promotion is costly, and the needed resources don't grow on trees. Scarcity demands priorities, and the setting of priorities requires assessing the consequences of alternative strategies. Human rights promotion calls for hard choices about which promotion efforts actually work, rather than relying on aspiration, publicity, or public outcry. What's needed is a decision-making process of triage.[18] Like the brutal medical process of triaging battlefield wounds, it requires concentrating resources where actors can make a difference. Making triage effective requires collecting the data needed for the careful and constant reassessment of priorities.

The stakes are high. As UN secretary-general Kofi Annan once said, "We will not enjoy security without development, we will not enjoy development without security, and we will not enjoy either without respect for human rights."[19] He was right. What's needed is a strategy that links that aspiration to the clinical data and practical experience about what really protects human rights.

## Step by Step through the Book

The challenges in human rights promotion are many and complex. I start by looking at what's known about why people (notably leaders of governments and their envoys) commit abuses. That's part I, and it's important because instruments for promoting human rights won't work well unless they are based on knowledge of why people commit abuses and the social contexts that encourage abuse.

In part II, I look at the international human rights legal system that has emerged over the last six decades. That system both declares a growing number of rights and aims to hold governments (and sometimes individuals) accountable. One of my chief concerns about that system is that it has led to an explosion of rights and procedures without eliciting much compliance from states. One of the chief challenges for more effective rights promotion is to slow the swelling; doing that requires understanding why legalization of rights has exploded in the first place.

Part III examines what governments themselves are doing to advance human rights abroad. It is fashionable today to look beyond governments to other actors, notably nongovernmental organizations, that promote human rights. Those many nongovernmental actors are important, but governments are essential. In part III, I especially focus on the governments that have proved most crucial in backing human rights when the international legal system, on its own, can't elicit compliance with the law. These steward states all use their power and other resources to advance human rights overseas. Key to the better deployment of that power is localization and triage of scarce resources.

## Part I: The Calculus of Abuse

The ultimate goal of this book is to understand when and how international law and state power can protect human rights. For scholars, those questions are important because the broad field of human rights is one of the most heavily legalized areas of international relations. For practitioners this is significant because human rights abuses are pervasive and more effective policy strategies are needed. Choosing better policies requires understanding, first, the many, complex, and often-veiled motivations for acts of abuse. That is the task of part I, which brings together insights from criminology and psychology on why people (as individuals or working in groups) commit crimes and other deviant acts. It also examines research in political science and sociology that has revealed the many different contexts that can encourage abusive behavior.

The central idea in this part of the book is that human rights abuses are not the work of socially or mentally abnormal madmen (or madwomen) who can't control themselves, although mental illness and other factors do play roles at times. Instead, abusers are normally ordinary people responding to the incentives and opportunities in their environment. Abuse is abhorrent, but it's typically a calculated act. It reflects deliberate and seemingly reasonable (in the eyes of abusers) calculations of the benefits and costs. Abuse is a gamble that its perpetrators think is worthwhile given the stakes. Once under way, reinforcing factors—such as rationalizations and group incentives—make it hard to stop. This perspective on abuse suggests that the task for law and other policy instruments examined later in this book is to make violators of human rights redo the calculus that guides their behavior.

For students of international law and international relations—like myself—much of the research surveyed in this part of the book will be new. I consider the research from two perspectives.

First, chapter 2 looks at the contexts that lead to abuse. There are some settings that all but guarantee large human rights abuses. Those include pervasive conflict, such as full-blown civil war, where the incentives working on leaders and rebels are short term in nature, and most formal governing institutions have broken down. Illiberal rule is another context that is ripe for abuses since illiberal rulers are not, by definition, broadly accountable to the public. Government institutions that generally are the most ardent defenders of human rights—such as courts and ombudsmen—can't operate independently of the elites who control government. These contexts are major catalysts for abuse, yet extremely difficult to manipulate. Chapter 2 focuses on six contexts that are particularly worrisome.

Chapter 3 looks more closely at individuals and the choices they make. It explores the rationales that allow people to justify their behavior.

Usually abusers are not biologically or psychologically abnormal people when they start up. They do what they do because they believe—rightly or wrongly—they will gain something: power or support, a victory over their rivals, information, money, resources, a job, a sense of superiority or satisfaction for following orders, control, or respect. With a sense of the benefits and risks in mind, perpetrators make choices that, to them, appear practical, rational, lawful, and even morally justifiable.[20] The institutions in which abusers are embedded often reinforce such rationales. Abuse usually involves many people, actions, and institutions; it's not a particular problem created by one rogue person, act, or situation. It can, says sociologist of crime Joachim Savelsberg, "involve collective action, with front-line, low-level actors who executed the dirty work as well as leaders whose hands remain untainted by the blood for the shedding of which they bear ultimate responsibility."[21] He was speaking about mass atrocities like genocide. But child labor, discrimination, censorship, tyranny, and election fraud also find their roots reinforced by institutions. Many diverse actors, each responding to local incentives, reinforce such behavior. They convince themselves and their peers that their actions—some of them crimes under law—are acceptable. Stopping the behavior requires disrupting an entire network of group conduct, which is quite a challenge.

## Part II: International Law

The most visible response to the problem of abuse has been efforts to create and spread norms through a growing system of international laws and procedures. Part II considers that international human rights legal system, its practical impact on human suffering, and the many ways that system could undergo reform.

On December 10, 1948, the UN General Assembly proclaimed the Universal Declaration of Human Rights. It endorsed this statement, which at the time was widely seen as radical: "All human beings are born free and equal in dignity and rights." It vowed to protect the "equal and inalienable rights of all members of the human family" by entitling every person "to all the rights and freedoms set forth in this Declaration, without distinction of any kind."[22]

Since that day, the international community has built a vast network of legal instruments designed to turn these universal goals into practical reality. At the core of this system is a body of fundamental principles of international law ("compelling law") that apply universally to all states and are nonderogable (meaning there is no lawful excuse to violate those norms). This canon of compelling law includes norms on genocide, slavery, and torture.[23] Other treaties establish other norms, such as criminalizing acts of torture or protecting economic, social, and cultural rights. Some focus on certain groups of people, such as women, migrants, and the disabled. Chapter 4 looks at the origins and operation of this system at the global level (under the auspices of the United Nations) as well as in the three regions of Europe, the Americas, and Africa. (There is not yet any meaningful regional human rights legal system in Asia or the Middle East.)

The growth of this system is seen as evidence that the values associated with the promotion of universal human rights and government account-ability are spreading.[24] Indeed, every government has made promises to uphold at least some aspects of the system. There are certainly holdouts—the United States has not ratified the UN treaties outlawing discrimina-tion against women or protecting children, for example. (Despite that, the US record in this area is strong.) Most countries have ratified most of the highly visible international human rights treaties, such as those protect-ing civil and political rights along with economic, social, and cultural rights, eliminating discrimination against women and protecting chil-dren. Many have also joined treaties that protect racial minorities as well as outlaw torture and other cruel, inhuman, or degrading treatment or punishment, the death penalty, the use of children in armed conflict, the sale of children, child prostitution, and child pornography. Others have promised to protect the rights of migrant workers and their families and prohibit genocide. The overwhelming majority has ratified multiple trea-ties, which create legal obligations for them and give concrete expression to universality.[25]

One hole in this system is enforcement, since there is no global police force or criminal justice system to put these laws into effect. Chapter 4 surveys the international human rights legal system and considers some of the many efforts to fill the enforcement hole. In a few jurisdictions, notably in Africa, the Americas, and Europe, there are special regional human rights courts with some enforcement powers. The European Court of Human Rights and the Inter-American Court of Human Rights are examples. Since 2002, the International Criminal Court (ICC), a per-manent tribunal, has been empowered to prosecute genocide, war crimes, and crimes against humanity committed not only by representatives of the treaty's participants but also by other governments, like Sudan, that never agreed to participate.

Viewed in totality, the emergence of this system is an extraordinary accomplishment. Chapter 4 also explores how scholars and practitioners think the system is supposed to function. For some, international law works through coercion by focusing incentives to reward good behavior and punish deviations. For others the law is about persuasion and the creation of shared understandings, trust, fairness, and legitimacy. Persua-sion can encourage compliance if people follow the rules willingly out of a conviction that the law is valuable. Later chapters revisit these two perspectives—coercion and persuasion—since they help reveal exactly how international legal mechanisms and other forces can alter the calculus of abuse I describe in part I.

According to many observers, making this system more effective requires more international principles, courts, treaties, and procedures that could strengthen the nets of legal protection and accountability. This mission drives activism, policy, and research, especially in the West; it is also a guiding principle inside the bureaucracies of the international organizations that manage the growing human rights system. According to this perspective, called "global legalism," one of the central goals of human rights promotion is creating stronger international legal norms and extending legal coverage to more—ideally all—nations and peoples for all manner of rights.[26] A key feature of global legalism is an open-door policy: just about any country can participate.

The many and varied advocates of global legalism fully understand that legal obligations alone will never stop all abuses. They seem convinced, however, that expanding the scope and membership of international law is an essential step in the right direction. Indeed, international institutions are already responding to this demand. The General Assembly of the Organization of American States (OAS) has drafted new treaties against racism, discrimination, and intolerance, and also for the protection of the rights of indigenous peoples.[27] The United Nations has also drafted new treaties protecting all people from enforced disappearance and promoting the rights of persons with disabilities.[28] Still other new agreements are in the works, too.[29]

Whether expanding an open-door international human rights legal system should be the core of a strategy for advancing human rights depends, in part, on whether the existing system is actually working—that is, whether human rights are improving. It's hard to make a definitive assessment, but chapters 5 and 6 scrutinize what is known from two major perspectives.

Chapter 5 examines the scholarly research—especially the systematic studies that utilize global historical statistics and hunt for associations between international legal agreements and actual changes in the protection of human rights. Research using such methods has the advantage that it doesn't cherry-pick sensational examples of success or failure. Instead, it is clinical in its effort to examine exactly which kinds of international treaties, courts, and other legal institutions have had some relationship to actual protections for human rights. Professor Beth Simmons, for example, explains in one such study that "under some circumstances, a public international legal commitment can alter the political costs in ways that make improvements to the human condition more likely." She also observes that "governments are quite unlikely to comply with their international treaty obligations with respect to human rights if it is not in their interest to do so."[30] A wide array of studies like hers has also uncovered how (and when) treaties and international courts have an influence. Most of the research suggests that the international human rights legal system works in a lot of different ways. One way is by motivating interest groups to organize and lobby governments; other ways are through fostering dialogue, shaping elite agendas, national constitutions, and legislation, or supporting domestic litigation.

The bulk of the evidence discussed in chapter 5 shows that participation in the international human rights legal system is associated with human rights protections only in a limited number of contexts. To have much relationship to actual protections for human rights, international laws and procedures must creep into domestic affairs, be taken up by local advocates, and applied by local courts.[31] Those conditions are present mainly in reasonably developed and stable or some budding democracies. In those countries, leaders control their security forces, are constrained by their legislatures and courts, face scrutiny from a free press along with active civil societies, and care about their global image. Since the advanced democracies, for the most part, would probably protect many human rights without the presence of reinforcing international legal norms, the conclusion from the scholarship is that international legal norms probably are having an effect mostly on a subset of newly democratizing countries. That is, they are having an impact on those countries with the right conditions in place to be influenced by international law, yet not already sure to internalize international legal norms on their own. Outside that group, the effect of international law on actual protections for human rights is probably small compared with other factors that international law doesn't much influence, such as the presence of war, an organized domestic political opposition, and institutions for accountability.

The systematic, scholarly research also reveals that despite all the efforts devoted to the international human rights legal system, the people most at risk still are not getting much relief. Even in fledgling democracies, where researchers now think that international legal institutions could probably help to protect some human rights, many victims go unaided by the law. And outside this group of countries is a large group where autocrats rule over cloistered, poor, war-torn, or unstable countries. There, millions of people suffer, and the perpetrators of human rights abuses have little to fear or learn from international law. According to professor Mark Massoud, "[International] law is not enough—and is potentially dangerous—in the insecure and impoverished areas where the international aid community has been encouraging it to flourish."[32] While most of the research pointing to this finding comes from scholars working in political science and law, similar conclusions emerge from anthropology, sociology, and other disciplines.[33]

Systematic, statistical research is helpful, but it also has flaws. That's why chapter 6 complements the statistical insights with a second perspective: the experiences of practitioners who work inside and around the system. Those insider views—many of them from lawyers who have one foot in academia and another in the practical efforts of NGOs and international legal bodies—point to many similar findings. They see a system in which legal obligations and membership have expanded much faster than the capacity to yield practical improvements in human rights. The legal system, many of these practitioners say, has been tremendously successful at declaring universal values, yet has fallen quite short in practical implementation.

Looking across chapters 5 and 6, it is clear that the open-door approach to international law has amplified the attributes of the system that impede its ability to turn bold international legal norms into actual human rights protection. The system is open to (in fact, welcomes) chronic lawbreakers. These governments formally adopt treaties on human rights and then violate their obligations without sanction from the system because the international legal system's enforcement structures are weak. In most cases, shaming is the worst that can happen, and it often falls on deaf ears.[34] Other instruments of coercion are largely unavailable within the international legal system. Nor is persuasion that easy to mobilize because the system lacks legitimacy in the face of so much open defiance of its norms. Because its doors are open, the institutions that administer these international laws are mired in politics and bureaucratic dysfunction with many actors especially keen to avoid holding states and individuals accountable. Indeed, within the international legal mechanisms that provide oversight and accountability, the inclusion of rampant lawbreakers has led to a growing number of irresolvable cases—and defiant decision makers—that waste the system's scant resources.

These downsides of the existing system are now gaining popular attention. For instance, journalist David Rieff, also a board member of the Arms Division of Human Rights Watch, has concluded in a high-profile assessment that "the human rights movement has assumed that establishing norms will lead to a better world. But can anyone be confident that developing the 'right' norms will lead to effective enforcement? It sometimes appears as if it is extrapolating from the experience of civil rights legislation. You establish norms, and they're unpopular, but eventually people acquiesce. But what if the model is not civil rights law, but drug law, in which the norms have not led to obedience but to mockery of the law itself?"[35]

Law professor Anne F. Bayefsky sums it up: "Somewhere along the path the international legal response to the protection of human rights has lost its way. Half a century after the project of developing and adopting human rights treaties began, the ultimate goal of alleviating human suffering remains elusive."[36]

The messages from chapters 5 and 6 are sobering. From two related perspectives, the international human rights system faces deep challenges. Before looking to alternatives, perhaps a major effort at reform could make the system more influential. That's the question examined in chapter 7. People often say that reform is needed, and they may be surprised to learn in chapter 7 just how much reform has already been attempted over the years. There have been many efforts, for example, to clarify legal obligations and set more precise expectations. The result is that universal norms, obligations, and boundaries for the international human rights system are already well defined. The problem today is not the lack of collectively articulated principles; quite the contrary, some people even talk of "norm fatigue."[37] Rather, it is that the institutions designed to manage and implement those principles cannot much affect the causes of the behavior they aim to change—not directly. They can't enforce the law using only coercion and they're not very persuasive. Facing this reality, a lot of reformers call for stronger enforcement mechanisms, including courts that would oblige all governments and people to defend human rights.

Chapter 7 doesn't just survey these reforms; it also looks practically at just what kinds of reforms are achievable in the real world along with their likely impact. Already states have adopted some of those reforms, notably through the creation of the ICC, which has the authority in some places to judge crimes such as those against humanity or genocide. As of 2012, about 60 percent of the UN members had recognized the ICC's jurisdiction on paper.[38] (Some notable exceptions include the United States, a country that strongly endorses values such as the promotion of human rights, but is wary of empowering this new court to enforce them.) Of those governments that recognize the court's authority, many have ignored its guilty verdicts and never enforced its rulings. In July 2009, the entire continent of Africa refused to acknowledge the ICC's arrest warrants against Sudanese president Omar al-Bashir even though his rule has seen tens of thousands killed and the death of many more through starvation and infection.[39] Some people even fear that the court's arrest warrants make things worse—indicted leaders are more inclined to fight it out, because once a leader loses power, they are more prone to arrest and accountability. Others worry the court deters intervention by other states.[40] The validity of those fears is debatable.[41] But the experience with the ICC—a massive reform similar to the kinds of reforms that the perspective of global legalism envisions for the future of the international legal system—is a reminder of the fundamental problem. A system that is universal in scope has some of the biggest abusers as formal members. Those countries in particular have strong incentives to frustrate reform agendas and undercut the efficiency of the system's procedures for making decisions.

Part II offers a baseline for just what's been achieved with international law as well as perspectives on whether those laws are working and the array of efforts at reform. Almost nobody thinks those reforms are enough, but chapter 7 suggests that they're all that is achievable. Part III outlines what else might be done by channeling state power.

## Part III: A Stewardship Strategy

Part III looks at what governments might do to fill in the many areas where international human rights law, on its own, isn't having much impact on the calculus of abuse. For better or worse, some states—including some of the most rich and powerful—are also willing to promote human rights through their foreign policy. They try to create incentives that can protect human rights. Although these incentives exist quite apart from the international human rights legal system, they can reinforce its legal norms. They can also backfire, by undermining the law, provoking resentment of universal norms, exacerbating motivations for abuse, and offending human rights stakeholders.

As with international law, experts and advocates often think that state power can get a lot more done than is likely in the real world. That is because they imagine that state power is readily available for any issue. In fact, even for the most sympathetic governments, the promotion of human rights overseas is just one of many foreign policy goals. Thus, a starting point for any evaluation of how steward states could actually better promote human rights requires looking at what they do already. That is the task of chapter 8, which discusses the punishments and rewards that steward states use as part of their foreign policy to advance human rights today. That chapter leads to two big lessons about how stewards can more effective: one concerns localization, and the other is about setting priorities.

One lesson from chapter 8 is that stewards could have a much bigger impact overseas if they invested more in the process of localizing their efforts at diplomacy within the countries they are actually trying to influence. Localization matters because it affects the full range of incentives that abusers ultimately face. If foreign human rights pressures are localized in national courts, for example, then abusers must fear the legal consequences of deviant action at home. Localization is also crucial to the processes of persuasion and building trust, for a well-localized strategy helps create and support interest groups within a country that advance the message of human rights promotion. It builds legitimacy and thus is a keystone for making stewards' policies more influential.

Chapters 9 and 10 look in depth at localization, and how it might work. Chapter 9 explores how engagement with nongovernmental organizations, or NGOs—such as local chapters of multinational human rights organizations and especially homegrown NGOs—can lead to localization. Chapter 10 examines localization through national human rights institutions, or NHRIs. These institutions are important because they have formal roles in public debate and the policy process as well as direct linkages to government.

The other lesson from Chapter 8 concerns priorities. Stewards frequently squander resources on efforts that are misplaced, targeted on perpetrators that will never be swayed, erratic and ephemeral rather than sustained over the long term, and generally not well informed by the underlying causes of human rights abuse. Chapter 11 offers a new approach for resource allocation. Its central message is that human rights stewardship requires difficult discussions—and also policy evaluations—that today are treated as taboo. It involves acknowledging that stewards often make choices about where they devote their scarce resources for human rights without a transparent or coherent set of guidelines. It advocates a process I call "triage" that requires investing more heavily in areas where the evidence indicates that human rights promotion is most likely to work. Chapter 11 doesn't offer detailed answers for exactly what stewards should embrace and avoid. It is a framework for each steward to make its own choices, not a formula that determines the answers.

The combination of localization and triage is a strategy that steward states can use to make their own human rights promotion more effective. That stewardship strategy, on its surface, will appear to be the antithesis of universalism in international law, for it requires making choices instead of treating all abuses as equal. It prizes effectiveness over open doors. It embraces what power can do to promote norms.

## The Road Ahead

This book is intended mainly as a hard-nosed look at the human rights situation today. It is analytical throughout and written in part to help analysts from different backgrounds understand the important, relevant debates in other fields. However, the arguments here also have some broader implications for public policy and the international order.

The concept of human rights arose mainly through the stewardship of states and NGOs that have built an elaborate system of international legal norms and procedures, and backed it, at least in some places, with their own substantial resources. It has now spread so widely that the very universalism of international human rights law poses one of the system's central challenges. What should the advocates that historically have been the main advocates for better human rights protection actually do in this circumstance? This question arises not just for human rights but also in many other areas of international cooperation where international law plays a central role, such as protection of the environment, labor, and promotion of human welfare through economic growth from trade liberalization.[42] Across such issues, the role of international law as an ordering principle faces great challenges. Global diplomatic talks on new legal agreements concerning matters as far ranging as trade, climate change, and financial coordination have ground to a halt. Making progress on such topics, I suggest in chapter 12, lies not in viewing law and power as substitutes but rather complements.

An international order that relies on law and power working in tandem won't happen automatically. It necessitates building institutions and capabilities—notably the ability of stewards to measure and assess whether their human rights promotion efforts are actually working. And it requires those stewards to invest more heavily in the frameworks needed to work together.

Critics might wonder why I put emphasis on states that are central actors in this book. After all, even the most democratic and constitutionally liberal of them can be hypocrites. They create false appearances of virtue—telling others to respect values they wittingly violate when convenient. People often make this claim about the United States, a country that advances policies that are filled with contradictions, but it's true for many other countries as well.[43] I focus on states willing to promote human rights around the world, not because they are morally upstanding or perfect advocates for human rights—they certainly are not—but because some have unique resources and personalities that give them an interest in along with influence over human rights. Their challenge is to use their power to greater effect—becoming better leaders and reducing more suffering. I put emphasis on states—not just democracies, but any state that seeks to promote human rights abroad—because international law requires the active support of states to get much done.

Still, states have their own interests, and their resources are scarce. Even the most ardent promoters of human rights face many other priorities and public pressures. We shouldn't pretend otherwise. Their efforts to spread human rights values involve motives other than altruistic compassion. No strategy that relies on governments for action can avoid risks that other matters of self-interest will intervene or that states will use their resources unwisely. These are inevitable dangers of any strategy that looks for change in a world where international law, on its own, can't achieve what's needed without the power of states.

## Conclusion

This book will articulate a strategy that is based heavily on identifying what works for actually reducing abuse of human rights.[44] That approach requires setting priorities—realistically, human rights can't be universal or indivisible in the efforts to promote and protect them. Some issues and countries will attract lots of attention; others will be impossible to manage for the resources and leverage available. Not everyone can be helped. Contending with this fact responsibly requires localization (a process for building legitimacy) and triage (a process for assessing priorities to maximize protection of human rights).

I rely heavily on steward states alongside international legal procedures because the practice of open-door universalism has made the legal system dysfunctional and less legitimate. The participation of lawbreakers is one of the most central problems in the international human rights legal system today.[45] Lawbreakers degrade the quality of international legal procedures; they clog treaty bodies with hopeless cases that squander resources to little effect, and they thwart reform. Even where efforts have been focused on making stronger enforcement mechanisms, as a practical matter many of these new structures are often hamstrung.[46] They are limited in who, what, and how they can punish.

The legal norms that are needed for promoting and protecting human rights already exist. That is a tremendous accomplishment. Creating more open-door legal procedures is not the best way to translate these bold norms into action—already these procedures have put the legal bureaucracy into gridlock. Foreign policy efforts could help translate legal norms into action, but these efforts easily are distorted. Some do more harm than good. Some undermine the spirit of the law. For law and power to work together for human rights, both need greater legitimacy. This book is a search for ways to build that legitimacy.

# PART I

# The Calculus of Abuse

This book is about how international law and state power can change the benefits and costs of protecting human rights. Before we look to law and power, however, we must understand why abuse arises in the first place and why abusive practices persist. That's the task of chapters 2 and 3. In them, I adopt the perspective that the perpetrators of human rights abuse act in ways similar to other criminals. That vantage point not only helps us understand when and how law and power might have an impact on abusive behavior—tasks taken up in other portions of this book. It also opens the door for human rights scholars and practitioners to incorporate some of the lessons from fields such as criminology. Those insights include practical lessons and techniques—such as crime avoidance, prevention, and deterrence—that could have a large impact on the patterns of human rights abuse. In addition to the important field of criminology, I also draw on insights from law, politics, sociology, and psychology.

Chapter 2 examines the context for abuse—that is, the various settings, such as pervasive civil war, that allow or even encourage abuse. Chapter 3 centers on the rationales that individuals use when committing and justifying human rights abuses—how they calculate, to the best of their knowledge, the advantages and disadvantages of abusive behavior. One insight from that chapter is that once abuse begins, perpetrators often find devices to deflect their own responsibility while convincing themselves that their behavior is acceptable. Rationales matter because they help explain why abuse, once it begins, is so persistent and difficult to reverse, as well as the role of punishments in reversing and deterring such behavior.

While my purpose here is to explore the similarities between human rights abuse and other forms of crime, obviously there are important differences. Most criminology sees the criminal and the state as separate entities. The big challenges in human rights, though, usually don't allow for such neat categories since the state apparatus frequently abets (or even commits) the crimes that degrade human rights. In criminology, much of the attention is on how to make state-based enforcement smarter and more powerful; in human rights, a central task is constraining state institutions and ensuring that the agents who perform state functions remain in line.

Two themes run throughout this part. The first is that the point in considering these broad literatures is not to excuse human rights abusers but instead to understand the calculus of human rights abuse. Criminology is a particularly rich source to draw on because it involves inquiries into so many different forces—including the influence of legal norms, psychological tendencies, and the group political, social, and cultural forces—that shape human behavior in ways closely analogous to the challenge of protecting human rights. There's a lot that human rights advocates can learn from this field.

The other theme is that the fuller picture of the root causes of criminal behavior can aid in more effective human rights promotion. That picture allows for a detailed look at how two broad mechanisms—coercion and persuasion—influence human behavior. Later in this book, I'll look at those mechanisms in more detail and link them directly to efforts to promote human rights, but first it is necessary to understand why abusers behave as they do.

# Contexts

People break laws for many reasons. The most basic is opportunity, not biology or mental illness.[1] People want something (a benefit from law-breaking) they believe they can obtain with tolerable consequences. Indeed, even seemingly ordinary or upstanding citizens may choose to break laws given the chance.[2] To be sure, some criminal behavior arises from less reasoned circumstances—on a whim, out of delusion or anger, or in response to fear. But human rights abuses usually are not so impulsive. Normally they are planned and organized, and they frequently engage networks of people and institutions—not as a single impetuous action by one person or institution, but rather as a series of decisions and actions by many interrelated participants.

The broad literatures related to criminology have devoted much attention to how the general environment in which people operate shapes their opportunities for breaking the law and deviating from other social norms.[3] Certain situations, like war or poverty, create larger incentives and more opportunities for people to abuse human rights. Certain positions, like the head of government, business, or family, give some people more power to wield. A leading criminology textbook argues that criminal behavior is learned and thus specific to a context and association with others.[4] I call such factors "contextual."

The literature that is broadly on the contexts that allow for human rights abuses does not fit in a small number of neat boxes. Instead, it covers a broad array of factors. Yet six factors connect most strongly with abuse and thus are most relevant to the study of human rights.

## Conflict and Cultures of Violence

War and other forms of systemic conflict, whether fought internationally or at home through civil war and insurgency, are perhaps the most familiar and important triggers for human rights abuses. War creates opportunities for abuse along with cycles of violence that shape people's understanding of acceptable behavior.

Somalia is but one of many examples where civil conflict and struggle for power have led to massive violations of human rights. The country has not had a permanent national government since 1991, when repressive dictator Mohamed Siad Barre fled as he lost his grip on power.[5] The political vacuum plunged Somalia into deep conflict as rival groups have vied for control. In 2009 alone, fighting resulted in the killing of thousands of innocent civilians and displaced more than one million.[6] Armed militias are so pervasive that personal quarrels and clan disputes frequently escalate into killing sprees.[7] Pervasive conflict has undermined state institutions and created strong incentives for power grabbing and revenge. To people in that situation, the benefits of abuse can seem large and immediate—guaranteeing survival—while the absence of the rule of law lowers the risks of legal prosecution.

Conflict prompts abuse of human rights for at least three reasons. First, conflict helps to legitimize abuses by making them seem justified—an unfortunate necessity for a greater good—or even noble. Waging war abroad provides leaders with goals that can rally support locally. Times of conflict also make it easier for leaders to curb freedom of speech or other human rights to secure the country or their hold on power.[8] For instance, the USA Patriot Act, passed after 9/11, provides law enforcement officials the powers to track suspected terrorists, including through the use of roving wiretaps.[9] Such factors create a local context that is open to abuse; in turn, that context can be exported to other countries. When US officials arrested terrorist suspect Maher Arrar, a Canadian engineer who was born in Syria, they sent him back to Syria where he was tortured and subjected to brutal interrogation by the government.[10] Extraordinary times, leaders tell themselves, call for extraordinary measures, including human rights abuses and infringements on personal liberty.[11]

Second, all forms of violence—perhaps especially the extreme violence of war—teach and breed cycles of aggression in a society, much like violence in a home creates cycles of violence in a family. Children who grow up in an environment of abuse, for instance, are about 30 percent more likely than others to engage in crimes as adults.[12] Similarly, societies at war are also more likely than those at peace to commit human rights abuses; cultures of violence tend to reproduce violence.[13]

Third, conflict erodes social ties while creating crisis environments and cultures. The combination of these forces—weaker social links coupled with crisis—can erode the normal social controls exerted by family, friends, and work.[14] Research on social disruptions of many different types—such as through divorce, isolation from peers, and unemployment—shows that as people become less embedded in their social networks and institutions, the likelihood of criminal behavior rises.[15]

## Illiberalism

While conflict creates many opportunities and incentives for abuse, a wide array of other contexts can yield similar outcomes that are also bad news for human rights. One is the type of government—often categorized as "liberal" or "illiberal." By and large, liberal democratic governments are better at protecting certain human rights, especially civil and political rights, than illiberal or nondemocratic ones.

Liberal democracy is a type of government that recognizes the inalienable right to human dignity. It makes the protection of human rights not merely politically desirable but also a moral and social priority that applies to all citizens.[16] Most leaders rule in countries that have no such tradition. Human rights protections and freedoms are not essential to the identity of those nations; those states' rulers pursue other priorities instead, such as accumulating resources or holding on to power through patronage to certain elites. Some see human rights abuses as a way to preserve their power and personal security. A massive centralization of unchecked power provides both motives and opportunities for the state to use its capacity to crush those in its way.[17]

Among the many examples is the situation in Myanmar (formerly known as Burma), which has been ruled by a junta since 1962. Protests for democracy in 2007 grew into enormous demonstrations.[18] In response, the government cracked down. The security forces broke up crowds with rubber bullets and then live ammunition. Injuries mounted, more than a hundred were reported killed, and as many were said to have disappeared. Monasteries were raided and wrecked, homes were invaded, and people were snatched. People who were later released reported having been beaten and tortured.[19] Myanmar is starting to reform, partly because other countries took note and imposed severe pressure on the regime.[20]

Liberal democracies are usually better at protecting civil and political rights because abuses are more difficult to hide and more likely to be costly for rulers. The incentives built into liberal democracy usually encourage transparency and the protection of rights. They offer judicious means to resolve the types of internal tensions that otherwise would degenerate into conflict.[21] In functioning democracies, ordinary people have information about government behavior and can sanction their rulers for inappropriate or undesirable behavior by voting them out of office. Such systems create strong incentives for leaders to seek to satisfy their electorate by protecting its rights or at least by not violating them. Most autocracies and other forms of illiberal government, by contrast, are less dependent on their citizens' wishes (even when they hold elections), and so they are more likely to scare them into obedience by at least occasionally resorting to abuses.[22]

The type of government affects the norms, peer networks, and incentives that, according to the literature on criminology, reinforce law-breaking or law-abiding behaviors.[23] Crimes can be learned or culturally transmitted, and peers can influence a potential criminal's opinion of how likely they are to be caught and punished.[24] Liberal constitutional democracy provides a national (if not personal) social and peer environment that supports, teaches, and legitimizes protections for people's rights and freedoms. Such incentives work alongside other rights-protecting tendencies of liberal democracies—such as electoral incentives for leaders to protect rights (discussed above) and the so-called rule of law that comes from a judicial system marked by independence and relatively easy access for individuals who think their rights have been violated.

These are just tendencies. Democracies, of course, are far from perfect protectors of human rights. They have been oppressive colonizers.[25] Liberal democracies also commit atrocities during wars.[26] They are often protective of some core human rights (e.g., the right to vote) while not always championing the full gamut of others (e.g., economic rights).[27] Some are good at protecting the rights of a sufficiently large electorate to keep leaders in power yet poor at protecting small or disorganized minorities.

Despite these caveats, the evidence is undisputable that the type of government has a big impact on human rights. For example, statistical studies show that censorship, torture, and mass killings happen much more frequently in countries with illiberal governments and no access to free and fair democratic political representation.[28] The governments that are the best protectors of most human rights are the most liberal and stable of democracies: the countries in which the chief executives are chosen competitively, the executive branch is subject to checks, the political process is open to social groups, and binding rules govern political participation.[29]

Even so, evidence is mounting that a state's "democrativeness" and respect for human rights are not strictly proportional. Two leading political scientists have found, for example, that there are thresholds: only the most liberal and established democracies regularly protect human rights.[30] Moreover, political science research is discovering that democratization—that is, a country's progress toward democracy—is not necessarily good for human rights in the short run.[31] Democratization can threaten leaders, who then resort to abuses in order to hold on to power. Threatened leaders can also encourage nationalism, which in turn can lead to conflicts and abuse.[32]

## Political Dissent

Conflict and illiberal rule contribute to human rights violations partly because they can lead to political dissent. Dissenters, especially when governments feel insecure in power, are ripe targets for abuse.[33] To stay in power, officials under attack censor, arrest, or otherwise constrain their political opponents, and the methods they use are often abusive.[34]

Leaders can use coercion to suppress dissent. They can also use it as a deterrent signal—to groups inside and outside the conflict—that the government will not tolerate threats that might destabilize its authority. Deterrence, by design, aims to readjust the calculus of dissenters. Yet successful deterrence often requires extreme acts for officials to signal credibly that they will do what it takes to stay in power. The Iranian government did just that by trying to quash the vast waves of protest that erupted after the contested June 2009 presidential elections. In 2011 and 2012, Syrian army and security forces cracked down on antigovernment protesters, detaining and killing tens of thousands of civilians.[35] Similar patterns of deterrent-signaling abuse happened in Libya and Bahrain.[36] A rational abuser weighs the costs and benefits of chronic abuses against political opponents with the larger deterrent value of prominent and egregious abuse. According to this calculus, human rights abuses are not deviant acts to be hidden but rather prominent signals to the political opposition that the only path to political control leads through a minefield of still more abuse.

Because the local details of each case are important, it is hard to draw general conclusions about exactly when and how dissent leads to a context in which human rights abuses proliferate. Yet some of the statistical research that aims to reach systematic conclusions has found that governments are more likely to commit human rights violations when political dissent is both significant and violent.[37] Other research suggests that the more varied the forms of dissent are, the sooner governments tend to reach their tolerable limit and respond with repression.[38]

## Poverty and Inequality

Robert McNamara, former US secretary of defense and former president of the World Bank, correctly observed: "There is an irrefutable relationship between violence and economic backwardness."[39] The causes probably run both ways, but certainly the strains of poverty and inequality can breed violence and behaviors that undermine human rights.[40]

Criminologists have long known that some crimes are driven by poverty or dire socioeconomic circumstances. In fact, most theories of crime are rooted, in part, in the view that economic inequality and poverty are "criminogenic."[41] Compared with wealthier populations, poor people are more likely to commit crimes, especially those involving the theft of property or other resources.[42] Economic disenfranchisement is frequently associated with oppositional cultures that define status through lawbreaking.[43]

Poverty tends to highlight scarcity and breed competition for resources. In response, unrest and conflict encourage governments to abuse rights to restore order, or take a bigger piece of the pie for themselves. In Sierra Leone, child labor is rampant, and even those laws that attempt to restrict it—such as by protecting children from hazardous conditions and keeping them in school—are not enforced largely because severe poverty provides incentives for families to send their children to work.[44]

According to economists Alberto Alesina and Roberto Perotti, who specialize on the relationship between economic activity and political behavior, economic inequality generates social discontent and political instability.[45] In contexts of inequality, political science research also teaches that "there are incentives for the 'haves' in society to engage in rent-seeking behavior within governmental institutions, to maintain control of their resources, and to exclude access to those resources by the 'have nots' in ways that use coercive means that undermine the protection of personal integrity rights."[46] Inequality can also result in the abuse of economic, social, and cultural rights. Myanmar, for instance, once violently relocated civilians to accommodate a gas line project whose royalties would largely flow to the government and elites.[47] Nigeria's government brutalized its Ogoni community in an effort to exploit oil reserves.[48]

Economic, social, and cultural rights are frequently violated in developing countries where poverty and inequality are endemic.[49] For example, Peru's maternal mortality rate is among the highest in the region, despite the country's moderate to high average economic growth and strong official stances in favor of protecting a wide array of human rights. This high rate of mortality is disproportionately concentrated in rural indigenous populations because many women do not receive essential obstetric care. Many indigenous women refer to their health clinics as "houses of death."[50] Policy fails to provide them with equal access or quality health care, and local health centers reportedly discriminate against them.[51] The context of poverty in rural indigenous communities yields, in effect, large transgressions against the human rights of women.

Of course, there is no lockstep correlation between income and the protection of human rights. Human rights are violated in most wealthy places too. But the systematic research in this area finds that abuse—especially those violent acts such as murder and torture—is highly correlated with poverty.[52]

## Intolerance and Dehumanization

In addition to links between certain types of governments or economic contexts and respect for human rights, some studies suggest that the prevalence of certain ideas in a society can undermine human rights.[53]

Racism, religious fundamentalism, political factionalism, and other such ideas can dehumanize people by stripping them of their dignity or individuality, making them seem to be less worthy of respect. Hate crimes, often a cauldron of human rights abuse, are driven by intolerance.[54] Many studies of genocide and other mass atrocities show that the victims had been the objects of prejudice.[55] Stereotypes that make people out to be worthless or a menace to prized values can inspire even otherwise-reasonable citizens to commit abuses.[56] Dehumanization allows abusers to downplay or ignore otherwise-powerful moral barriers.[57]

Government policies can also reflect, create, or reinforce these prejudices. Take, for example, the decades of violence between Hutu and Tutsi ethnic groups in Rwanda that peaked in the 1994 massacre of eight hundred thousand Tutsi women, men, and children as well as Hutus who opposed the genocide.[58] The fighting and hatred was reinforced by policies such as the decision to retain identity cards that classified Rwandans based on their ethnicity, which were originally distributed by Belgian colonists who favored Tutsis, and educational and labor policies that excluded Tutsis from benefits enjoyed by the Hutus.[59]

## Crime and Abuse Systems

These circumstances help explain why human rights violations are so often an insidious, system-level problem—a group of collective or interrelated actions that form a complex structure.[60] Rarely is one person in a government responsible for abusing human rights for one personal reason. Instead, many acts of abuse—and many perpetrators along with their delegates and institutions—coexist and even depend on one another like an ecosystem. Governments like Zimbabwe's that routinely repress their political opponents, for example, must involve many different people and institutions in their quest, including security officers to arrest their opponents, prison workers to jail and torture them, and members of the judicial or legislative system to ensure the government's impunity for these crimes. While some of these people operate in isolation, many are acquainted and knowingly collaborate in a system of abuse.

Part of what makes fighting human rights crime difficult is that an abuse system can take many forms and is often self-healing. Removing one element without changing the whole system doesn't have much impact. Individual agents of abuse can be organized in many different ways. A crime system can be hierarchical, like a family tree, with a ringleader as well as many underlings and their subordinates. In such systems, the central actor issues, implements, legitimates, or hides orders to violate human rights to further the goals of the organization.[61] Other systems include spirals that lack central authority and hierarchical interconnections between perpetrators. A crime system can even be chaotic or only loosely networked, with competing ringleaders and fuzzy chains of command, which is what we find in many collapsed and failing states.

Systems of abuse are quite numerous. They are not always easy to map out because perpetrators often are clandestine and keen to avoid external scrutiny. Different system structures require different strategies for isolating and removing abusive elements along with avoiding the tendency for a networked system to self-heal.

## Conclusion

Contextual factors do not directly cause people to commit human rights crimes. Nevertheless, they create situations and perceptions that allow people to believe that abuses will get them what they want at a price they are willing to pay. Many of these incentives depend on the type of government in place, for that partially determines whether abusers will be identified and held accountable for their actions. Wars, illiberalism, political dissent, poverty and inequality, and intolerance also provide contexts that are ripe for abuse.

As crucial as it is to understand the contexts that can encourage or allow perpetrators to commit human rights crimes—the topic I've explored in this chapter—it is equally important to understand how people convince themselves that engaging in these crimes is acceptable and why abusive activities, once they get started, often are really difficult to stop. That topic is what I turn to now in chapter 3.

# Rationales

A now-famous experiment studied the reactions of twenty-four male volunteers from junior colleges when they were given abusive tasks. The volunteers were tasked with punishing, with what they thought were painful electric shocks, another group of students if they made poor collective decisions. Some of the targets of this abuse were described as being "rotten"; others were labeled perceptive and understanding; and still others were given neutral terms. The group administering shocks had never met the other students, but its members gave stronger shocks to the students who had been portrayed in the most pejorative terms.[1] Of course, this study was on college students, not actual perpetrators of human rights abuses. But it suggests that even apparently normal, educated people who hold conventional moral values and socially acceptable roles in society are capable of violence toward others in some circumstances that are not even dire or extreme. With little prodding, average people will become abusive if they can justify their behavior.

This chapter helps explain such deviant behavior by looking at how people convince themselves that abuse is acceptable. In addition to the contexts that lead to human rights abuses described in chapter 2, this perspective is important not just because it offers a fuller explanation of how abuse arises and persists. It also has possibly large implications for policy. Often it is extremely difficult to change the contextual factors that lead to abuse; war, illiberal government, poverty and inequality, intolerance, and other such contextual factors don't change overnight. Indeed, some policy strategies aimed at addressing these factors—such as forced democratization or military intervention—can backfire and lead to even more abuse. Yet perhaps it is easier to work at the individual level—such as with government leaders, their employees, gang members, and the like. Large literatures have emerged around the question of how individuals weigh the costs and benefits of abuse (and criminal behavior more generally) and how they justify their choices. Understanding those individual calculations could lead to policy instruments that yield a new calculus with less abuse.

My goal in this chapter and the previous one is to rectify the view pervasive in some accounts of crime and mass atrocity that perpetrators are insane, irrational, or psychologically (or biologically) abnormal.[2] This is common, for example, in studies and popular depictions of Adolf Hitler along with his motivations for implementing the Holocaust.[3] Some criminology books even still advance the argument that some people are biologically predisposed to crime.[4] Most criminology, though, has shifted to the perspective discussed in this book: criminal activity is largely a function of various rational and social logics. Whether Hitler was in fact insane is a much-debated subject.[5] But it is easy to see the superficial appeal of the "crazy man" hypothesis and the more general idea that human rights abuses are acts of madness or uncontrollable urges. It is uncomfortable, yet essential, to realize that sane people could deliberately commit such horrible acts.

Here I look at two perspectives. I start with the many ways that perpetrators rationalize their actions since nearly every account of systemic, long-term abuse includes a large role for rationalization. From there, I look at other particular perspectives that psychologists, sociologists, and economists interested in criminology have adopted—such as the individual costs and benefits of criminal abuse.

## Rationalization

One reason why people commit acts of human rights abuse is because they believe they are doing their job. Exceptional, stressful, life-threatening circumstances require it. Especially when it comes to abuses carried out under the orders of a government, military leader, or some other organizational authority, the hands-on perpetrators who carry out the dirty deeds are often looking for ways to please their superiors, save their own lives or livelihoods, or protect some deeply held conviction. But they know the decisions are morally questionable so perpetrators look to particular political, economic, or cultural norms when justifying abusive practices.[6] Torture, for instance, has frequently been used by "well-meaning, even reasonable people" when they believe that torture is necessary to preserve civilization or their form of government.[7] And one of the lessons of social psychology is that people tend to favor their own social group, conform to their peers, and prejudice "outgroups."[8]

One implication of this is that perpetrators often act knowingly. They hurt others because they believe they will gain something from the abuse, not because they do not realize what they are doing.[9] This perspective helps explain why retrospective accounts that study perpetrators usually find they are ordinary people who embraced various rationalizations to explain their behavior.[10] This is just as true for the people who order the abuses (e.g., government leaders) as the security forces or other foot soldiers who implement abuse. In the next three sections I look at three particular ways that perpetrators rationalize their crimes: exceptional circumstances, avoidance, and routinization.

## EXCEPTIONAL CIRCUMSTANCES

The process of rationalization is a powerful one that follows a common pattern. First, perpetrators—usually, ordinary individuals under a variety of strong social pressures—begin acting in seemingly trivial ways, using insults and name-calling, for example. As they become accustomed to this behavior their actions grow in severity and soon include abuse and degrading treatment. Although the perpetrators are in control of their actions, they might not realize their seriousness and even criminal nature. Some might even believe that the subjects of their mistreatment deserve it wholly, and that their actions are justified and even venerable.[11] In exceptional circumstances, even ordinary people can resort to abuse.

Postwar studies of atrocities committed during the Holocaust, for instance, found that many of the Nazis responsible for these acts were basically normal people who were originally not inclined toward violence.[12] In fact, the psychological profiles of these Nazis were similar to those of their ordinary US contemporaries.[13] Similar conclusions emerge from studies of the Greek military officers behind abuses such as heinous acts of torture that marked the military junta's rule in the late 1960s and early 1970s. Aside from their position in the military, nothing psychologically unusual distinguished these military men from other Greek men their age.[14] They were not diagnosed as mentally ill. They did not believe (or at least didn't report believing) that they were doing evil when they committed the abuses; under the guidance of their military commanders, they appear to have believed they were doing what was best for their nation. Likewise, a US Army commission of inquiry found that the soldiers in the Eleventh Brigade who raped, tortured, or murdered hundreds of Vietnamese civilians in the My Lai massacre were "generally representative of the typical cross-section of American youth assigned to most combat units throughout the Army."[15] These men had not been out of control in their everyday lives; they were, on the face of it, ordinary folks. But during the Vietnam War, some reacted to unusual situations—sometimes believing they were following orders—by doing terrible things.

The same might be said of the human rights violations committed by US soldiers against Iraqis at the Abu Ghraib prison during the war in Iraq.[16] These crimes were heinous, but there is plenty of evidence to show that otherwise-average people would commit similar acts when placed in similar circumstances—this according to the now-famous 1971 Stanford prison experiment and many others that followed.[17]

For fifteen dollars a day, several dozen US and Canadian college students participated in the Stanford prison experiment. They were an average group of healthy, bright, middle-class young men. By the flip of a coin, half were anointed as prison guards and half were assigned the role of prisoner. The prisoners, who were no different than the guards before the experiment began, were locked up in cells in a makeshift prison in the basement of Stanford University's psychology department building. The students playing guards were not trained on how to be guards but instead were told that they could do, within limits, whatever was necessary to keep law and order. Within a few short days, about one-third of the guards began to harass and intimidate the prisoners, and were aggressive, arbitrary, and creative in their forms of prisoner humiliation. According to the study's leader, professor of psychology Philip Zimbardo, "These guards appeared to thoroughly enjoy the power they wielded, yet none of our preliminary personality tests were able to predict this behavior. . . . How could intelligent, mentally healthy, 'ordinary' men become perpetrators of evil so quickly?"[18] After only six days, the prison simulation, which was planned to last two weeks, was called off because the experiment grew out of hand. The roles assigned to these students explain some of their behavior, but rationalization was also a major factor in explaining how individuals could justify remaining in positions that they knew, at least initially, were abusive and criminal.

That was just an experiment, but these things also happen in real life. In Poland, during the Second World War, for example, the men of reserve Police Battalion 101, ordinary in just about every way, killed Jews in cold blood. Years later, some were tried for these crimes. Their stories were documented in their own testimony as well as court and investigation records. Using these sources, historian Christopher Browning shows the series of actions, circumstances, and personal reactions that led up to the killings. By his account, they had no special dispositions for these crimes. Most followed orders to shoot and kill that they, at first, found objectionable.[19] Something happened that let them overcome their objections.

When the young US soldiers at Abu Ghraib prison were asked to explain their actions, most saw themselves as acting morally given the circumstances. Their acts were surely morally wrong and in some cases have been found criminal, but many of the soldiers perpetrating the crimes appear not to have seen it that way. Instead, they claimed that their actions would protect their nation and freedom more generally; they were doing "nothing out of the ordinary," or were just following orders. Lynndie England, a young US private who was convicted for abusing prisoners at Abu Ghraib, put it this way: "I always aim to please. . . . But what happens in war, happens. It just happened to be photographed and come out. . . . They were the enemy."[20]

Of course, not every person who could become a perpetrator actually engages in abuse. Not all the guards in the Stanford prison experiment became cruel, and not all US soldiers at My Lai or Abu Ghraib became abusive. In war, for example, soldiers oftentimes don't shoot their weapons for reasons that sociologists have tied to particular social, physical, and emotional factors.[21] The research is not terribly convincing at explaining why, even in high-stress situations, some people resort to crimes while others do not.

What the research does explain, however, is that people who do become perpetrators tend to be, psychologically and biologically, not much different before the abuse from other people who do not engage in such behavior; they tend not to fit the profile of a clinically insane or mentally ill person but rather an average person reacting to circumstances, to the situational contingencies facing them.

Recent work on terrorism is beginning to shed light on why some people who find themselves in exceptional circumstances that create opportunity for such crimes choose not to engage in them. That work supports basic principles of modern criminology. The context people find themselves in, along with opportunities and peer pressure, shape their choices about whether or not to commit a crime.[22] But so do regular interactions with potential victims and early (family-based) teaching on how to make choices in such situations.[23]

## AVOIDING RESPONSIBILITY

One reason that abuses are so common and enduring is that perpetrators are quick to disengage morally from their behavior, or to redefine right and wrong. Some justify their behavior as acceptable. Others come to believe that they are not responsible for it but that someone else is instead.

Perpetrators often reclassify their hurtful actions as admirable, or even lawful, moral, or good.[24] Torturing a terrorist might seem entirely justified if it produces information that can boost national security or save lives. Crushing a political protest might seem defensible, even desirable, if it lowers the threat of social unrest and political instability. While acts of torture and political terror may be widely perceived as wrong, perpetrators frequently claim that such measures are appropriate in the specific situations at hand. Either they don't see the abuses as crimes, or they believe that committing them is for the greater good or may avert even more egregious crimes.

Avoiding responsibility often includes redefining the level of abuse at stake. Perpetrators are prone to downplay the extent of the pain and suffering they have inflicted, arguing that the abuses they committed were not as bad as is claimed or as the abuses that others would have committed. In tandem, abusers may change their opinions of their victims, telling themselves that victims deserved the treatment they got or that they are somehow less than human.[25] Sometimes perpetrators also deny any direct connection between their actions and the consequences. For instance, a prison warden who orders guards to detain a prisoner without trial and force a confession may not feel responsible for the hands-on abuses their underlings carry out as a result of their orders. And the guards who act on the warden's orders may feel that they were just doing their job, behaving as best they could, given the situation. The Nazi official Klaus Barbie—on trial in 1987 for having once tortured Jews and members of the French Resistance, and deported them to death camps—defended himself by saying: "I was simply doing my job. . . . I respected the Resistance. . . . War is war."[26] Hugo Garcia, a torturer in Uruguay from 1976 to 1979, explained in an interview: "I am a victim too. . . . [M]y superiors who got me into this. They made me do it. They told me things that were not true. . . . I never took the initiative to start torturing somebody. I was given the orders."[27] More recently, the head of the most infamous Khmer Rouge detention center, known as Duch, stated during his trial in Cambodia that he had supervised the torture and execution of more than fourteen thousand people partly because he feared sanctions from his superiors if he didn't.[28] The implication is that Duch wasn't at fault.

As Roy Baumeister, a professor of social psychology, puts it, perpetrators

> do not see things in the simple, black-and-white absolutes that victims and lawmakers are fond of. To them, events are complex and morally ambiguous. They may see something wrong in what they did, but they also see how they were affected by external factors, including some that were beyond their control. In other cases, perpetrators see themselves as having acted in a way that was fully appropriate and justified. Perhaps most important, perpetrators typically do have reasons and motives that make sense to them. Victims may see random, gratuitous acts of cruelty, but perpetrators rarely see their own acts that way."[29]

Moral ambiguity, which often plays a role in avoiding responsibility, depends on how perpetrators view the legitimacy of law and other institutions that establish social norms. While efforts at policing and incarceration convince some people to obey the law out of fear of reprisal—topics I will examine in more detail later when I turn to the calculus of abuse and compliance—we also know that people more readily obey laws they see as legitimate and fair. In fact, explains professor of psychology Tom

Tyler, "legitimacy is crucial if the authorities are to have the discretionary power they need to fulfill their roles."[30] When people believe in the law—learn to value it—they are more likely to obey the law.[31]

ROUTINIZATION

As perpetrators engage in more abuse—aided by their ability to rationalize their actions and avoid responsibility—actions become routines. Criminologists learned long ago that prior crimes raise the odds of subsequent deviant behavior.[32] One of the biggest predictors of human rights abuse is earlier behavior.[33] And plenty of research—especially in psychology—shows that as perpetrators commit more violations, they use increasingly intense violence or repression, and commit the acts with increasing ease.[34] Actions that were once difficult for individuals to rationalize become easier—in part because perpetrators come to think that they are acting appropriately. "As perpetrators evolve, the feeling of responsibility for the welfare of other humans . . . diminishes."[35]

Routinization depends, in part, on incentives. Group leaders usually perpetrate abuses by ordering others to carry out the crimes. Some hands-on perpetrators, especially those who displace responsibility for their wrongdoings onto others, believe that they stand to benefit from obeying orders to carry out abuses.[36] Obedience brings them feelings of accomplishment and appropriateness or praise from superiors, among other benefits. And it provides motivation to displace personal responsibility for their actions on to superiors.

The desire to obey can be a powerful personal motivation that leads to routines in behavior.[37] Laboratory studies show that people not otherwise inclined to abuse will freely administer pain to others if they are instructed to do so by someone they perceive to be an authority figure. As shown in the Stanford prison study, that tendency to deference exists even when abusers do not believe that they will get any specific reward for following orders or be punished for disobeying them.[38]

## Calculus of Abuse

Rationalization based on circumstances, avoidance of responsibility, and routinization of abuse help explain how abusive patterns emerge and are sustained. But they don't fully reveal how abusers think they will benefit in the first place from a course of abusive action. Over the next four sections, I will look at four such benefits—starting with psychological superiority—before considering the costs associated with efforts to achieve these benefits.

## SUPERIORITY

Perpetrators may get, or hope to get, various psychological gains from committing abuses. Among those are satisfying a sense of idealism, increasing their own or their group's security, ideological superiority, and necessity. Some perpetrators believe that they are making the world a better place. Several accounts of the Holocaust emphasize that at least at first, the average Nazi was not driven by any intense hatred of Jews but instead by the strong conviction that participating would lead to a superior society.[39] The Jews and other targets were gradually devalued and dehumanized.[40] As German society increasingly scorned them, many individual perpetrators abused them out of revenge for some perceived earlier harm and slowly developed a sense of superiority, sometimes even moral righteousness, over the oppressed groups.[41]

## INTELLIGENCE

Many of the benefits of abuse to the abusers—real or imagined—are about collecting information. The hope that abuses might yield useful or so-called actionable information was a big part of the Bush administration's explanation for using torture after 9/11. Popular TV shows like *24* pose the dilemma of whether government officials should abuse personal rights for the supposedly larger social gain of avoiding catastrophes such as nuclear terrorism. In addition to obtaining information, abuses might intimidate and deter victims as well as other potential enemies.

As Julio Cesar Cooper, a former officer in the Uruguayan military and torturer, explained in an interview: "In my own case (and I would consider it typical of the general attitude of an officer at the time) torture was regarded as a means to an end. The objective was to obtain a confession from the detainee, pure and simple. The authorities constantly enjoined on us the need to obtain confessions in order to save the lives of military personnel who might be in danger of attack of revolutionary groups." Cooper also noted that "subsequently the idea began to lose its force and changed into the application of torture for its own sake, as part of a routine, and also as an act of vengeance against the detainee."[42]

## REVENGE

As Cooper's statements reveal, revenge is another reason people commit these crimes. Revenge is a form of reciprocity and thus helps explain why earlier abuses lead to still more abuse. It's a reciprocal mentality that can both motivate and justify human rights violations: they did it to us, so they deserve it in return. Allen Joseph Boyce, who was in the US Army company that took part in the My Lai massacre, explained: "We were all 'psyched' up because we wanted revenge for some of our fallen comrades that had been killed prior to the operation."[43] As I write this book, a new government in Libya is replacing Muammar el-Qaddafi's, and evidence is emerging of revenge killings by both rebels and the military regime.[44]

## MONETARY BENEFITS

So far, I have focused on psychological and political gains. Yet human rights abuses, like many other crimes, can yield economic benefits as well. Perpetrators may depend on committing abuses for their livelihood. They may plunder resources from their victims that are forced to hand over money or other valuables. Or they may get paid for the abuse. When discussing his role for the Uruguayan military in torturing people, torturer Hugo Garcia described some of his position's benefits: "I could say I had a good job, good salary, a lot of fringe benefits—free taxis, free hotels if I wanted. I could get a lot of things for free, presents from businesses."[45]

## PENALTIES

The calculus of abuse depends on costs as well as benefits.[46] Perpetrators usually abuse human rights because they expect some advantage, but abuse can carry the risk of penalties. Here I focus on those penalties, and in the next section I examine whether such penalties actually deter criminals. Evaluating those costs, much more than the benefits, has been a central element of the scholarly literature—especially the literature that has focused on the economics of crime.

The possible penalties for human rights abuses are familiar. For example, suppose government officials are guilty of abusing human rights—of, say, ordering the imprisonment of their political opponents without trial, torturing dissidents, censoring journalists, and outlawing public protests and strikes. The military or some other official institution could put them in prison for breaking the law, or a rebel might punish them by killing or hurting them or their family. In a contestable democracy, the officials might be voted out of office. NGOs might mobilize public opinion against them, leading to riots, the destruction of property and other economic losses, and eventually, the officials' removal from office. Other governments could punish the officials through sanctions—by withholding aid or cutting back on trade (which harms the government and indirectly a nation's leaders)—or impose travel bans or freezes on bank accounts aimed at targeting costs personally. An international organization such as the United Nations might publicly shame the officials or ban their government from participating. In particular, scholars who have focused on the specific incentives at work related to international human rights norms have devoted considerable attention to naming and shaming as a mechanism for imposing penalties on human rights abusers.[47]

## DETERRENCE

A central question in the study of criminal penalties is the credibility and effectiveness of deterrence. Just as some people do not drive drunk because they fear the consequences of breaking the law, some obey laws outlawing specific human rights abuses because they fear the consequences of being caught and punished.[48] This, of course, is the idea behind international criminal laws and courts, like the ICC as well as some aspects of national human rights trials that hold individual people accountable.[49] It's also part of the idea behind other human rights courts like the inter-American or European courts that hold governments accountable. Long ago, criminologists started looking at how law works and focused on the fact that deterrent effects depend less on the size of possible punishments than the certainty that punishment will be delivered.[50]

When it comes to ordinary criminals, people have long debated the merits of deterrence—that is, punishment as a way to prevent other people from committing crimes.[51] Some people have no regard for the legal (or other) consequences of their actions; they simply do not think about getting caught or punished.[52] This is especially apparent in criminals who act impulsively and hence have not thought through the consequences of their actions.[53] And some people are inhibited from crime by considerations other than punishments, such as morality or other social norms.[54]

Even so, the evidence from criminology is overwhelming that "at least some active offenders do pay attention to sanction threats at least some of the time." Moreover, even "persistent criminal offenders do consider the risks involved when both committing specific crimes and in deciding when to commit the crime 'business.'"[55] Both policing and incarceration tend to reduce crime.[56] And with some exceptions, various other criminal justice punishments seem to help deter crime too.[57]

Much like the benefits of human rights abuse, however, deterrents against abuse are in the eyes of the beholder. Some perpetrators seem willing to risk greater penalties than others. Some don't seem to feel hurt by bad publicity; others desperately want to be liked. Some are more willing to risk death if committing abuses means that they have a better chance of getting what they want. Some put their families at risk. Others never take the risk that far.

In this way, abusing human rights is a bit like gambling. A lot depends on the gambler and what they are willing to risk—information that is usually private to the gambler. For any given perpetrator of abuse, the costs of abuse depend partly on their perception of the likelihood that they will be found out and sanctioned. When the risk of being caught and punished seems low, or the punishment seems small, a potential perpetrator might decide that committing abuses is a reasonable gamble because they expect—rightly or wrongly—to get away with impunity. This is especially likely when abuses are done on impulse.

In the shock study described earlier, the intensity of the shocks that the students administered depended in part on how much personal responsibility they thought they might bear for their actions. Subjects gave much higher shocks when they believed that all members on their team would be held jointly responsible than when they thought they would be held individually accountable. As accountability was diffused their reservations about commiting abuse declined.[58]

When perpetrators commit abuses, most are probably not aware of the real benefits and costs of their actions. But they decide to act based on a calculation that is informed by perceptions and guided by heuristics. When they choose to abuse, it is often because they think that the prospective gains outweigh the prospective costs; either the gains seem greater than the costs or the gains seem more likely to accrue than the costs. Or the gains are simply worth the costs. This is why, in the eyes of many perpetrators, abuse appears to be a practical means to achieve a desirable goal, not an unjustified criminal act. And since heuristics are formed by experience, it is why calculations for (or against) abuse depend so much on past behavior.

## Conclusion

This chapter and the previous one weave together a particular view of the reasons why people engage in human rights abuses. I've suggested that most perpetrators of abuse reason and rationalize; they are not biologically or mentally disabled, and most are not impulsive criminals acting on whims. They have goals, shaped by the contextual circumstances discussed in chapter 2. And they calculate, to the best of their knowledge, the advantages and disadvantages of various ways of accomplishing it. Frequently, they are part of systems of people and institutions acting collectively, supporting the behavior. They rationalize their decisions, and convince themselves that their behavior is acceptable and even just.

This vision of human rights abuse has a major policy implication: responses to human rights abuses that are based on telling perpetrators that their actions are immoral or illegal are unlikely to be effective unless the

e seen as legitimate and backed up by believable consequences
breaking. I discuss these two different mechanisms for influencing
ulus of abuse—coercion and persuasion—in much more detail
in chapter 4 in the setting of international law. How those mechanisms
actually work to change the calculus of abuse is the task of the rest of
this book.

# PART II

# International Law

In part I, I explored why people commit human rights abuses and other crimes. I now look at the international legal agreements and procedures that governments and NGOs have created with the goal of spreading norms that curtail abuse. In response to human rights atrocities such as the Nazi Holocaust, over the last six decades governments have elaborated an entire structure of doctrines, treaties, courts, and organizations—a network of obligations, norms, and procedures that make up the international human rights legal system.

The breadth of the international human rights legal system is extraordinary. Its existence is the result of people's efforts to turn their highest aspirations for fairness and human dignity into an array of obligations that apply across the globe to every person.

At the end of the nineteenth century, international legal institutions did not much focus on protecting universal human rights. Instead, international law was principally concerned with managing the rights and obligations of states toward one another. To the extent that international law did address the rights of individuals, it was during the special circumstances of war and concentrated on special categories of people: prisoners, combatants, and civilians.[1]

The roots of today's international human rights legal system were established after World War II and with the creation of the United Nations. One of the United Nations' first tasks, which it completed in 1949, was to update the Geneva Conventions to add additional protections for people who weren't active combatants yet might be harmed by the atrocities of war—such as civilians, medics, aid workers, the wounded, sick and shipwrecked troops, and prisoners of war. In tandem, UN members also unanimously adopted the Universal Declaration of Human Rights in 1948.[2] The declaration launched modern international human rights law with its aspiration to protect all individuals at all times—not just in war—and make states accountable for this protection. In the decades since, dozens of treaties have been created to further acknowledge and protect human rights. They aspire to universal application. Human rights are for everyone, and they should be every government's obligation.

There is now no region or culture in the world that isn't subject in some way to this system. While this part of the book will look closely at where and how this system actually works to improve respect for human rights, it is important to recognize, first, the extraordinary accomplishment of just creating the system. These new norms and institutions have redefined the frontier of international law. By setting shared understandings of standards according to which governments ought to treat their nationals—and those of other states—in many respects the human rights legal system has redefined state sovereignty, long the cornerstone and an almost-sacred, absolute aspect of international law. Unlike international law that dates back to the nineteenth century, which focused just on special rights in special circumstances, the postwar human rights legal system is universal and timeless in aspiration; it is also broad in the array of rights it aims to protect.

This system now inspires human rights advocates to reach further. For example, Belgian courts claim they have universal jurisdiction over some crimes committed outside Belgium by and against non-Belgians. They recently sentenced Ephraim Nkezabera, a Rwandan *genocidaire*, to thirty years in prison after finding him guilty of crimes against humanity on Rwandan soil during the 1994 genocide against the Tutsi.[3] And there is a move by NGOs and some governments to recognize new rights, such as the "responsibility to protect": a universal norm that would prevent and stop genocides, war crimes, ethnic cleansing, and other crimes against humanity.[4]

Chapter 4, written for the nonexpert, explains the legal and organizational nuts and bolts of that system—looking at not only the various UN-based approaches to human rights, which have global application, but also the varied regional parts of the system. Chapter 4 also explains why so many countries have joined this system and explores how the system aims to influence the behavior of the perpetrators who might abuse human rights.

The nuts and bolts of the system are a starting point for a lot of research and debate about whether that system actually does much to protect human rights and what might be done to make it more effective. I analyze that research and debate from three perspectives over three chapters. Chapter 5 centers on what rigorous academic research has learned by studying the human rights legal system and discusses in plain words whether human rights laws are statistically correlated with actual protections for human rights. Research of this type is controversial, not least because it has implications for whether human rights law actually works to improve respect for human rights. Thus, chapter 5 also concentrates on the difficulties in learning the right lessons from statistical research. Chapter 6 takes a more hands-on approach. It looks at what people who have spent careers doing practical work to promote human rights—such as heads of human rights organizations along with legal experts who have built careers studying and advancing human rights law—actually think about the strengths and especially weaknesses of the system. The strengths are important, but I will focus on the weaknesses because they provide a road map for making improvements.

Together, chapters 5 and 6 offer a foundation for thinking about where the existing international human rights legal system is in solid shape and where reforms are needed. Indeed, a rich debate on possible reforms has emerged, and chapter 7 reviews and assesses those ideas. These reform proposals have arisen in the context of a legal system that has expanded rapidly. Chapter 7 explains why that legal system is unlikely ever to have universal reach for the full list of human rights.

The message from these chapters is that the international human rights legal system that has emerged since the late 1940s is an impressive accomplishment. But the evidence—from scholars and practitioners alike—suggests that law is closely associated with human rights protections in some areas but not others. It probably works best to foster respect for human rights for a few kinds of countries and settings, but its practical impacts are few in the areas where many of the worst or most human rights abuses actually occur. And as the system expands, it is becoming increasingly crucial to think strategically about how it interacts with other ways to promote human rights.

# 4

# The International Human Rights
# Legal System

This chapter, written for nonexperts, is an introduction to the most important nuts and bolts of the international human rights legal system. Most of those human rights laws are intended to regulate governments themselves. Yet some also apply directly to individuals who perpetrate human rights abuses—also known as international criminal law. International legal norms come in many different types. I concentrate on two that have attracted the most scholarship and political attention.

One type of law—the most visible kind—is treaties. Today's human rights legal system includes many treaties. These are a form of contract that governments willingly sign among themselves and then ratify at home, usually through their legislative (or in some cases executive) branch. One peculiarity of the international human rights legal system, and a marked difference from domestic legal systems, is that treaty law originates through a process that is largely consensual. Most of international law, especially binding treaties, consists of obligations that states voluntarily consent to being bound to. There is no global police force or international criminal justice system to enforce them; as I will show, however, there are some courts whose reach and influence is growing.

In addition to treaties, states embrace legal norms through consistent behavior—by repeatedly respecting a given practice or decrying deviations from it by other states. Such behavior, when buttressed by a widespread perception that it is obligatory, forms the set of rules known as customary international law. Treaties often systematize and codify existing customary international law. Both these forms of law give considerable power to governments to shape them. That same authority also allows governments to opt out or derogate from some binding norms. The opportunity to escape binding norms isn't always available—so-called peremptory norms of customary international law, also known in legal jargon as *jus cogens*, are norms from which no derogation is allowed, and to which no state or person can ever take exception no matter what their reason.[1] Which subset of international legal norms belongs to this group is a contentious matter, but several relating to human rights—genocide, slavery, and torture, among others—are generally included. Although peremptory norms are strictly binding as a matter of law, their enforcement still depends on institutions such as courts and ultimately governments. Thus the practical application of customary law also often depends heavily on the consent of governments.

This chapter gives an overview of the international human rights legal system in three steps. First, the bulk of the chapter surveys the nuts and bolts of that system and its component parts. Broadly, that system consists of the UN-based laws and bodies that have global reach because the United Nations is a universal organization. It also includes some criminal courts along with various regional laws and organizations that work in tandem but are distinct. The system isn't organized as a hierarchy; rather, these different laws work in conjunction, overlapping in some areas and not others.[2] Second, I explain why these laws have been so popular. A striking attribute of international human rights law is that so many countries voluntarily join the system. Even some countries with horrendous human rights records sign and ratify binding treaties that prohibit the very abuses they commit. Understanding why this system has been so popular will be essential for the analysis that follows later in this book, for one of the challenges in making human rights law more effective involves getting countries that are keen to join these agreements to also honor them. Third, I explain how these laws are supposed to influence behavior. By design, law is intended to coerce and persuade individuals and governments to alter their behavior. (Whether it actually works is examined in more detail in chapters 5 and 6.)

## Universal Human Rights Law and Institutions

For the most part, the international human rights legal system resides within the structures of the United Nations.[3] The core of that system is the International Bill of Human Rights. In addition to that core, which consists of three documents, the UN has also created many other agreements, special bodies that manage its treaties, and procedures to collect information about the fulfillment of legal commitments.

### THE INTERNATIONAL BILL OF HUMAN RIGHTS

If there is a manifesto for international human rights, it is the 1948 Universal Declaration of Human Rights. The first major global acknowledgment that all people have the same fundamental and inalienable human rights and freedoms, this declaration is the basis of international human rights law today. The norms it declares—such as nondiscrimination, equality, and fairness—apply to all people, in all places, for all time.

Like other declarations, principles, guidelines, and recommendations passed by UN members or other international organizations, the Universal Declaration of Human Rights is not legally binding in itself.[4] Governments do not ratify it or make any formal legal promise to agree with its terms in the way that they do with treaties. But the document does detail the fundamental freedoms and human rights expressed more generally in the Charter of the United Nations, to which all UN members have formally committed.[5] And many lawyers believe that it has become part of customary international law.[6]

The Universal Declaration of Human Rights arose in a special context. It was negotiated in the aftermath of the Second World War with wartime atrocities fresh in minds. Governments in the Western and Eastern bloc nations were attempting in various ways to cooperate, and the nonbinding nature of the declaration made it relatively easy for governments to agree. The Cold War, which opened right as the declaration was finalized, changed all that; for the subsequent decades, diplomacy on human rights was a lot harder to manage because the Cold War blocs could not agree on much at all.

From the late 1960s, as it became clear that the Cold War was not merely a passing fad, the two blocs of nations slowly and tacitly framed compromises on where and how they could cooperate. Eastern nations sought to codify new economic rights; the West sought stronger civil and political rights. Slowly, negotiations searched for common ground. Of course, these two geopolitical blocs weren't the only ones that influenced UN negotiations. Many of the goals in codifying new economic rights, in particular, also resonated with the increasingly vocal group of developing countries and their vision of a New International Economic Order. The result, finally, was two new treaties: the International Covenant on Civil and Political Rights, and the International Covenant on Economic, Social, and Cultural Rights. Both define keystone rights and are widely ratified by governments. These two treaties, along with the Universal Declaration of Human Rights, make up what is known as the International Bill of Human Rights.

Under the International Covenant on Civil and Political Rights, which came into force in 1976, participating governments agree, among other things, that no person should be subjected to torture, or cruel, inhuman, or degrading treatment or punishment, be held in slavery, or be arbitrarily arrested or detained. This covenant also enshrines the right to freedom of thought, conscience, and religion as well as freedom of expression.[7]

The International Covenant on Economic, Social, and Cultural Rights, which also came into force in 1976, requires governments to recognize people's right to work along with freely choosing their jobs. The treaty also guarantees everyone's right to safe and healthy working conditions, and to form and join trade unions freely. It holds that primary education should be compulsory and freely available. It guarantees the right to food, water, and a healthy living environment, housing, social security, and respect for cultural rights, such as the protection of religious practices.[8]

With these two treaties also came oversight bodies: the Human Rights Committee and the Committee on Economic, Social, and Cultural Rights. The practice of creating oversight bodies is a pattern that has continued in the decades since as the UN system has invented new organizations to manage an array of new human rights challenges. (Altogether, today there are almost a dozen operating treaty bodies, which engage over one hundred experts serving from many dozens of countries.) These bodies act as administrators—they don't have powers to impose fines or award damages like civil courts do. Rather, their job is to monitor.

The Human Rights Committee is the body of independent experts that was established with the International Covenant on Civil and Political Rights to oversee the implementation of that treaty.[9] Prior to the creation of the ICC (which I discuss below), some believed that it was "the closest the world has ever come to an international court of human rights."[10] In operation now for more than three decades, the committee has developed a large body of case law. It reviews periodic reports in which states that are parties to the treaty detail their human rights problems and activities.[11] It has commented on more than four hundred of these reports, and produced what are known as "concluding observations" for a couple hundred. It has also registered almost two thousand communications from individuals alleging violations in about eighty states and expressed "views" on about one-third of those communications.[12] It is usually made up of eighteen representatives from around the world, all elected for a four-year term by secret ballot; every party to the treaty gets to vote on a list of people that governments nominate.[13] They meet in Geneva or New York several times a year.

In spring 2009, the committee considered state reports from Australia, Rwanda, and Sweden, for example.[14] In their concluding observations on Australia, members expressed concern that despite positive developments toward recognizing the land rights of aboriginals and the Torres Strait Islanders, the Australian government had not adequately resolved these peoples' title claims. They also worried that law enforcement officials had been reported to use excessive force (such as "tasers") against indigenous people, minorities, and persons with disabilities as well as young people, and voiced their regret that investigations into allegations of police misconduct were carried out by the police.[15] These kinds of observations are routine. They also are feasible in part because NGOs now play an important role in the compilation of some reports submitted to the Human Rights Committee.[16]

The Committee on Economic, Social, and Cultural Rights is the body of eighteen independent experts created by the UN Economic and Social Council to oversee the implementation of the International Covenant on Economic, Social, and Cultural Rights. Among other tasks, it too reviews the periodic reports that governments submit.[17] Committee members, who are nominated by their governments and elected by treaty member states to serve a four-year term, meet in Geneva a few times a year.[18] During its May 2009 meeting, the committee considered, among other things, a report by the government of Cambodia. It noted with concern that a 2001 land law providing for the granting of land titles to indigenous communities had not been implemented effectively, and urged the government of Cambodia to do so without further delay.[19]

## OTHER HUMAN RIGHTS LAWS AND TREATY BODIES

The discussion above has focused on the most prominent international agreements that comprise the International Bill of Human Rights and their two treaty oversight bodies. In addition to these, there are many other visible treaties, including:

The Convention on the Prevention and Punishment of the Crime of Genocide, in effect since 1951, states that genocide, whether committed in a time of peace or war, is a crime under international law.[20]

The International Convention on the Elimination of All Forms of Racial Discrimination, in force since 1969, prohibits any distinction, exclusion, restriction, or preference based on race, color, descent, or national or ethnic origin.[21]

The Convention on the Elimination of All Forms of Discrimination against Women, in effect since 1981, condemns any sort of discrimination against women and sets an agenda for national action to end any discrimination.[22]

The Convention against Torture and Other Cruel, Inhuman, or Degrading Treatment or Punishment, in effect since 1987, requires its participants to take effective legislative, administrative, judicial, or other measures to prevent acts of torture and other cruel, inhuman, or degrading treatment, even in times of war.[23]

The Convention on the Rights of the Child, in effect since 1990, requires its participants to protect children from all forms of abuse, including sexual exploitation, the sale of children, and the involvement of children in armed conflict.[24]

The International Convention on the Protection of the Rights of All Migrant Workers and Members of Their Families, in effect since 2003, specifies the application to migrant workers and their families of rights included in the core treaties, including, for example, protection against slavery and servitude, the right to social security, favorable work conditions, rest and leisure, and education.[25]

The Convention on the Rights of Persons with Disabilities, in force since 2008, clarifies and qualifies how all categories of rights apply to persons with disabilities.[26]

The International Convention for the Protection of All Persons from Enforced Disappearance, in effect since late 2010, protects individuals against forced disappearance regardless of any justification such as war or any public emergency, defines enforced disappearance as a "crime against humanity," and requires member states to take measures to hold accountable any actor responsible for this crime.[27]

With the exception of the treaty outlawing genocide, all of these treaties have created a separate committee or group of experts to oversee their implementation.[28] These bodies also review reports by member governments describing abuses and efforts to redress them. They ask the governments to respond to their observations, and occasionally they make specific recommendations about reforms.

Although procedures vary in their details, these treaties generally allow allegations of violations to be brought to the attention of the treaty bodies in one of three ways: through individual complaints, state-to-state complaints, or inquiries initiated by the treaty bodies in response to accusations of abuse.[29] For example, the review bodies set up to monitor enforcement of the treaty outlawing torture along with those protecting civil and political rights, economic, social, and cultural rights, the rights of women, the rights of disabled persons, and the rights of racial minorities all have the authority to review individual complaints (provided member governments expressly permit this). The Convention against Torture also allows governments to file a complaint to the relevant treaty body about alleged acts of abuse by other countries. So far, none of the state-to-state complaints procedures have been used.[30]

Some treaties also allow review bodies to open investigations on their own so long as they have serious reason to believe that a country is guilty of grave or systematic violations.[31] For example, since its establishment over twenty years ago, the Committee against Torture has used its inquiry authority to investigate human rights violations in Brazil, Serbia and Montenegro, Mexico, Sri Lanka, Peru, Egypt, and Turkey.[32] These inquiries, however, can only take place if the government of the accused country has recognized the relevant committee's competence to make them— meaning that governments can agree to honor a treaty protecting human rights, but at the same time refuse to be investigated for alleged violations.

Some treaties have additional optional protocols. These extend the list of activities prohibited under the treaties, such as the death penalty or the use of child soldiers.[33] Or as discussed above, they designate certain organizations to serve as watchdogs and oversee the treaties' enforcement. By changing the array of norms that a government formally declares it will follow, these optional protocols also influence the activities that the treaty bodies oversee and even the procedures that these bodies follow. For instance, governments that ratify the First Optional Protocol to the International Covenant on Civil and Political Rights, recognize the Human Rights Committee's authority to consider complaints from individuals who claim to be victims of violations under the treaty.[34] Likewise, parties to the Optional Protocol to the Convention on the Elimination of All Forms of Discrimination against Women agree to recognize complaints that individuals can file through a panel of independent experts that meets several times a year. Soon, an optional protocol to the International Covenant on Economic, Social, and Cultural Rights will come into force, allowing its treaty committee to review individual complaints too.[35]

## UN OFFICE OF THE HIGH COMMISSIONER FOR HUMAN RIGHTS

There is no shortage of universal laws that are part of the UN system, including the International Bill of Human Rights. But these legal standards, along with their oversight bodies, can't perform the full task of protecting human rights. To help, the UN system has created a number of additional oversight bodies that work in tandem with the treaty-specific bodies. Much of this additional oversight capacity emerged only after the main agreements and treaties were in place. In this section and the next, I focus on the two additional oversight bodies that are most visible and important today.

To promote and protect the rights guaranteed by the Universal Declaration of Human Rights, in 1993 the UN General Assembly created the Office of the High Commissioner for Human Rights (OHCHR).[36] Headed by the high commissioner for human rights, the OHCHR is headquartered in New York and Geneva, has twelve country and twelve regional offices, and employs several hundred human rights officers in UN peace missions. It has become the focal point of the United Nations' human rights machinery, providing the main hub for research, education, information, and advocacy for human rights in the UN system.

The OHCHR helps governments build up their human rights capacity so they can perform tasks such as ratifying and implementing international human rights treaties. In 2009, for example, the local office in Uganda trained several hundred local council members in human rights protection, thereby raising awareness of the national, international, and regional human rights mechanisms available to the people of Uganda.[37] The OHCHR also works with NGOs and human rights advocates to help them in their campaigns to promote human rights. It draws attention to abuses around the world and offers potential solutions to victims.

## THE HUMAN RIGHTS COUNCIL

The OHCHR also provides technical and substantive support to the newly created Human Rights Council, a body of representatives from UN members and the main intergovernmental body in charge of human rights today.[38] The UN General Assembly established the council in 2006 as a replacement for the long-standing (and controversial) Commission on Human Rights. Its core mission is to identify human rights abuses, expose perpetrators, and make recommendations on how to stop their crimes.

The Human Rights Council, like the commission it replaced, uses various procedures to scrutinize abuses. It can decide to focus on specific issues, such as minorities and terrorism. To aid its efforts on those topics, the council appoints working groups or individuals—the latter known as special rapporteurs, special representatives, or independent experts. These specialists respond to complaints, carry out studies of violations, and provide guidance and support in the effort to stop abuses.

One such specialist is Radhika Coomaraswamy, of Sri Lanka, who served as the special rapporteur on violence against women from 1994 to 2003. In that capacity, she collected information about the causes and consequences of violence against women from governments, treaty bodies, specialized agencies, and women's organizations, sometimes through fact-finding missions (for example, she visited Afghanistan, Brazil, Cuba, Indonesia, Poland, Rwanda, and South Africa).[39] Coomaraswamy issued urgent appeals to governments regarding alleged cases of violence.[40] She also submitted annual reports to the commission on different topics, including violence against women during armed conflict and human trafficking.[41] She also recommended strategies to eliminate the causes of the violence and remedy its consequences. Informed by specialist advisers, the Human Rights Council can then pass resolutions expressing its concern and urging governments to respond.

In addition to such issue-driven activities, the Human Rights Council also oversees an ongoing Universal Periodic Review of the human rights records of all 193 members of the United Nations. This review is based on the national reports that states submit as part of their obligations under each individual treaty as well as other information from treaty bodies and stakeholders, including NGOs, NHRIs, and academics. (The role of NHRIs as a source of this information is particularly important, and I discuss them in much more detail in chapter 10.) UN secretary-general Ban Ki-moon has remarked that the Universal Periodic Review "has great potential to promote and protect human rights in the darkest corners of the world."[42]

## Universal Criminal Law and Tribunals

Nearly all human rights law focuses on governments. When governments become parties to treaties, the new obligations they undertake typically get incorporated into domestic law—sometimes also giving individuals the right to sue for violations in domestic courts.[43] For example, the Convention against Torture and the treaty norm against torture have been evoked in Spain's courts, though the government itself still has not implemented the UN Committee against Torture's recommendations to bring Spanish legislation in line with the treaty.[44] The cases in Spain and a few other countries, however, are still exceptions. And in other places where governments violate their citizens' human rights, individuals have no recourse through their own country's legal system. Where domestic courts fail, historically there have not been many alternatives at the international level. For much of the last century, the only freestanding international court was the International Court of Justice, which was designed to hear disputes between states (rather than cases involving individuals), or issue opinions about international law at the request of the United Nations or international organizations.

Partly with this problem of individual accountability and enforcement in mind, international criminal law has developed in fits and starts since World War II. The process began with the Nuremberg and Tokyo trials, which were set up to try key functionaries in the defeated parties for war crimes and crimes against humanity. The defeated governments could not adequately hold the responsible individuals accountable, and military courts managed by the occupying armies were too narrow for the abuses at stake. The Western powers hoped these war trials would establish individual accountability for civilians and military personnel alike. Following those trials, though, there was little progress in establishing international criminal accountability through international courts until the 1990s—at the end of the Cold War, when a new political environment along with instances of heinous abuses allowed for the creation of additional ad hoc tribunals. New ad hoc courts were created to judge international criminal violations committed during the conflicts in the former Yugoslavia (the International Criminal Tribunal for the former Yugoslavia) and the genocide in Rwanda (the International Criminal Tribunal for Rwanda), among others.[45]

Based on their experience, these ad hoc tribunals—which proved cumbersome to create and thus available only in special circumstances—contributed to long-standing pressure for a permanent, established criminal mechanism. In 1998, the ICC was created as a freestanding, permanent court that would soon have jurisdiction over cases involving genocide, war crimes, and crimes against humanity.[46] In 2010, the states parties of the ICC's founding agreement—the Rome Statute—adopted an amendment that expanded the list of actionable crimes to include "crimes of aggression"; at this writing, however, the amendment is not yet in force.

The ICC's designers intended the court to act when national courts cannot or do not. As such, it's a backup court. The ICC, which sits in The Hague, in the Netherlands, is not part of the UN system, though it is open to membership by all governments.[47] It is funded by its members (121 states, as of April 2012) as well as charitable donations from governments, international organizations, individuals, businesses, and other groups.

The court only has jurisdiction over citizens of countries that recognize it, or on a referral from the UN Security Council, a member government, or the ICC's prosecutor. So far, Uganda, the Congo, and the Central African Republic have referred cases to the ICC—and in all those instances, the referrals were based on crimes committed on their territories, mainly by rebel groups that the referring governments were keen to punish. The UN Security Council has also referred the situation in Darfur, Sudan, to the ICC, despite the government of Sudan's refusal to recognize the ICC's jurisdiction. The Security Council has also asked the ICC to look into allegations of criminal abuse in Libya, and the ICC prosecutor has requested—and pretrial chambers of the court have opened—investigations in Kenya and Côte d'Ivoire.[48]

With the emergence of special criminal tribunals and the ICC, a convergence is under way between the norms and procedures for state and individual accountability. In a few regions a similar convergence has already taken place.


## Regional Human Rights Laws and Institutions

Along with the global human rights rules and procedures described above, several regional legal institutions also aim to promote and protect human rights. These institutions were set up to help enforce specific regional principles and treaties, many of which focus on rights that are also described in the Universal Declaration of Human Rights. Nevertheless, the architects of these regional institutions purposely designed them differently, and thus these institutions are distinct bodies of law. They are not subsidiary to the UN. Each of the regional mechanisms, especially in Europe and the Americas, relies more heavily on a single core treaty and its protocols than does the United Nations, which relies on many more. They tend to put more emphasis on individual complaints procedures and rely less on state self-reporting as a tool for supervision. They also have supervisory bodies with judicial (or quasi-judicial) powers that can make decisions and even award damages. While the UN system of treaties, procedures, and bodies has swelled, the regional mechanisms have remained leaner.

Here I look at all the main regional institutions. I devote more space to the institutions in Europe and the Americas, however, because they have developed more integrated and elaborate bodies of law. They also have devoted more substantial resources to building independent courts that can oversee implementation of these human rights obligations.

## EUROPE

The most active regional system by far is the European one. The Convention for the Protection of Human Rights and Fundamental Freedoms—created by the Council of Europe and in force since 1953—requires its (currently forty-seven) members to protect a wide range of human rights for all people within its jurisdiction. These rights are similar to those codified in the UN-based agreements—especially those protecting civil and political rights. While the Convention for the Protection of Human Rights and Fundamental Freedoms (also known as the European Convention on Human Rights) is the core of this regional legal system, governments have also adopted several supplementary protocols that, among other things, guarantee people's rights to education and free elections and freedom of movement. Governments have also adopted distinct treaties that augment the convention. Those include the European Convention for the Prevention of Torture and Inhuman or Degrading Treatment or Punishment, in force since 1989—a treaty that creates not new norms but instead an enforcement regime based on unannounced visits to detention centers.

At its start, this regional system was a means by which Europe's liberal democracies could defend themselves from threats of authoritarianism and communism. It was based on state-to-state relations, with a grievance process that states controlled. Today, however, its role has changed, having moved away from an expression of identity and solidarity for Western Europe, and toward a constitutional model for an entire and quite diverse continent. Its model is no longer one of state complaints but rather individual justice. Under this new model, people seeking to protect their rights can bring governments before an international court in search of justice.[49] That court, the European Court of Human Rights, was formally established in 1959 as part of the Convention for the Protection of Human Rights and Fundamental Freedoms. Seated in Strasbourg, France, it has been working full time since 1998.[50] Any person, group, or NGO claiming to be a victim of violations under the convention can, subject to some conditions, lodge a complaint with the court, so long as they have exhausted available remedies within the country where the abuse was supposedly committed, filed their complaint within six months of the final domestic decision, and the court has deemed their complaint admissible.[51] Despite these demanding requirements to file complaints, the court has become extremely active. It delivered about ten thousand judgments in its first fifty years and by late 2008, nearly one hundred thousand applications were pending its judgment.[52]

*McKerr v. the United Kingdom* (2001) is one example of the many individual petitions that have come before the court.[53] In this case, Eleanor Creaney accused the government of the United Kingdom of Great Britain and Northern Ireland of failing to effectively investigate her husband's death. Police officers shot her husband, Gervaise McKerr, while in transit in his vehicle in 1982. The court unanimously found the government in violation of the right to life under Article 2 of the European Convention and awarded the surviving family ten thousand pounds sterling in damages, in addition to twenty-five thousand pounds sterling in costs, plus interest.

Governments that have ratified the treaty can also lodge complaints against one another. About twenty-two states have done so, and several of those have been relevant to the development of the court's jurisprudence. One example of an interstate complaint was filed by Cyprus against Turkey in 1974 accusing the Turkish government, after it occupied Cyprus in 1974, of depriving missing and displaced Greek Cypriots of their rights to life, home, and property, decent living conditions, and free elections.[54] The court found Turkey to be in violation of several international obligations under the European Convention and ordered the government to complete an investigation regarding the fate of missing Cypriots. Although Turkey cooperated with an investigation carried out by the UN Committee on Missing Persons, the court deemed it ineffective, and ordered further investigation on the cause of death and responsible parties for those missing Cypriots.[55] In 2008, Turkey had still not complied with the court's order for an investigation.[56] The court's judgments, which are binding, can also require states to enact laws to stop future violations and pay compensation to victims.

The European system does not have a state self-reporting mechanism for its main conventions, but the Council of Europe's Commissioner for Human Rights is vested with the authority to carry out investigative visits and monitor member states.[57] The commissioner's monitoring mandate is broad; it chooses countries based on theme. In practice, it has focused on human rights issues it deems as particularly serious, or when requested to do so by the European Parliament or the state itself. Since 1999, the commissioner has visited each of the forty-seven member states of the European Convention on Human Rights (plus Kosovo) at least once.[58] Turkey stands out as having received the commissioner a total of six times between 2001 and 2011. The European Council also publishes correspondence between the commissioner and foreign government officials following the visits along with follow-up reports.

THE AMERICAS

Though older, the human rights legal system in the Americas is less active than the European one. The American Declaration of the Rights and Duties of Man was drafted in 1948, several months before the UN Universal Declaration of Human Rights. Like the UN declaration, the American declaration is not a legally binding treaty, but many believe it is a source of obligation for the thirty-five governments of the OAS, much like the UN declaration is a source of obligation for all UN members.[59]

In 1959, the OAS created the Inter-American Commission on Human Rights to encourage its members to protect human rights. That body now oversees the American Convention on Human Rights, a treaty that came into force almost two decades after the OAS created the commission and is the region's first human rights treaty. Its obligations are far ranging, and include a prohibition against torture as well as cruel, inhuman, or degrading punishment. It also covers civil, political, economic, social, and cultural rights, including children's rights and the rights to life, personal liberty, a fair trial, freedom from ex post facto laws, privacy, conscience and religion, expression, assembly, free association, and progressive development, among others covered in the UN treaties and more.[60] Subsequent regional treaties cover the rights of persons with disabilities, women, and indigenous peoples along with protection from forced disappearances and the death penalty, and even the intersection between the environment and human rights. The breadth of these treaties underscores that while the regional mechanisms are distinct, they often reinforce universal law.[61]

To enforce these obligations, the convention created the Inter-American Commission on Human Rights and vested it with the power to suggest that member states pass laws protecting human rights. The commission also prepares reports asking governments for information, assessing their performance, and offering them advice on how better to protect human rights.[62] The seven members of the commission—who meet several times a year, often in their Washington, DC headquarters—also actively engage in their own fact-finding, typically undertaking a few dozen on-site evaluation missions per year.[63]

Although any resident of an OAS government that ratified the convention can file a complaint with the commission, this regional arrangement shares with the UN treaties the fact that governments can block investigations that pertain to their country. Complaints may be lodged with the Inter-American Commission on Human Rights after all other avenues have been exhausted under the accused country's domestic law. The complaints mechanism and the commission's staff are active; in 2007, for example, about fifteen hundred such complaints were received. Nevertheless, the commission resolves only a fraction, submitting just a dozen or so each year to the regional court (discussed in the next paragraph). And the commission's reports, proposals, and recommendations are not legally binding.[64]

The nonbinding nature of the commission's work reflects that the commission was designed to provide staff support that would make human rights practices more transparent. For binding adjudication and enforcement, the convention created a second body, the Inter-American Court of Human Rights. Though the court's discussions are off the record, its judgments, which are final and cannot be appealed, are public. The court may issue orders, and even award compensation to victims for their financial losses, emotional harm, and litigation costs. Unlike the ICC, however, it can only hear cases against governments that have ratified the convention and willingly accept the court's authority; some governments in the Americas, including the United States, still have not done so.[65]

The case of *Garrido and Baigorria v. Argentina* provides an example of individual petitions that have been filed before the commission and submitted to this court.[66] In the late afternoon on April 28, 1990, near General San Martin Park in Mendoza, Argentina, a police officer detained Adolfo Argentino Garrido and Raúl Baigorria, who were driving a car. Although their family members located the car at police precinct number five in Mendoza, they were told that the men were not being held at any police facility and that the car was picked up at San Martin Park where it had been abandoned. Like many Argentines during and after the military dictatorship, it appeared that Garrido and Baigorria had been forcibly disappeared. For five years, their families unsuccessfully brought the case to local and national courts, appealed to governmental authorities for assistance, and searched for the men at judicial, police, and medical facilities. Having exhausted all domestic recourse, they petitioned to the Inter-American Commission of Human Rights that their case be considered by the court for violations of Garrido's and Baigorria's rights to life, personal safety, personal freedom, and a fair trial under the American Convention of Human Rights. The commission investigated the case and then handed it to the court. In 1993, the court sentenced the state of Argentina to pay financial reparations in the sum of more than seven hundred thousand US dollars to the family members of both Garrido and Baigorria, investigate the events leading to their disappearance, and prosecute the responsible parties. By 2007, a majority of the reparations had been paid. The court ordered that outstanding payments be made and that the state provide a detailed report on its compliance with the 1998 sentence in order to close the case.

Despite cases such as *Garrido and Baigorria v. Argentina*, the inter-American court has been much less active than its European counterpart. According to legal scholars Laurence Helfer and Anne-Marie Slaughter, from its inception in 1979 until 2005, the court issued only 97 judgments, 17 advisory opinions, and 148 orders for provisional measures—most of them after 1990.[67]

## AFRICA

The Organization of African Unity, the predecessor of the African Union, adopted the African Charter on Human and Peoples' Rights—a treaty that came into force in 1986.[68] The charter, ratified by over fifty African governments, promotes many of the rights already enshrined in the UN treaties. The treaty requires its members to submit reports on legislative or other measures taken to fulfill human rights and freedoms enumerated within the charter.[69]

The treaty created the African Commission on Human and Peoples' Rights, a quasi-judicial monitoring body similar to the UN Human Rights Committee.[70] The commission has the authority to collect documents, study human rights problems in Africa, hold educational meetings, and encourage the work of national and local institutions concerned with human rights. It reviews reports on abuses and has the authority to appoint a special rapporteur to study a particular theme, problem, or country. After exhausting local remedies, any person, treaty member government, or organization can submit a case to the commission alleging violations.[71] By 2003, the commission had received 120 communications; of the 46 they found admissible, the commission determined there were violations in 44 cases. The commission can make recommendations to governments, but these have no binding legal power.[72] The charter and rules of procedure also don't provide for follow-up on the fate of the commission's recommendations.[73]

The system in Africa also includes the African Court on Human and Peoples' Rights. The court, which came into being in 2004 (though judges were first elected in 2006), is unusual compared to other human rights courts in that it can give an opinion about violations of not only the regional charter but also other international treaties, including UN ones.[74] It can consider complaints at the request of its commission when the accused government accepts the court's jurisdiction. Its decisions are binding. The Council of Ministers of the African Union, which includes representatives from each of the organization's members, monitors the implementation of the court's judgments.

This court has not been active like the other regional courts. In 2004, before the court had ever heard a case, the African Union decided to merge it with the African Union's principal court: the African Court of Justice. A formal legal instrument creating the new court was adopted in 2008.[75] The result, the African Court of Justice and Human Rights, has not yet entered into force. When it does, it will have one section for general disputes and a separate section devoted specifically to human rights cases. For now, efforts are still under way to put the African Court on Human and Peoples' Rights into operation until the new court is fully established.

Some of the newest and most exciting developments in Africa are taking place not in these human rights institutions but rather in subregional economic organizations such as the Economic Community of West African States. Although its core mission is to promote economic integration among its fifteen members, the Economic Community of West African States' Court of Justice has competence to rule on human rights violations. Since 2005, citizens have been allowed to file complaints directly with the court, even if local remedies have not been exhausted. The court made a groundbreaking decision in 2008 on slavery, convicting the government of Niger for violating its obligations under international and national law to protect Hadijatou Mani from slavery, and obligating Niger to pay about twenty thousand (US) dollars in reparations.[76] More recently, the court ruled that all Nigerians are entitled to the right to education.[77] A tribunal in another economic organization, the Southern African Development Community, recently ruled against Zimbabwe for failing to pay compensation to torture victims. Barry Gondo and other victims of torture by security agents sued the state in Zimbabwe court, and then took the case to the Southern African Development Community when the government never paid the damages owed.[78]

## THE ISLAMIC WORLD AND ASIA

Europe, the Americas, and Africa are the only regions with their own human rights treaties as well as their own courts. Other parts of the world have only begun to move in the same direction. The Organisation of Islamic Cooperation, which comprises fifty-seven states on four continents, was created to protect the interests of the Muslim world and promote international peace. In 1990, its member states signed the Cairo

Declaration of Human Rights in Islam, which proclaims, "All men are equal in terms of basic human dignity and basic obligations and responsibilities, without any discrimination on the grounds of race, colour, language, sex, religious belief, political affiliation, social status or other considerations."[79] The Cairo declaration also affirms that human rights come from Shari'a, Islamic religious law and ethics. Like the UN Universal Declaration of Human Rights, this declaration is not binding law. Although there are no formal institutions empowered to enforce this declaration, Organisation of Islamic Cooperation member governments have been quite successful in promoting their group's views inside the UN Human Rights Council, which allows access to more elaborate monitoring and enforcement mechanisms. For example, the Human Rights Council, in three separate 2008 resolutions, condemned Israel for its military attacks and incursions in Occupied Palestinian Territory along with its disregard for and removal of Palestinian settlements.[80]

In Asia, the Human Rights Charter, created in 1998, endorses the UN International Bill of Human Rights and other international instruments for the protection of human rights and freedoms.[81] This charter proclaims that international human rights norms and institutions should not be ignored in the name of state sovereignty. But the Asian charter was created by NGOs, and it has no binding value on governments in the region. There is also an Asian Human Rights Commission, an independent nongovernmental body, but it has no legal authority over governments.[82] These institutions were born of citizen advocacy, and are not part of the formal international or regional human rights legal system.

Recently, the Association of Southeast Asian Nations, an organization created to accelerate economic growth, social progress, and cultural development in the region, has taken up institution building related to human rights. It inaugurated an Intergovernmental Commission on Human Rights in 2009. The commission's mission is to assist association members in addressing human rights concerns, ensure that international laws are observed and implemented, and help ensure that people have a common understanding of universal human rights issues.[83] It makes decisions by consensus, meaning that each of its members can veto inconvenient decisions. Individual governments can appoint or dismiss commissioners at their discretion.

## Popularity of International Law

Even countries accused of awful human rights abuses, including many in which their leaders have masterminded atrocity, have chosen to participate in the legal system designed to prohibit these behaviors.[84] Today, just about every state in the world is a party to at least one international or regional treaty protecting human rights. The result is that this system serves different, sometimes-incompatible functions for its members.

This section explores this puzzle. It aims to explain why so many countries—even those largely unable or unwilling to comply—have ratified universal and regional human rights laws. It aims for general observations about these patterns, although obviously the details matter a lot as well. Ratifying (or joining) a treaty can be easy or hard, depending on the state's internal political process, and how many people and agencies are involved in passing a treaty into law. Sometimes, joining can also be personal. Egypt, for example, ratified the Convention on the Elimination of All Forms of Discrimination against Women in 1981, after the president's wife showed a special interest in the issue.[85] Mindful of those individual details, some general patterns have emerged.

Governments participate in these international human rights laws and procedures for different reasons. Some join the system with the goal of following the rules. They either want to set a good example for other countries or reassure their own people that they are committed to human rights.[86] For instance, countries with a historic commitment to democracy, those on the path to democracy, and societies closely linked to Western cultural mores and practices, such as Christianity, have ratified some human rights treaties more readily.[87] Perhaps they believed in the treaties' values and their own capacity to fulfill the treaty obligations.

Imitation is another powerful motivation for participation in the system. Governments have been more inclined to ratify some treaties if their neighbors have done so.[88] Social camouflage intended to hide duplicitous behavior is one possible interpretation; social pressure from neighbors (with whom governments have many other interactions) to conform to worldwide norms of treaty participation is another.

Certainly, some countries join this system duplicitously for public relations purposes, with no intention of respecting the rules. As law professor Oona Hathaway puts it, "The ratification of a treaty functions much as a roll-call vote in the US Congress or a speech in favor of the temperance movement, as a pleasing statement not necessarily intended to have any real effect on outcomes."[89] Many governments ratified the International Convention on the Elimination of All Forms of Racial Discrimination, for example, to communicate their disapproval of apartheid in South Africa, but had no intention in their own territories of combating racism.[90] Others participate to secure specific benefits: to stay in the good graces of neighbors or trading partners, manage political pressure (India ratified the Convention on the Elimination of All Forms of Discrimination against Women after Pakistan publicized abuses taking place in

Kashmir, an area that the two countries contest), or increase their chances of joining an organization (many European states have joined treaties to advance their case for membership in the European Union).[91] Latvia and Croatia are illustrations.[92]

The combination of these reasons helps explain why governments increasingly are joining the international legal system for human rights in large numbers. Some of this membership is automatic. All 193 members of the United Nations have, by virtue of their membership, already accepted the Charter of the United Nations, which enshrines fundamental human rights and the dignity of every person.[93] Not all of them have promised to obey every single UN human rights treaty, though over time, the vast majority has been ratifying more of them.

In Africa, the Americas, and Europe, a growing number of governments are states parties to their regional human rights convention. All members of the Council of Europe have promised to put its Convention for the Protection of Human Rights and Fundamental Freedoms into practice, and all are subject to the authority of the European Court of Human Rights.[94] Many European countries have promised to implement the human rights laws of the UN part of the system too. Some also recognize the jurisdiction of the ICC. In the Americas, twenty-five governments are states parties to the American Convention on Human Rights (although fewer than half allow the Inter-American Commission on Human Rights to receive and examine communications in which one member government alleges that another has violated the convention).[95] This means that many countries in the Americas have made commitments globally, through the United Nations, and regionally, through the OAS. Some have also recognized the jurisdiction of the ICC. Meanwhile, the African Union's members, from Algeria to Zimbabwe, have ratified the African Charter on Human and Peoples' Rights.[96] A couple dozen countries, including Kenya and Mauritania, have ratified the protocol that created the African Court on Human and Peoples' Rights.[97] More than half of African countries—Kenya and Uganda among them—have also accepted the jurisdiction of the ICC. These governments represent many regions of the world and many different types of political systems.

The international human rights legal system has grown rapidly. Just as most advocates had hoped, it has attracted more states parties to a growing number of treaties, procedures, and obligations.

## How Law Works

Finally, before I turn to assessing the practical impacts of the international human rights legal system—a task that is taken up in the next chapters of this book—it is important to understand how this system was intended to function, or what I call its "mechanisms of influence." Answering that question isn't easy because there isn't a single architect of the system who can be consulted. Fortuitously, however, a body of legal and social science literature has emerged that tries to understand how legal institutions are intended to influence behavior, and much of that research has focused especially on human rights. That work points to two main explanations: coercion, such as fines, sanctions, and other forms of payment or punishment, which can have a direct impact on behavior while also deterring abuses in the future. And persuasion, such as techniques that foster socialization, shared understandings, and information as well as legitimacy. These factors overlap, to be sure, but laying them out starkly and distinctly helps set the scene for my evaluation later of how the international system for human rights actually performs in practice.

First is coercion—a model in which international law works, in part, much as domestic legal systems operate through monitoring and enforcement along with the meting out of penalties for deviant behavior. Some international human rights laws and institutions were designed to coerce governments as well as their accomplices to improve their human rights practices—that is, compel compliant behavior by force, intimidation, or authority, and deter noncompliance by the presence of credible punishments. Coercion has a sunnier side as well, for it can include rewards to governments and individuals that engage in good behavior. Increasingly, the international legal system is developing procedures designed to change perceptions about the costs of violating human rights (and the benefits of compliance) in order to punish and deter crime.[98] Most of such efforts focus on ways to raise the costs of abuses through defining the law, monitoring, and publicly exposing violations.[99] International adjudication is supposed to raise the costs of abuses for specific perpetrators who are caught and tried, and it could deter other potential criminals if they fear similar punishment—such as fines or even jail time.[100] This, in turn, should help or encourage domestic courts to hold their own government representatives legally accountable for violations of international human rights laws.[101] And institutions such as the United Nations could empower global activist networks, interest groups, or citizens to insist that their governments live up to international legal norms, or if they do not, then punish them—by voting leaders out of office.[102]

Second is persuasion—a model in which international law works, in part, through socialization, the creation of shared understandings, trust, and learning. The goal of building coercive power has inspired many of the legal institution-building efforts I have discussed above—notably the creation of independent tribunals, investigative commissions, and the like. But coercion is not the core of the international legal process. The international human rights system cannot enforce the law using rewards and punishments alone; it needs willing obedience.[103] International human rights law was designed to improve state practice partly through a transnational process that spreads information about the global norms that protect human rights, stirs up debate and interpretation of those norms, shames violators, and eventually teaches people to value those ideas as part of the legitimate social order in which they live while embedding those values in society's institutions.[104] The goal of persuasion is self-regulation—people abide by the law because they think they should, regardless of whether they think they'll be punished for lawbreaking.[105] This active teaching and internalization process is time consuming because it works by changing people's minds about what they are doing. Persuasion makes actors behave differently, not because they stand to gain money or power from following the rules, and not because they are deterred by the possibility of jail time, but rather because they learn the proper way to act, and come to believe in the values of the human rights system along with the legitimate authority of the law as well as its procedures and arbitrators.

International human rights laws and institutions—even courts—were intended to work this way by providing government representatives with opportunities and venues to debate and define the issues, pressure one another, and learn. They also provide information and opportunities for activists and the media to take up dialogues with governments about abuses happening in their countries.[106] They are supposed to get more people, especially legal professionals and business interests, involved in the human rights movement and give them access to more mechanisms, such as using courts and other legal avenues, to pressure governments to protect human rights and interpret legal norms. They are meant to foster conversations between activists, legal professionals, and governments.[107] And they are intended to prompt diplomatic exchange between governments, create authoritative expertise, and foster peacemaking communication to teach governments about as well as convince them to take up global human rights norms locally.[108]

This second mechanism—persuasion—relies heavily on interaction, dialogue, and debate. When government officials consider ratifying a human rights treaty, they must debate—and may therefore come to believe in—its merits.[109] Monitoring abuses and reporting on them can help distinguish the accidental and tolerable abuses from the deliberate and terrible ones, and that should promote an exchange of ideas about how best to punish or prevent the worst abuses.[110] One reason that there is so much evidence that international laws are particularly influential in some types of democratic governments—a topic I examine in more detail in chapter 5—is that democracy, by design, promotes this kind of dialogue and electoral accountability.

International legal mechanisms can help the persuasive process in many ways. For example, bringing in new information about abuses through monitoring should also trigger government representatives to think care-fully about their actions and force them to explain themselves. This pro-cess of reflection and justification could change their beliefs about what is tolerable behavior and create new values to guide their future actions.[111] Information about other countries' efforts to take up global human rights norms could prompt government leaders to think about their own ac-tions and encourage them to endorse these values, too.[112] Even declara-tions that have no binding legal effect, such as the Universal Declaration of Human Rights, were designed to have moral force and offer a compass to guide what actions are legitimate.[113]

So far I have looked at two different (though complementary) views of how law works: one based on coercion, and the other rooted in acts of persuasion through the spread of information, debate, the creation of shared understandings, trust, and socialization. For persuasion especially, legitimacy is central to the process. By creating legal customs and a re-sponsibility to obey them, legitimate international human rights laws and institutions could seep automatically into governments' agendas, poli-cies, and practices as well as people's ways of thinking about their ac-tions.[114] In an environment rich with legitimate norms and procedures, it is hoped that potential perpetrators will experience pressure to follow the rules: the psychological or social costs of breaking these rules (shame and isolation) is higher than if international law were widely seen as il-legitimate, as are the benefits of compliance (praise and social status).

Legitimacy is important, as well, because it might lead people to com-ply even when governments have not ratified a treaty. The existence of the international human rights legal system by itself should influence how governments as well as individual perpetrators think about the accept-ability of abuses. A good example of this is universal suffrage, which spread almost like a virus once it began, giving women almost every-where the right to vote. According to this view, the human rights legal system works by broadcasting the best human rights practices, which could create an environment conducive to improving respect for human rights.

## Conclusion

With human rights norms now defined by many international treaties, enforced by several international and regional courts, and accepted on paper by governments just about everywhere, many people are convinced that further legalization, ideally global legalism, will lead to a better, safer, more peaceful world. The way forward, they envision, is making more law open to participation by all governments. More perpetrators of abuse will be brought to justice. More will abide by the law because they fear the consequences if they disobey. More people in more countries will come to see these obligations as legitimate, and so obey them willingly because they will learn to believe in them and trust that law represents the right values. And the culture of law will become a culture of rights.

These are the hopes behind the international human rights legal system and its growth. How well, in fact, does this vast array of existing international legal institutions protect human rights? They could coerce or persuade perpetrators to stop committing crimes, and dissuade others from trying. But in reality, do they? The next two chapters provide answers.

# Scholarly Perspectives

The last chapter outlined the large and growing system of international laws and procedures that is tasked with protecting human rights. The next three chapters, from different perspectives, will look at whether those legal institutions are actually associated with protecting human rights. No single vantage point can capture the richness of experience with human rights law. All three perspectives, however, suggest that the actual implementation of the system's norms is highly uneven. Compliance with international norms is highest in countries already primed to protect human rights—notably in some established and emerging democracies. Yet human rights abuse continues apace because most countries are, with a few exceptions, not fully implementing most international human rights legal commitments.

This chapter examines scholarly research on international human rights law. That work takes many different forms, but I concentrate on research that is highly systematic—most of which is based on historical statistics and carried out by social scientists. As more governments join the international human rights legal system a wealth of statistical evidence has amassed. Scholars have seized on that data and learned a lot about how the international human rights legal system actually works.

While there are weaknesses in such research, scholarship that is systematic, impartial, and statistical also offers many strengths. It is a good starting point for an unbiased assessment of whether (and perhaps how) human rights law is linked with the actual protection of human rights. It allows for the identification of big trends that aren't readily visible in single examples or case studies.

The systematic, scholarly study of international human rights law fits broadly into two main categories. First are studies on the process of international law, such as on how judges in human rights tribunals make decisions. Second are studies that look for relationships between the presence of law (and laws of different types) and actual changes in human behavior. Some of that work also helps reveal which of the causal mechanisms discussed in chapter 4—that is, coercion and persuasion—are at work under different circumstances. I devote most of this chapter to this second category of research because it raises the largest questions surrounding when and how the law actually affects human rights violations. I also look at the main weaknesses of this kind of statistical research. My goal in focusing on weaknesses is not to disparage such research—in fact, much of my own research uses these methods—but rather to explore where this kind of research leads to robust conclusions and where other perspectives (which I examine in chapters 6 and 7) are needed for the full picture.

## Legal Process

The first area of systematic research on international human rights legal institutions concerns the processes through which laws are made and adjudicated. That work has looked, principally, at two main aspects of legal process. One is the UN-based decision-making system, and the other is the work of judges. In both those areas, one of the central findings is that decisions made within the human rights legal system—perhaps as with any legal system—are quite political and sometimes even personal. Decision making within these legal processes exhibits a variety of biases reflecting the values and positions of key decision-making individuals as well as some of the ideologies and political interests of the states that appoint or elect them. Decision making is also infused with strategy: key decision makers, aware that others are also making decisions, maneuver to increase the influence, relevance, and legitimacy of their own institutions.

### UN DECISION MAKING

The research shows plainly that decision making about human rights in the United Nations has a long track record of favoritism. For example, consider the practice of shaming—one of the most important activities of the (now-defunct) Commission on Human Rights and most other international bodies that oversee human rights. Until it was replaced by the Human Rights Council, the commission was the principal intergovernmental body within the UN system responsible for promoting human rights, and much of its work was through the mechanism of shaming. By making abuses public, it was thought, the commission would generate peer pressure and also mobilize domestic actors to pressure governments to change their behavior.

For decades, the commission made decisions to engage in confidential investigations of alleged violations of human rights by countries, issued statements of consensus expressing concern about alleged violations, and passed formal resolutions publicly condemning abuse. And for decades it let particular countries off easy. For example, systematic research has shown that countries that participated in UN peacekeeping operations were less likely to be criticized, perhaps as a quid pro quo for their contributions to these missions. Moreover, commissioners were frequently reluctant to target the governments of other commission members or powerful countries, even when there was evidence of human rights abuses.[1]

Decision making in another body, the Human Rights Committee—the UN treaty body responsible for civil and political rights—has been just as irregular. It does not give equal treatment in making rulings or requiring compensation for all victims, and it is erratic in how it oversees the different bodies of human rights law. Claims that a government has violated a person's due process rights, civil liberties, or political freedoms have been the most likely to lead to a ruling in the victim's favor. But the committee has tended not to rule in favor of victims for claims pertaining to suffrage or the rights of women or children. Meanwhile, it has found democratizing countries to be in violation much more often than other countries—including countries where abuses were much worse. It has also exonerated these democratizing countries of wrongdoing at much lower rates than other categories of abusers.[2]

JUDGES

Perhaps these findings of favoritism simply reflect the political realities of the United Nations. If favoritism were the by-product of the UN system, then perhaps less favoritism would be evident in settings that are removed from the UN system—such as regional parts of the human rights legal system, whose members tend to have closer cultural, economic, and political ties. Similarly, perhaps there is less favoritism in those regional institutions where decisions are controlled by supposedly independent judges.

In fact, research suggests that even judicial appointments to regional human rights courts are shaped by political considerations, and these considerations influence the work of the courts. For example, some judges on the European Court of Human Rights have taken a more activist stance about the reach of the court than others. This judicial philosophy is systematically linked to the political ideology of the appointing government: left-wing governments have been more likely to appoint activist judges than right-wing governments. Similarly, aspiring EU members and governments that favor integration within Europe tend to favor activist judges; right-wing governments and those with no aspirations to join the European Union, by contrast, appoint judges who are more conservative about the scope of the court's jurisdiction.[3]

The fact that national political agendas are reflected in the judicial appointment process raises the concern that judges on these courts can't be trusted to resolve disputes impartially.[4] Indeed, research on judicial decision making on human rights courts shows that these judges have not always been evenhanded, although scholars disagree over whether judges reveal a systematic national bias in rulings. On the European Court of Human Rights, judges rarely have been lone dissenters in favor of their own government when it was accused of human rights violations. But they have been more likely to rule in favor of their own country when other members of the bench join the decision, although that favoritism has rarely been pivotal in cases. Judges close to retirement have tended to favor their own government, as have judges with diplomatic backgrounds—perhaps because such judges are more inclined to act like bureaucrats and fear the future consequences for employment back at home if they make inconvenient decisions. Judges have also been more inclined to favor their own government when ruling on issues that concerned the security of their country.

Clearly, ideology and political maneuverings have played a role in how the system's judges, commissioners, and governments make decisions about human rights. This insight helps to explain why, as I'll discuss in the next section, the impact of international law has been muted in some settings, especially when the law is highly politicized and conservative governments reign. It also helps to clarify why the impact of legal procedures appears to be much more noticeable in states that are newly democratizing and keen to join Western political groups such as the European Union. These are the very settings where governments are already more inclined to allow their abuses to be investigated and their judges on international tribunals to behave independently.


Legal Effectiveness

Now I turn to research that has examined the topic that is ultimately most important: the relationship between international law and human rights behavior. There is no doubt that lawbreaking is widespread; human rights treaties and norms are not universally or broadly obeyed. The questions that matter most, though, are what conditions determine when human rights behavior corresponds with legal norms, and how legal norms influence behavior. Scholars have used statistical techniques to explore these questions. Of course, this kind of statistical research is extremely complicated, and caution is needed when interpreting the results. The exact mechanisms at work can be hard to pin down, and they vary by type of government. Nonetheless, over the last decade, scholars employing statistical methods have made a lot of progress. Their work has examined both the broad categories of human rights that make up most of the canon of human rights law: civil and political rights, on the one hand, and economic, social, and cultural rights, on the other. I now evaluate what we have learned in both.

## CIVIL AND POLITICAL RIGHTS

Statistical studies have revealed the most about civil and political rights, perhaps because these rights have been of keenest interest to the organizations that collect the most useful global, historical data on human rights.[5] That statistical research shows, with high confidence, that as countries become more democratic they tend to do a much better job of protecting civil and political rights. A maturing or advanced democracy also tends to be better at adopting the national procedures needed to comply with international legal obligations. It appears that democratic countries that ratify human rights treaties are quite likely to obey those laws for two reasons: democratization leads to internal political contests that foster accountability, and it also improves most country's ability to comply with international law.

The record of democracies in adhering to international human rights laws doesn't simply reflect that democracies are always prone to protect human rights whether or not they are inscribed in international law. Compared with mature democratic governments that don't ratify treaties, the ratifying democracies have even better human rights records. For example, the European Convention for the Prevention of Torture and Inhuman or Degrading Treatment or Punishment is associated with less torture in democratic countries that have formally joined this international law. Countries in the Americas that ratify the Inter-American Convention to Prevent and Punish Torture also torture less than those American countries that do not ratify the treaty.[6] (That finding holds so long as ratifiers have strong domestic civil societies that actively participate in international NGOs.)[7] In addition to these findings regarding torture, statistical research points to the same conclusion in terms of countries that join the UN Convention on the Elimination of All Forms of Discrimination against Women.[8]

In short, most advanced democratic countries that agree to obey human rights laws abide by them relatively well. That outcome is probably partly a matter of coincidence, since some would act the same even without international laws. But it also partly reflects self-interest, given that some don't want to be found in violation of international law when political parties must face open national competition in elections. The good compliance record of these countries probably also partly reflects national identity, because protecting human rights is an essential feature of liberal democracy. The democracies most willing to observe legal norms also may be the ones most willing to join the system—a topic I discuss more below in regards to legal norms prohibiting torture.

There is some indication that international human rights legal norms might also encourage advanced democracies to make human rights issues a larger part of their foreign policy agenda. This effect has been explored notably in activist democracies—countries that tend to do a good job of protecting rights at home while also devoting resources to helping victims in other parts of the world by putting pressure on other governments to respect human rights. (I look at the behavior of those steward states more closely later in this book.) Two political scientists from Columbia and Princeton universities recently conducted a survey of several thousand US residents. They wanted to know whether international human rights law influenced people's decisions to support US government action to protect human rights in Myanmar. They found that Americans were more willing to support actions intended to punish Myanmar's military junta when they were aware that a government had violated nonbinding legal principles spelled out in the Universal Declaration for Human Rights. (Interestingly, this willingness did not increase when people were informed that the conduct also violated a specific treaty commitment—suggesting that it matters a lot more for voters whether a norm exists than if it is written into binding treaty law.) The effect of the law was most evident for lesser crimes, such as forced labor without compensation. Still, Americans were unwilling to support any punishment if they believed that might undermine other US interests, regardless of the law.[9]

It isn't surprising that international law is associated with protections for civil and political rights in advanced democracies; after all, those are the countries that are often driving the formation of international human rights law and already have the conditions in place to protect human rights at home and push them abroad. Yet a body of statistical evidence has emerged showing that international law is also associated with protection for some human rights in some countries that are democratizing and at earlier stages of economic development (which itself frequently correlates with democratization).[10] For example, Beth Simmons concludes that international law has improved protection of human rights in countries "in flux," with some democratic experience, where, she argues, law sparks political mobilization.[11] Those like Chile that have ratified treaties—protecting civil and political rights as well as women, and outlawing torture—are the more likely ones to grant rights to freer religious practices, improve educational opportunities for girls, and use less torture. This may be because the treaties influence the policy agendas of policy elites in these countries, pave the way for domestic human rights litigation, or provide information or other tools around which advocates mobilize politically. The scholarly research in this area is clear in showing some association between law and human rights protection, but it has been a lot harder to pin down the causal reasons for that association.

That's all good news.

Behind these upbeat associations between some treaties and some human rights in some countries at various stages of democratization, the statistics also show that the laws generally don't relate well to protections for human rights in settings where rights are most in jeopardy. Many governments that have ratified human rights treaties fail to comply. They do not protect human rights—including the rights to be free from murder, torture, forced disappearance, and political imprisonment—any more than do governments that have not ratified these treaties.[12] Even many years after governments ratify these treaties there isn't any apparent corresponding change in behavior—at least not that the statistics can distinguish. Scholarly studies have devoted much attention to understanding which types of governments display these worrisome patterns.[13]

Figure 2 summarizes what we know about changes in levels of government-sponsored murder, torture, political imprisonment, and forced disappearances as well as other violations of political rights and civil liberties, including censorship and the suppression of political association along with workers' rights.[14] These data make it possible to track over time whether reported levels of abuse improve, degrade, or stay about the same. Figure 2 does that with a twist: it links those data to ratification of the principal global treaty that outlaws such abuses: the International Covenant on Civil and Political Rights. Some countries' human rights protections improve (solid lines); others decline (dashed lines). Yet there is little change—for better or worse—even decades after most countries ratify. As the dotted lines show, the vast majority of countries keep acting the way they did before they ratified. (Because this chart looks backward in time—at the number of years since countries ratify the treaty—there is a strong tendency for all lines to slope downward. As is normal with treaties, total ratifications of this covenant have grown with time, and thus there are many fewer countries that have been ratified members of the treaty for the full thirty-six years since that treaty has been in effect than those that have joined more recently).[15]

Of course, this is just an illustration of the relationship between two trends—that is, membership in a particular treaty and changes in the reported presence of human rights abuses. It doesn't tell us much about the other forces that play into these trends; nor does it reveal what would have happened without the covenant. Other statistical techniques, however, do allow for more precise statements about the relationship between participation in laws such as this treaty and actual human rights behavior, while controlling for lots of other factors that are at work as well.

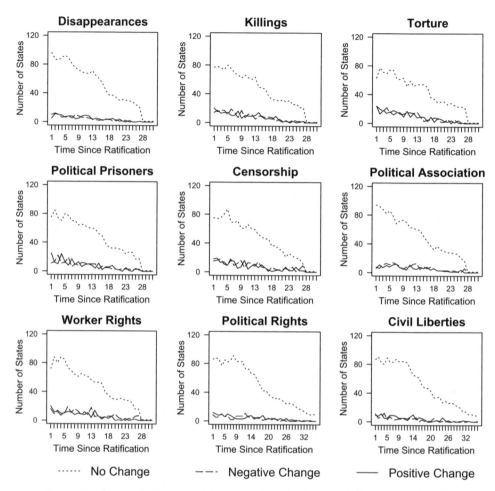

Figure 2. Changes in human rights violations in the member states of the UN Covenant on Civil and Political Rights, over time since ratification.

In a groundbreaking statistical study, law professor Oona Hathaway found that for most ratifying countries, treaties outlawing torture or protecting civil and political rights did not clearly relate to improved human rights practices such as the incidence of fair trials or the protection of civil liberties.[16] Democracies may be generally (though not always) respectable law abiders, but Hathaway's research shows that many other states have a long history of breaking these laws. Most countries don't obey international laws they readily endorse. Among the many countries with weak legal systems (for example, Angola, Belarus, Cameroon, Myanmar, and Tajikistan) or endemic abuse (say, Bangladesh, Colombia,

Ethiopia, and North Korea), treaties do not correspond with protections for human rights.[17] These kinds of places, with perhaps a few exceptions, seem largely immune from the influence of most international human rights laws; at the very least, the laws are not associated with growing protections for human rights.

More disturbing is the evidence that participation in some treaties correlates with worse human rights behavior. That is, some countries that ratify some treaties actually engage in violations of those rights more frequently after they ratify than countries that do not ratify.[18] Autocratic governments (like Sudan) that agree to abide by treaties protecting civil and political rights actually murder, kill, torture, and take political prisoners more often than countries (like Qatar) that don't ratify.[19]

Sometimes, these upticks in violence happen during a crisis. In such circumstances, one of the central challenges for legal mechanisms is to offer enough flexibility so that governments can manage the transient crisis while not letting governments use that flexibility as a means of permanently avoiding human rights obligations. Several human rights treaties do this by allowing states to derogate—for example, a temporary suspension of certain civil and political liberties—in response to an emergency. The drafters of these treaties placed restrictions on derogations, and they also required states to notify others about their use of derogations and follow monitoring procedures to help reveal whether they are complying. The statistical evidence suggests that most democratic governments derogate when facing a severe crisis and don't usually keep derogations in place indefinitely. Autocratic governments, such as Sudan, also derogate from their legal commitments. But they are much less likely to provide information about which of their treaty commitments they are suspending and also prone to keep suspensions in place for years.[20] Moreover, when these countries derogate, they tend to step up human rights violations of many types—even of those peremptory norms against murder and torture that are not derogable.[21]

These facts fly in the face of what the architects of the human rights system had originally envisioned. Their vision was that states would agree to treaties; through that process they would also come to internalize those obligations into society, politics, and local legal custom. And where architects added flexibility in treaties—such as through derogation mechanisms—the flexibility would be used to make human rights law more effective and not as a disingenuous escape mechanism.

No one really knows why treaties sometimes correlate with worse human rights. Maybe treaties allow leaders to do even more terrible things than they would if there were no treaties. Perhaps advocates inside and outside such countries put a spotlight and pressure on governments to join treaties, but the spotlight shifts once the government joins. Maybe the presence of binding treaties inspire people openly to fight for their rights, prompting more government crackdowns.

Whatever the reasons for this poor (or even inverted) link between some human rights treaties and actual protections for human rights, the systematic scholarly research paints a dismal picture of the ability of international law to protect human rights among the world's most vulnerable populations.[22] In 2011 Freedom House, an independent watchdog organization that advocates for democracy and human rights worldwide, released its annual report identifying the world's worst human rights abusers, where, it explained, "state control over daily life is pervasive, independent organizations and political opposition are banned or suppressed, and fear of retribution for independent thought and action is ubiquitous."[23] There were nine states on that list—Burma (Myanmar), Equatorial Guinea, Eritrea, Libya, North Korea, Somalia, Sudan, Turkmenistan, and Uzbekistan. Eight more were on the threshold—Belarus, Chad, China, Côte d'Ivoire, Cuba, Laos, Saudi Arabia, and Syria. Every single one of these states outright violates at least one or more global human rights treaty that it has formally ratified and committed to honor.

While the systematic research on dictatorships is quite robust, the problems aren't restricted to just those countries. Even democracies are provoking concern. Many close their eyes to some human rights obligations—not just obligations to protect economic, social, and cultural rights but even, at times, their promises not to engage in torture. Emilia Powell and Jeffrey Staton believe that the key to this problem, which they have studied in the context of torture, lies with an effective domestic legal system to protect human rights.[24] Enforcement of human rights laws generally occurs in domestic legal systems, where local trials for past human rights violations might deter some future abuses.[25] The problem is that the countries with the most effective judicial systems have been hesitant to join international treaties outlawing abuses because they don't want to be held accountable. The very factor that raises compliance (an effective judiciary) discourages the ratification of international treaties. Such research suggests that efforts to improve the quality of domestic legal systems might have little impact on the effectiveness of the international human rights legal system, although clearly judicial strengthening has many other benefits as well.[26] The answer to the problem of human rights may not be more international law but instead more accountable domestic legal systems.[27]

These nuanced conclusions about compliance with human rights law might surprise readers who mostly have heard about the system's big victories, such as attempts to prosecute mass murderers like Augusto Pinochet and Charles Taylor.[28] And they might make you wonder whether international courts have more influence on human rights than weakly enforced treaties or broken local courts. After all, international courts like the ICC were created to hold the perpetrators of certain crimes of concern accountable to the international community. They were designed to work precisely in settings where domestic legal remedies have been exhausted or simply don't exist. These courts are supposed to be influential even without their own police force, in part through deterrence created in high-profile cases, in part through redefining the meaning of law.[29]

There is growing systematic research on how these courts work and whether they are actually linked, as intended by their architects, to growing protection for human rights. There is some global, historical evidence that states under their jurisdiction act differently. Democracies in the ICC, for example, have been less likely to sign agreements not to surrender US citizens to that court; some scholars interpret this as proof that the ICC constrained these states' behavior.[30] (The United States is not a signatory to the ICC and has attempted to get other countries to sign side agreements that would nullify the effect of the ICC for US citizens, such as US soldiers.) Among the few dozen nondemocratic states in the ICC, membership in the court has been associated with a hiatus (or even termination) of civil war and more durable peace accords, although it's unknown whether the court actually provoked those improvements.[31] In general, reliable facts and assessments of the influence of the ICC are scarce, in part because the court is relatively new, few warrants have actually been issued, and even fewer cases have been tried—all of which makes it hard to do the kind of statistical analysis that is really needed to determine whether the ICC is actually connected to certain outcomes or the correlations are merely spurious.

There is more reliable information about the two regional courts—in Europe and the Americas—that have been in operation for longer and are also more active. The emerging statistics, although still in short supply, reveal that there is some relationship between the operation of regional legal mechanisms and actual protections that governments offer for human rights. In Europe, for instance, the European Court of Human Rights has produced many judgments on lesbian, gay, bisexual, and transgender issues. Such rulings have increased the probability that countries, including defendants, adopt legal reforms to expand these human rights. Nonetheless, implementation of the court's rulings remains partial and imperfect. There is only a small chance that a government will actually implement a fully compliant policy after a court ruling.[32] Compliance with the court's rulings on most allegations of human rights abuse has been politically divisive and frequently unpopular.[33] Overall, states have been more likely to take action in response to the court's orders when it has been easy to do so, such as by paying judgments that involve only small sums of money or covering court costs. They have been less willing to react when the court ordered them to amend, repeal, or adopt new laws, punish perpetrators, or restore rights to victims. When the court's orders have been costly, countries have rarely implemented them.[34] Similar findings hold for the inter-American court, where states with serious human rights problems rarely have complied all the way, no matter how the court's judges have crafted their decisions.[35]

## ECONOMIC, SOCIAL, AND CULTURAL RIGHTS

We know less from the statistics about what role international laws play in the protection of economic, social, and cultural rights. In part that is because there is no consensus on how exactly to measure these violations.[36] This relative scarcity of systematic empirical research also reflects that most international courts don't actually take up these issues.

Despite these obstacles to systematic, scholarly research, some analysts believe that laws such as the UN International Covenant on Economic, Social, and Cultural Rights motivate people to hold their governments accountable.[37] The underlying logic for why international law may be associated with protecting these rights is similar to the logics described earlier. In democracies, for instance, voters favor politicians that adopt policies that tangibly improve social welfare and align with established, legitimate norms. The presence of courts—both within countries and to a lesser degree international courts—can lead to greater accountability as well.[38]

One example is Colombia. On February 3, 1997, the National Human Rights ombudsman, Jaime Córdoba Triviño, filed an appeal with the Constitutional Court of Colombia against the Ministry of Environment and Occidental Petroleum, Inc., on behalf of the U'wa indigenous group.[39] The appeal aimed to revoke Occidental's license to develop an oil project on indigenous lands. The ombudsman alleged that because the community had not been consulted about the project, its fundamental rights—including property and environmental rights—had been violated. The Constitutional Court decided in favor of the U'wa, "on the principle that participation through consultation [is] a fundamental right, because it is an essential way to preserve the ethnic, social, economic and cultural integrity of indigenous communities and, thus, to ensure their survival as a social group."[40] It ordered a consultation between the relevant parties. Dissatisfied with the conditions of the consultation, the U'wa filed a petition before the Inter-American Commission on Human Rights. The commission requested that the project not be carried out on sacred indigenous land and initiated a negotiation process to remedy the conflict. In 2002, Occidental Petroleum reported that it would abandon the effort, at least temporarily, due in part to the costs of the U'wa issue.[41]

While this anecdote is encouraging, others suggest that governments often violate these international legal norms and face few penalties within courts or politics. Norms that should be incorporated into domestic legislation generally are not honored. People who have their economic, social, and cultural rights violated are usually among the most disadvantaged and thus usually do not have the resources to obtain legal redress. Litigation, when it occurs at all, frequently addresses narrow issues, leaving in place the fundamental causes in the abuse of economic, social, and cultural rights.[42]

New work in social epidemiology is beginning to look carefully at the role that law can play in facilitating the human right to health—a right articulated in the UN International Covenant on Economic, Social, and Cultural Rights.[43] But the systematic research done on this topic is focused much more on domestic conditions, including the role of law within a society and other organizing factors. Such research confirms what was already widely known, which is that laws on the books do not translate easily into practices on the street and the behavior of key actors such as law enforcement officers. When it comes to drug policy, for instance, many police are ignorant about their legal obligations, and simply providing them with more accurate information does not change their enforcement behavior to conform to the law.[44]

Work of this type is suggestive, but it still hasn't advanced to the point where there is much of a demonstrable relationship between international legal obligations and actual protections for economic, social, and cultural rights within most countries. The work that has been done in this area indicates that the relationships are likely to be similar to what I concluded in my evaluation of the research on civil and political rights, which is that for some states, international law leads to protection for human rights, but in the places where the abuses are most prominent, the law probably has the least rapport. If anything, the relationships are probably even weaker in the area of economic, social, and cultural rights because the rights are harder to translate and measure. Moreover, domestic factors—such as cultural norms and the organization of the national economy—are of paramount importance and probably swamp the particular influences of international legal norms and procedures.

MECHANISMS OF INFLUENCE

Whether the rights in question are civil and political, or economic, social, and cultural, international laws probably influence protection of human rights behavior in different ways. Chapter 4 looked at those mechanisms broadly under the headings of coercion and persuasion; here I consider what's been learned from research that has tried to identify exactly which of these mechanisms is actually at work under different conditions.

A central insight from this research, not surprisingly, is that it's pretty rare for the international human rights legal system to deliver coercive punishments like jail time, economic sanctions, or fines. Such forms of coercion, though unusual, have worked best when they have been applied in countries with well-functioning domestic institutions, such as independent courts, and in cultures where behavior is already broadly in alignment with global norms. When the authority making the threats—an international court, for example—signals that it is willing and able to follow through on its threat, the intimidation is more likely (although not sure) to work. The perpetrator is more apt to believe that punishment is actually possible and hence start worrying about the consequences.[45] Such threats also have worked best when they have been directed in support of widely accepted norms, such as those embodied in the central canon of international human rights treaties and declarations, and where the judicial branch of government is independent from political control.[46] Likewise, enforcing the law through coercion has been more likely to work when domestic interest groups are mobilized and they exert pressure on liberal democratic governments—the ones most likely to listen.[47]

Scholars have given special attention to the ways that domestic legal actions—such as litigation—can enforce international human rights laws. That research suggests that prosecutions lead to improvements in human rights both through coercion and persuasion—they can even create a deterrence effect across state borders.[48] However, the judiciary's ability to affect government practice is constrained not just by the lack of judicial independence in many countries but also the availability of the particular types of information needed to prosecute abuses. Whether victims and their advocates can introduce legally admissible evidence of abuses and the standards of proof needed for conviction of abusers varies by the offense. When it comes to accusations of murder and torture, legally admissible evidence can be especially difficult to obtain. Standards of proof are quite stringent, and secondhand knowledge of crimes may not be admissible as evidence in court. This helps to explain why so many governments engage in acts of political terror even though they participate in treaties outlawing these crimes. Even if domestic courts wanted to, they couldn't do much to punish these offenses reliably. For other types of rights—such as the freedoms of speech, association, and religion—court-admissible evidence can be more readily available and standards of proof are often lower. That helps explain, too, why membership in human rights treaties more often corresponds with actual improvements in freedoms of speech, association, and religion among their adherents: domestic courts have a better shot at enforcing them.[49]

Despite all these difficulties, national courts in some countries are highly active in meting out coercive punishments against abusers—especially in countries where the legal system is allowed to function independently of the rest of government.

At the international level, the evidence for coercion as a mechanism of legal influence is much thinner. Scholars have been interested in this mechanism because it is, in theory, the closest parallel between international institutions and well-functioning national judicial and enforcement systems. But that interest in coercion far outstrips the reality of how coercive incentives might actually operate through the international human rights legal system. Indeed, most of the international human rights legal system has little coercive power at its disposal, and thus truly coercive threats delivered by this system are rare. Even courts like the ICC so far have had a hard time delivering such threats in a convincing way because governments (and rebels) just ignore them. Of all the international courts working on human rights, the European Court of Human Rights has been the most active; yet it, too, lacks any direct means of inducing states to obey its rulings.[50]

Harold Koh, former dean of the Yale law school, assistant secretary of state for democracy, human rights, and labor at the US Department of State, US delegate to the UN General Assembly from 1998 to 2001, and legal adviser to the US Department of State, has expressed little faith that international mechanisms will ever offer picture-perfect enforcement of human rights law. Even though governments have built a whole international legal system to compel each other to act in accordance with the Universal Declaration of Human Rights along with many treaties that codify its principles, the realities of international politics and intergovernmental institutions make serious enforcement unlikely. The conventional view, says Koh, is that "the overall picture of this standard enforcement story is one of impotence, ineffectiveness."[51] Instead, he argues, human rights laws have at times been enforced through a transnational legal process of persuasion through debate, interpretation, and internalization by domestic legal systems.

One example of Koh's logic is found in the international norms on torture. The United States for a long time hesitated to ratify the UN Convention against Torture and Other Cruel, Inhuman, or Degrading Treatment or Punishment. Still, the norm against torture has become internalized, as US courts defined a law of torture under the Alien Tort Statute, and Congress enacted a Torture Victim Protection Act that helped to convince skeptics in the government eventually to ratify the treaty. Through both the courts and Congress, the UN treaty had influence long before the country was a formal member. The United States, says Koh, internalized international legal norms, and that process is now a powerful motivation to obey. Yet he reminds us that "this process works sporadically, and that we often most clearly see its spectacular failures, as in Cambodia, Bosnia, and Rwanda." It requires norm entrepreneurs along with stable, legitimate social, political, and judicial institutions.

In terms of the law's influence, persuasion is a process that is more in line with the real-world capabilities of the international human rights legal system. While there is a lot of scholarly writing on the importance of persuasion as the core mechanism by which international law has influence, systematic empirical research is rarely conducted.[52] That's partly because it is so hard to measure the elements of persuasion and track exactly how they influence the ultimate behavior of their targets. Of course, the mechanisms of persuasion don't work in all contexts. Persuasive mechanisms, notably, have not much penetrated into the parts of the world where abuses are most widespread. Attempts at persuasion have sometimes come with accidental material and symbolic costs to the people who suffer—visible supporters of human rights are often exposed to the nasty machinery of their government's regime, even putting them in physical danger.[53] As I discuss in greater detail in chapters 9 and 10, attempts by the human rights system's advocates to spread norms through persuasive tactics also occasionally backfire, insulting people whose rights are in question rather than convincing them of their status as "victim."

In different ways, studies on the various means of persuasion rely heavily on learning and legitimacy as a means of changing values as well as behavior. Learning is hard to measure, however, and evidence is scant that either coercion or teaching fairness or legitimacy of the law has played a major role in making the international human rights legal system effective or relevant in many cases. By and large, these debates have been academic and not yet able to deliver practical applications.

## Shortcomings of Statistical Research

At this juncture, some critics will contend that this mountain of statistical research is wrong. Because it relies on quantitative information, which is difficult to compile, it is prone to be based on thin or bad data. It makes things look worse than they really are, especially if such studies hinge on statistical techniques that make the wrong assumptions about how human rights treaties affect behavior. Such statistical studies, by design, are prone to search for robust relationships and too quick to reject claims that law works in lots of complicated ways that aren't amenable to statistical probing.

These criticisms merit genuine consideration.[54] The statistical methods and data being applied to research on the international human rights legal system provide valuable tools that have given scholars the power to discover historical trends and important associations; in some cases, they have allowed scholars to draw inferences about the mechanisms at work and even make predictions. Nevertheless, as with any body of empirical research, the limitations are as important as the insights. The statistical research on human rights does indeed suffer from two central shortcomings that should give us pause to put this research into the right context.

The first shortcoming is the uneven quality of the existing data that are used to measure actual human rights practices. It is difficult to obtain accurate information about human rights violations since perpetrators have strong incentives to hide that information. In addition to those built-in limitations of government self-reported data, the main data-collecting organizations that produce independent data and reports on abuse as well as the NGO staffers and scholars who assess those reports all face well-known difficulties of limited resources.

Such difficulties suggest that most (though not all) of the data on human rights abuse allow, at best, only broad assessments of general trends by year and country. For most data sets, it is impractical to make a close examination of specific instances of mistreatment, specific perpetrators, or specific locations. They do not allow for a careful look at all the types of abuses committed, which means the evidence cannot reveal when and how governments might substitute one abuse for another. Nor do the data reveal when, as with the practice of rendition, abuses are ordered by one government but carried out by another or by paramilitaries elsewhere.

Scholars don't have much statistical information on some countries, especially from small ones that seem insignificant to data-collecting organizations—say, Vanuatu. Moreover, most of the information on human rights comes from a limited number of sources that are generally headquartered in Western countries and heavily funded by Western sources. NGOs like Amnesty International and Freedom House along with government agencies like the US Department of State—all major sources of human rights data—could unduly reflect an elite Western view of the world. The statistical data also compress crucial differences. When studies use ranked data, they face a problem of comparability.[55]

Still, data on human rights abuse reveal important patterns. Those include the fact that the human rights legal system frequently doesn't relate well to actual protection of human rights—a pattern that is probably robust since it appears across so many distinct data sets and studies. Amnesty International and Freedom House, two of the main sources in use, are NGOs; they're certainly not neutral organizations, but their reports are among the most credible and well respected we've got. Nuance is certainly lost in the reporting process and by aggregating a lot of information into single numbers, such as ranks.

While data quality is always an issue, innovations are also allowing for more reliable evidence and interpretation. For example, new data sets facilitate more nuanced rankings in national human rights practices.[56] And statistical advances are addressing some of the problems that in the past have resulted when scholars tried to combine information about different kinds of abuses.[57]

In short, while the statistical data aren't perfect, they are probably reliable gauges for significant (though not minor) changes in human rights behavior over time, and that is the context in which we can interpret the statistical findings explored in this chapter.

The second shortcoming is research design, which remains for the most part correlational.[58] Some studies, for instance, compare the trajectory of actual human rights practices before and after a country ratifies a treaty with the average trajectory in nonratifying countries. Although it is tempting to draw causal inferences from correlations and make statements like "that treaty caused improvements," many of the important associations produced by this research do not prove causation. Instead, the best that most of this research achieves is showing that one process, such as participation in a treaty or court proceeding, correlates systematically to another process, such as respect (or lack thereof) for human rights in some circumstances. A relationship, however, is not conclusive proof that one process has caused the other.

The complexities and limitations of research design help explain why statistical research on the influence of international human rights treaties has been controversial. Consider, for example, the recurring finding that participation in some treaties actually correlates with worse human rights behavior—a finding I explored earlier in this chapter. This correlation could have many causes. Treaties may have caused more violations, they may have had no influence on human rights, or the human rights performance of participants may have been even worse without treaties—yet none of the existing research provides a satisfactory explanation for the underlying cause of this correlation.

The distinctions between correlation and causation are as old as the field of statistics, and scholars are acutely aware that correlations don't prove causation. The big news in scholarship is that this problem is beginning to dwindle with the expanded use of sophisticated research techniques—such as the use of matching followed by statistical regression and experiments—that allow for more genuine causal inference about the international human rights legal system.[59]

## Conclusion

The most generous conclusion one can draw from the vast statistical evidence today is that international human rights laws, principles, and institutions correspond to protections for human rights in some situations in some places—notably in political settings that are already primed for accountability. But the evidence is overwhelming that they do not relate well to genuine protection for or improvements in human rights in many places—certainly not among the world's most vulnerable populations.

All the evidence we have points toward the conclusion that the establishment of the rule of law, stable democratic political institutions, and economic development matter much more for human rights protection. Participation in the international human rights legal system, which has limited coercive power by itself, has done little to persuade most leaders into believing in or protecting human rights. That legal system, also, hasn't done much to improve the capacity of governments to comply. The presence of these laws has resulted in lots of commitments to treaties, but much less adherence in practice.

The statistics come with many limitations, of course. Looking beyond those limitations requires other methods, to which I now turn in the next chapter. Those other methods offer a mass of finer-grained evidence, much of it based on the personal experiences and observations of people working inside and around the system. These two approaches—systematic, mainly statistical research of the type presented in this chapter, and the more personal narratives discussed in the next one—suggest that the system is distressed.

# 6

## Practitioner Perspectives

The battery of statistical associations described in chapter 5 suggest that participation in the international human rights legal system doesn't always relate well to actual respect for human rights. It relates best in particular contexts—notably in the presence of factors that are strongly associated with democratic rule, such as a well-functioning independent national legal system and organized civil society that can hold governments accountable through elections or other mechanisms. But the statistical research can only reveal so much. It is best for looking at broad patterns, and it's only as good as the quality of the underlying data. Crucially, it has a hard time revealing exactly what causes the associations between law and human rights behavior. For additional insights I look to other perspectives, and in this chapter I explore the personal experiences and observations of human rights practitioners working inside as well as around the legal system. I won't review all that practitioners have written; instead, I concentrate on their critiques that shed light on the most worrying findings from the statistical research examined in chapter 5. Looking at the two perspectives together—the statistical scholarly research, and more anecdotal but in-depth examination of particular laws and procedures from the perspectives of the people most closely familiar with them—helps set the stage for later parts of this book. They help reveal what international law can achieve, and where other approaches to promoting and protecting human rights will be needed.

In 1999 and 2000, law professors Christof Heyns—the UN special rapporteur on extrajudicial, summary, or arbitrary executions—and Frans Viljoen carried out an innovative study of the impact of the UN human rights treaties and their supervisory bodies. Working in collaboration with the UN OHCHR, they looked at twenty countries in Africa, the Americas, Asia, and Europe.[1] They picked countries where human rights treaties were most likely to have made a difference, favoring countries that had ratified the treaties and avoiding countries at war that were hopeless cases for international law.[2] In each place, they sent in country specialists, including academics, members of NGOs, and legal practitioners, to conduct hundreds of interviews with relevant governmental and nongovernmental actors. Together, the specialists, guided by a questionnaire for each treaty, produced more than two thousand pages of observations. They looked for evidence of "any influence that these treaties may have had in ensuring the realization of the norms they espouse in the individual countries," including "reporting, individual complaints, or inquiries, or because treaty norms have been internalized in domestic legal systems or cultures."[3] They were not looking for perfect results, just some indication that the treaties had influence.

From the many facts they gathered on the ground in these countries, Heyns and Viljoen drew two central conclusions that, as this chapter recounts, have since been confirmed by many other observers. The first was that the international human rights legal system has raised awareness of some individuals and institutions. This awareness has shaped how some countries "understand" the presence of basic human rights as well as the need to protect them. Second, they found a vast difference between the actual and potential impact of the human rights legal system.

The system, Heyns and Viljoen observed, has had the least impact on those governments that sign on to the treaties while making no effort to integrate the legal norms into domestic law or practices. Echoing the findings of the statistical research discussed in chapter 5, they found that the governments most likely to abuse human rights were the least likely to be put in the spotlight by the UN monitoring bodies. (One of the chief means of enforcement in the international human rights legal system is the shaming and pressure that follows from putting a country's poor record under scrutiny.) While most in need of reform, those governments were least likely to be criticized because despite being formal ratified members of the human rights system, they choose not to participate in most enforcement procedures or simply ignored inconvenient rulings. For them, the commitments to laws on paper are deceptions.

The Heyns and Viljoen study is unusual because it is so thorough and extensive. There are other studies that also look at elements of the system, however, along with a wealth of narratives by practitioners who have experience with the system. And like the systematic scholarly work, these narratives offer good news and bad news. I start with some good news and then turn to more troubling findings. The good news is important—a lot has been written about the system's achievements—but I focus on the bad news because it helps explain the most disconcerting findings in chapter 5 and also sets the agenda for possible reforms, which I examine in chapter 7.

## Good News

Most of the good news about the effects of the international human rights legal system comes, as Heyns and Viljoen emphasized, through effects within countries. In particular, the studies have stressed two main effects: on national law (including constitutions) and on domestic politics.

EFFECTS ON CONSTITUTIONS AND NATIONAL LAW

International treaties were designed to affect government behavior partly by shaping domestic law. On this account, international law—especially the set of norms embodied in the Universal Declaration of Human Rights—has played a clear and significant role in shaping how national authorities draft some national constitutions. The governments of Colombia, Estonia, Finland, the Philippines, Romania, Russia, and South Africa, for example, all borrowed wording from various human rights treaties when they drafted or revised their constitutions. In Estonia and Lithuania today, there are constitutional guarantees for human rights through general clauses on the domestic applicability of treaties.[4] The South African constitution instructs courts to have regard for human rights treaties in their interpretation of the bill of rights.[5]

Looking beyond constitutional effects, international treaties and legal customs also have an impact on national legislation. Ecuador, Egypt, and Senegal, for instance, have all abolished certain repressive laws and practices following recommendations by the UN Human Rights Committee.[6] In Australia, the treaty protecting women's rights appears to have shaped the Sex Discrimination Act of 1984. In Finland, the treaty against racial discrimination informed the Amendment to the Penal Code. In South Africa, both treaties protecting women and children informed the Domestic Violence Act, and there are other examples too.[7]

In some circumstances, international law can have particularly powerful effects on how national courts interpret and apply the law through litigation. Treaties, especially some regional ones, have influenced the decisions of some domestic courts, particularly in countries like Australia, Canada, Finland, and South Africa, as the jurisprudence of treaty bodies has gradually come to be recognized by courts in these settings.[8] The Heyns and Viljoen study, for example, found that "in some isolated instances, treaties have been used as an independent basis on which the substantive outcome of cases in domestic courts has hinged," or more frequently, "as interpretative guides to clarify legislative provisions, such as those of the national bills of rights."[9] The Supreme Court of Canada recently stated that the "values reflected in international human rights law may help inform the contextual approach to statutory interpretation and judicial review."[10] The Inter-American Court of Human Rights' declaration that Peru's amnesty laws were incompatible with the principal American human rights treaty led to prosecution of rights violators that the government had previously protected from legal proceedings.[11]

Of course, these effects are evident only in some settings. Most of the world doesn't yet act like Canada and Peru. Court decisions in places such as India, Iran, Romania, Russia, Egypt, and Zambia, to name just a few, have so far made limited references to international human rights treaties.[12] This is at least partially a result of the different processes by which governments incorporate international treaties into domestic law and also due to the constitutional authority of the treaties. In Iran, for example, Islamic law is superior to treaties and overrides their authority. Even in Europe, which has the most active regional human rights court, an analysis by human rights lawyer and professor Steven Greer suggests caution in proclaiming the effectiveness of that legal system. According to Greer,

> There can be no doubt that laws and practices in many member states have been changed as a result of successful litigation by individuals before the European Court of Human Rights . . . [I]t is not clear that individual applications provide the most effective means of dealing with systemic or structural compliance problems—such as gross violations stemming either from an authoritarian culture in certain public institutions, struggles over the identity of the state, or intractable institutional problems such as those relating to delays in national judicial processes.[13]

DOMESTIC POLITICS

Much of the human rights legal community has focused, as discussed in the last section, on how international law has affected the content and application of national law. Yet practitioners also have found many positive effects of the international human rights legal system on domestic political processes. It has affected both the process of setting national policy and political activism.[14] These effects are not present everywhere. Instead, the international human rights legal system has the largest domestic political impacts on governments that incorporate international legal norms into their domestic law through constitutional and legislative restructuring and that take their reporting obligations seriously. In the main, those countries are some budding and established democracies with effective domestic judicial systems and strong civil society—a finding that resonates with the statistical research discussed in chapter 5.

NGOs, for instance, have periodically used the system to bolster their own efforts to put the screws on governments. In settings like Denmark and Finland, according to Martin Scheinin, professor of law, former member of the UN Human Rights Committee, and also a special rapporteur on human rights and counterterrorism, NGOs have "made systematic efforts" to use the system's reporting procedures to focus public attention on issues of concern.[15] They have lobbied some governments, such as those in Switzerland, Croatia, and Moldova, pressuring them to implement recommendations made by treaty bodies that the governments then implemented.[16]

The legal system has also relied on the expertise of NGOs. One example, given by Andrew Clapham, law professor and former representative of the watchdog group Amnesty International at the United Nations in New York, is Peru. In that country, many bills were filed before Congress relating to false charges and convictions of crimes of terrorism.[17] Amnesty International produced a report for the UN Human Rights Committee, and a local consortium of NGOs (Coordinadora Nacional de Derechos Humanos) spoke out against laws that granted amnesty to Peruvian officials involved in fighting terrorism from 1980 to 1995. The consortium invited members of the committee and an Amnesty International researcher to discuss the context of the offenses, and the United Nations coordinated a meeting in Geneva. As a result, members of the committee recurrently made mention of Amnesty's materials during their formal review of Peru's report and eventually produced concluding observations that reflected several of the NGO's concerns.[18] In effect, the local consortium of NGOs was a conduit that altered domestic politics within Peru and also helped spread information into international legal procedures. As a result of these actions, there is evidence that the Peruvian government has looked more seriously at these legislative proposals. By late 1996, almost a hundred political prisoners wrongly accused of terrorism had been released.[19]

The international human rights legal system also shapes the public discourse and opinion within nations when the media publicizes its activities. Admittedly, says Philip Alston, law professor and former chairperson of the UN Committee on Economic, Social, and Cultural Rights during the 1990s, "the work of the treaty bodies rarely provides grist for the mills of the British Broadcasting Corporation's *BBC World*, Cable News Network (CNN), and their like in other languages. Nor can it be said that the media coverage attracted by most treaty bodies in most cases is as strong as it should be."[20] Still, according to Alston, there have been cases of encouraging media publicity. Some of Canada's reports to the UN Committee on Economic, Social, and Cultural Rights have drawn extensive media coverage inside Canada, as have some Australian reports to the UN Committee on the Elimination of all Forms of Racial Discrimination.

Bad News

Despite its achievements, the international human rights legal system, according to practitioners, suffers from an array of deep problems. Even in settings where the system has gained some traction and has an effect on behavior through the coercive and persuasive mechanisms identified in chapter 4, there have been major impediments to the effective or timely implementation of the rules. Legal commitments are broken. Many victims are never heard. Bureaucratic backlogs, ambiguity in the norms, and overlapping requirements limit the system's influence, downgrading its capacity for deterrence and its legitimacy.[21] Multiple reporting requirements—a separate report for every treaty in the United Nations— means "the countries that most often end up being singled out as human rights violators are those that are engaged. Within the system, more criticism seems to be the reward for a higher level of engagement."[22]

The rest of this chapter puts into plain words the specific and practical details surrounding the system's main problems. While these narratives don't paint a complete picture of all practitioners' views, they largely resonate with the systematic, impartial, and statistical findings explored in chapter 5. And unlike the studies discussed in chapter 5, they offer practical insight into the reasons for the system's troubles. The literature in this area is large and complicated, but it points to nine major impediments.

IGNORANCE

The legal system requires participation along with a sense of legitimacy to function effectively. Ignorance is a barrier to both. As a reader who is now deep in a book on the human rights legal system, your level of knowledge about the organization of international law is extremely rare. Many people know little about this subject.[23] A recent survey in the United States showed that 93 percent of the respondents had never even heard of the Universal Declaration of Human Rights, the cornerstone of international human rights law.[24] An even smaller portion probably knows about the specific treaties and supranational courts that are the other building blocks of the international human rights legal system. Knowledge of the individual complaints procedures under the various treaties is also scarce—perhaps especially in emerging democracies and developing countries where these complaints procedures could have a large effect on protection of rights—which makes public awareness campaigns and training important. For example, the UN Committee on the Rights of the Child reports that illiteracy in Uganda exacerbates the lack of public awareness about rights and a generally negative attitude toward the rights of children.[25] This is a common observation from the treaty bodies. If people do not know a law exists, or do not know that they can file complaints about violations of that law, they cannot themselves engage in the treaty process or mobilize around the laws (or procedures) as a way to demand greater protections for their rights. Absent such information, it is hard to internalize legal norms.

Speaking about the UN Convention on the Elimination of All Forms of Racial Discrimination, Chris Maina Peter, member of the UN Committee on the Elimination of Racial Discrimination and law professor at the University of Dar-es-Salaam, explains, "[It is] a fact that among developing countries very few of them take the time to popularize the Convention. Therefore, there is a clear lack of awareness of the existence of this important legal instrument among the members of the civil society in developing countries."[26] Such problems are hardly insurmountable. Indeed, some NHRIs, such as the Human Rights Commission of Sri Lanka, have taken on the task of improving local knowledge about the international legal system.[27]

Not surprisingly, the people most likely to be familiar with human rights treaties are young urban lawyers, academics, and NGO staffers. Familiarity is also high among some government officials, especially those who work in foreign affairs—although many officials who play key roles in the process remain woefully uninformed.[28] NGOs, often working with modern communication and information technologies, are providing easier access around the world. But people everywhere—especially in poor or closed countries—are still in the dark about their rights as enumerated by international law and the international institutions designed to protect them. That is also true for many of the people who actually carry out acts of abuse.

Even when people know something about the law, not all human rights command equal attention. Knowledge of international law tends to resonate when the same challenges are present in local politics. In places where race, ethnicity, or religion is a politically divisive issue—for example, in Australia and the Czech Republic—the treaty outlawing racial discrimination is quite well known, according to the Heyns and Viljoen study, though it is still virtually unknown in other countries. In general, there is a much higher awareness of the treaties protecting women and children, perhaps because these are groups seen as needing protections.[29] According to other accounts, migrant workers and indigenous peoples get less public attention than women and children—in part because NGOs tend to focus more effort on those investigations—while issues such as poverty, hunger, and famine get even less consideration.[30]

The role of the media in the education process is highly variable. Of the twenty countries studied by Heyns and Viljoen, only media sources in Australia, Canada, and Finland had published significant articles on the system itself. Media in the other countries reported little, if at all, on the laws. Many countries in their study did not have a free press, and even in those countries with independent media, few journalists had human rights training.[31] Complicating the problem is that the treaty bodies themselves generally have made little effort to publicize their work beyond the UN press office, which helps explain why most major press venues have not been enthusiastic about reporting on the system's activities.[32] Within the regional parts of the system—especially in Africa and the Americas—the same pattern of low publicity prevails.

Language barriers are also a problem. Most treaties and supporting documents are primarily translated into English, French, and Spanish, but not into many other languages, particularly indigenous or minority languages. Still, translation is not the only problem; the Universal Declaration of Human Rights is now translated into hundreds of languages—presently almost four hundred versions.[33] Despite these translations, most people don't seem to know anything about it, even in a relatively well-educated country like the United States.

Of course, spreading knowledge of the human rights legal system is not enough to ensure that the system will offer recourse for those who seek its support. Yet ignorance all but guarantees that uninformed victims won't benefit much from the system. Moreover, ignorance undermines some of the ways that international legal mechanisms can lead to changes in behavior through persuasion. Even so, other, more austere problems inside the system stem from deeply rooted institutional dysfunctions and quirks, including decisions made decades ago that seem irreversible today.

OPEN MEMBERSHIP

Another major challenge is that the international human rights legal system for the most part has no minimum standards for participation. Its doors are open. A government can ratify a treaty even when it routinely violates the treaty's norms. For treaties sponsored by the United Nations, the only condition for participation in most instances is that a country is a UN member. In the regional parts of the system, the only condition in most instances is that the country must be located in the related territory. Universalism is a powerful ideal, rooted in the belief that systems with open memberships are prone to be representative of a wide array of members and thus also more legitimate than restrictive systems. It is based on the belief that while membership in a system through ratification of a treaty isn't a magic potion that works overnight, it is a step in a process toward better human rights. By participating formally, states are brought into conversation, information is made more readily available, and the salience of human rights issues rises for the government and interest groups inside the country that mobilize to protect human rights.[34]

While those benefits of membership can be important, open membership also imposes high costs. As more authoritarian and chaotic governments flood into the legal system, the laws suffer from more breaches.

Lower compliance erodes legitimacy; legal systems that are flooded with large numbers of noncompliant members struggle not only to earn authenticity but also to convince their more compliance-prone members that compliance is in their self-interest. The erosion of legitimacy wears away one of the key reasons people willingly comply with the law—because they feel they ought to do so because others do the same.[35]

Consider the International Covenant on Civil and Political Rights. Of the almost 170 states parties to this treaty, fewer than half are functioning democracies.[36] The majority openly deny people basic rights to representation and dignity—a direct violation of the treaty's central obligations. A similar story emerges when looking at other treaties. Notably, there are 160 member states to the International Covenant on Economic, Social, and Cultural Rights. Each commits on paper to promote and protect rights such as access to education, decent work, social security, health, food, and water.[37] As with the International Covenant on Civil and Political Rights, most do not fully honor those commitments. Some don't want to honor their commitments; some simply can't. A wide array of states with poor records protecting these rights are members. In Chad, where weather fluctuates between drought and floods, the state leaves millions of people without adequate access to basic necessities such as water, food, and firewood—severe stresses that contribute to the country routinely violating its people's rights to an adequate standard of living.[38] In Iraq, the government still does not provide adequate health care to its most vulnerable populations; the result is high levels of infant and child mortality despite treaty commitments to protect children.[39] The Turkish government has long discriminated against Kurds, whose right to express and identify with their culture has been repressed.[40]

The trend is similar for the other human rights treaties and institutions. More than 60 percent of the governments that are parties to the UN Convention against Torture aren't democratic, and the vast majority of them are also reported to use torture.[41] These patterns are true not only for the treaties but also the institutions such as treaty bodies that oversee human rights law. They suffer from allowing countries with poor compliance records to play formal roles. Today's UN Human Rights Council—an organization designed to be a leading advocate for the promotion of universal human rights—includes as its members not just countries with reasonably good human rights records but also countries that regularly commit serious human rights crimes. Ivan Shearer, once a member of the UN Human Rights Committee, explains that the result of this situation is that "some poorly performing states tend to be given an easy time [by the council] in their oral examination by other poorly performing states, which will stress their accomplishments in the face of alleged economic or political difficulties rather than shortcomings. . . . Adverse findings and recommendations are expressed in moderate language, and harsh condemnation is avoided."[42]

The situation is not much different in the regional parts of the system. Europe looks best, although this good record hasn't always marked the European system. When the European Convention on Human Rights first came into force (in 1953), of the ten original participating states, only three (Denmark, Ireland, and Sweden) allowed individuals to bring forth complaints of abuse. Since 1998, however, a protocol has made it compulsory for all member states.[43] Now the European Convention includes countries such as Poland, Romania, Russia, Turkey, and Ukraine, where human rights abuses continue to be a problem. Since these countries joined the European part of the human rights legal system, the number of cases involving graver human rights violations has shot up; in 2007, those five countries accounted for about 60 percent of the court's docket that year.[44] This rising caseload is a sign that the European part of the system is being allowed to perform as intended. Nonetheless, these countries are far from deeply internalizing European legal principles. Their judges also sit on the court, responsible for ruling on cases that involve the actions of countries with much better human rights records, like Britain—not surprisingly, that's been a source of controversy.[45] The European part of the system offers a partial model for how broad membership that initially includes many countries with poor records might, over time, lead to better protection for human rights—although it is important to keep in mind that broader political reforms in Europe following the collapse of the Soviet Union and the expansion of the European Union probably explain much of that improvement in rights protection.

In the Americas, some countries that pride themselves on their human rights records, such as Belize and the United States, have not fully accepted the authority of the Inter-American Court on Human Rights. By contrast, others recognize the jurisdiction of the court and still get away with human rights abuses unpunished.[46] Of the 462 remedies ordered within the inter-American part of the system from June 2001 to June 2006, 50 percent were met with noncompliance, 14 percent with partial compliance, and 36 percent with total compliance.[47] This record—with half the remedies leading at least to partial compliance—might sound like a good one. But on close inspection, the vast majority of those remedies that achieved partial or total compliance were monetary in form as well as relatively easy for governments to honor.[48] When remedies require bigger changes that are more complicated for governments to implement—such as changes in law, policy, or public administration—compliance is rare.

The situation in Africa is a special concern, where many governments have signed on to the African Charter on Human and Peoples' Rights despite pervasive violations of the charter. Oddly, though, despite being members of the charter, most of these governments refuse to recognize the jurisdiction of Africa's regional human rights court—even though that court is mostly nonfunctional anyway. Only some African states have joined tribunals that address human rights issues as part of regional economic organizations in Africa; some of those tribunals could have some effect.[49]

As Anne Bayefsky, an activist and a law professor with extensive experience on human rights delegations, puts it, "The emphasis placed on universal ratification of the major human rights treaties is a mistake. . . . Disrespect for international laws is exacerbated by sustaining the false claim that ratification is laudable in itself. The system does not work, at bottom, because it presupposes democratic impulses on the part of states parties which in reality are not shared."[50]

## INSUFFICIENT RESOURCES

The United Nations spends less than 3 percent of its regular budget operating its many human rights treaty bodies.[51] Yet the tasks that its various human rights bodies must perform grow in complexity every time new standards are made or new countries join its treaties.[52] Despite a growing workload, resources for meetings and staff have mostly stagnated or contracted.[53] Open membership, discussed in the last section, amplifies these problems because it generates a workload that grows exponentially and has quickly outstripped what the system can adequately handle. Many complaints and investigations lead nowhere. Yet the norms of universality require treaty bodies to give all members comparable and constructive attention. Despite severely scarce resources, the organizations that manage these complaints and provide other functions to the growing membership usually don't have the authority to adopt strategies, such as triage, that might allow them to marshal their resources more effectively. As with the bodies that actually manage each treaty, the oversight committees that are an integral part of many treaties face similar challenges. Each is typically run by only a handful of people who are specialized in that one treaty.[54] The system's foremost experts are not given the time or capacity to study all the relevant background materials for every case, and key issues frequently don't get passable scrutiny.[55]

Judge Elizabeth Evatt—the first Australian to be elected to the UN Human Rights Committee and former chairperson of the UN Committee on the Elimination of All Forms of Discrimination against Women—explains:

Insufficient resources have been a constant problem for the treaty bodies. Despite provisions in some instruments that "the Secretary-General of the United Nations shall provide the necessary staff and facilities for the effective performance of the functions of the Committee" it has long been recognised that the funding of the treaty bodies and their resources are inadequate to allow them to carry out their mandate effectively. Too few professional staff have been assigned to treaty body work, and even those staff who have been assigned to this work have sometimes been seconded to other work. Some meetings have been cancelled, interpreting has sometimes been restricted and summary records are sometimes not prepared. Far from improving, this situation threatens to get worse. Limits have been imposed on documentation and delays in translations have been chronic. Petty restrictions on the distribution of documents have frustrated the work of the Human Rights Committee (HRC). These demoralising restrictions have come at a time when the increase in ratifications, in the number of communications and in the length of reports, together with the Committee's attempts to make its procedures more effective, have increased the workload of the Secretariat.[56]

The problem of scarce resources is most acute when human rights legal institutions aim to perform the widest array of functions in the service of human rights—that is, when they try, truly, to operate as a system. Such elaborate and interlocking tasks can't be performed well on a shoestring, and when one part of that system falters the rest suffers as well. These problems are, ironically, most acute in the regional part of the system that has been most active: Europe. According to professor of human rights law Steven Greer, who has looked closely at the European system,

The individual applications process is incapable of delivering individual justice. . . . Given the current application rate, there is not the remotest prospect that every applicant with a legitimate complaint about a Convention violation will receive a judgment in their favour at Strasbourg. With one judge per member state ([47] in total), the Court's capacity is limited to about 1,000 judgments a year. Currently about 98 per cent of the 40,000 or so who apply every year are turned away at the door without judgment on the merits, although 94 per cent of those lucky enough to have their case adjudicated on the merits receive a judgment in their favour.[57]

In 2009, the European court's backlog had reached 119,300 applications.[58] This upsurge, according to Rolv Ryssdal, the former president of the court, has swelled in part because people look to the court "to seek redress for their grievances in sometimes very ordinary situations, far removed from the concerns to defeat totalitarian dictatorship and genocide that motivated the Convention system's founders."[59]

The inter-American part of the system, though much less active, also cannot meet its workload. According to James Cavallaro, clinical professor of law as well as petitioner and advocate in dozens of cases litigated before the Inter-American Commission and the Court of Human Rights, and Stephanie Brewer, international legal officer for the Miguel Agustín Pro Juárez Human Rights Center in Mexico: "Although the Court now resolves a significantly increased number of cases each year, we emphasize that it remains an organ of extremely limited access for the vast majority of victims of human rights violations."[60] From inauguration through 2007, it issued determinations in fewer than a hundred contentious cases. This sluggishness reflects a lack of political support from its parent organization—the OAS—and its member states.[61] In 2000, the court's president pleaded for greater funding, explaining that the annual budget of just over one million (US) dollars "permits the Court to function only with the minimum of resources, with a consequent deterioration in the services required for the proper operation of the Court."[62] Four years later, judges of the court sent a letter to the secretary-general of the OAS—without effect—warning that the court was about to break down due to budgetary cutbacks. As of 2008, the court's annual budget remained under two million (US) dollars, just 2 percent of the annual OAS budget. The court's main financier in the past has been the European Union.[63] In addition, a handful of Latin American governments, including Mexico and Colombia, have given individual contributions on the scale of a few hundred thousand (US) dollars—contributions that account for such a significant share of the budget that they might put the court's independence in jeopardy.[64]

The only regional part of the legal system that isn't overextended is the African regional court. That's because it is essentially dormant.

INSIDER POLITICS

Another barrier to a more effective human rights legal system is insider politics. There is no question that the system is staffed with some dedicated human rights advocates working hard to spread protections for human rights, and many of them are quoted in this book. Still, the membership of the treaty bodies tends to take a certain bent. The election results for positions on committees—even expert committees—reflect many factors, often with human rights qualifications playing a subsidiary role. Prominent roles on the committees have been given to politicians, such as foreign ministers, ambassadors, and other officials, with little track record or expertise on human rights.[65] Insiders working on their own agendas partially explain why the treaty bodies operate in "splendid isolation" of the rest of the system; for example, the people who head UN field operations aimed at improving how treaties are implemented on the ground often have had little contact with the treaty bodies in Geneva.[66] And there have been accusations that committee members lack objectivity, which is not entirely surprising given that the system's committees are composed of bodies of experts whose nomination and election depends on states that, according to law professor Yogesh Tyagi, also chairperson of the Center for International Legal Studies as well as director of the Center for Promotion of Human Rights Teaching and Research at Jawaharlal Nehru University, have "no incentive to enhance the independence or performance of those experts."[67]

Anne Gallagher, a former special adviser on human trafficking to the OHCHR, observed during her tenure at the United Nations that the

> world's human rights problems are presently being addressed, at the international level at least, by a group of (mostly male) lawyers and diplomats. . . . This has led to a situation where the so-called "constructive dialogue" is often little more than a diplomatic exchange between government and legal elites who, for the most part, speak the same language—a language which is not well understood by those officials, private individuals, agencies and groups on whom the day-to-day burden of protecting rights invariably falls. Numerous other negative work practices can be traced, at least in part, to the homogenous composition of the treaty bodies and the delegations which come before them. These include the failure to identify appropriate national structures on which to focus attention and the failure to propose realistic solutions to genuine obstacles.[68]

## CUMBERSOME TREATY REPORTING MECHANISMS

Another big problem lies in reporting—one of the main strategies for eliciting the information needed to enforce human rights treaties and encourage societies to internalize legal norms. In 1970, there was only one UN treaty body charged with monitoring compliance with just one treaty (the International Convention on the Elimination of All Forms of Racial Discrimination) that had only a few dozen members.[69] Today, as chapter 4 described, the human rights legal system has been transformed, with many more treaties, treaty bodies, and members.

The troubles in reporting are numerous. Some stem from bureaucratic redundancy and overlapping jurisdiction among the treaty bodies.[70] Every country that has ratified a UN treaty, for example, is required to submit periodic reports on its human rights practices to the relevant treaty body. A country that has ratified six treaties owes six different reports to six different UN treaty bodies—in addition to any obligations they may have to the other parts of the system. Compliance with the requirement to write so many reports puts an administrative burden on countries, especially small and impoverished ones with relatively few bureaucratic resources and many competing priorities.[71] In some systems redundancy leads to more robustness, but redundancies in the human rights reporting system for the most part are just inefficient because different treaties recognize the same right yet require different reports.[72] In addition to these treaty requirements, the various other committees and special procedures add to the growing demand for states to provide human rights information. Despite this surge in reporting requirements, the reports often don't seem to lead to results that matter. The consequence is a system with strong incentives for states to spread available resources thinly rather than invest in high-quality reporting.[73]

The result, explains Felice D. Gaer, vice chair of the UN Committee against Torture and member of the US Commission on International Religious Freedom, is that "many States parties simply don't report."[74] They do not turn in their periodic reports or provide them years late, making it hard for the treaty bodies, NGOs, or other observers to monitor the government and press them for reform. It is telling that none of the twenty countries in the Heyns and Viljoen study fulfilled their reporting obligations on time—not even the established democracies with good records promoting human rights. On average, they were at least two years late, but some never fully complied with their reporting requirements.[75] This is a problem that still extends to almost every UN member and treaty today.[76] By mid-2007, more than fourteen hundred reports expected by the United Nations were overdue.[77] Even the landmark Human Rights Committee—which many observers would expect to have much better reporting because it has such a high profile and is a keystone to the UN legal system for human rights—suffers from widespread missing reports.[78]

Governments have refused to file or have been late filing their treaty reports for several reasons. Lack of political will is one explanation, as some governments think reporting is not a political priority. Another is the perception that multiple and overlapping reporting and review obligations are too burdensome. In 2007, there were thirty-five states being reviewed in more than one treaty body at the same time, and that is an encumbrance on governments.[79] Still another reason is the lack of capacity or expertise to write reports. Other factors also explain the difficulty in submitting useful reports, such as disagreements within governments along with unforeseen events and political instability. New governments have withdrawn reports submitted by old ones.

Even among countries that eventually hand in reports, there are problems. Sometimes junior officials or outside consultants write them instead of leading government experts. That diminishes one of the chief supposed effects of reporting: central engagement with the national policy process. Few people read the reports.[80] Officials who present the reports to the United Nations have not always participated in the drafting process, which impedes the full international dialogue that reports are supposed to trigger.[81] Some are evasive during questioning.[82] Most reports, which are submitted by governments that are evaluating their own performance, are not critical or honest enough about real policy challenges—thereby making it harder for the reporting and review process to yield practical information about needed policy reforms.[83]

The new Universal Periodic Review procedure—the process discussed in chapter 4 designed to ensure equal treatment for every country when their human rights situations are assessed—may help to resolve some of the problems with the current reporting systems. The Human Rights Council responsible for the review, however, is deeply politicized. According to Olivier de Frouville, professor, vice chair of the UN Working Group on Enforced or Involuntary Disappearances, and member of the French National Consultative Commission on Human Rights, the process "has failed to live up to the expectations. . . . States who want to take it seriously will be very much involved in the process and will certainly profit from it. . . . But on the contrary, it is very doubtful that the UPR can be of any use in the case of those who are not really willing to participate and who only will be striving to escape criticism as much as they can."[84]

Explains Scott Leckie, former executive director of the Center on Housing Rights and Evictions, director of NGO Displacement Solutions, and participant in the UN Committee on Economic, Social, and Cultural rights: "In short, the failure of many states to submit reports, on time or at all, the frequent presentation of reports of poor quality, the failure by states to follow reporting guidelines established by the relevant committee, the overlapping of reporting obligations and the reluctance by states to use the reporting process as a means of divulging particular problems or short-comings typify the system as it now stands."[85]

Reporting problems are related to not just the writing and submission of reports but also the treaty bodies that struggle to review and assess reported information in a timely way. In 1994, for example, it took the UN Committee on the Elimination of All Forms of Discrimination against Women an average of three years to give feedback to governments.[86] That record has since improved, but not much. And when committees finally do issue observations, they are often too few, too vague, and too forgiving.[87] According to Gallagher, "The overwhelming majority of proposals and suggestions made to or about states parties are so broad as to be verging on the platitudinous."[88]

One reason that review and assessment falls short is that the universal treaty bodies depend on committees rather than professionalized secretariat staff to play central roles in the management of the reporting process. Committee members work for governments; many are paid little (or nothing) to perform this job and not selected for their expertise. Most work part time on the treaty body committees for several months a year and hold primary (and paid) jobs back at home. Yet these committee members oversee the review process—albeit with the help of already overstretched Secretariat staffers who aid with administrative functions. It is no wonder that the treaty bodies' observations are frequently short, variable in relevance and quality, and often years late.[89] A UN study once determined that if the Committee on the Elimination of All Forms of Racial Discrimination reviewed all reports that states were required to submit by 1996, it would take the committee more than twenty-four years to do so.[90] Many concluding observations lack clarity and are written in legalese that isn't easy to decipher. Some seem to have no relationship to the relevant treaty, while others demonstrate a fundamental misunderstanding of the law.[91]

In addition to late and thin analysis of state reports, the treaty bodies' observations also rarely translate their work into indigenous languages (and sometimes not even into major UN languages), making it difficult for many domestic human rights groups to hold the state accountable.[92] Yet accountability is the central goal of reporting systems. Some of the UN treaty bodies have begun to post reports and recommendations on the Web. This is a major step forward, but the government processes that use the UN information generally remain opaque. According to the Heyns and Viljoen study, the Indian government discussed the feedback from the Human Rights Committee behind closed doors. The governments of Jamaica and Iran sent the recommendations to some government departments, but not to those responsible for making policy changes. In Zambia, the Department of Foreign Affairs simply shelved the recommendations.[93]

Reports and observations, by themselves, can only do so much. There is substantial evidence that governments, when they receive these recommendations, often pay no attention to them.[94] This problem arises even with the governments that are traditionally the most ardent promoters of human rights. Australia ignored recommendations about ending discrimination against indigenous peoples and improving protections for women's rights. The US government, which has ratified the International Covenant on Civil and Political Rights, still disregards the portions of the treaty related to the death penalty even though those norms are intertwined with the treaty's object and purpose.[95] After a treaty body called on Japan to abolish the death penalty, the number of executions in the country actually rose.[96]

On some occasions, the review of human rights performance has worked exactly as intended, and governments have complied in response to observations and recommendations from UN treaty bodies. Partially in response to comments received from reviews of its human rights reports, the Colombian government abolished armed civilian groups it had helped establish to fight guerrillas; the Egyptian government once released people it had held under its Emergency Act. These reactions are unusual, however; more common is for governments to ignore or brush aside recommendations that conflict with their interests or cultural practices.

Similar patterns are evident in the regional parts of the system, with one important difference: in general, regional human rights institutions are less dependent on state self-reporting. (Africa is an exception.) Instead, they rely on ad hoc country reports carried out by commissions. In Europe, the system of monitoring allows for follow-up procedures that provide additional sources of information, thereby offering a fuller, timelier, and probably less biased picture of human rights abuses. Moreover, the European commissioner plays a central role with special visits and requests for data. For instance, in his 2006 follow-up report to his visit a few years earlier, the commissioner reported that the Greek government had complied with his recommendations regarding reform of the justice system.[97] Local NGOs and the Greek ombudsman also remarked that since the commissioner's visit, the efficiency and responsiveness of the administration to members of the public had improved.

In the Inter-American part of the system, the regional commission has published more than fifty country reports in the last four decades.[98] Although some of them have been revelatory, in general they are not consistent or efficient sources of information. The OAS has the authority to condemn a state based on the information that appears in these reports, which could provide a political incentive for states to improve. But such condemnations are few and far between. Country-specific condemnations are limited—to the tune of one in forty-one years.[99]

Africa is an exception because unlike the other regional systems, which gather their own information, the African part of the system relies much more on state self-reporting. In this part of the system, most states do not report on time and some never report at all. As of May 2010, no state had turned in a report from 2008 onward, and many have only submitted one report over a period of ten or so years.[100] Rwanda has submitted the most reports, tallying four since 1990. In the early 1990s, the African regional commission recommended that the Assembly of Heads of State and Government adopt a draft resolution on overdue reports allowing states to submit one consolidated report covering all the years they owed.[101] Thirty-two of fifty-three states submitted consolidated reports.[102] The content and format of submitted reports varies so widely that reports are not always useful to the commission. For example, in 1998, Algeria submitted a report of ninety-six pages while Mozambique submitted just a seven-page document.[103] The Seychelles submitted merely a copy of its national constitution as its report. The commission has few options but to respond to states through observations and resolutions that seek more and timely information. State compliance with these resolutions has been called "sketchy" when not in the context of a dispute and "low" when in the context of a dispute.[104]

## UNDERUSED OR INEFFECTIVE COMPLAINTS MECHANISMS

In theory, complaints are an important mechanism for enforcing treaties. In practice, they are underutilized and often ineffective.[105] These complaints can work in three ways in the UN part of the system: states complaining about other states, individuals complaining about states, and inquiries initiated by the treaty bodies in response to accusations of abuse.

In the interstate mode, the complaints system is stillborn. Several of the UN human rights treaties allow participating states to utilize this procedure, which permits states to allege that another participant has violated a treaty.[106] At its creation, this procedure was foreseen to be "the keystone of the implementation clauses," the "crux" of the legal system, and the "best" means for its effective implementation.[107] But that vision was never fulfilled, and the state-to-state complaints procedure has never once been used in the United Nations; it has been used a few dozen times in Europe, rarely in the Americas, and only once in Africa.[108] States are reluctant to formally lodge human rights allegations against each other—perhaps because few states are immune to counterclaims, and because states have many varied goals, not just human rights, when they interact—and those states that are willing to call attention to compliance in other states have learned that interstate complaints are not a useful way to do that.

There's better news in how individual complaints are handled. Under several UN and regional treaties, a person can file a complaint against a government, and this procedure has led to some victories. It prompted the Canadian government to amend the Indian Act to remove discriminatory provisions. Quebec changed its law, allowing outdoor commercial signs in both French and another language. Some states have even paid compensation to victims. Norway acted promptly to remedy violations in an education case for infringements on religious freedoms, including amendments to its Education Act. In several cases, states have granted relief even before the complaints procedure was completed. For example, in a Bolivian detainees case, the government released seven detainees even after the Human Rights Committee found the complaint inadmissible.[109]

In theory, the complaints mechanisms are one of the most important innovations in international human rights law. They allow the ultimate beneficiaries of human rights protections—the people with the most intimate knowledge of when and where the law is failing—to shine a spotlight on abusing governments. Yet gaining access to the international human rights system is a prohibitively costly affair for many victims of human rights violations. Given the nature of the human rights at stake, many of those bringing the claims are more likely to come from disadvantaged backgrounds. If they contemplate a complaint, they face barriers within their own governments as well as social and pecuniary costs. (Some efforts have been made by the regional parts of the system to allow greater participation and easier access. Among these is the Inter-American Human Rights Legal Assistance Fund. In addition, NGOs have played important roles in mobilizing complaints and paying the often-high costs.)[110]

Despite their potential benefits, the individual complaints procedures suffer from acute limitations. In the UN part of the system, people cannot file a complaint without the approval of the accused government.[111] When victims can file complaints, not all do; many do not have the resources or knowledge to access the system. Since its creation, the UN Human Rights Committee has received only about two thousand cases, compared to the much more active European system, which despite covering a smaller population, received over fifty thousand complaints against forty-six states in 2009 alone.[112] When complaints are filed, they frequently sit in backlogs for months and sometimes years before they are reviewed.[113] Meanwhile, when a complaint is filed it triggers requests for information from states, which often don't respond—leading to even longer delays.

Not one of the twenty countries in the Heyns and Viljoen study—not even the democracies—had its citizens use the individual complaints mechanisms effectively or frequently. Some governments did not allow individual complaints. In part, the authors found, the problem was ignorance, as I've discussed already. People, including many lawyers supposedly expert on matters of human rights law, were not fully aware of the option to file an individual complaint; in some places, like Zambia, copies of the treaties that explain these procedures were not readily available. Money was also a problem. Many countries lacked the resources (say, a legal aid group) that could help individuals file a complaint.

One outcome of the complaints procedures is that by and large, the countries that already have a strong tradition of protecting human rights are the most prone to be the targets of individual complaints because these host governments are most likely to allow or encourage the process to function properly.[114] And the countries with the worst records are the least likely to be the subject of complaints because most of these governments do not allow complaints, victims fear vengeance at home if they file, awareness of the complaints procedures is low, and people cannot afford to bear the cost.[115]

Even when a formal complaint is launched, noticeable changes in state behavior generally do not follow. Australia, Canada, and Spain all made legislative amendments or took administrative steps in response to some individual complaints against them. Canada, Finland, and Spain compensated some individuals for their losses. But many countries in the Heyns and Viljoen study did little or nothing in response to complaints. They just ignored them.[116] Canada, France, and the Netherlands all have refused to accept the Human Rights Committee's views in some cases triggered by individual complaints. Once, the Netherlands even thought about denouncing the First Optional Protocol to the Convention on Civil and Political Rights in objection to the committee's far-reaching application of the nondiscrimination principle.[117] From the perspective of the complainant, the benefits from launching this costly UN process are usually low.

Even in the regional parts of the system, especially in Europe where the complaints mechanism is much more active, the benefits to complainants are muted because the system cannot keep up with the workload. Even the European Court of Human Rights—"the crown jewel of the world's most advanced international system for protecting civil and political liberties," says Laurence Helfer—is hampered by bureaucratic problems.[118] As the number of governments under the court's jurisdiction has grown alongside the number of aggrieved Europeans filing complaints, a backlog of 170 thousand cases had accumulated by 2011.[119] (Such problems of gridlock arise at a time when the court is also accused of being staffed by judges from undemocratic countries such as Russia and Armenia that are passing judgment on established democracies.[120] If it could deal with its huge backlog, would the judgments be viewed as legitimate?) The court receives complaints on all kinds of human rights issues, but mainly has found violations on a limited set concerning the right to a fair trial and unreasonable delays in the administration of justice. That emphasis in its caseload explains why, astonishingly, Italy has had a much higher national violation rate than Russia or Turkey. Moreover, though the court does order compensation, it has been reluctant to direct states on exactly how to remedy their violations.[121]

In Africa, the new court is not yet operational, and the old one (the African Court on Human and Peoples' Rights) has only ruled just once—in that case, the court found that it lacked jurisdiction.[122] Meanwhile, the

African commission, the quasi-judicial supervisory body that is supposed to promote and protect human rights as set out in the African charter, has failed to issue clear and specific findings—which would be nonbinding anyway—on particular complaints.[123] The individual complaints mechanism envisaged by the charter lacks clarity.[124]

OVERLAP AND INCONSISTENCY

As the system has expanded its procedures, obligations, and participation base, many inconsistencies have emerged between provisions in different parts of the system. These inconsistencies create problems for the interpretation of the law. They open loopholes for governments seeking legal norms and procedures that most suit their own goals, rather than the ones most likely to be effective or in the best interests of victims of abuse.

Eric Tistounet, chief of the Human Rights Council Branch of the OHCHR and former secretary of the Human Rights Commission, has considered the problem of inconsistent, sometimes-overlapping obligations in detail. According to Tistounet, there are duties under the International Covenant on Civil and Political Rights—for example, to protect the right to participate in the conduct of public affairs, a general nondiscrimination clause, and the rights of minorities—that do not have direct counterparts in the European Convention on Human Rights. There is a body of UN principles for the Protection of All Persons under Any Form of Detention or Imprisonment, which contains provisions that overlap with articles of the International Covenant on Civil and Political Rights. The philosophy behind the Convention against Torture was to limit its scope to acts committed by or at the instigation or consent of public officials (or people acting in an official capacity), not by ordinary individuals. But that legal norm is inconsistent with the UN Convention on the Rights of the Child, which takes up issues like corporal punishment regardless of who instigates the abuse. And other treaties—the Convention on the Elimination of All Forms of Discrimination against Women, the Convention on the Elimination of All Forms of Racial Discrimination, the Convention against Torture, the Convention on Civil and Political Rights, and the Convention on Economic, Social, and Cultural Rights—cover some of the children's rights articulated by the Convention on the Rights of the Child.[125] The latest UN treaty—the International Convention for the Protection of All Persons from Enforced Disappearance—overlaps with existing obligations in other treaties, such as the International Covenant on Civil and Political Rights and the Convention against Torture.[126]

Overlapping obligations might create more opportunities for victims to seek out and achieve compensation—to "shop" for a venue or rule that will most alleviate a victim's suffering.[127] The effects of complex, overlapping laws and forums can also work in the opposite direction by weakening the coherence of the system's obligations. Divergence creates ambiguities that governments can exploit to water down their own commitments; in the face of multiple interpretations the already-overstretched treaty bodies are unable to make consistent recommendations for improving human rights. For example, when considering the problem of police brutality against foreigners in Germany, the Human Rights Committee once recommended that the government establish an independent body to investigate, while the Committee on the Elimination of Racial Discrimination only asked for better training and stricter disciplinary actions. When considering the plight of children in Guatemala, the Human Rights Committee once drew particular attention to street children abused by the authorities while the Committee on the Rights of the Child never raised this issue, focusing instead on the impact of armed conflict on children.[128]

In addition to inconsistent interpretations by treaty bodies, governments themselves don't interpret or manage their legal obligations coherently. States, for instance, often enter reservations for one treaty but fail to make similar reservations in others. A state might reduce (through a reservation) its obligations to provide equal rights with regard to the nationality of children under the Convention on the Elimination of All Forms of Discrimination against Women, yet not make the same reservation in the International Covenant on Civil and Political Rights. The result is a legal irregularity and normative incoherence that can make it harder for governments (and other key actors in the system) to set priorities. As the system has grown in its obligations and participants, these problems have mushroomed.[129]

Legal redundancy makes the system less efficient. Some think it also creates the wrong incentives for governments that might otherwise live up to the human rights standards they have endorsed. Helfer, looking at a version of the problem in Jamaica and Trinidad and Tobago, has demonstrated how redundancy has diminished the status and impact of international human rights law.[130]

Both countries had signed on to the UN and inter-American treaties protecting civil and political rights. Both also allowed individuals to file complaints under the two parts of the legal system—the UN Human Rights Committee and the Inter-American Commission on Human Rights. Both countries are members of the Commonwealth of Nations, and each recognizes the Judicial Committee of the Privy Council as their court of last resort.

In the 1980s, as crime rates soared in Jamaica and Trinidad and Tobago, so did death penalty sentences. Death row inmates increasingly filed complaints with the UN Human Rights Committee, the Inter-American

Commission on Human Rights, and the Privy Council. But rather than help, these distinct procedures yielded conflicting rulings. In 1993, the Privy Council found that prolonged detention on death row beyond five years constituted inhuman punishment. But neither the UN Human Rights Committee nor the Inter-American Commission on Human Rights could process complaints quickly enough to respect the five-year rule set by the Privy Council. As a result, petitions rose sharply from death row inmates, and reviews carried out by the UN and inter-American bodies took even longer. The Privy Council ruling became a de facto ban on the death penalty—even though neither the UN treaty nor the regional one banned the practice.

Meanwhile, with the death penalty a popular policy in both Jamaica and Trinidad and Tobago, public opinion in both countries started to condemn the international human rights legal system for undermining national efforts to fight crime. The governments of Jamaica and Trinidad and Tobago tried to revise the rules of the human rights tribunals to meet the Privy Council's new deadline, giving them a timetable for action. When the tribunals refused to follow the timetable, Jamaica and Trinidad and Tobago denounced their treaty obligations.

In 1997, Jamaica pulled out of the First Optional Protocol to the International Covenant on Civil and Political Rights, the UN treaty that gave individuals the right to file complaints about abuses of their political and civil rights to the Human Rights Committee. In 1998, Trinidad and Tobago pulled out of both that UN treaty and the American one. It soon tried to rejoin the UN treaty, but with a reservation that would have prevented the Human Rights Committee from reviewing petitions from its death row inmates. The committee rejected the reservation, and in 2000, Trinidad and Tobago pulled out of the treaty altogether. These two experiences, probably rare, demonstrate how an overlegalized system can give governments incentives to opt out of legal systems that otherwise could have an influence on the protection of human rights.

These outcomes are hardly surprising in a system where treaty bodies are largely independent from one another. The result is that "the substantive quality of the work of each treaty body depends on the individuals who are elected to these bodies, and those who provide administrative support from within the UN human rights system. This type of system is therefore dependent on fluctuating subjective factors which produce unforeseeable variables."[131]

WEAK ENFORCEMENT

In any country with a well-functioning criminal law system a police officer can arrest a scofflaw, courts can punish the offender, and the criminal justice system can usually see to it that the court's orders are carried out. International treaty bodies, such as the Human Rights Committee, are different. They are empowered to oversee the reporting process and complaints procedures, but they have no way to ensure that governments implement their observations and conclusions. Governments get to decide whether and how to react. Much of the time, governments simply ignore these international bodies.

UN war crimes expert Mahmoud Cherif Bassiouni puts in plain words the problem of enforcement. He served as the independent expert for the Commission on Human Rights on the Situation of Human Rights in Afghanistan, chairperson of the Drafting Committee for the Diplomatic Conference on the Establishment of an ICC, chairperson of the UN Security Council's Commission to Investigate Violations of International Humanitarian Law in the Former Yugoslavia, and chairperson of the Drafting Committee of the UN Treaty on Basic Principles of Justice for Victims of Crime and Abuse of Power. Bassiouni explains that

> there is an inherent tension between the object and purpose of the human rights treaties and the procedures for their enforcement: on the one hand the treaties and their mechanisms are meant to recognize and vindicate rights, and on the other hand the strength and effectiveness of their enforcement relies wholly on the will of the State parties, the same States who are themselves responsible for the violations identified in the treaties. In this entire process the affected individual has little or nothing to do with the process.[132]

This tension pervades almost every aspect of human rights law. Over a decade ago, the UN high commissioner promised to give special attention to implementation of the Human Rights Committee's decisions and recommendations.[133] But according to a legal expert on the committee, "There is little change in reality, and parts of the High Commissioner's promise have remained unfilled. At the same time, an initiative to involve other organs of the UN system to handle a grave human rights situation is not appreciated by some members of the HRCttee [Human Rights Committee] itself."[134] Though treaty bodies can express their views on human rights, most have no real power to carry out visits, conduct inquiries or investigations during the consideration of individual communications, or provide or seek advisory opinions from the International Court of Justice.[135] They cannot give legal aid to victims making complaints, and their comments, observations, and decisions are not legally binding. Thus, their suggestions for remedies seldom "threaten state interests sufficiently to bring about prompt compliance."[136] That helps explain why the International Law Association's UN reform study group has expressed the view that "the present situation of monitoring and enforcement of human rights through the UN is far from fully effective in attaining wider observance of human rights at the global level, and indeed even at the local level of some relatively well resourced and otherwise well-meaning states."[137]

Mindful of the enforcement problem, experts hoped that international courts would create a deterrent effect, just as domestic courts, trials, and criminal justice systems deter some crime. Prosecution would send a message to potential future perpetrators that they might be held accountable. In practice, however, there is no such thing as a world human rights court or police force that covers all the treaties' norms. Deterrent effects are notoriously hard to measure, but the absence of reliable international courts makes it unlikely that such effects are strong. The ICC has a narrow jurisdiction, and does not cover most of the norms in the UN or regional treaties. According to legal scholars Julian Ku and Jide Nzelibe, international criminal courts, and the ICC in particular, are not actually likely to deter human rights abuses, especially in the "weak states" where many human rights perpetrators come from, because perpetrators there are almost certain to suffer much worse local punishments—torture or death—than the ICC could inflict.[138] Even Bassiouni, chairperson of the Drafting Committee for the Diplomatic Conference on the Establishment of the ICC, is "quite doubtful" about the court's ability to deter abuse or bring about justice.[139] And though the court has a budget of over a hundred million (US) dollars a year, the chances of being held accountable before this court, despite all its resources, are extremely low.[140] Worse, the failures of such courts to impose penalties in their signature cases—such as ICC's long-standing unfilled warrant for the arrest and trial of Sudan's President al-Bashir—could send a signal to tyrants that is exactly the opposite of deterrence.

Some regional courts have greater authority and jurisdiction, but even they must ultimately rely on governments to cooperate, participate, and implement their decisions. If a government does not want to implement, generally, it does not.[141] States in the regional systems comply, if at all, mostly with the least costly of court orders—paying reparations to individual victims—but often refrain from adopting more difficult and costly reforms such as changes in legislation.[142] In Africa, the human rights court is still mostly inactive, so there has been little in the way of binding court rulings to actually comply with. Compliance with the recommendations of the African Commission on Human and Peoples' Rights has been rare, as governments like those in Angola, the Congo, and Sudan have just ignored its suggestions.[143] In the Americas, "where respect for human rights is not entrenched, supranational tribunals are unlikely to enjoy the automatic implementation of their decisions, particularly when these decisions call for a significant political or financial commitment or implicate endemic human rights problems."[144]

It is tempting to see the European part of the system as uniquely competent. It is more accessible and active, and more effective. By most accounts, it is poles apart from the rest of the international human rights system. Yet even the Council of Europe—the body of countries that are members of the European Convention on Human Rights—lacks any direct ways to enforce the rulings of the European Court of Human Rights. There are no obligations rooted in the European Convention that make judgments of the court executable within the domestic legal system of the convention's participants. In general, rulings by the European court aren't like a domestic court; they are, instead, of a declaratory nature stating only to what extent a protected human right under the European Convention has been violated.[145] Many national courts don't accept the judgments of this court as binding on them—in 2002, more than twenty European constitutional courts actually declared themselves not to be bound by the European court's rulings, though many acknowledged that they are influenced by them anyway. Not all states have effective ways to litigate accusations of violations in domestic courts.[146] Yet the European Court of Human Rights has not been able to provide a reliable alternative to domestic courts because it has problems gaining traction exactly in the countries where there is a weak commitment to the rule of law, and where people lack confidence in the management of their own courts and law enforcement.[147] And where a sense of European identity as well as independent judicial and legal cultures have not taken hold, the status of the European Convention in the legal and constitutional system seems beside the point.

Consider Turkey, a participant in the European Convention and subject to the jurisdiction of the European Court of Human Rights. The court has consistently found that Turkey violates international human rights law at a high rate. Until the 1990s, however, Turkish courts didn't much refer to those findings. Today that situation is changing as Turkish courts formally consider European judgments more often. That shift has led to some tangible improvements in Turkish human rights along with new rationalizations and strategies by the Turkish government when it does adopt policies that are abusive; instead of abusing dissidents, the Turkish government has dissolved political parties that advocate a federal solution to the Kurdish question.[148] According to Neil Hicks, the international policy adviser for the NGO Human Rights First in Turkey, "many prosecutors and judges still believe, and are willing to state as much to representatives of human rights organizations, that their first priority is to support the security forces in maintaining national security. If the security forces break Turkish law and violate international human rights instruments in pursuit of this goal, then they are willing to overlook it and even to condone it."[149]

The problem isn't just Turkey. Constitutional courts in long-standing members of the European Union, such as Portugal, lack awareness of the European Court of Human Rights' case law. In Greece, domestic courts have rarely applied the convention to actually remedy problems. In France, there has been a historical reluctance by domestic courts to apply the convention's standards.[150]

Although these regional courts aren't like well-functioning national courts,[151] they do have some impact. Knowing that they can't draw on strict enforcement, they can craft clever strategies to attract states' cooperation and encourage intervention by other states on behalf of the court.[152]

Enforceability has never been the strong suit of international human rights law. Moreover, as I discussed in chapter 4, coercive enforcement isn't the only mechanism by which human rights law can have an effect; persuasion also plays a role.[153] Still, the fact that the international human rights legal system doesn't have reliable enforcement mechanisms means that it can't easily compel uninterested (or even hostile) states to comply.

CULTURE AND HISTORY

Finally, there is perhaps the fundamental challenge to the cherished goal of universalism. Not every universal human rights value is accepted universally or interpreted in the same way into different local customs and practices. Global treaties sometimes conflict (in reality or appearance) with local cultural and religious traditions, such as the caste system in India and authoritarian family structures in Iran. Though the Convention on the Elimination of All Forms of Racial Discrimination argues that untouchables suffer discrimination, the Indian government and much of Indian society disagrees. In Iran, treaties such as the Convention on the Rights of the Child are subject to Shari'a law. In short, some of the laws proclaimed universal are not seen as universally legitimate.

Asian governments have been especially vocal on this subject. When ministers and representatives of Asian states met in Bangkok in 1993 to prepare for the World Conference on Human Rights, they agreed that "while human rights are universal in nature, they must be considered in the context of a dynamic and evolving process of international norm-setting, bearing in mind the significance of national and regional particularities and various historical, cultural and religious backgrounds."[154] Some leaders even suggested that Asian values are more communitarian and less individualistic than the human rights norms championed by Western governments.[155]

Yet the UN human rights treaty bodies, according to anthropologist Sally Engle Merry, tend to ignore local cultural differences. They often have no choice. These bodies evaluate many countries in short periods of time. Their staff members are not anthropologists or country experts; frequently, they are not trained in or are reluctant to recognize the complexity of particular situations. The dominant culture among human rights lawyers and advocates is the application of universal norms rather than tailoring (and sacrificing) those ideals for local circumstances.[156]

One example, says Engle Merry, is the practice of *bulubulu* in Fiji—a village-based form of apology and settlement, used to settle cases of rape as well as a wide range of conflicts and for arranging marriages. The Committee on the Elimination of All Forms of Discrimination against Women has urged Fiji to eliminate the custom, which they have viewed as an unacceptable response to sexual violence that actually provides legitimacy to rape. Yet the government of Fiji has objected to this criticism because it views *bulubulu* as a process that is essential to village life. The Fiji minister for women herself explained to Engle Merry that the committee did not understand how important this custom is for the people, that the village could not function without it, and that the people of Fiji would not give this custom up.[157]

Other times, treaties are associated with out-of-favor issues, such as the abolition of the death penalty in Jamaica or the treatment of Gypsies in Spain, making it easier for governments and even NGOs to overlook the treaties. In the Czech Republic, the treaty protecting economic, social, and cultural rights was long associated with the country's brutal Communist period, and so shunned. In some places, a general feeling that the United Nations is powerless, isolated, and a tool of Western imperialism discredits the treaties altogether, undercutting the laws' legitimacy.[158]

## Conclusion

While aspirations run high, many of the hard facts and expert impressions about the international human rights legal system paint a troubling picture. The system's ability to get countries to implement its norms is highly uneven and generally low. Its capacity for coercion and deterrence is low; persistent noncompliance and uneven treatment suggest that legitimacy of the system is low, which probably diminishes the extent to which international human rights law leads countries to comply through persuasion.

Looking mainly from the perspective of practitioners working inside the international human rights system, this chapter has looked at some good and especially bad news about how that system actually functions. While there is good news, there are also many troubles. The problems include ignorance, bureaucratic dysfunction, resource strain, and weak enforcement.

Together, chapters 5 and 6 paint a consistent picture, albeit from two very different perspectives. They suggest that what matters most for the effective protection of human rights is domestic stability and a well-functioning, independent national legal system along with political systems that encourage accountability and public dialogue. Where those are lacking—where much of the world's population happens to live— international treaties, courts, and other human rights institutions don't seem to factor much into the decisions that governments, perpetrators, and victims make, and local courts have little power to take up the legal principles.

The next chapter picks up where this one leaves off. The list of nine troubles documented in this chapter is, perhaps, also a list that can guide reformers. Chapter 7 looks at what they have done to make the system work better.

# System Reform

While the aspirations for the international human rights legal system are high, the facts on the ground about how the system actually functions are worrying. Chapter 5 suggested, from the vantage point of systematic scholarly research, that the system most corresponds to human rights protections in a subset of countries—democracies, and some "in flux"— which are generally not the leading abusers of human rights. Chapter 6 echoed this message, along with a lot of detail from practitioners who work inside the international legal system and know it well. Mindful of those chapters, what can be done to make the system work better?

Before I look to reform, obviously it is important to keep things in perspective. In some contexts, it is unlikely that the international human rights legal system will have much effect on actual protections for human rights no matter how its components are designed. These settings include contexts where government has failed completely. They also include contexts where government is run by a highly centralized state that devotes resources to suppress the accountability that comes from an active civil society, stacks courts with cronies, breeds inequality, and kindles prejudice. Such contexts, the research I surveyed in chapter 2 suggests, are likely to yield abuse.

With that in mind, nonetheless there may be places where reforms could make the international legal system more effective, and this chapter is devoted to that topic. My starting point is chapter 6, which identified nine shortcomings of the international human rights legal system. These range from ignorance and inadequate resources to fragmented legal norms and weak enforcement. Such shortcomings erode the potential influence of international law in circumstances where the law could be effective, such as in countries where national courts and civil society groups are healthy.

System-savvy human rights experts have proposed an array of reforms that might strengthen some of these weak spots. I first focus on the reform proposals themselves. Second, I look critically at what reform might actually accomplish in light of the many real-world constraints that slow and limit the practical implementation and effects of reforms. And third, I explore strategies that could increase the success of reform efforts. A central message from this chapter is that although reforms are needed, they won't have much impact on the fundamental challenges for the international human rights legal system. They won't have much impact on the contexts and rationales that drive most abusive behavior. Moreover, the many existing reform efforts are a reminder of the severe challenges that face future efforts to make the international legal system more effective. Overcoming those challenges will require other strategies, which I take up later in part III of this book.

## Reform Proposals

To a system outsider, reform seems like a dull topic of conversation. Despite its bland flavor, though, reform is central to the future health of the international human rights legal system. Without repairs, the numbers of noncompliant governments that are formal members of the system will continue to swell—legal obligations will become more fragmented, and procedures will become more complex and conflicting. The legitimacy of the system, already a major concern, will erode further. The result will be more lawbreaking and greater frustration. Reform, if done well, could make a difference for a subset of countries—a significant contribution, even if reforms can't fix the troubles in the places where abuses are worst.

Human rights experts for decades have been advocating reform, and there is a close interaction between scholars who study the system, NGOs that agitate for the system to do better, and the practitioners who steer the system through their roles in governments, the United Nations, and other official postings. Veteran scholar-practitioners, such as Philip Alston, have joined many NGOs and human rights practitioners in calling for reform.[1] When UN High Commissioner for Human Rights Navanethem Pillay reached out to the global human rights community asking for proposals to improve the system, experts around the world responded. Drawing on advice from dozens of organizations and regional consultations, Pillay has offered a wealth of ideas for reform that echo what the community has been saying for a long time.[2] While Pillay focused on the United Nations, experts have also urged reforms in the regional institutions in Africa, the Americas, and Europe.

In short, the system is hungry for reform and overflowing with ideas. While there's no single menu for reform, the ideas that have emerged fit broadly into four categories. First are notions about how the broader public might become more aware that the system exists, and also more fully engaged with human rights legal procedures at home and internationally. Such ideas speak especially to problems that stem from public ignorance of existing human rights laws and procedures. Second are reforms aimed at streamlining the human rights legal system—a concern identified by experts who have observed the proliferation of laws and procedures over the recent decades. Streamlining proposals have focused on the content of treaty law as well as the varied reporting and complaints procedures that are in need of repair. Third is the professionalization of the system, especially the UN treaty bodies and Secretariat, which could lead to a more independent and even-handed oversight and implementation of human rights law. And fourth is investing in credibility, such as by setting minimum standards for participation so that treaty registers are not filled with countries whose governments have no intention of obeying the law. Because a more credible system is also probably a more legitimate one, such efforts could overall make human rights law more effective. I look at each of these four types of reform in turn.

PUBLIC OUTREACH

Ignorance, chapter 6 explained, is a genuine problem for the effectiveness of international law. On this front, experts have offered many proposals to better equip the human rights legal system to promote awareness about its values, obligations, and procedures.[3] Such reforms could make government leaders, agencies, ministries, and bureaucrats at all levels— along with the general public—more aware of the system. Simply providing information will not, of course, automatically inspire compliance with human rights laws and norms. Like all the reforms discussed in this chapter, efforts to promote awareness aren't a silver bullet of effectiveness. Still, they can raise the odds that the legal system will have an impact.

The system could better educate and train members of national legal communities—judges, lawyers, and legal aids—about human rights obligations and international legal procedures and opportunities.[4] This community within countries is crucial, for the best hope to protect human rights is not for an international court to prosecute human rights offenders; usually, recourse to an international court is a last resort that isn't available in most circumstances. Instead, a functioning domestic justice system is essential to ensuring that domestic law protects human rights and punishes criminal offenders.[5] Better awareness of international rights and procedures can help national legal systems evolve in ways that are consistent with local legal cultures and jurisprudence yet also supportive of international norms.[6]

The system might also have more impact if more victims and their representatives knew about the array of remedies available at home and abroad. With these goals in mind, experts have proposed expanded media and communications outreach, including the translation of legal materials into forms (and languages) that are more accessible to nonspecialists. Some also recommend more coordination and outreach efforts to engage regional and local media, even through instant social media such as Facebook and Twitter that can reach people directly in formats popular with younger generations.[7] Some informational reforms also focus on perpetrators. Police officers, prison guards, security forces, and other agents of violence, many of whom are responsible for carrying out orders that result in human rights violations, perhaps would be less likely to commit these crimes if they understood their obligations and the possible consequences.

Experts know that reforms of this type must be sustained and system-wide. Providing information or training to one element—say, journalists—is less effective than engaging the complementary parts of a network, such as lawyers, NGOs, and police. Repeated efforts—and repeated visits to a country by consultants—are more effective than one-shot reforms.[8]

## STREAMLINING

Reformers have often urged greater consistency—to avoid creating mixed signals and incentives—as human rights standards proliferate. Where redundancy is unavoidable, better coordination across the system can give key players within each component fuller information about how the rest of the system works.[9] Such ideas have been advanced not just in the United Nations but also across the regional treaty bodies. At their core is the idea that inconsistency and confusion undercut the efficiency, credibility, and efficacy of international law.

Some of these reform proposals focus on reducing inconsistency in the substantive content of international law. Such efforts, it is thought, might ameliorate problems such as confusion in jurisdiction. Some focus on particular legal procedures—for example, a requirement (understandably controversial) that member states cannot make incompatible reservations to different treaties with overlapping content.[10]

Most reform efforts aimed at streamlining have focused on the system's varied information reporting processes. Making reporting work better is important because reporting—along with the effects of international law on litigation in domestic courts—is perhaps the most significant mechanism for international human rights institutions to have a practical impact on abusive behavior. To work as intended by its creators, the UN part of the system relies heavily on governments to self-report on their efforts and limitations in protecting human rights. (Some regional parts of the system, such as in Africa, have similar self-reporting obligations. The most active regional parts, notably in Europe, rely less on government self-reporting and more on individual complaints.) Self-reporting forces governments to assess their own policies and practices—when it works it leads to self-monitoring, learning, and a focusing of attention on areas where government needs to improve its performance. It can be a resource for other stakeholders, such as NGOs, who use these reports to shame governments. Given all the evidence that even the best-performing governments hand in late and incomplete reports, perhaps reforms could lead to reporting systems that provide more useful information and a greater practical effect on human rights abuse.

Reforms have sought to streamline existing requirements while also requesting more useful information. Reformers have also looked for ways to raise the cost of nonreporting and failures to follow reporting procedure. One proposal in this spirit would allow treaty bodies to use other sources of information when they review the record of nonreporting governments. Publishing such reviews could give nonreporting governments a strong incentive to offer their own account.[11] The UN Committee on Economic, Social, and Cultural Rights switched to this procedure a while ago, and the result was that overdue reports "suddenly materialized."[12] What remains unclear, however, is whether these extra reports have actually led to better protections for human rights.

A more effective international reporting system might also work better in tandem with the elaborate systems that a few countries use to provide information on human rights abuses around the world. Every year for the last three decades, the US Department of State has published a report on the individual, civil, political, and worker rights set forth in the Universal Declaration of Human Rights for countries that receive US assistance or are UN members.[13] These reports, presented to Congress, are widely circulated, published online, and inform US foreign policy and public discourse.[14] (The United States also puts online the self-reports it provides to the United Nations.)[15] The UK Foreign and Commonwealth Office publishes an annual report on human rights containing detailed information on other countries' records.[16] The NGO Amnesty International also reviews human rights practices around the world, and publishes its own annual reports on countries' practices.[17] Another NGO, Freedom House, independently reports on civil and political rights.[18] Some people believe these reports might pressure governments to improve human rights, although that is a question of intense debate.[19] Such reports are not a replacement for individual governments to participate in the treaty reporting process, but they are another source of information.

Some problems with self-reporting are rooted in state capacity, which active investments in capacity building can help address. Many experts seem convinced that making governments write separate reports for every law is a burden on them.[20] That burden may help explain why there are thousands of late reports due to the United Nations.[21] In light of all the challenges with the existing reporting requirements, experts are particularly wary of new treaty obligations that would expand reporting obligations—especially for small or poor states.[22]

Perhaps the most important reforms to reporting are efforts, notably with streamlining, that would make it easier for governments to comply. One proposal, supported by UN secretary-generals Kofi Annan and Ban Ki-moon, would consolidate existing reporting requirements by merging the UN treaty bodies.[23] Where almost a dozen treaty bodies now work, one or two might suffice.[24] Nico Schrijver, law professor and vice chair of the UN Committee on Economic, Social, and Cultural Rights (and member of the Senate of the Dutch house of parliament), has even proposed the eventual creation of one worldwide human rights treaty with an integrated reporting system.[25] The idea behind these various proposals is the same. Instead of writing many second-rate and redundant reports for many different committees, a government would write one or two comprehensive reports. Treaty bodies would combine their resources, expertise, and administrative capacity to review those consolidated reports in a timelier and more comprehensive manner.[26] Such integration and streamlining would resonate with the reforms that the UN has already made, notably the creation of the Universal Periodic Review I discussed in chapters 4 and 6.

Integration and streamlining would allow treaty bodies to be more strategic in how they deploy scarce resources. For example, with more accurate and timely information these bodies might help focus the individual complaints process on the most serious cases. A more strategic sense of overall levels of abuse and policy reforms that might address abuse could help treaty bodies and individual governments identify the complaints and policy reforms that would be most important to pursue.

PROFESSIONALIZE THE SYSTEM

While streamlining could make the universal and regional parts of the system more efficient, the system also needs more resources and professionalization.[27] There simply are not enough people, time, or resources to process all the reports, or for all the committees that review the reports to issue responses that are detailed enough to be helpful.[28] If more governments ratify more treaties and file more reports, the system could come to a near standstill unless it is given new professional capacity. The treaty bodies need extended and more frequent sessions to review the reports. In the United Nations, meeting times have expanded a bit over the years, but much more is needed.[29] The Secretariat needs more resources. And experts contend that the treaty body committees need greater professionalization, independence, impartiality, and expertise—achieving such outcomes will require greater use of performance assessments, improved remuneration, and better training.[30] More money into the system might have an impact on its ability to improve the monitoring process by paying and training professional committee members to work on a full-time basis.[31]

Professionalization could work in tandem with many other proposals to streamline decision-making. Some have suggested an end to the United Nations' consensus decision-making process that eats up a lot of time. Another recommendation is to reduce the need for expensive translation services by requiring that main documents be submitted in an official language—if possible, a major world language; this is contrary to ideas discussed earlier in this chapter to increase translations.[32] Meeting times, some propose, could be used more efficiently, with less duplication in questioning. And intersessional periods could be used more effectively for follow-up, which doesn't much happen now.[33]

Hand in hand with more professionalized treaty bodies are proposals for reforms that would give a stronger, central role to the UN Secretariat. For example, the Secretariat might provide committee members—some of whom are nonexperts in human rights or the law—with more support, including a better understanding of law and practice in the reporting states they review. There have also been calls to create more professional flexibility inside the Secretariat, away from the hyperspecialization that can produce tunnel vision and amplify communication problems between different parts of the system. For instance, more Secretariat staff could be made responsible for multiple treaties and issues.[34]

A more professional human rights legal system with a stronger Secretariat would also benefit from improved communication within the system. Improved communication is needed between governments and treaty bodies, between treaty bodies, and between different parts of the system. Reports and other sources of official information and evaluations, for example, could be stored in searchable databases that would provide useful information at all stages of the legal process.[35] Experts have also recommended making that information (including anonymized individual communications) publicly available so that anyone can obtain details about the nature and status of cases.[36] Still others endorse greater participation by and reliance on NGOs for information and expertise.[37] Materials from NGOs, if properly communicated in advance, might help treaty bodies improve the quality of their discussions and recommendations.[38]

Another recommendation is to better coordinate the treaty bodies. To this effect, the United Nations already holds some intercommittee meetings, which bring together representatives from each of the treaty bodies to discuss their work and consider ways to enhance the effectiveness of the system as a whole. Among the topics those sessions have explored is modernization of reporting procedures, harmonization of work methods, and obtaining new financial resources.[39] Still, there are problems of over-lap, redundancy, and inconsistency along with a plain lack of knowledge between all these bodies. The many proposals for the coordination of treaty bodies usually go hand in hand with efforts to streamline reporting systems, since the management of reports and complaints is one of the chief functions of these bodies.

Streamlining and professionalization might allow the system to be-come more strategic in how it uses its resources. Notably, experts have recommended a host of different reforms that could, in some settings, boost the system's limited capacity for enforcement. There have been calls for committees to follow-up on their observations and recommen-dations.[40] At present, once these observations and recommendations are made, they often disappear as priorities; a more strategic and professional human rights legal system could help ensure more follow-up. Some experts, similarly, have advised that the committees engage in consciousness-raising about their own recommendations and even create training pro-grams to help ensure that recommended reforms within governments are implemented.[41] Others have advised the committees to set priorities, identifying their most urgent and important recommendations to follow up on within a set time frame—say, a year or two.[42] And there are pro-posals that the treaty bodies all periodically undertake country visits, in consultation with civil society and NHRIs, in order to directly witness whether their recommendations are being applied—something that is only done regularly in the European part of the system.

INVEST IN CREDIBILITY AND LEGITIMACY

Experts also believe that reforms can help raise levels of compliance while making the system more reflective of local circumstances, which can give it credibility and legitimacy—something the system currently lacks in much of the world. One idea is to have the different parts of the system hold more meetings outside of headquarters as well as in places where treaties could have traction in local politics.[43] This might give local media a reason to cover the international human rights legal system, leading to greater local familiarity with international human rights procedures. A more familiar system might be more accessible, and it might also lead to better local engagement.

The largest challenge to credibility and thus legitimacy comes from the countries that are formally members of human rights treaties yet are rampant abusers of human rights. A government has to do something ter-ribly bad, like commit major atrocities, before the UN General Assembly will even consider recommending that the government be excluded from agencies like the Human Rights Council. For example, it took decades and the outbreak of civil war before the General Assembly suspended Libya in 2011.[44] In Africa, the Americas, and Europe, states continue to participate as members in their regional institutions despite having committed major atrocities. Since the door has been open for decades it's probably far too late, today, to impose formal standards for participation in most existing institutions. Yet there may be ways to start building in standards moving forward.

Increasing the competitiveness of the election process in the United Nations is one possible step. Membership on the Human Rights Council was envisioned by the General Assembly as a competitive process, given that an absolute majority of the General Assembly is needed to elect a candidate. The General Assembly is supposed to "take into account the contribution of candidates to the promotion and protection of human rights and their voluntary pledges and commitments made thereto."[45]

There are positive signs that election to the council is becoming more selective as NGOs play a larger role in expanding access to information about the human rights violations of candidates. Since 2007, coalitions of NGOs have waged successful campaigns against the candidacies of Belarus, Sri Lanka, Azerbaijan, and Iran; none of these countries has obtained a seat on the council. The picture is not entirely positive, however, as membership is still framed in terms of the five UN geographic regions, and authorities from each region can game the system—for example, by proposing only as many new council members as there are seats allocated to each region—in ways that give the General Assembly few or no choices.[46]

## Prospects for Reform

These four broad types of reforms are ambitious. Are they practical? Answering that question requires looking at the reforms that have been going on for years. Here I first examine that history of reform since it helps set a baseline for what is achievable. Then I explain why reforms, in practice, probably can't have much of the intended effect.

### REFORMS HAVE BEEN MADE

It's a common misperception: the United Nations is a bloated, corrupt, glorified talk shop that never changes.[47] In fact, the United Nations is constantly changing itself, expanding its scope of action and the interpretation of its powers. These shifts are particularly evident in the human rights part of the UN system, which has been in flux since its inception. The United Nations and its leading experts have created new treaty bodies and agencies, such as (in 1993) the OHCHR, along with an array of other reforms aimed at improving the system's performance.

The UN Human Rights Committee—one of the leading treaty bodies—is an example of how the UN apparatus has attempted to identify and repair its flaws. In the 1990s, the committee created a working group with the goal of expanding its resources and crafting new, more effective procedures.[48] Those changes have included new rules for reporting as well as efforts to improve the efficiency and credibility with which the committee issues its concluding observations. For many years, the committee operated with the philosophy that implementation of its observations was a matter of goodwill and its role ended once it had articulated its findings. These reforms were inspired by a more strategic vision for how the committee should operate. In the 1990s the committee, no longer content to rely on goodwill, created a new follow-up procedure asking states to submit information on how they have responded; today that procedure comes with time limits that are measured sometimes in just a matter of months.[49] Additional reforms are in the works. In 2011, the committee adopted reforms, triggered by its own internal special rapporteur, that will lead to country-by-country reviews of state compliance with the treaty that the committee oversees: the International Covenant on Civil and Political Rights. At the same time, it also made progress on reforming how the committee handles individual communications.[50]

The reforms at the Human Rights Committee aren't unique. Essentially all the other elements of the human rights legal system have made efforts to reform themselves over the years. In 2002, for instance, the United Nations held its first inter-committee meeting to try and address some of the problems associated with overlapping jurisdiction along with a lack of communication and coordination between its human rights treaty bodies. This meeting now happens twice annually. The United Nations replaced its own Human Rights Commission with the Human Rights Council in a 2006 effort to fix some of the problems with its highly politicized predecessor. The council created a new procedure—the Universal Periodic Review—with the goal of enhancing the monitoring process for all treaties. And the United Nations had already made other efforts. It had strengthened its human rights capacity, improved its system of special procedures, posted some committees' reports and state responses online, translated the Universal Declaration of Human Rights into many more languages, and reduced (a bit) the backlogs in consideration of some reports.[51] Whether these reforms have had their intended effects is another matter, but clearly the United Nations has some capacity for change.

This chapter has focused a lot on UN reforms because the United Nations is at the center of the international human rights legal system. Reform is hardly unique to the United Nations, however, as the regional parts of the system have also been a locus of massive reform efforts. The Europeans, notably, have been responding to their changing circumstances created by the end of the Cold War and the expansion of the European Union. In the 1990s, they even abolished their own Commission on Human Rights, which was relatively weak and cumbersome, and replaced it with a single, full-time human rights court—the European Court of Human Rights—with compulsory jurisdiction and individual rights to petition.[52] In part, such reforms were intended to address the rising application rates and complexity of cases associated with the growing number of states participating in the system. In practice, these reforms aimed at streamlining the system, shortening proceedings, and improving judicial quality haven't been enough.[53] Less than a year after the overhaul, Luzius Wildhaber, the president of the court, admitted that the system was under pressure and faced "asphyxiation" from the backlog of applications.[54] An array of further reforms emerged and came into effect in 2010 after Russia finally ratified a plan.[55] Worries that this new plan also wouldn't be adequate led the Council of Europe to push for additional reforms.[56] In 2010, a ministerial-level conference on the future of the European Court of Human Rights ended with all forty-seven member states adopting another plan with still more reforms, including proposals related to filtering applications and implementation of the European Convention on Human Rights at the national level.[57]

The human rights community lavishes much attention on Europe for these big (and important) renovations, but reforms also have been made in the Americas. New procedures are in place to make more efficient use of hearings as well as to make the court's jurisprudence more accessible to the public.[58] For instance, new regulations came into force in 2010 that, among other things, will speed up the process through which victims and governments can question witnesses and experts and the system can deliver final judgments. These reforms have also created a new role of "inter-American defender" to represent victims who don't have legal counsel along with legal assistance that will support victims otherwise unable to afford bringing claims through the inter-American process. Gone, as part of these reforms, is the earlier practice by which a state being sued could appoint its own judge to the court—a clear conflict of interest. Still other changes include the granting of precautionary measures and referrals to the court in new ways that are likely to boost protection for human rights.[59]

Africa, too, has made big changes, although tracking these reforms and anticipating their effects is extremely difficult. Once there was an

African Court of Justice, created when the Organization of African Unity became the African Union, along with a totally separate African Court on Human and Peoples' Rights. The existence of these two courts created confusion over their powers and jurisdictions, which contributed to these courts' impotence.[60] Eventually the two courts were merged to form the African Court of Justice and Human Rights, which will be based in Tanzania.[61] No one really knows how the new African Court will work in practice. Meanwhile, an African Commission on Human and Peoples' Rights has been operational for decades, and in that time, a variety of reforms have been implemented to improve how it functions.[62] Longtime observers of the system are skeptical that the reforms will have much practical impact.[63]

THE LIMITS OF REFORM

The extensive record of active reforms within the United Nations and all three of the regional parts of the system would appear to bode well for future reform efforts. After all, reformers have already, it appears, accomplished a lot. The hope is that attempts to identify the full range of flaws in the system—such as those summarized in chapter 6—could lead to still more reforms that, in turn, lead to practical improvements in human rights in some contexts.

Unfortunately, the potential for deep reform is probably limited. There is a colossal mismatch between what governments are agreeing to on paper and what they are doing in practice. Experts have thought a lot about reforms. But the most consequential changes are generally the least achievable, and many of the reforms that have been undertaken aren't having the expected effects—they're not making the system more legitimate or powerful.

Reform requires money and other resources. The system already relies heavily on contributions from members and is stretched thin. James Crawford, professor and member of the UN International Law Commission, explains, "No informed observer believes that any substantial injection of resources for the system as a whole is likely."[64] Many envisioned reforms would require more coordination between the treaty bodies and Secretariat, which is practically difficult. Regrettably, says Chief Justice Elizabeth Evatt—once chairperson of the UN Committee on the Elimination of All Forms of Discrimination against Women and also special rapporteur on the Human Rights Committee—"there is often tension between these two groups, and this has been added to by the way in which restructuring has proceeded." She also explains why getting much more out of the United Nations' general budget is probably impractical. The whole system is perennially short on resources; despite a lot of talk and urgent pleas, the United Nations hasn't put much more into the human rights portion of its total budget. And she warns that it would be "unwise to develop plans which made the treaty bodies dependent on direct funding by states parties."[65] They need independence from the states they evaluate. Most parts of the regional system are impoverished too.[66]

Reform also requires various kinds of political agreements. Even people working on UN committees who are inclined to adopt reforms often can't agree on the actions that are essential to implementing practical reforms. While these insiders now discuss methods of harmonization between their groups, for example, they are divided on questions such as whether a unified body would actually make the system more coherent and effective. Some committees seem to like the idea; the Committee on the Elimination of All Forms of Racial Discrimination has been favorable to the plan, which reformers hope would reduce documentation, reporting burdens, overlapping competences, and inconsistencies. Others, including those committees overseeing women's, children's, and migrants' rights, have been opposed.[67] People worry that the plan could sneak in a hostile agenda to weaken the system, squander diversity, and neglect and de-prioritize some rights.[68] Some call the idea of consolidation "irresponsible."[69] Most African, Asian, and Pacific countries as well as Russia and the United States have at one time or another joined in disapproval of the plan.[70]

Even the world's leading human rights steward states—the countries most committed to protecting human rights abroad—disagree over the most basic reform initiatives. Some support streamlining the reporting process by eliminating comprehensive periodic reports; others oppose reforms that would yield a comprehensive report and favor, instead, reforms that just focus on specific aspects of the reporting process. Without a concerted push from the countries that care the most and devote the largest resources to international human rights, major reforms are unlikely to follow.

Reform is difficult not only because advocates disagree. Any serious program for reform must confront the reality that some countries oppose making the system more effective. Human rights abusers have an interest in keeping the system from working better; vested interests, which are pervasive in a system as large and old as this one, often oppose change of any kind. Indeed, the treaty bodies, already packed with violators, have responded to most of these requests mainly with silence, unwilling to make the big reforms or restructure the system to make it more effective.[71] The UN General Assembly, which receives the concluding observations and reform recommendations from the UN treaty bodies, also tends to avoid big structural changes. Many of the governments in the General Assembly, and even some that sit on the Human Rights Council or have representatives on the treaty bodies, are the cause of the problems in the first place.[72]

These challenges help explain why some well-intentioned reform efforts turn into dead ends. Some feel the new Human Rights Council, for instance, has become a venue for Islamic countries to criticize Israel by passing resolutions condemning the government for its occupation of the Golan Heights, settlements in the West Bank, and treatment of Palestinians.[73] Some have argued that Israel has unfairly received a disproportionate share of the council's attention and condemnation, while others maintain that such attention is merited.[74] Regardless of whether these claims are true, there is little doubt that the council itself has become highly politicized. As a result, it is widely seen as illegitimate, much like its predecessor (the Commission on Human Rights). It's not clear that the massive effort, which came at a massive cost, to replace the commission with this new body has led to better results because those reforms haven't (and can't) change the underlying fundamental difficulties.

Reflecting on the process around the creation of the Human Rights Council, Françoise Hampson, professor of law and member of the UN Subcommission on the Promotion and Protection of Human Rights, believes that "reforms were needed. However, the reason why the process was embarked upon had nothing to do with improving the human rights machinery. The context in which the negotiations [were] being conducted [was] not conducive to improving the protection of human rights." From her perspective "it looks as though, like Alice in Wonderland, the Council will have to run very fast to even stand still. Currently, it does not appear that the Council is running fast enough to achieve that. This is hardly a surprise. The circumstances surrounding the initiation of the reform process bade ill for a successful outcome. To maintain the status quo would be a triumph."[75]

Looking across all these challenges—the difficulty of raising resources, getting reformers to agree on the most important reforms, and managing the inevitable political obstacles—it is hard not to be pessimistic about what reform can really achieve. The big fixes for the limitations of the system must all confront in various ways the central challenge that by design, human rights law aims to curb state power and autonomy. Scott Leckie, longtime UN insider, explains that a treaty body "can only be expected to have a limited impact upon the actual enjoyment of human rights in countries over which it has occasional supervisory jurisdiction. This is true no matter how far the Committee may improve its methods of work or how intensively it may strive to address serious human rights infractions."[76]

Still, there are good ideas on the table. And those ideas could help to modernize a system that has potential to become more effective in at least some settings, if not the settings that generate the most abuse of human rights. That alone makes reform worth pursuing. The question is, how?

## Making the Most of Reform

It's frustrating to realize that the immense system created to promote human rights faces so many obstacles that prevent it from actually protecting human rights in so many situations. And it's all the more aggravating to know that ideas aren't being used that might clear some of those obstacles. Short of imagining the impossible—like the end of infighting and turf battles inside the system's different parts—this chapter concludes by offering some practical ways to raise the odds that serious reforms can be implemented. It should be clear that I don't think the international human rights legal system, even with achievable reforms, will be adequate for enforcing human rights norms. That's why later in this book I suggest some additional approaches that could make human rights protections more effective. But international law has an important role to play. Efforts on two fronts can make reforms of the international legal system more consequential.

### STOP EXPANSION

It probably sounds counterintuitive, but halting the production of more such laws, bureaucracy, and treaty bodies might pave the way for giving the international legal system more force and reach. The existing obligations and procedures could do more. Expansion, especially in the context of an already thinly stretched bureaucracy, probably will lead to more lawbreaking, and further erode the credibility and legitimacy of the system. Thus, the first way to make reforms more feasible is to stop the system's swell of obligations and procedures. A pause would give reforms a better chance to work.

The case against expansion is based on the evidence from chapter 5 and narratives from chapter 6 that the current system has struggled to put its expression of collective values into practice. An open-door human rights legal system has empowered abusers, letting them participate in the system with little rebuke. Fixing that system won't come from opening still more doors—with more treaties and procedures accessible to every government, no matter its record on human rights. My argument isn't that no new laws will ever be merited. Before adding new obligations, however, the existing system must meet two criteria.

First, the existing system needs legitimacy. Greater legitimacy requires greater fidelity to the law. Achieving that in the existing system, let alone an expanded one, will be difficult because weak enforcement mechanisms make it hard to enforce compliance against the growing number of treaty members that already break laws. Most of the human rights legal system offers few tangible benefits for governments that follow the rules; instead, it publicly criticizes those governments trying hardest to follow the most rules.[77]

Second, expansions must be put on hold until the system has a viable plan for obtaining the resources it would need to meet the responsibilities of more obligations and members. Only once it has shored up its ability to better promote the protection of core rights in the countries where it has a decent chance of having an impact should the system take on harder, more peripheral cases and rights. Expansion in a world of fixed budgets guarantees that a thinly stretched system will dissipate even further.

The danger of dissipation is especially evident in the resource intensive area of enforcement. The ICC was a big step toward more enforcement of global norms, but as noted earlier in this part of the book, it's not a global solution. At best it's a backup that, so far, hasn't actually been used much. Many reject its authority. Many countries that accept its jurisdiction on paper ignore it in practice. The ICC's jurisdiction is also limited to the most shocking crimes; it has no ability to prosecute the crimes of discrimination or inequality, for example. The ICC might be able to shape the behavior of elites in coherent and democratizing states who are dependent on global trade, aid, and other transnational linkages, although it hasn't actually been tested in those settings—only in war-torn parts of Africa. But it has done little so far to protect even the most basic human rights to security of the person when national passions are high, authoritarians are in charge, or the state is in decay. In such circumstances, like the civil war in Syria that unfolded in 2012, immediate political survival for government leaders seems to trump any fears of future indictment in The Hague. Moreover, the ICC can interfere with crucial national processes, such as reconciliation. The ICC investigation of atrocities committed in the context of the twenty-year civil war in Uganda has been inconclusive since it was begun in 2005. Numerous NGOs and international bodies have condemned the ICC investigation of war crimes there, arguing that it has come too soon— that reconciliation and peace must come before justice. They fear that meddling by the ICC is likely to disrupt current peacemaking efforts, and prosecution of repressive leaders won't resolve the profound injuries that the war has inflicted on society.[78] These are complex and controversial subjects. Yet clearly there is no immediate plan for a more general human rights police force or a court with broad jurisdiction and truly global reach. That means that if universal treaties and institutions were expanded, the current enforcement problems will remain and probably get worse.

So far, the best hope for judicial enforcement that is effective lies with domestic courts, not at the global level.

My pessimism about the enforcement capacity and legitimacy of the current legal system applies not only to the universal level but also essentially to all the regional parts of the system. In Africa, the courts of a few regional economic organizations, not the regional human rights courts, are taking all the landmark actions. Even so, those regional organizations have handled only a few cases despite a vast supply of terrible violations. Even in Europe, where the regional part of the system has been quite successful in bringing cases to court—so successful that many tens of thousands are backlogged—legal procedures leave possibly millions of victims without help and many perpetrators go unpunished.[79] These courts spend little time on the worst of the crimes. And they have no jurisdiction in many of the places where terrible abuses take place.

In short, with every new repressive country that joins and right that is enshrined, the legal system itself becomes increasingly hamstrung. Swelling the system before fixing these problems will make future reforms harder to craft and implement. A temporary moratorium on the expansion would help prevent existing problems from getting worse.

## COORDINATION FOR REFORM

Another way to nudge reform forward is for the countries with the strongest interest in promoting human rights abroad to form a coherent bloc that pushes for repairs to the system. Such a bloc would need not just coordination and focus but also a commitment to sustain the effort. The coalition that now pushes reforms into place is often formed ad hoc—with strange bedfellows like the United States and Russia at times taking the same side—yet disappears just as quickly when the next reform agenda arises. Instead, what's needed is a group of states (and experts and NGO advocates) that remains aligned and strategic so it can advance major, integrated reforms.

So far it has been difficult for reformers to agree on the best approaches. Governments, even willing human rights stewards, are skittish about creating legal structures and processes that might hold them accountable as well. It's easier to boss others around than to constrain oneself too.[80] Those concerns are understandable. The human rights stewards are unnecessarily splitting hairs on minor issues, though, and those disagreements have undercut the larger goals these governments share in trying to make the system more effective. Worse, as with many problems of collective action, it is hard to keep all members focused and contributing. Even altruistic human rights stewards have incentives to "free ride" on each other's efforts, with some shouldering less than their fair share of the burden.

Solving these problems isn't easy, but working in small groups of like-minded countries and NGOs could make them a lot more practical to manage. I revisit this "club" notion again in chapter 11 as I consider how steward states can better harness their own power for human rights. Even in the best of circumstances, however, reforms face deep resistance from the many dozens of states that routinely break the law, and have packed treaty bodies and courts with their agents. Coordination by those who care most can help shut doors when needed and concentrate resources on the reforms that will be most important yet are often most resisted.

## Conclusion

In this chapter I argued that reformers have lots of good ideas. Reform is a worthy agenda; without it, the system will stall. Such reform efforts will be more consequential if reformers themselves are more strategic, such as by working in smaller groups and resisting the drumbeat of expansion.

Even with better reform strategies, it is important to keep a sense of perspective. Reformers must know where the human rights legal system can have an impact and where, no matter the expense and effort, even a reformed system will have little purchase. Reforms might help ensure that treaties and legal procedures have more impact in some contexts—mainly in democratic and some democratizing countries. Elsewhere, such as in contexts where leaders clamp down on groups and institutions that try to monitor them, and where wars, poverty, and inequality incite violence, these efforts to mend the international legal system probably won't have much effect without a transformation of domestic institutions and cultures. People in positions of power and authority will continue to violate the law, often with impunity.

So what else can be done to spread the values of the international legal system when the legal system itself just can't do it? Part III looks to state power and diplomacy.

# A Stewardship Strategy

While the international human rights legal system has achieved much, it also leaves substantial room for improvement. Some of the very attributes that make this system so attractive in theory—that it aims for universal coverage and aspires to protect a growing list of rights—also limit the system's practical influence on the calculus of abuse. Parts I and II of this book explained why the system is likely to work best to improve respect for human rights mainly in special circumstances. People with incentives to break the law are inclined to obey legal norms most when they fear the consequences (coercion), or learn that law represents a legitimate authority along with a widely held social expectation they trust and value (persuasion). On both fronts, the practical effect of the international legal system is probably small in the countries that account for most abuses. The consequences for abusing human rights are few and uneven; penalties are severe only in unusual circumstances, and good behavior is not well rewarded. Compliance is low, and the institutions that manage the legal process are deeply politicized—which helps explain why international law is seen as illegitimate or simply irrelevant in some contexts. Better legal institutions could help, but as chapter 7 shows, real world experience has proven that those reforms are extremely difficult to organize and implement. Reform, even in the best of circumstances, will yield a legal system that corresponds to actual protections for human rights in special contexts. The existence of the international human rights legal system is an extraordinary achievement, but making the most of law requires knowing not just when it works but also the many instances where the law alone can't change the calculus of abuse.

In part III, I look at the roles that states, acting in their own self-interest, play in advancing the cause of protecting human rights in other countries around the world. The power of steward states, I argue, offers many advantages. It can be used to complement the law and especially is useful where the international legal system can't have much influence on its own. These states have already proved they are willing to devote substantial resources to protecting human rights. Indeed, these stewards are the main engines for the expansion of the international human rights legal system. I suggest they adopt a new human rights promotion strategy—what I call a "stewardship strategy"—and focus, particularly, on places where state power can make a difference.

For enthusiasts of the human rights legal system, opening a large role for state power is controversial. Law, after all, is supposed to operate independently and remain blind to power. Yet the reality is that law on its own can't achieve ambitious goals to spread human rights protections in many contexts. States already meddle in others' human rights affairs whether they belong to treaties or not. A new approach could better align these two forces: state power and international law. I make this argument in three steps.

First, in chapter 8, I look at the status quo—a broad array of policies that stewards already adopt—and map them to the two mechanisms of influence described in chapter 4—coercion and persuasion—that can change the calculus that drives abusive behavior. These policies, I will suggest, are not strategic and effective enough to maximize protection for human rights. But they are useful as a baseline that reveals what states are already willing to do. Such a baseline helps ensure that proposals for making better use of state power remain in line with what states can (and will) actually do. While steward states tend to be democratic and wealthy, in fact any state can play a stewardship role. These states already do a lot to promote human rights; a more strategic use of that power has enormous potential to make those efforts more effective.

Next, I discuss how steward states can use their power to "localize" the protection of human rights more effectively. The most visible uses of state power involve deployment of military assets, but for many states that option isn't available, and even powerful states mostly don't work with gunboats. Instead, when it comes to promoting human rights, the most effective uses of state power lie in how states help localize norms and incentives in other countries. Localization is not a new concept, but it plays an important role for a strategy, such as the one I advocate in this book, that relies heavily on a few key countries to advance the cause of human rights in other countries. Localization can give legitimacy to the use of foreign power, and legitimacy is central to effectiveness. Effective localization helps link the international legal system and the use of power to reliable local information; it also can create pressures internal to states to align behavior with international legal norms. It is a keystone to making international aspirations a reality within countries, and thus is crucial to ensuring that stewardship works in tandem with widely adopted international legal norms. Chapter 9 looks at localization through NGOs in foreign lands. Chapter 10 examines localization through NHRIs. There are lots of ways to localize, but these two options—partly complementary and partly rivals—attract the most attention and hold the most promise.

Chapter 11 develops a strategy for how steward states (and other key actors, such as NGOs and reform-minded experts working within the international legal system) can pick and choose the issues as well as settings where they have greatest leverage. The strategy is built on the concept of triage, and it will be controversial because it is fundamentally different from the universal norms that underpin international law. Triage requires choosing where power and law, working in tandem, can achieve results. It also requires recognizing the settings where they will have little impact. While I focus on how triage can help steward states focus their power on the places where it can do the most, the triage strategy is equally important for NGOs and other actors that make choices about how to devote scarce resources to the goal of advancing human rights. A lot has been written about the importance of NGOs, but more attention is needed to how these groups can deploy scarce resources strategically.[1]

The strategy outlined in these chapters—on the punishments and rewards that steward states are willing to deploy (chapter 8), and making localization (chapters 9 and 10) and triage (chapter 11) work—offers a picture of where and how states can use their power to advance human rights more effectively.

8

# The Status Quo

Where the international legal system can't have much impact on abuse, the policy of states that are willing protectors of human rights could play a special role. Governments in these states are willing to invest substantial resources in protecting human rights abroad. Often these states also face strong public pressure at home from human rights organizations, religious groups, and other groups to use their power in this way.

This chapter looks at how two especially active stewards already use their political authority, resources, and reach to promote human rights. I focus on the US and EU, but they're not the only stewards. Steward states are a minority, but, says professor Alison Brysk, "good samaritans" are more than exceptions.[1] In settings where there is enough stability—notably, when civil wars and other conflicts are absent—stewards can offer the discipline, leadership, and education functions that the international legal system, on its own, can't adequately provide. Even when these favorable contexts don't exist—such as in civil war—stewards may also be able to intervene, though such instances and the records in those settings are much thinner. Stewards aren't merely altruistic samaritans. Rather, they see stewardship as a matter of national interest.

Later chapters will explore how stewards can be more influential in how they deploy their resources. The task in this chapter is to describe what stewards already do today. That reality is a helpful starting point for discussing how states could use their power more effectively in the future. It also helps calibrate any discussion of new actions to the reality of what stewards are already willing to do.

Stewards work in many different ways. Here I focus, broadly, on two. One is how steward states punish other governments (and individuals) who break the law. The other is the many varied rewards that stewards offer for good behavior. Together, punishments and rewards can change the calculus of abuse. They can also fail or backfire.

## Punishment

I argued in part I that human rights abuses are crimes—moral offenses and usually also violations of law. A standard way to fight crime is to catch and punish criminals, which can isolate deviant behavior and also deter future offenses. That's harder to do when the culprits are the same organizations—governments—that in well-functioning societies are also charged with making and enforcing laws. Human rights stewards try to address that problem by threatening (and at times actually punishing) abusive governments. Actors within the international legal system, such as courts, also try to perform this role, although in practice that is difficult when perpetrators are governments that can block or readily ignore international legal pronouncements. Stewards can help by punishing some culprits that international courts and shaming processes cannot reach. The most prominent examples involve military intervention, and thus I start there. But in practice the punishments that are most important and practical are those of the nonmilitary type that are less costly to deliver.

## MILITARY INTERVENTION

Human rights are most endangered during wars, genocides, and other power struggles between groups violently seeking control. A government embroiled in civil war hopes to maintain its power by clamping down on or eliminating its challengers, often in brutal ways. Meanwhile, the challengers frequently use violence as a strategy for protest, publicity, and grabbing power. These conflicts can spread far beyond the political class to implicate innocents, leading to ghastly violations of human rights. In the extreme, a government or group engaged in genocide aims to destroy another ethnic, racial, religious, or national group.

In such contexts, where the national rule of law has failed, it is particularly difficult for most international human rights law to play any direct role. It does not matter whether states belong to treaties outlawing torture or discrimination against women, for example, because the state apparatus has failed or is mobilized against the goal of equal protection for human rights. Stopping these crimes requires, as a first and necessary step, brokering peace and reestablishing order, and then in time, empowering independent law enforcement institutions. Little of the international human rights legal system was designed to play a direct role in the peacekeeping or peacemaking process. Nor does it have much impact on the complicated process of institution building that ideally follows peace. Those roles are mainly the prerogative of governments, acting alone or together through organizations such as the North Atlantic Treaty Organization (NATO), the African Union, or the UN Security Council.

One way that steward states punish perpetrators is through military intervention. The goal is to make continued repression so costly that perpetrators and their supporters are compelled to stop. This approach, followed only in some cases, is fraught with difficulty. It is prone to complications, often fails, and at times even backfires.[2]

Governments have tried many times to use military intervention to stop mass human rights violations, with mixed results. After the government of Somalia collapsed in 1991, the United States led a UN military mission to stop the turmoil. US troops were dragged to their deaths through the streets of the capital.[3] US and Canadian forces were accused of the torture, rape, and summary killing of Somali civilians.[4] When foreign troops withdrew two years later, after at least three hundred thousand people had been killed in the war, Somalia was still in chaos. Ethiopian forces invaded the south in 2007, and Somalia today still has no permanent national government.[5]

Military intervention, especially in the most abusive contexts, may sometimes be the only method that can change the calculus of abuse. Similarly, muscle-bound peacekeeping missions may be essential to creating a durable peace, which is necessary for the protection of human rights after civil war.[6] Following the US-led action in the first Gulf War, there was, at least temporarily, improved protection of human rights for Iraqi Kurdish minorities.[7] According to Samantha Power, professor and senior director of multilateral affairs at the National Security Council, "Thanks to the allied effort, the Iraqi Kurds were able to return home and, with the protection of NATO jets overhead, govern themselves."[8] Military intervention in this instance changed both the context that allowed for severe abuse and the rationales of the abusers.

Yet there have been unintentional, harmful side effects from these kinds of humanitarian interventions.[9] In some circumstances, military interventions make things worse by aggravating existing tensions and catalyzing still more aggression.[10] In the former Yugoslavia, a lopsided war between Kosovar Albanians and Serbs was triggered in the late 1990s when the Kosovar Liberation Army (KLA) rebelled. It appears that the KLA rebellion was inspired, in part, by the hope that the international community would intervene to protect Kosovar Albanians against bloody retaliation.[11] Dugi Gorani, a Kosovar Albanian negotiator, said, "The more civilians were killed, the chances of intervention became bigger, and the KLA of course realized that."[12] In 1999, NATO did finally bomb Yugoslavia to stop ethnic cleansing by Serbian security forces against civilians in Kosovo—as the KLA had hoped. Today, the former Yugoslavia is at peace, but subsequent investigations suggest that the interventions, which eventually led to a peace process and the protection of human rights, may have escalated human rights abuses during the bombing.[13] In Sudan too, hopes of humanitarian intervention may have worsened the crisis by emboldening rebels—although it's hard to know for sure. Indeed, rebel groups rejected peace plans (in 2006 and 2007) that could have brought the conflict to an earlier end. According to Jide Nzelibe,

> These case studies reveal a consistent pattern. First, rebel or victim lead-ers engage in provocative actions against a dominant group largely (or partly) because they hope to attract humanitarian intervention against the dominant group. The dominant group then responds by aggres-sively committing even more atrocities against the victim group. In the end, however, the humanitarian intervention either does not come or comes too late to prevent the bulk of the atrocities from happening.[14]

Human rights stewards have watched terrible atrocities take place without using their own militaries to intervene. In Rwanda, genocide rap-idly occurred while the world stood by. Steward states did not promptly intervene in part because there was little public pressure at home for in-tervention and in part because past military action elsewhere (in Somalia, for example) had failed.[15] The mass killings, rapes, and other human rights violations that have taken place in Sudan attracted more attention than Rwanda, but military intervention nonetheless has not followed, partly be-cause of fears that military action would be costly and could fail.[16]

Rwanda and Sudan are reminders of how difficult it can be to mobilize military intervention. It is not a surprise, therefore, that even the most ardent stewards of human rights who believe they have a responsibility to protect nonetheless often don't favor military intervention, even in the most tragic situations where human rights are under attack. The full range of interventions needed—not just an initial intervention to stop the conflict, but also peacemaking, peacekeeping, and peace building—is im-practical except in special circumstances partly because political interest at home is insufficient to make intervention sustainable. And even when intervention is an option, it is hardly a guarantee of peace, stability, and protections for human rights.

## NONMILITARY PUNISHMENTS

In settings of extreme violence, military involvement may be the only way to change the calculus of abuse. But human rights stewards use many other, nonmilitary strategies for punishing abusers. Many—although usually not the worst—human rights abuses take place in less intense contexts where perpetrators might be persuaded by an array of nonmil-itary punishments.

For example, such punishments helped change human rights abuses in Guatemala in the 1990s. After president Jorge Serrano Elias dissolved

Congress and the Supreme Court, and suspended the Constitution in a self-coup in 1993, the US government suspended millions of dollars in economic and military aid, and threatened to block loans to Guatemala from the World Bank, the International Monetary Fund, and the Inter-American Development Bank.[17] Japan, Germany, and the European Communities also suspended millions of dollars in aid.[18] In addition to the penalties actually delivered, the United States also threatened suspension of the country's trade benefits under the Generalized System of Preferences (GSP) and the Caribbean Basin Initiative—a diplomatic move that would cost Guatemala at least two hundred million (US) dollars in lost exports.[19] Together, all these measures did not topple the government, which was using its power to abuse human rights—notably the rights of its opponents. But they helped reinforce anti-Serrano protests inside Guatemala while also creating stronger incentives for the country's elite to restore political order as well as human rights protections.[20] With the support of the Guatemalan Army, which was hurt by the cut in military aid, the Constitutional Court declared the coup illegal, paving the way for the military to oust Serrano and replace him with the defense minister.[21] That action was insufficient to quell dissent, and the Guatemalan Congress finally elected Ramiro De León Carpio, the nation's human rights ombudsman, to serve out the rest of the president's term.[22] Democracy was restored. As a reward, the US government did not suspend trade benefits, and it gave Guatemala thirty million (US) dollars in economic aid. Japan and the European countries also lifted sanctions and restored aid.[23]

As often happens, Guatemala's human rights troubles were not a singular event. New violations appeared in the late 1990s, including the 1999 murder of a union official along with attacks on the union of banana workers and more than a hundred complaints about similar crimes.[24] The United States was also concerned about evidence that Guatemala employed child labor. Washington issued an ultimatum that included, once again, threats to limit Guatemala's benefits under the GSP. The government of Guatemala, which had done little to stop these abuses until then, resolved a labor dispute involving hundreds of workers who had been illegally fired and charged twenty-two people in the attacks on the banana workers' union leaders.[25] And the government also made efforts to cooperate with the International Labor Organization (ILO), accepting a direct contact mission from the organization, and undertaking reforms that gave Guatemalan unions more freedoms and protections, plus brought the country in closer compliance with international legal standards. A special prosecutor for crimes against unionists and journalists was appointed to investigate and prosecute past as well as ongoing crimes. And then, in 2001, the Guatemalan Congress enacted labor code reforms. The United States withdrew its GSP threat, but also promised to monitor compliance closely. A few months later, Guatemala ratified the ILO Convention concerning the Prohibition and Immediate Action for the Elimination of the Worst Forms of Child Labor.[26]

Stewards have used actual and threatened punishments of this kind in many places, sometimes with substantial effect. In Mauritania, for instance, US pressure helped along a movement to rein in abuses that included the failure of the government to recognize trade unions.[27] In March 1993, early in the Clinton administration, the United States threatened to and then suspended Mauritania's benefits under the GSP.[28] Mauritania amended its labor code, and in early 1994 recognized some unions.[29] The US government, seeing that its threats had influence, pushed harder. In summer 1996, with the status of Mauritania's GSP benefits still in limbo, the US House of Representatives passed a resolution condemning slavery in the country.[30] Congress also passed an act that required the US president to withhold essentially all assistance to Mauritania until the country enacted and enforced antislavery laws.[31] The government of Mauritania removed a magistrate from the bench for refusing to accept provisions of Mauritanian law abolishing slavery.[32] It also launched a national debate on slavery and ratified the ILO Forced Labor Convention.[33]

Starting in 1997, Washington began to consider reinstating Mauritania's GSP benefits as the country made reforms—it recognized another trade organization and 155 new NGOs, signed an agreement with the UN high commissioner for refugees to help resettle refugees, and created a new cabinet post, the Commissariat for Human Rights, Poverty Alleviation, and Integration, to address slavery.[34] Mauritania's president also received the assistant US secretary of state in charge of democracy, human rights, and labor for talks on trade relations and human rights practices.[35] By 1999, President Bill Clinton informed Congress of his intent to end the punishment by restoring Mauritania's GSP benefits.[36] Of course, Mauritania's improved human rights record wasn't the only reason. It also began to support the Middle East peace process, established relations with Israel, and distanced itself from Saddam Hussein's regime in Iraq.[37] Nonetheless, punishments linked to tangible actions on human rights played a central role. Shortly after Clinton's 1999 announcement, the Mauritanian government joined the ILO Convention concerning the Prohibition and Immediate Action for the Elimination of the Worst Forms of Child Labor.[38]

The experiences of Guatemala and Mauritania are illustrations of how states use targeted political and economic punishments to help reinforce international human rights norms in settings where abusing governments, acting alone, would not have much incentive to comply. Even without the use of military force, abusive practices were met with large penalties. These experiences underscore some lessons that practitioners have known for a long time. They include the lesson that targeted punishments work much better than sweeping, all-purpose penalties such as broad-based sanctions. Such pressure works best when the target government is vulnerable yet also has the means to change policy within its grasp.

These are by no means the only nonmilitaristic instruments that stewards use to shape human rights practices, but they demonstrate some of the punishments stewards use to promote human rights.[39] Punishment, like other forms of coercion, works by changing how abusers calculate costs and benefits. Thus, it also tends to encourage tactical changes in policy—such as reforms that placate human rights advocates, trade partners, aid givers, or investors—rather than persuading governments to adopt fundamentally new perspectives on the kinds of behavior that are appropriate. That's why punishments, once threatened or applied, must often remain in place so that the target government doesn't revert to abuse when it recalculates costs and benefits. Yet tactical concessions can interact with persuasive mechanisms—as a first step toward long-term improvement for human rights that can eventually transform a nation's politics and alter what is acceptable behavior.[40]

## THE LIMITS OF PUNISHMENT

Punishments cannot solve all human rights problems, just as incarceration cannot stop all crime. To work, punishments must hurt perpetrators of abuse where it counts, which isn't easy. Delivering punishments that are painful enough to make perpetrators change their behavior can be costly even for the richest stewards of human rights, and not all stewards are rich. That cost helps explain why punishment strategies—even those that don't rely on military intervention—are particularly difficult to organize when the target is large or strategically important. China is an important example. No human rights steward has ever successfully used punishments to convince the Chinese government to make substantial improvements in human rights for its people. In fact, in 1994, US president Clinton broke a campaign promise by extending most favored nation trade status to China despite Beijing's lack of real progress on human rights. He explained that "this decision offers us the best opportunity to lay the basis for long-term sustainable progress on human rights and for the advancement of our other interests with China."[41] He may have been right, but the US government simply could not sustain the political and economic costs at home that would accompany cutting trade with countries like China.

A punishment strategy also doesn't work well when targets can find ways to lessen the sting. For example, a common problem with economic sanctions is that sanctioners must coordinate and present a unified front lest the targets shop around for new partners who are less picky about human rights.[42] Attempts by Western countries to threaten sanctions in Africa, where many mineral-rich countries also trade with China, is an illustration. Chinese trade, which reached fifty billion (US) dollars on the continent in 2006, comes with no requirements to protect human rights.[43] Countries such as Sudan can lessen the burdens from sanctions that human rights stewards impose by instead working with Chinese firms.[44] In turn, China has placed billions of dollars in investments in Sudan's oil industry while supplying Sudan's repressive government with diplomatic protection as well as Chinese-made weapons, tanks, and fighter planes, fueling civil violence.[45]

Similarly, punishment may have little impact when individual people and their institutions are less susceptible to outside pressure. For example, the rationalization processes that tend to accompany abusive behavior (such as the denial and displacement of responsibility, as explained in chapter 3) and social structures that reinforce abuse (as described in chapter 2) can make people blind to the risks they take by committing violations of human rights. Some—terrorists, for instance—may commit crimes of belief that aren't easily influenced with policy instruments that alter how people weigh risks and punishment.[46] When punishment comes from foreign sources, a national public is often rallied around local flags—even when local officials are abusive. That phenomenon, studied long ago when foreign sanctions against white-ruled Rhodesia actually made the illegitimate Rhodesian government stronger, is a perennial reason why human rights stewards struggle so much to earn legitimacy, especially when diplomacy is punitive.[47]

Punishments don't necessarily need to be severe to work, but research on crime and punishment suggests they do need to be swift, credible, and sustainable so that criminals can see a clear link between their behavior and the consequences.[48] Yet swift policy action is not always possible because the machinery of foreign policy choices frequently moves slowly. And when perpetrators make tactical concessions—implementing new policies to avoid retribution—stewards may relax the punishment, sending mixed signals about the credibility of future punishments. When abusers are embedded in deep networks, making punishments effective can place huge burdens on stewards who must not only be swift in their punishment but also sustained, consistent and systemic in punishing the entire network. Since most of the biggest stewards now are advanced democracies, they also face changes in policy at home as new leaders take power. A consistent foreign policy is often at odds with the political process inside contested political institutions. The old maxim that foreign policy stops at the water's edge usually doesn't apply to human rights, because a steward state's decision to back human rights depends heavily on its internal motivations as well as its willingness to bear costs at home, such as lost trade.

## Rewards

Because punishments—whether of a militaristic nature or not—are difficult to mobilize and often, by themselves, don't work, there's another class of strategies that stewards also use to alter the costs and benefits of abuse. Rewards are less conventional in discussions of criminality, which tend to focus on punishment, but they have a role to play here and can be convincing.

Paying criminals to act properly—rewarding progress instead of threatening deprivation—sounds offbeat. But human rights stewards give out a lot of rewards. They open their pocketbooks for people and governments that abuse human rights, partly because it is so difficult to make punishments work. European nations have been especially active with this policy approach. When used to full effect, such rewards change the calculus of abuse and put a premium on human rights. They can also create and bolster interest groups within abusing countries that favor better protection of human rights.

There are many examples of this approach, although experience reveals that stewards rarely rely on rewards alone. Almost always there is a threat of punishment lurking behind these offerings. For example, the US government rewarded the monarchy of Oman in 2005 for agreeing to protect some human rights by signing a free trade agreement that had long been under discussion. When the negotiations began, Oman was known to abuse human rights that were a special concern to the United States. Its laws, for instance, did not allow workers to create or belong to labor unions, or strike and bargain collectively. Reports showed that many foreign workers, who made up half the country's workforce, toiled under conditions considered forced labor.[49] By dangling the prospect of a trade agreement, the United States nudged Oman toward better protections.[50] Oman—keen to use trade as a way to help diversify its economy beyond oil and gas—made reforms.[51] As negotiations were under way, Oman's government amended its labor law, improving labor rights for some workers. In early 2006, after the trade agreement had been negotiated, but before it had become law, the government of Oman sent a letter to the US House Ways and Means Trade Subcommittee Minority Staff admitting that Oman needed to protect workers' rights to bargain collectively.[52] It also opened talks with the ILO on providing technical assistance to help Oman better comply with certain international labor standards.[53] The Omani government also worked to address the problems of forced and child labor. It issued a royal decree revising Omani laws on workers' rights and embracing some international protections it had been ignoring for years, giving workers the right to form and belong to labor unions, bargain collectively, and take part in union activities. It set punishments for blocking such activities as well as the use of forced labor of any kind.[54] All of these actions were taken after members of the US Congress promised to approve Oman's trade deal if the government made such changes.[55]

While it remains to be seen whether these new domestic laws and standards of conduct will be fully implemented, they are a starting point in a country that has historically repressed workers and others by denying them basic human rights. Some improvements in Oman are evident already, and more are likely.[56] Without the reward, Oman would be less exposed to international human rights legal norms, and its government probably would not have taken all these actions on its own.

I raise examples from US foreign policy because the United States is very active in its effort to promote human rights, especially rights associated with workers. However, other human rights stewards have also used rewards, and not just in an effort to protect workers' rights. The European Union has repeatedly given aid, trade, and political benefits to Turkey as a reward for particular human rights reforms that the Turkish government probably would not have implemented otherwise.[57] While Turkey's human rights record is far from perfect, it is much better for the European Union's involvement as well as the dance that the two political bodies have done over economic and political integration. Turkey first applied for membership in the European Union (then the European Economic Community) in 1959. The ultimate reward is full EU membership and its many perks.[58] But one of the prices for Turkey is broad-based reform of human rights.[59] In 2000, for example, the European Union outlined specific goals for Turkey's government and made negotiations for membership conditional on compliance.[60] Turkey was asked to strengthen legal and constitutional guarantees for freedom of expression as well as provisions against torture, maintain a de facto moratorium on the death penalty, and remove laws preventing citizens from broadcasting in languages other than Turkish.[61]

Some reforms followed quickly, including approval in 2001 by the Turkish cabinet of a plan to implement the *acquis communautaire*—the European Union's accumulated legislation, laws, and court decisions that include protections for human rights. Turkey's parliament amended the constitution to improve protections for freedom of expression.[62] An array of other reforms also followed—such as better publication of information on torture as well as more active prosecution against that form of abuse—that affected the lives of millions of people.[63] With reform under way, the European Commission recommended in 2004 that Turkey enter into open-ended negotiations toward full EU membership. But that new prospect of reward came with still more demands, such as requests for more legal reforms including a new law on associations, a new penal code, and reforms to the judicial police.[64] Turkey adopted them all, and on October 3, 2005, the European Council decided that it would, indeed, open negotiations for full EU membership.

Today, Turkey is still not a member of the European Union (and the Eurozone is in severe crisis, which is a particularly inopportune time to discuss large expansions that might affect the European labor market).[65] But it has obtained rewards through more trade, financial assistance, and closer diplomatic ties with Europe. Expecting that Turkey will improve human rights even further, the European Union has guaranteed billions of euros of financial assistance targeted at development and social aid projects.[66] The money has funded projects like "Call, Don't Be Silent!" a hotline for victims of domestic violence and a public awareness campaign combating violence against women in Turkey.[67]

The stream of rewards—many delivered and still more promised—has played a crucial role in convincing the Turkish government to make the protection of human rights a greater priority at all levels of government. It has improved the judiciary, civil–military relations, and protection for political and cultural rights; Turkey's reforms have even included fuller dialogue with political parties and civil society to address discrimination against Kurds.[68]

Of course, not every government acting as a steward for human rights can offer carrots as large and compelling as EU membership. But carrots come in many sizes and varieties, and the cases of Oman and Turkey illustrate how such rewards can help countries improve their human rights records by changing the calculus of abuse.

## THE LIMITS OF REWARDS

Just like punishments, there are limits to what steward states can accomplish with rewards. Some of the difficulties are strategic, since governments often dangle or deliver rewards in ways that aren't the most effective for the protection of human rights. Some are tactical because perpetrators stop violating human rights when they believe that the rewards for their complicity outweigh the benefits of abuse. In some settings, such as when a government fears losing power, those benefits can be perceived as quite large. And some, of course, relate to geopolitics. No policy—whether anchored in punishments, rewards, or both—has yet effectively used trade, aid, investment, or diplomacy rewards to seriously boost human rights in China, partly because no single government will or can on its own provide rewards important enough to sway the Chinese government to stop practices such as political imprisonment, torture, and censorship that the ruling party feels are essential to retaining power and order.

A reward strategy is also difficult to implement and sustain. Once a reward has been granted, for instance, the abuser often has strong incentives to renege. If they can get away with it, perpetrators will gladly take rewards for making some human rights concessions while switching to other forms of abuse. An example is a tyrant rewarded for holding elections who uses the scrum of electoral contest to abuse political opponents, harass voters, and even kills protesters.[69] The result is that one hallmark of democratic rule—the holding of elections—becomes more prevalent even as others suffer.

Even in the cases that are ripe for an effective reward strategy—such as in smaller countries that are ruled by governments that are vulnerable to the demands of stewards—many difficulties arise. In Oman, the US strategy of trade rewards was hardly as influential as it could have been. The policy was never comprehensive or bolstered with corresponding efforts to support human rights stakeholders within Oman. The US congressional mandate under which the George W. Bush administration negotiated rewards for Oman's human rights protections strengthened the policy efforts because it made them more credible. But once the rewards were given, the pressure on Oman relaxed. A greater ongoing impact would have been possible if the US government had followed up its original trade agreement with a string of further conditional rewards. And while the US trade strategy does appear to have encouraged the Omani government to improve legislation protecting workers' human rights, many problems remain. Women continue to be discriminated against and practices such as female genital cutting are common, refugees are vulnerable to rights violations, homosexuality is illegal, and speech and press remain censored.[70]

Turkey, in many ways the most prominent example of a successful rewards strategy, also reveals many limitations in rewarding perpetrators for reform. Despite the European Union offering the prospect of membership, today the Turkish government still fails to fully protect human rights. Security forces commit unlawful killings, beatings, and torture. Troubles in the judicial system are legion, and the government still limits freedom of expression.[71] In part this is due to the government's continuing obstinacy against fully embracing human rights principles. In part it is due to the complex, interlocking nature of domestic political, legal, and social institutions; reforming these institutions is not an overnight affair. In part the troubles also reflect a common problem with large rewards: making them credible. Voters in the European Union have big reservations about granting Turkey membership, and many outright oppose it, no matter how much membership might help to consolidate democracy and the protection of human rights in Turkey.[72] Turkish leaders know this, and the periodic cold shoulder from the European Union dampens Turkey's interest in reform.[73]

## Conclusion

Governments are already using their muscle and money to advocate for the protection of human rights abroad. This chapter has only touched the surface of what they do. Their efforts to change the calculus of abuse fall into many categories, but I surveyed two—punishments and rewards—intended to coerce and persuade abusers to change their behavior. For stewards states—not only the United States and the countries of the European Union, but also any state that makes human rights a significant part of its foreign policy—the challenge is to make these policy instruments, and others like them, work much better.

One insight from this chapter is that foreign policy tends to work when targets have few other options (e.g., US economic pressure on Guatemala) or when the rewards are so huge (e.g., EU membership for Turkey) that abusers have few options but to notice. Yet that insight is troubling because it suggests that foreign policy will be highly limited in its impacts and often costly to mobilize. One reason for this is that punishments and rewards tend to be tactical. They change the calculus of abuse. But they have lesser (and occasionally negative) impacts on the process of persuasion. Efforts to promote human rights through rewards and punishments encounter great skepticism—and at times, outright hostility—from local communities and governments. Fixing that problem requires looking inside countries and finding ways to make foreign pressure less "foreign." The key to that, I suggest in the next two chapters, is localization.

# Nongovernmental Organizations

Governments already use their power as stewards for human rights. They discuss human rights at the highest levels of diplomacy, doling out punishments and rewards. They try to be persuasive. Chapter 8 surveyed some of their efforts to help protect human rights and illustrated what works, even in contexts where international laws usually don't get direct traction. Chapter 8 also described some of the challenges and dangers.

A central challenge with all these attempts is that they are seen, within the target country, as foreign governments imposing "their" interests on the rest of the world. Such troubles arise not only when steward states use the punishments and rewards discussed in chapter 8 but also with seemingly less threatening activities, such as the funding of human rights advocates and programs in an effort to empower victims. Viewed from the inside, the local fit isn't good. The use of state power to promote human rights is seen as illegitimate or misguided, based on alien motivations or understandings that are out of synch with the needs and perceptions on the ground. That explains why efforts by steward states to use their power to promote human rights often flop—even at times catalyzing antihuman rights sentiment.[1]

The remedy is not for stewards to avoid using their power, for that would be devastating for human rights. Instead, they must find ways to use power more effectively. That requires efforts to localize their stewardship: translate human rights promotion efforts in context, indigenize foreign efforts within particular communities, and develop "congruence with local beliefs and practices."[2] When trying to promote human rights from the outside, such localization strategies are essential.

This chapter explains why there is value to legitimizing the use of state power (and thus advocacy) in a local context, and explores practical strategies that foreign stewards can use to localize how they wield their power for human rights. It looks especially to locally based actors, concentrating on the roles of NGOs. The next chapter takes the same perspective, but focuses on another main organization that can aid localization: NHRIs.

My argument is that NGOs (and in the next chapter, NHRIs) can directly assist in implementing foreign-backed punishments, rewards, and other forms of diplomacy that are intended to promote human rights, while raising the odds that those policies resonate with local issues, customs, and practices. These local organizations can broadcast, endorse, and legitimize foreign efforts within their community even as they appeal to local stakeholders without whose support foreign efforts to improve human rights will fall flat.

The first part of this chapter articulates how localization—whether through NGOs or NHRIs—actually leads to legitimacy and the congruence of local with international policies around human rights. Second, I describe what NGOs actually do and put their operations into perspective. Third, I examine some of the troubles that arise when NGOs play these roles. For example, local NGOs have their own agendas that often don't align well with outsiders who seek to promote human rights. Localizing human rights is crucial for giving legitimacy to foreign diplomatic efforts such as those explored in chapter 8—a challenge that is now well understood and can be navigated.

There are many arguments for localizing human rights. Mine is that it allows stewards to use their power more effectively and therefore elevates the protection of human rights. A localization strategy poses a great threat to the human rights abusers because it can unite their local and foreign adversaries and boost the legitimacy of human rights by championing them from within.

## Legitimacy, Congruence, and Implementation

One reason that international human rights legal norms don't get incorporated into domestic politics and social behavior is that they, and their supporting institutions like the UN human rights bodies or the United States government, often lack local legitimacy. Foreign governments and other organizations that originate and transmit the norms are seen as alien or disingenuous. Or the norm feels out of place, even offensive, to the local community.[3] To be sure, there are lots of other reasons why human rights are abused—among them the fact that they are inconvenient at times for local governments that want to stay in power. But legitimacy is essential for making human rights protection sustainable for the long term.

Gay McDougall is a lawyer and longtime human rights advocate. She has served as an independent expert on the UN body that oversees the Convention on the Elimination of All Forms of Racial Discrimination as well as a special rapporteur on rape, sexual slavery, and slavery-like practices in armed conflict, and was named the first UN independent expert on minority issues. From all her experience, she's learned that "many human rights professionals come from elite backgrounds. More often than not, the leading human rights activists in any country belong to a privileged class or social group. This is particularly true in resource-poor environments, where the human rights field has become something of a last-chance business—and may represent one of the few sectors where paid, professional jobs are still available."[4]

Chidi Anselm Odinkalu, lawyer and human rights advocate, describes a similar perception in Africa. "Instead of being the currency of a social justice or conscience-driven movement, 'human rights' has increasingly become the specialized language of a select professional cadre with its own rites of passage and methods of certification. Far from being a badge of honor, human rights activism is, in some of the places I have observed it, increasingly a certificate of privilege."[5]

This exclusivity, explains sociologist and former staff member of Human Rights Watch James Ron, surged when the international development community embraced human rights in the 1990s. Foreign funding poured in. These new funds were concentrated on a single template, rooted in the goal of getting as many countries as possible to embrace international law, which created significant problems for ground-level interpretation, integration, and acceptance of universal human rights.[6] In turn, this approach has catalyzed concerns that foreign actors—both governments and internationally based NGOs—are using universal human rights talk to impose control over other societies and cover for political goals. Those apprehensions have made it much easier for some local actors to dismiss norms and policies that originate from foreign countries and multilateral organizations.[7]

Beyond just skepticism about foreign ideas, in some communities the fact that human rights are advanced through official language and legal procedures also generates deep suspicion. After all, legal code is frequently correlated with corrupt or abusive governments as well as bureaucratic sclerosis that impedes the effective protection of individuals—in short, all the things that local human rights organizations are trying to avoid. "Although rights-based language is attractive to those familiar with its ideological background, it sounds bizarre when spoken out of context," says Ron.[8] In Spanish, *derechos* means "rights," but it also means "laws," and those are not trusted in settings like Bolivian barrios. In Bolivia, the legal protections afforded defendants can be perceived as undermining indigenous conceptions of justice and security.[9] In China, it's not controversial to speak about a person's legal rights, but speaking about human rights often provokes "a nationalistic response."[10]

This dissonance poses a challenge for foreign stewards of human rights. When stewards use their power to coerce or persuade—without attention to the local context, perspectives of local partners, or preexisting normative frameworks—they increase the risk of failure and even back-lash.[11] Promotion efforts fail if they alienate potential local partners or those whose rights are violated. It is crucial to get community support for diplomatic efforts—a task that NGOs, notably those locally based, can help address.

## NGOs in Perspective

You've probably heard about Amnesty International and Human Rights Watch. They're global human rights NGOs.[12] While their methods and structures differ, these international human rights NGOs conduct human rights research, reporting, and advocacy wherever they deem it most necessary across the globe. They pressure governments seen as human rights violators as well as governments that might be inclined to use their power to promote human rights. And they are influential members of the international advocacy community.

Alongside these organizations are local NGOs promoting the rights of specific groups in their communities.[13] They exist in the thousands.[14] The first local human rights NGOs emerged in the 1970s and 1980s, and took up the atrocities committed by the era's dictators. They were at the forefront of emerging human rights movements, and worked especially to prohibit murder, torture, and other forms of extreme bodily harm while also aiding the victims of those crimes (and their families) as they sought justice. They sprang up first in Latin America, then Eastern Europe, and later in other parts of the developing world.[15] The communities in which they worked funded and supported them. And they were, by many accounts, influential—saving lives, winning access to government-controlled information, and shaming criminals.[16]

The end of the Cold War shifted the focus on to economic, social, and cultural rights. Prominent NGOs, which had previously concentrated on civil and political issues, broadened their mandates to take on new tasks such as ensuring that significant economic suffering like famines were not ignored simply because they did not formally invoke traditional civil and political rights.[17] Just as multinational NGOs embraced these new agendas, so too did local NGOs. Foreign donors gave generously. NGOs flourished, and the human rights mission began to overlap with poverty alleviation and development.[18] Today, these organizations work all over the world to promote all kinds of human rights for all kinds of people.[19]

In El Salvador, the Committee of the Mothers of the Disappeared (Comadres) is the country's first (and longest-running) human rights NGO.[20] It formed in response to government-sanctioned disappearances and killings in the years preceding El Salvador's civil war. During the war, Comadres grew to a membership of over five hundred women from across the country. It documented atrocities, and fought for the release of political prisoners, the return of the disappeared, and government accountability for torture. After the war, the organization has continued calling for perpetrators to be brought to justice, spotlighting ongoing human rights concerns, and conducting human rights education.

Women of Zimbabwe Arise! (WOZA) began in 2003 as a civic movement.[21] It gives women a platform and the empowerment to speak out against the injustices facing them on a daily basis. The group mobilizes in defense of rights (particularly civil and political) where and when the need arises. They have targeted police brutality, state propaganda, and widespread hunger.[22] The organization now has a membership of seventy-five thousand Zimbabwean women and men (the latter affiliated with WOZA's wing called Men of Zimbabwe Arise! or MOZA). Thousands have been arrested for their protests of government-condoned injustices. In 2006, WOZA held listening sessions in hundreds of local communities to hear and document what Zimbabweans wanted in a free and fair Zimbabwe. This input is reflected in the WOZA-drafted People's Charter that many other NGOs and civil society groups—including Zimbabwe Lawyers for Human Rights, the Progressive Teachers Union of Zimbabwe, and Zimbabwe National Students Union—have also endorsed.[23]

In India, dozens of activists from across the country have allied in response to the government's disregard of the 1989 Prevention of Atrocities Act. Through this legislation, India had made commitments to address human rights abuses stemming from "untouchability" in the caste system, but in practice it had done little to comply. These activists formed the National Campaign on Dalit Human Rights.[24] This campaign raises visibility of the issue by collecting millions of signatures that call for an end to untouchability and government recognition of caste discrimination as a crime. Such efforts attract media coverage and provide grassroots training, alliance building, and documentation of rights violations.

There are many types of NGOs. Local NGOs such as WOZA are less visible to foreign audiences yet crucial, and they can advance localization in lots of different ways.

## How NGOs Can Localize Foreign Stewardship

NGOs can play central roles in localizing foreign stewards' efforts—such as those surveyed in chapter 8—and thus boost the odds that stewardship from the outside leads to actual improvements in human rights on the ground. One way they help localize pressure is by seeking out foreign promoters—a strategy, core to some NGOs, that has become known as the "boomerang" pattern.[25] Some local activists don't have the resources or power to sway the governments they'd like to go after directly, so they invite sympathetic foreign actors to join their cause. In turn, the foreigners—both international NGOs and steward states—use their power to influence abusers by forcing them to pay attention to and heed the local community's cause. The prime mover for this boomerang is inside the country in the form of local human rights promoters who set the agenda, but much of the power is conveyed via sympathetic, foreign stewards. The impact of these foreign stewards depends in part on the ability of local agents to ensure that the foreign efforts are aligned within the local situation.

The Mothers of the Plaza de Mayo is an example of one group that has used this boomerang strategy. The group first mobilized in Argentina during the period of government repression in the 1970s and 1980s. At a time when public dissent was forbidden, these women marched every Thursday in Buenos Aires' central plaza to demand accountability for the disappearances of their children. The group faced risk of brutal persecution for their activism.[26] Given the dangerous climate for organizing, they looked globally for support. They provided information to international human rights NGOs like Amnesty International, which in turn lobbied foreign governments to get involved as well. The group also forged alliances with civil society organizations abroad. Mothers, lawyers, and faith-based communities elsewhere mobilized in solidarity with this movement, and pressured their own governments to act in order to hold Argentina's government accountable.[27] In addition to providing information, the local Argentine group also traveled to the United States and Europe, where they met with officials, the press, and human rights organizations. This outreach translated into press coverage and funding opportunities along with more foreign pressure on the Argentine government.[28] For example, the group urged the United States to suspend military and economic aid to Argentina's dictatorship, and lobbied both the United Nations and the Inter-American Commission on Human Rights to condemn what it considered to be government-sanctioned human rights abuses.[29]

Some governments responded. In February 1977, the US secretary of state announced that the Carter administration would reduce the amount of military aid to Argentina by over half, and the Argentine government responded by refusing all military aid.[30] Then in July, the US Congress passed a bill that cut all military assistance to Argentina.[31] The French and Swedish governments condemned the Argentine junta's violations of basic rights. The Inter-American Commission on Human Rights visited Argentina in September 1979; despite the risk of reprisal, thousands lined up outside the commission to give testimony.[32] The Argentine government proved to be sensitive to the tarnishing of its image.[33] While foreign intervention didn't bring about immediate structural change, the advocacy network is credited with saving lives.[34] Involuntary disappearances in Argentina declined from 3,098 in 1977 to 181 in 1979; the government also released political prisoners and restored some measure of political participation.[35]

The boomerang needn't be a passive process in which the steward states simply await calls for help and then respond. Foreign governments can seek out local activist organizations that share their goals. And they can work together to localize their policy objectives, which are shaped and adapted by these organizations to fit the local environment.[36]

Once local NGOs are engaged, they can help localize stewardship through the better deployment of state power in three ways. First, they can give a steward's policy legitimacy. Through efforts to advertise and explain favorably foreign efforts at coercion and persuasion, they can mobilize local public support. Failures of foreign policy are particularly likely when local stakeholders are not engaged. The lack of engagement with local NGOs, for example, helps explain why US sanctions against Cuba have failed to yield political change; instead, sanctions have mostly alienated the Cuban people.[37]

Second, NGOs can guide foreign stewards on the appropriateness of their approach as well as reactions from potentially allied local groups. They can help craft language, incentives, and procedures that fit with the community's needs and situation. Crucially, they can counsel against policies that are sure to backfire. Almost certainly this type of guidance doesn't happen enough. Greater congruence, in turn, can lead to improved legitimacy. These benefits apply not just to individual steward states that are trying advance their own foreign policies but also to international institutions working to protect human rights. Indeed, many NGOs have a formal status in international organizations such as the United Nations that give them the ability to provide consultations and make public statements.[38]

Incongruities between international agendas and local circumstances often arise. Efforts to protect gay and lesbian rights have been among the many examples. Ndubisi Obiorah, a lawyer and policy adviser with the Human Rights Law Service in Nigeria, explained at an ethics conference in 2002 that despite the positive working relationship that many international human rights NGOs had with local human rights activists, pushing for gay and lesbian rights at that time would be unwise, given local cultural beliefs and attitudes.[39] In a world where resources for promoting human rights are quite scarce, such advice on places where resources might be spared is invaluable.

Third, in some circumstances local NGOs can play a central part in implementing projects that foreign governments and multinational NGOs craft or fund. This role for local NGOs helps build legitimacy while yielding tangible changes on the ground—something that is particularly hard for outsiders to do in cases where local politics are likely to backlash against foreign involvement.

One example where all three of these roles for local NGOs—in promoting legitimacy, improving congruence, and implementing projects—is on display is the international movement to abandon female genital cutting, the cultural practice of partially or totally removing the external female genitalia. The practice has no health benefits. In some societies it is considered part of raising a girl properly: a way to ready her for marriage while promoting particular ideals of femininity and modesty. For some, the ritual is part of their ethnic or cultural identity or religious practice.[40] According to the World Health Organization, however, it "is recognized internationally as a violation of the human rights of girls and women."[41] It's a form of discrimination against women, and because the practice is nearly always carried out on young girls it violates the rights of children. Some also consider the practice as cruel, inhuman, or degrading treatment as well as a violation of a person's right to health. Over a hundred million girls and women have been cut.

Female genital cutting attracts a lot of attention from human rights promoters. But foreign pressure by steward states to do away with the practice hasn't had much effect. In fact, in some settings foreign pressure has actually strengthened local determination to continue the ritual. People, including the women being cut, have perceived these foreign efforts as insulting. Speaking about the practice in Somalia, one woman explained, "If Somali women change, it will be a change done by us, among us. When they order us to stop, tell us what we must do, it is offensive to the black person or the Muslim person who believes in circumcision. To advise is good, but not to order."[42]

This backlash against foreign involvement is now abating, notably where local NGOs have played key roles. *Tostan* means "breakthrough" in the West African language of Wolof. Since 1991, it's also been the name of an NGO whose mission is to empower African communities through community education.[43] It is supported by a wide range of foreign donors and credited with the widespread abandonment of female genital cutting in Senegal. Its approach implements community-targeted education programs in national languages, engages in communication through extended social networks, and supports public declarations for the abandonment of cutting. Collaboration with religious leaders has been a central part of Tostan's strategy, as local imams have joined the movement to abandon cutting.[44] Rigorous evaluations have found that the program increased knowledge as well as changed attitudes and behavior in the participating communities. Among thousands of participating villages, the prevalence of female genital cutting in Senegal dropped by approximately 70 percent. Mothers with uncut girls were three times more likely to report that they didn't plan to have their daughters undergo the procedure. And there was a slight reduction in the prevalence of marriage of girls under fifteen years old.[45]

The government of Senegal eventually took up Tostan's approach in its national action plan to implement a ban on female genital cutting by 2015—the ultimate sign of successful localization.[46] The approach is being piloted in Gambia, Burkina Faso, and elsewhere.[47] And it provides a model for working with activist organizations to localize international norms through community engagement, communication, and education.

Of course, these roles for NGOs frequently require collaboration both locally and with international partners. One example of effective grassroots mobilization that resulted in nationwide reforms is Amnesty International's Sierra Leone campaign to fight maternal mortality. In 2008, UNICEF identified Sierra Leone as the country with the highest child and maternal mortality rates in the world.[48] Inspired by Millennium Development Goal 5 (to improve maternal health) and the belief that health is a basic human right, Amnesty International (based in London) targeted Sierra Leone as one of its launch points for a new campaign to promote socioeconomic rights such as health.[49] Working in tandem with other international NGOs and UN agencies, Amnesty and its local branch (Amnesty International Sierra Leone) worked with local partners to mobilize national stakeholders. It organized a caravan that brought the message of health as a basic right to villages across the country; it used community-oriented techniques including plays and a pop song performed by a famous Nigerian actress to highlight the problem of maternal mortality.[50] This combination of centrally managed international coordination and local mobilization resulted in the implementation of a new Free Care Initiative by the national government, which offers free medical care to all pregnant women, breast-feeding mothers, and children under five.[51]

## Some Troubles with NGO Localization

Local NGOs can provide legitimacy, congruence, and local implementation skills for foreign-backed human rights stewards. Playing these roles, NGOs can help increase the effectiveness of foreign efforts to coerce and especially to persuade governments to protect human rights. The bad news is that those same close relationships that explain how local NGOs lead to more effective foreign diplomacy can also undermine their capacity to localize international promotion efforts. When NGOs depend on foreign support they must walk a fine line. That support, on the one hand, is a signal that can raise an NGO's status and influence.[52] On the other hand, it can also compromise their reputation or ability to operate in the local settings, and play central roles in making international human rights norms more legitimate and influential.[53]

One danger for NGOs is that a large role for foreign funding can make local governments feel insecure. Aggravated by a rise in local community activism and afraid of losing control, local governments can respond with intimidation that undermines the ability of local NGOs to operate effectively.[54] The effects are felt not only by NGOs but also among citizens who, fearing revenge or other consequences, become more prone to disengage. For example, the government of Ethiopia froze the bank accounts of two local NGOs—the Ethiopian Women Lawyers Association and the Ethiopian Human Rights Council.[55] Retroactively, it charged these NGOs with violating legislation that requires organizations engaged in human rights or governance work to raise 90 percent of their funds from local sources.[56] Both organizations opted to reregister as charities—and thus avoid the requirement for local funding—but each nonetheless sustained budget and staff cuts.[57] The Ethiopian government accused these NGOs of making false claims to the US Department of State and Human Rights Watch that the government violated human rights and misused foreign aid.[58] In a similar story of local government backlash against foreign-linked NGOs, President Robert Mugabe of Zimbabwe banned all NGO operations in 2008, just before his presidential election runoff; the ban disrupted emergency food aid from foreign donors to millions of people.[59]

NGOs can also find their influence diminished when foreign funding creates perceptions of collusion and opportunism; dependence on foreigners can distort local social movements by introducing external agendas and accountability.[60] When foreign money and prestige are available, some NGOs crop up looking for jobs, publicity, or status rather than actual change in human rights practices. They take up an international agenda tactically—as a source of funding—rather than truly aligning their activities to the needs of the local community. Foreign funding can also reduce local oversight and accountability.[61] NGOs don't need to solicit support from or work to stay in tune with the community they are supposed to be helping.[62] Dependent on outside resources, they're seen as deputies peddling alien agendas, without the local credibility that is essential to raising awareness and acceptance in their own community.[63] Such dangers may be especially troublesome in former colonies where NGO practices can be seen as an opportunity for volunteers and employees to gain extra status or set themselves apart from those they are educating by collaborating with colonizers.[64]

Law professor Obiora Chinedu Okafor describes how foreign funding has affected the legitimacy of local organizations in Nigeria. There, human rights NGOs have flourished, propelled by foreign funders. Elite urban lawyers tend to run them. Many NGOs advocate for policies that are incongruent with the priorities of the communities they serve.[65] The Nigerian human rights community has emphasized civil-political rights, Okafor argues, to the exclusion of pressing socioeconomic rights. This is due to multiple factors: the legalistic mind-set of the lawyers involved in national NGOs, the groups' hierarchical structure and lack of membership bases, and the historical emphasis by Western NGOs of civil-political over socioeconomic rights (an approach which has been taken up by local organizations).

Anthropologist Harri Englund finds the same situation in Malawi, where foreign aid and human rights activism are impeding the process of democratization. One example, he says, is the National Initiative for Civic Education, an EU-funded project to promote democracy. Although founded on noble principles, in practice this project has divided staffers (who depend on foreign income) from the people they were hired to serve.[66]

Of course, engaging local NGOs—even when done well—is no guarantee of successfully coercing or persuading a path to better human rights. Local activists and government can be hard to persuade; they may be skeptical of the agendas promoted by foreign partnerships with governments or internationally based NGOs. Many in Arab states, for instance, view the human rights agenda as biased toward Western interests and cultural norms. The fact that major human rights organizations like Amnesty International and Human Rights Watch are based in the West, and mainly publicize findings for a Western audience, leaves some activists elsewhere feeling excluded and suspicious of international human rights discourses.[67] One example is homosexuality—a practice that leads to such ostracism in Egypt that local human rights organizations do not defend gay rights. Hisham Kassem, director of the Egyptian Organization for Human Rights, explains: "What could we do? Nothing. If we were to uphold this issue, this would be the end of what remains of the concept of human rights in Egypt. . . . We let them [homosexuals] down, but I don't have a mandate from the people, and I don't want the West to set the pace for the human rights movement in Egypt."[68]

## Navigating the Troubles

These difficulties of working with foreign-linked, local NGOs are well known. There is no infallible method for managing the tension between the need for foreign powers to link their efforts into local NGOs and communities and the fact that those very linkages are a potential source of suspicion and misaligned incentives. Yet there are a few rules of thumb for establishing successful partnerships with local organizations with the goal of advancing a steward state's influence on human rights. I will discuss four.

One benchmark rule is resonance. The objective—say, to combat child soldiering, or reduce illiteracy among girls and women—must fit with the localizer's mission and expertise. Where possible, the local NGO should be located near its constituency, while working to maintain an open dialogue with the community's needs.[69] Resonance helps NGOs localize a policy through framing. That is, it helps guide the creation of shared interpretations of a norm that legitimates and inspires community support rather than imposing foreign concepts that are completely alien.[70]

Another benchmark is community buy-in. Law professor Abdullahi An-Na'im explains that if all "funding for local NGOs comes from foreign organizations, that is where their accountability lies."[71] When some backing comes from the local community, the NGO represents that community. The community is more invested in guiding the organization's work and seeing its programs succeed. Even when local funding is small, the result is NGOs that are more qualified localizers because they have closer ties to their community. By necessity, they have to be accountable to the people supporting them.

A third condition is the presence of in-house assessment and accountability. The partner NGO should have procedures to plan, monitor, and evaluate its activities so it knows when its efforts to engage local communities and implement projects are working as expected.[72] Local partners must be transparent in their operations, and be prepared to demonstrate how they are obtaining the expertise they need and soliciting feedback from local stakeholders.[73] Organizations unaccustomed to or wary of impact evaluation, or with a cloudy decision-making structure or chain of command, usually make for unreliable allies in the localization process. Of course, the real world poses difficult trade-offs for foreign stewards because ideal local partners don't always exist. In such cases, a foreign human rights steward may identify the organizations most likely to help localize and then invest in making them more accountable—such as by helping the NGO develop sound evaluation mechanisms, auditing for accountability, and other programs.[74]

Access is another important attribute of local partner organizations.[75] Localization requires an NGO to have a persuasive rapport with the public or government sphere necessary for the specific human rights advocacy they're engaged in. Access helps create opportunities for social movements.[76] It determines the openness of a political system to social movements seeking change.[77] This frequently involves "networks of contacts and collaborations" across traditional boundaries of family, ethnic group, and location.[78]

## Conclusion

The previous chapter explained ways steward states use their power in an effort to promote human rights—through punishments and rewards as well as an array of other policies such as funding for advocacy campaigns. Those governments have proved that they are willing to devote substantial resources to the cause of protecting human rights around the world. Unfortunately, those efforts frequently don't work well and can easily be seen as illegitimate uses of foreign power.

This chapter has taken up the challenge of making state power more effective. It has argued that state power will have more influence on improving human rights when international norms and state policies are seen as legitimate, sufficiently congruent with local attitudes and implemented locally. These three crucial attributes—legitimacy, congruence, and local implementation—can sometimes be met by coordination with local NGOs as partners.

NGO partners can play essential roles. Yet they also come with many flaws. I have suggested some benchmark rules that, if followed, can help foreign stewards make the right partnerships with local NGOs. Where these benchmark rules, which are based on the actual history of foreign governments working with local NGOs, are not followed, the results can be wasted resources and even counterproductive to the mission of protecting human rights.

When ideal local NGOs aren't available, fortuitously foreign stewards have other options. They can invest in improving or even creating their local partners. And they can also look to different types of institutions—notably NHRIs—the topic I address in the next chapter.

# 10

# National Human Rights Institutions

Chapter 9 looked at how governments that are keen to promote human rights abroad can use their power more effectively by working with local NGOs. This chapter discusses localization of a different type: through national human rights institutions (NHRIs). Unlike NGOs, these organizations have formalized roles in public debate and the national policy process. States create and mostly fund them; in most instances they are accountable to legislatures.[1] Like NGOs, they are abundant and active— existing in more than a hundred countries.[2] They work through reporting, educational programs, media campaigns, networking, and involvement with civil society and other stakeholders.

This chapter looks, first, at the many different types of NHRIs and puts them into perspective. Second, it explores how NHRIs could actually help localize foreign efforts aimed at advancing human rights. Third, while NHRIs hold much promise, they also pose many challenges, which I explain while also offering some strategies for navigating those difficulties. Fourth and finally, I discuss how NGOs and NHRIs interact since the most effective forms of localization usually require cooperation among these different types of national institutions. I focus on when the NGO– NHRI relationship leads to synergistic behavior that boosts human rights protections and when it is prone to unproductive conflict.

## NHRIs in Perspective

NHRIs come in many forms, but two are dominant.[3] First, ombudsmen, such as those operating in Albania and Bermuda, work to improve "the performance of the public administration and the enhancement of government accountability to the public."[4] Those operating in Slovenia, Georgia, and Peru also receive individual complaints about human rights violations committed by government agencies, and sometimes by private agencies fulfilling public services.[5] They act as mediators to resolve the complaint. Some ombudsmen are more active than others, taking on investigative and promotion roles, engaging in public awareness activities, and publishing opinions about how public policy and government decisions are affecting human rights. By design, an ombudsman works to interface between public institutions and the public itself. But their mandate tends to be narrow, and usually an ombudsman's efforts are not triggered until a member of the public complains or there is evidence that government institutions have failed to perform their duties.

The second type of NHRI consists of human rights commissions such as those working in New Zealand, Canada, Australia, India, Malaysia, Afghanistan, and Chile. Their procedural mandate, typically wider than most ombudsmen, gives them the tasks of both human rights protectors and also promoters. They often carry out broad investigations into local human rights situations, monitor government compliance with international human rights obligations, and educate, train, and sometimes review individual complaints about human rights violations. Many states, such as South Africa and Sri Lanka, have established both types of NHRIs—ombudsmen offices and human rights commissions. And in some countries, such as Ghana and Russia, NHRIs are singular institutions that perform both kinds of functions.

One example of an NHRI is the Defensoría del Pueblo, a human rights ombudsman operating in Peru.[6] Under Alberto Fujimori, the government created the ombudsman position in the 1990s after a military death squad disappeared and then murdered nine students along with a university professor. The position was written into the Constitution.[7] Fujimori is no longer in power, but the ombudsman still operates today, with wide public support.[8] The ombudsman investigates complaints (the office received more than half a million complaints from the public between 1999 and 2007), reports on issues, intervenes in constitutional processes (through amicus curiae), presents policy drafts to Congress, and publishes other statements.[9] The office even collects data on its own productivity in performing key tasks such as reviewing and settling complaints as well as the effectiveness of its efforts to cooperate with state agencies.[10] The ombudsman also coordinates community-based legal and social mobilization for human rights in Peru through more than two-dozen local offices in the country.[11]

Public education is a core function of the ombudsman. The office promotes human rights through television and radio spots—a radio program called *By the Ombudsman's Hand* is transmitted throughout the country.[12] The ombudsman covers issues from the right to adequate health services to children's and women's rights to be free from domestic violence. In addition to spreading messages in Spanish, the ombudsman office also works in indigenous languages such as Quechua, Aymara, Ashaninka, and Shipibo. Through an initiative called Defensoría del Pueblo, Closer to the People, the ombudsman also sets up human rights workshops for the public, educating the poor about their human rights and the ombudsman's services.

Another example is the office of the ombudsman in Namibia, mandated to protect, promote, and enhance respect for human rights along with the fundamental freedoms enshrined in Namibia's constitution, which include civil, political, economic, social and cultural rights.[13] Like other NHRIs, it investigates allegations of human rights abuse; for example, it has reviewed complaints of racial discrimination, wrongful arrest and detention, assaults, ill treatment of prisoners, and delays in the justice system. It provides legal assistance to victims involved in litigation.[14] It also engages in public outreach and education, including public lectures, newsletters, and community meetings.[15] The current ombudsman, John Walters, has been working in different capacities in the justice system for over twenty years.[16] An advisory committee offers a forum for dialogue between his office and local civil society organizations, and has helped to coordinate local campaigns, such as the 16 Days of Activism against Gender Violence campaign to raise awareness about gender violence.[17]

NHRIs like these operate in many countries to locally promote and protect all kinds of human rights. They vary enormously in both their effectiveness and awareness of how they actually operate.[18]

## How NHRIs Can Localize Foreign Stewardship

NHRIs, by providing many of the same functions as NGOs to localize international norms—legitimacy, congruence, and implementation—can work with foreign steward states that want to advance the protection of human rights to use their power more effectively. Though NHRIs are national institutions, already many are connected to international organizations, activists, and foreign governments. The Australian Agency for International Development has provided financial support to the Asia Pacific Forum for NHRIs, which gives advice and technical assistance toward the establishment of NHRIs in places like South Korea, Malaysia, Mongolia, and Thailand.[19] Many NHRIs have ties with sister institutions in other countries. For example, the Canadian Human Rights Commission has provided technical assistance to NHRIs in China, Russia, Hong Kong, Cuba, Kenya, Sri Lanka, Vietnam, South Africa, and Cambodia; it has also facilitated exchanges with NHRIs in Indonesia, Benin, India, Madagascar, and Nigeria.[20]

NHRIs differ from NGOs in the scope of their activities. They are national institutions with mainly nationwide missions, while NGO operations range from village or community-based to regional or even global advocacy. They also have different stakeholders, which for NHRIs include civil society organizations (such as NGOs) as well as varied government agencies. As a result, the reach of NHRIs is different from NGOs, notably because of their direct connection to national government. As with NGOs, NHRIs can localize by legitimizing, guiding, and assisting in the implementation of foreign policy in their community.[21]

One example of an NHRI that has been particularly effective in promoting human rights is Ghana's Commission on Human Rights and Administrative Justice (CHRAJ). Created by Parliament and embedded in the national Constitution, its responsibilities include ensuring the accountability of the branches of government, investigating complaints, and educating the public about human rights.[22] It also has enforcement powers that allow the CHRAJ to bring an action before any court in Ghana to seek available remedies. Already, it has held senior Ghanaian officials accountable for violations of human rights.

Despite these official roles it is accessible to local communities to hear their complaints.[23] The CHRAJ carries out public education campaigns, mainly through seminars and workshops aimed at public officials, including military, civil servants, and even district assembly members. It has developed a close relationship with Ghanaian civil society, meeting regularly with NGOs to discuss priorities and strategy, and collaborating on human rights education. The local media widely reports on the commission's activities and verdicts. By many accounts, the CHRAJ has earned public legitimacy—an essential condition for effective localization.[24]

The CHRAJ has done a lot to promote human rights.[25] It's made headway on prison overcrowding and mistreatment. Its prison-monitoring program coordinates annual visits to scrutinize prison compliance with international and domestic human rights standards, and follows up with reports and recommendations to Parliament.[26] The program has had some success, although widespread overcrowding, poor sanitation, and slow justice remain persistent problems.[27]

It's also made progress against forced servitude and sexual abuse by curtailing *trokosi*: the traditional practice of involuntary labor in the service of local priests, who take in human beings, usually young virgin girls, and force them to work to atone for a crime or social misdeed committed by a family member.[28] Often, these girls are exploited and sexually abused during servitude.[29] To educate the public and open a dialogue with those who practice the ritual, former commissioner Emile Short formed a coalition with local NGOs, the National Commission for Civic Education, members of Ewe ethnic communities, and victims of *trokosi*.[30] The coalition worked to convince communities where the practice is prevalent that servitude is a violation of human rights. Thousands of women and children have since been released, and it appears that *trokosi* is now a dwindling practice in Ghana.[31] The government criminalized the practice, and the CHRAJ continues conversations with local priests and leaders on ways to stop the ritual.[32]

The CHRAJ has also had an impact on ministerial corruption. It has investigated and publicized allegations of bribery, illegal acquisition of wealth, and abuse of office by government ministers and presidential staffers.[33] Its investigations have prompted high-profile resignations by corrupt officials along with greater transparency and accountability.[34] In 2011, it also won an appeal against a high court ruling that prohibited the CHRAJ from investigating a scandal in which a UK construction firm, Mabey and Johnson, was accused of bribing Ghanaian government officials to win construction contracts in Ghana.[35] The investigation is still pending.[36]

NHRIs work best in settings where there is sufficient stability and adequate governing institutions that the NHRI has receptive points of entry into the courts, the national policy process, and civil society. While those conditions are ideal, NHRIs can also operate in countries that are much less stable. In Afghanistan, for example, there's the Afghanistan Independent Human Rights Commission.[37] Its programs cover human rights education, women's rights, children's rights, the rights of persons with disabilities, transitional justice, and monitoring and investigation. It reviews and resolves complaints, advocates for policy, and builds capacity through training, monitoring, and community outreach; in 2009, the commission investigated 99 percent of all the complaints that it received, and about two-thirds were resolved.[38] Its recommendations have been incorporated into the criminal procedure code, the Shia personal status law, a law on the elimination of violence against women, the family law, the law on control and audit, and the law on national audit, among others. It has nine regional offices, including a headquarters in Kabul along with six provincial offices. Its approach is to solicit widespread community support and participation.[39] For example, it developed its strategic action plan for 2010–13 through more than a dozen consultation sessions with hundreds of local government and nongovernmental stakeholders across the country.[40]

A core part of its mission is education, which has helped localize an understanding that human rights are not just a matter of international law but also a long-standing part of local ideology. In 2009, the Afghanistan Independent Human Rights Commission carried out dozens of human rights workshops and hundreds of awareness-raising meetings. One participant described a meeting: "For me, the topic on human rights and Islam was the most interesting, because I had a misunderstanding about the relationship between human rights (in particular women's rights) and Islam. I thought human rights and Islam are totally at odds in the case of women's rights. I am grateful to the AIHRC for such a useful workshop." Another said, "In the past I heard from others that human rights is something imported from the West. After this workshop, I changed my mind. Human rights is not alien, but something that exists, in a considerable measure, in our religion and culture."[41]

The practical effects of these educational activities have been many. For instance, one assembly—the Ulama Council of the Shibar District in Bamyan Province—issued a declaration that condemns and bans forced as well as underage marriages in the district while also supporting women's participation in public life, including their right to work. In Balkh Province, local religious leaders (mullahs) made speeches in the mosques about women's rights in Islam, underscoring women's right to justice. Across three provinces in the east (Khost, Paktia, and Paktika), there are reported declines in the number of "bad" marriages.[42] A UN evaluation found that the commission's women's rights unit has gained legitimacy for its awareness-raising activities with civil society while also drafting legislation to reduce domestic violence and underage marriage alongside the Ministry of Women's Affairs.[43] The commission also has assisted individual women through its complaints system. A woman came to the Mazar-i-Sharif office, for example, with serious burn injuries caused by her husband, who was subsequently prosecuted due to the commission's intervention.

The Afghanistan Independent Human Rights Commission has also launched campaigns to educate security and military forces about human rights. In 2009, Afghan Army recruits received about a hundred hours of human rights training over nine months; new police recruits received twelve hours over three months; and prison guards received sixteen hours over three months.[44]

## Some Troubles with NHRI Localization

NHRIs can play a large role in the localization process in part because they have special access to government institutions. At least to some degree, they are conceived and funded by national governments; they are embedded in governing institutions in ways that give them access that most NGOs do not enjoy. Yet the very strengths of this special structure can also generate problems—such as a lack of independence and autonomy—that can undercut the localization process.[45]

A central challenge is impartiality. Governments can constrain the power of NHRIs, such as by limiting their mandates and blocking them from engaging in state affairs. For example, the Algerian National Advisory Commission for the Promotion and Protection of Human Rights, the country's NHRI established by a presidential decree in 2002, is often perceived as just another "state institution."[46] The commission has focused on important questions—notably cases of forced disappearances—but independent NGOs lament their own lack of participation in investigations, the lack of accountability by state institutions, and the government's failure to offer monetary reparations and other forms of restitution.[47] The government has resorted to violence to prevent peaceful protests by civil society groups representing the family members of the disappeared.[48] In other countries, such barriers can be addressed when the NHRI has its own independent enforcement powers, but in Algeria the National Advisory Commission for the Promotion and Protection of Human Rights lacks substantial investigative authority.[49]

When NHRIs lack impartiality, they are unlikely to be helpful in localizing international norms or policies that contravene the government's wishes. Because at best they can promote policies and take positions on only a narrow band of approved issues, these NHRIs don't have much credibility or influence in the community. Just as collusion with foreigners endangers the trustworthiness of local NGOs, NHRIs' complicity with the national government can also diminish their trustworthiness.[50]

The NHRI of Bahrain illustrates this problem of co-optation. A royal decree created this institution in 2009, and members were appointed a year later. But after four months, its president, Salman Kamal Al Deen—a founding member of the Bahrain Human Rights Society—resigned under political pressure.[51] A coalition of locally based NGOs, including the Bahrain Center for Human Rights, the Bahrain Youth Society for Human Rights, the Women's Petition Committee, the Committee for Martyrs and Victims of Torture, and the Human Rights Office of the Freedom and Democracy Movement, has since condemned this institution and called for the development of a truly independent replacement.[52] NHRIs seen as shams have no credibility to localize global norms.

Another difficulty that arises when foreign stewards try to work with NHRIs is that these are national organizations whose mandates and priorities can make it particularly difficult for them to incorporate international policy agendas. Ideally, an NHRI would cover all rights in the Universal Declaration of Human Rights, with no hierarchy between different sorts. And they would have a wide range of powers and procedures. In practice, however, most NHRIs give priority to certain human rights issues that aren't always of paramount importance to foreign stewards. The international community has been vocal about violations of political rights in Indonesia, for instance. There has been widespread international condemnation of killings by Indonesian security forces, harsh prison conditions, abuse against religious groups, child labor, and the failure to enforce labor standards and workers' rights.[53] Meanwhile, the

National Commission on Human Rights in Indonesia (Komisi Nasional Hak Asasi Manusia, known as Komnas HAM) has put a high priority on land rights.[54] It has resolved disputes in which peasants lost their land tenancy to large corporations because they didn't acquire land titles when Indonesia gained independence. Similarly, the Northern Ireland Human Rights Commission focuses on issues that span the Catholic–Protestant divide—such as social and economic rights, women's and children's rights, and the rights of disabled persons—because of the volatility of civil and political rights in the local context.[55] Meanwhile, the global human rights community has been concerned with other topics, such as violence and insurgency.[56] In other countries, NHRIs prioritize civil and political rights over economic, social, and cultural rights.[57]

Of course, foreign human rights stewards can shop around for other local institutions—notably NGOs and other civil society groups—whose priorities might be more in line. Chances are, no matter what the goal or country, some local organizations also work for it. By contrast, the choices among NHRIs are many fewer. Worldwide there aren't as many NHRIs in operation as NGOs; not all countries have them, and those that do usually have just one or perhaps two. The problem of mismatched priorities is much more likely to arise when foreign stewards try to localize human rights by partnering with NHRIs.

## Navigating the Troubles

Navigating these challenges for localization requires accurate evaluations of what NHRIs can actually achieve for human rights, and attention to their many faults and limitations.[58] Such evaluations pose another challenge for stewards, in part, explains Peter Rosenblum, law professor who has worked within the OHCHR, because "the promotional project of expanding the number, resources, and access of NHRIs has colored the analysis of actual institutions and undermined any systematic evaluation."[59] That leaves stewards to make their own evaluation, and the risk is that stewards will partner with NHRIs that lack local credibility.

While there's no handbook for creating partnerships with NGOs for localization, the international community has developed a recognized manual for evaluating the quality of NHRIs: the Paris Principles, adopted by the UN General Assembly in 1993.[60] These guidelines support an international accreditation process that while far from perfect, can steer partnerships to the more effective NHRIs.

The OHCHR has used the Paris Principles to elaborate a toolbox for helping NHRIs become effective. That toolbox maintains that the mandate of an effective NHRI should be broad, and the institution should be given the competence to promote and protect human rights.[61] It should have a constitutional or legislative base to protect against arbitrary changes by the government, including intrusions such as closure.[62] It should be able to operate without interference—to draft its own rules, and have the capacity and freedom to handle daily business on its own. Membership should be representative of the society in which it operates. Though the NHRI is free to receive money from outside sources, the national government should provide adequate funding for its operations. And the NHRI should have authority to take up any issue within its competence, hear any person, and acquire any relevant information. Institutions that adhere to these principles can be granted certification through a UN-managed process that awards grades (A, B, and C) depending on the degree of compliance with the Paris Principles. In turn, the NHRI gets special rights that vary with its grade. An A-level NHRI, for example, participates as a voting member and holds office in the International Coordinating Committee as well as participates in sessions of the UN Human Rights Council, by taking the floor on any issue, making statements, and submitting documentation.[63]

The seventy NHRIs with an A-level UN status include, for example, the National Commission on Human Rights and Freedoms in Cameroon, the Procurador de los Derechos Humanos in Guatemala, and the National Human Rights Commission of Thailand.[64] According to Amnesty International, NHRIs that comply with these principles "enjoy a level of credibility and trust which facilitates their relationship with the executive, the judiciary and most importantly, the victims of human rights violations, and makes their work even more effective."[65]

Of course, not all NHRIs are of this quality. The B-status NHRIs, such as the National Human Rights Commission of Burkina Faso, are judged not fully compliant. They can only participate in the Human Rights Council as observers. The C-status ones, such as the Iranian Islamic Human Rights Commission, are judged noncompliant and so are given no privileges of involvement, although they can reapply for accreditation at any time.

The United Nations can change an NHRI's status over time. It can offer promotions; for instance, the National Human Rights Commission of Nigeria was promoted to an A status in 2011 after the government passed a law providing the institution independence and securing its funding.[66] Amnesty International hailed the act as a "landmark."[67] The United Nations can also devalue an institution; it recommended in 2011 that the Human Rights Commission in Azerbaijan be downgraded to a B due to concerns that it lacked independence in its investigations of torture and the appointment of the commissioner. The National Human Rights Commission of Algeria was downgraded to a B status in 2009 for concerns regarding the selection process for members, lack of cooperation with civil society, and failure to provide information about the commission's efforts to investigate enforced disappearances, torture, and impunity.[68]

Accreditation is far from flawless. Status can quickly fall out of date, as national circumstances evolve faster than the accreditation process. The United Nations evaluates NHRIs every five years (unless a member of the evaluation committee initiates an evaluation earlier), and a lot can happen in that time. There are also plenty of inconsistencies—a problem revealed by comparing the experiences of India and Austria, for example. In 2011, the United Nations gave the National Human Rights Commission of India an A status, despite a long list of concerns. There were problems with its appointment of senior membership, pluralism, influence of government, its relationship with civil society, and the way it handles complaints. It also hadn't addressed recommendations that the subcommittee made back in 2006.[69] By contrast, the United Nations downgraded the Austrian Ombudsman Board to a B status despite fewer areas of concern.

An A status also assigns the same rank to different types and qualities of institutions. Consider the Human Rights Commission of Malaysia. Its mandate is extremely limited, and independent expert human rights groups view the commission with suspicion, as a public relations exercise.[70] Still, the United Nations ranks it an A, or the same status it gives to the Canadian Human Rights Commission and the CHRAJ in Ghana, both stronger institutions.

In spite of these irregularities, governments that are stewards of human rights can use accreditation ranks as they search for partnerships with NHRIs that can help in the process of localization. The As and Bs are good places to start, while the Cs or unaccredited institutions should be avoided. For instance, Human Rights Watch, a global NGO, has called for the international community not to support the newly established Burmese National Human Rights Commission due to its lack of autonomy from the government; it is not yet accredited.[71] In countries where there aren't suitable NHRI partners, foreign stewards might seek alternative organizations—such as NGOs—to help with localization. Or they might invest in new or improved organizations.

Accreditation is the most important (albeit flawed) existing tool that can help foreign stewards find good NHRI partners. In addition, the same benchmark rules that apply to NGOs—discussed in chapter 9—also apply here. I won't repeat them in detail, but the keys are local policy resonance and community buy-in and reliance, when possible, on local partners for implementation of projects.[72] The goals of a foreign government that wants to advance human rights through the use of its power must resonate with the local NHRI's mandate and priorities. That resonance along with community buy-in are more significant than some of the factors that determine UN grading; even B-status institutions can localize effectively if they have buy-in from their own communities. When choosing a partner, the individual merits—including resonance, local buy-in, accountability, and access—must be weighed carefully.

## The Relationship between NHRIs and NGOs

Perhaps the most certain way for a steward state to localize its efforts to wield its power for human rights is though partnerships with both NHRIs and NGOs. This is not always possible, however, and NHRIs and NGOs sometimes work at odds.[73] In large part because of their overlapping functions, on the one hand, and variations in scope and stakeholders, on the other, the relationships that develop between NHRIs and NGOs vary in quality as well as effectiveness. They can be cooperative and synergistic—jointly focused on the promotion and protection of human rights, taking advantage of NGOs' awareness of people's needs as well as the NHRIs' closeness to governments and their policies. Or they can be competitive and adversarial.

A cooperative relationship arises when civil society organizations—including human rights NGOs—are included in the NHRI's activity planning and represented in its membership. Cooperation is also likely when NGOs act as implementers of an NHRI's activities to promote human rights. Where efforts are coordinated in this way, the whole array of institutions can maximize their impact. In its Social Justice Report of 2005, for example, the Australian Human Rights Commission described the gross inequalities in health care between indigenous Australians and the rest of the population, expressed its concern, and recommended ways to bridge the gap.[74] Out of this, the Close the Gap Indigenous Health campaign was formed. The campaign is led by indigenous leaders, and consists of their joint efforts with the Australian NHRI and more than forty NGOs to set targets to improve indigenous health; together they monitor the progress and implementation of government policy, run community education workshops, and liaise continuously with the government. The campaign has had success. Since 2008, the Australian government has committed five billion (Australian) dollars to the cause and has signed National Partnership Agreements to guide related policy implementation.[75]

By contrast, an adversarial and even competitive relationship arises when civil society sees the NHRI as alien to its own concerns—perhaps because it is co-opted by government interests. The National Human Rights Commission of India has recently come under ample criticism from the All-India Network of NGOs and Individuals Working with

National and State Human Rights Institutions (AiNNI).[76] In 2011, in a report to the UN International Coordinating Committee of NHRIs, AiNNI urged it to downgrade India's NHRI to a B status because, the group argued, the National Human Rights Commission lacks financial and political independence from the Indian government, its members are often appointed as political favors, it is largely inaccessible to Indians living outside New Delhi, it frequently disposes of individual complaints at random, and it fails to engage with civil society.[77] The NHRI responded aggressively, strongly denying the accusations.[78] Such a relationship illustrates the challenges that can arise out of the varying capacities and stakeholders of NHRIs and NGOs—challenges that can certainly undermine the goals of protecting and promoting human rights.

## Conclusion

State power to coerce and persuade for better human rights is most effective when it is localized—vetted, taken up, and spread through local institutions seen as knowledgeable and legitimate in context. Localization isn't a guarantee that foreign stewards will have an impact. The process of localization, while essential, is fraught with difficulties and dangers.

Foreign stewards have a choice of many different actors that can play roles in localization. I have explored the ways that two important types of local partners—NGOs and NHRIs—can aid with localization. These actors have many roles in national society, but for the purposes of this book, they are particularly notable for their ability to take foreign incentives and make them more legitimate as well as congruent with local circumstances; they can also implement foreign projects. While both NGOs and NHRIs can perform these functions, the roles of NHRIs are particularly intriguing because these institutions have formal roles in national governance processes, and thus might be particularly effective conduits between international pressures and national policy and behavior. Their ties to repressive government also undermine their independence and hence credibility.

Implementing this strategy of localization—through partnerships with NGOs, NHRIs, and other local actors—can make foreign stewardship for human rights more effective, but it also can strain the stewards. Delivering punishments and rewards and cultivating local support for them requires resources to spend. Yet resources are highly limited, which raises the question of how governments and other actors that want to promote human rights can be most strategic as well as efficient. The next chapter of this book offers some answers.

# 11

# Triage

This chapter further develops a stewardship strategy. Its central message is that the universality of human rights norms, which are the bedrock of the international human rights legal system and the core idea of the Universal Declaration of Human Rights, is not a tenable guide for the most effective implementation of human rights norms. The resources needed to protect human rights are scarce. No steward can or will try to make a difference everywhere. No reformer can fix every aspect of the international legal system. Constraints require choices. This chapter offers a framework for making those choices in ways that are more effective. It also engages with the troubling issues that arise whenever public institutions must allocate scarce resources on important human matters.

This chapter revolves around a central concept: the triage of scarce resources. Triage requires putting a priority on some situations while delaying action or even setting others aside. It necessitates active assessment and reappraisal to ensure that resources are devoted to areas with the greatest return on investment. Resources spent to no effect on human rights can make people feel good by tilting at seemingly worthy causes, but those resources could be used in other situations with greater impact. Waste is not just inefficient. It is indecent because the only people helped—the stewards who feel good about their efforts—are not the people who need support.[1] Triage is essential yet it is also deeply discomforting because it requires choices that are emotionally and ethically challenging, and also contrary to the core legal principles of universality and indivisibility.

Rooted in the experience of battlefield medics who must allocate scarce resources in conditions of extreme demand, triage is a process that can guide some of the most difficult choices in human rights promotion today. Applied to human rights, triage isn't just a clinical process. It's also political. A practical triage strategy requires attention to national interests because triage depends on support from the steward states. Any scheme for making choices that drifts far from their national interests won't be sustainable politically. Triage requires knowing what works (and at what cost) and also knowing which policies are fruit-less. Applied to human rights, triage combines a central role for national interest with the sober assessment of where the deployment of resources actually delivers the most protection to inform battlefield-like choices.

Most of this chapter will focus on what triage implies for how steward states use their power. The concept, though, is equally relevant for how these states interact with the international legal system, including how they advance reforms with the goal of rectifying some of the many weak-nesses of international law that this book has discussed.

One of the reasons that triage is discomforting is that it requires ra-tioning and exclusion. Rationing is essential to allocating scarce resources. Exclusion is the essence of stewards working unilaterally or in alignment with small numbers of other like-minded countries. Although controver-sial, rationing and exclusion have parallels to many other areas of public policy, such as health care. Professor of bioethics Peter Singer, thinking about health care in the United States, argues that

> setting a value on a human life is at least closer to what we really believe—and to what we should believe—than dramatic pronounce-ments about the infinite value of every human life, or the sugges-tion that we cannot distinguish between the value of a single human life and the value of a million human lives, or even of the rest of the world. Though such feel-good claims may have some symbolic value in particular circumstances, to take them seriously and apply them—for instance, by leaving it to chance whether we save one life or a billion—would be deeply unethical.[2]

Like Singer, I also believe that it is appropriate to target resources toward the reduction of human suffering where possible, and that where resources are scarce, the most principled practice involves allocating re-sources in a way that minimizes human suffering. That practice requires value judgments about which people should receive help. Quite apart from Singer, however, I start from the idea that all human life has intrin-sically the same value. Our rationalization of human rights promotion should not be based on, nor should it imply, an evaluation of the indi-vidual person's worth; instead, it should be based centrally on an evalu-ation of the potential effectiveness of intervention. Evaluating which of many choices is most effective is not immoral; it is essential to a frame-work that is both ethical and politically viable. And because these choices are political, getting serious about triage for human rights also requires being realistic about collective action and states' interests.

## Triage

A train has crashed, and hundreds of victims await help. A medical team, fresh on the scene, cannot help everyone and faces difficult choices. Some people are so badly hurt that they will probably die even if they receive treatment; others are likely to eventually recover without immediate treatment, though they will suffer while they await therapy; still others could survive only if they receive treatment right away, and even then some of them will die. This situation requires triage.[3]

We're used to thinking about triage as something that trained medical professionals do. But the ethical challenges in medical crises where demand for treatment far outstrips supply is not so different from decisions involved in human rights promotion.[4] Human rights stewards also operate with limited resources. They can muster an array of actions that could promote human rights and care for victims, but resources are insufficient for everyone. Human rights stewards face the decision of how to allocate their resources when not everyone can receive the attention they need or deserve.

Put that way, triage sounds like an obvious approach to promoting human rights. In fact, it is quite difficult to implement because it requires choices that are morally and politically hard to make. Thus, governments and human rights advocates often talk about triage when in fact they allocate resources largely in an ad hoc fashion. They rely on hope and bold aspirations rather than hard-nosed assessment of trade-offs.

Making triage a reality requires efforts on three fronts. First, national interest must be put at the center, for only when steward states see policies broadly in their interest is it possible to mobilize as well as sustain the needed resources for punishments, rewards, and other costly measures that steward states use to advance human rights abroad. Second, triage requires national governments to build mechanisms to assess which policies have the most effectiveness—what I call "leverage." Put simply, leverage is about maximizing the protection for abused populations with the most efficient use of resources. Leverage and assessment, tied closely to national interests, is how steward states actually do the picking and choosing among options that is essential to triage. Third is "coupling." The worst human rights abuses are usually the result of whole systems of abuse, and solving them requires working on many fronts in concert—a systemic effort rather than a discrete attack on particular elements. Coupling matters because it means that serious efforts to limit abuse usually require many actions—frequently implemented in coordination with other stewards—and sustained over time. Because actions must be coupled they are even more demanding of scarce resources; these extra demands redouble the need for a sober assessment of what actually works and can be sustained politically.

## WHY NATIONAL INTEREST MATTERS

A general law of politics is that people take actions they perceive to be in their interest. Fortunately, many governments, including some of the world's most powerful states, see human rights as a matter of national interest. This book is filled with examples of promotion efforts. Some stewards get involved in promotion because they share human rights challenges or sympathies with other nations, such as concerns about the protection of a specific religious or ethnic group, or citizens living abroad. Some get involved because abuses elsewhere create problems that affect them directly, creating refugees, labor competition, or regional instability. Some get involved because they have an economic, political, or moral interest in protecting human rights.[5] Some want to be seen as leaders on this issue. And some see security or economic implications.

Whatever the source of interests in promoting human rights, pursuing them comes at a price. For example, imposing sanctions can mean losing access to low-priced imports, disrupting a valuable political relationship, or diverting resources away from other priorities. This is one reason why governments have not been keen to place much real economic or political pressure on big trading states, such as China.[6] Since they'll pay a price for applying pressure, governments choose to do so only when it seems to serve their interests and they decide they can afford it.[7]

Nothing can erase the fact that all governments and societies are not motivated to intervene in all atrocities, crimes, and human rights violations. And nothing can alter the reality that governments will not act against their interests. Had Mauritania not supported Iraq during the first Gulf War, and had it supported the Middle East peace process and recognized Israel early on, the United States probably would not have bothered to sanction it for its human rights violations.[8]

In various ways, steward states tailor where they concentrate their investment in human rights based on how they conceive of their national interest. As of this writing, US secretary of state Hillary Clinton was traveling the world calling for greater respect for human rights, such as the release of imprisoned democracy campaigners like Burma's Aung San Suu Kyi, who was set free (partly due to pressure from stewards) in November 2010.[9] Ron Kirk, the US trade representative, was devoting resources from his office to monitoring and enforcing the human rights obligations under many US trade agreements.[10] The European Union was pursuing negotiations to link trade and aid with human rights mainly among its former colonies and regional neighbors—countries where the EU's members feel strong attachments. In 2010, the European Union decided to withdraw preferential trade benefits from Sri Lanka (a former British colony) due to "significant shortcomings" on human rights.[11] For years, the European Union has been providing money and assistance to convince Turkey to improve its human rights.[12] In Asia, over a dozen governments are working through the Asia Pacific Forum to build NHRIs and strengthen human rights protections in the region. In Brazil, candidates for president adopted ten commitments related to promoting human rights through foreign policy, including the promotion of human rights in bilateral agendas.[13] Qatar is promoting freedom of speech and expression in the Arab world through its broadcasting network Al Jazeera. All of these actions are driven, in large part, by national interests.

## LEVERAGE AND ASSESSMENT

No one wants to see their loved ones hurt. But imagine the consequences if medical professionals in emergency situations made decisions based on what bystanders or family members wanted them to do rather than what their expertise led them to believe was the most effective course of action. Steward states can easily find themselves in the analogous situation. They face pressure groups that demand action in particular situations—some that surely need and deserve attention—without regard for whether the efforts are likely to be effective or appropriate. That is a central tension in any practical triage strategy. Managing this tension requires intensive, periodic, and reflective assessments to determine how limited resources can be deployed for maximum leverage. Just as with medical triage after a train wreck, it's about knowing where scarce resources can go the furthest.

Assessments of which actions yield the most impact on human rights are particularly crucial because the domestic political processes within steward states tend to inspire human rights actions that are often prone to fail. Governments tend to get most involved in settings, such as crises, that attract public attention and outrage because abuses are often terrible and highly visible—exactly the settings where there is frequently the least amount of leverage.[14] It is no wonder that human rights promotion efforts fail to have much impact, especially when such massive deployment of resources is often done quickly in response to ephemeral public concerns and thus tends to ignore some of the lessons already discussed in this book, such as the need for long-term investments in localization. By contrast, situations involving perpetrators whose incentives can more readily be manipulated at lower cost generally command less public attention yet often provide settings where small amounts of foreign resources can obtain a large amount of human rights protection. Stewards need support from their publics to mobilize the resources for getting involved in foreign places. Yet investing resources to intervene in the most difficult situations to little effect often means forgoing investment in situations where efforts could have more traction. It means letting people suffer who could have been helped.

Done well, assessments of leverage require close scrutiny of the underlying causes and rationalizations behind abuse discussed in chapters 2 and 3. Particularly important is an assessment of where in the life cycle of abusive activities a steward is trying to have an impact. Preventing abuse may prove to be relatively easy, even though investments in prevention usually are not politically salient. But once abuses start, they are hard to stop. As I explained in chapter 3, perpetrators of abuse become inured to their own cruelty or learn to rationalize it over time. They learn to deal with the discomfort or guilt involved in hurting others. They downplay the pain they cause. They assure themselves that their victims were asking for it. They disengage morally from their acts or make them seem justifiable. Or they deny that the abuse is taking place at all. These facts about how abusers think about their crimes put a premium on stewardship efforts that begin early. Intervening later—after perpetrators have integrated the acts into their routines, and cruelty has become part of everyday politics and social life—is less likely to succeed, yet more likely to attract public attention and support at home.

A triage strategy requires facts, assessment, and specialization, so that resources can be devoted to areas where they can prevent or alleviate abuse. In addition to guiding the most effective interventions, those same facts and assessments are useful resources for stewards when they explain to their publics why intervention is important in some areas and impractical in others. Triage thus looks different from a strategy that focuses on situations that attract the most public attention. It looks more like the clinical job of medical professionals who select which patients to treat based on the likely effects of their treatment and other demands for resources.

COUPLING

In chapter 2, I explained how many human rights crimes are the consequence of whole systems, not isolated instances or abnormal acts. One insight from that discussion is that crimes such as human rights abuses often result from a network of practices rather than as discrete misdeeds by individuals acting alone. This systemic perspective also helps reveal how perpetrators can avoid sanctions—shifting their abuses, such as by disappearing opponents instead of killing them openly, using psychological instead of physical torture, or intimidating voters instead of banning elections. Since abusers themselves are often in control of governments, they can order their agents to hide their crimes more thoroughly, making them harder to spot and stop.[15] These kinds of human rights *jujitsu* can make it hard for steward states to have much impact, and often the attempt at making things better can actually amplify abuse.

A telling example is elections. The Universal Declaration of Human Rights provides everyone the right to take part in government and makes the will of the people, expressed through genuine elections, the basis of government authority.[16] Adherence to this right seems to be spreading on the surface; even autocrats all over the world now hold elections, or have passed legislation to increase pluralism or political participation. In reality, though, this strong electoral trend often affects just the veneer of governance; elected leaders now resort to other forms of abuse, such as political terror, that nullify the intended effects of genuine elections and keep incumbents in power.[17] They give people the right to vote, but throw their political opponents into jail or put them on the sidelines with a bullet. They intimidate or attack voters who support the opposition. They shut down the free media, and harass journalists and civil society organizations that air opposing views. They suppress public protests.

This problem—that perpetrators of abuse can substitute one kind of violation for another—is made worse when abuse is embedded within the means of government and the way that society is organized. In those situations, strategies for the protection of human rights are more effective when they are coupled and localized to create the right incentives at multiple levels of government and society. Spreading the right to vote does little to spread or protect human rights without also securing the rights for opposition groups to be free from murder, torture, political imprisonment, and forced disappearance, and civil society to freely disseminate information and organize. Partial efforts to force elections without other reforms can even backfire by creating stronger incentives for governments to abuse human rights.[18] That's why elections in autocratic and chaotic places so frequently breed human rights violations.

The challenges aren't just in thwarting abusers who substitute one form of human rights violations for another. They also include the need, where abuse is the result of a whole system, to saturate society with human rights promotion. Isolated promotion projects often don't have much impact. In 2002, the US Agency for International Development spent about eighty thousand dollars to support local organizations in Cameroon in their efforts to build democracy and human rights. The money was spent on seminars on the rights of disabled persons and a women's rights television documentary, among other projects. Protecting the rights of the disabled and women is surely essential in Cameroon; men keep a tight rein on women's rights to inheritance and employment, girls are subject to genital cutting, and some local customs consider women as the legal property of their husbands. But in a country where the government clamps down on free speech, press, assembly, and movement, where people are arrested and held arbitrarily, where security forces beat and torture people, and where the per capita income is stagnant, did these dollars yield any leverage?[19]

The need for systemic responses is widely understood in theory. Yet in practice, it is rarely observed.

Europe has taken a coupled approach in places like Turkey, with significant leverage. But these examples are rare in most of the world, where human rights promotion efforts tend to be spread thin and made without adequate attention to the underlying systemic incentives for abuse. The European Instrument for Democracy and Human Rights gives aid to local civil society organizations—for instance, its noble effort to spend one hundred thousand euros over the course of two years in Tajikistan to help provide girls access to secondary education.[20] But its success in changing behavior ultimately depends on providing those girls with opportunities and rights to utilize as well as continue their education—not matters that the European Instrument for Democracy and Human Rights can by itself tackle.

The lesson is that systemic human rights abuses require systemic responses—coupling—that link, for example, education campaigns about rights to legal aid programs along with training for military and police. The problem, of course, is that effective systemic responses are expensive, thereby redoubling the need for a triage strategy that can prioritize where to focus available resources.

## Working with Like-minded States

A lot of human rights stewardship can be done unilaterally by working directly in the countries where there is the greatest potential leverage on abuse. In some settings, however, the stewards would gain a lot by working together with other stewards. The practical value of working in small groups—what experts on cooperation often call clubs—is well known in other areas of international cooperation, such as in trade and arms control. Applied to human rights the logic is similar.

Among other things, clubs could help these stewards work around the problem that international treaty bodies are packed with disingenuous and weak governments. A small group of human rights promoters could identify other channels for influence, coordinate punishments and rewards, and offer a concerted front to help reform international legal procedures in cases where reform might actually make a difference. When governments (especially powerful ones) act alone, many others are suspicious of unilateralism and easily brand it as illegitimate. When governments work in teams—and when they take care to localize their efforts—such harmful side effects can be lessened.

A club-based strategy for human rights promotion has ties to two major strands of thought. One is the coincidence of calls from the "Left" and "Right" of the political spectrum to establish a meaningful concert of democracies.[21] The logic in favor of a "concert" is that democratic countries—those that are most likely to protect human rights at home and invest in human rights promotion abroad—tend to have similar views on many topics. A concert would make it easier for them to organize the use of force in humanitarian crises when they fail to get the United Nations to act. Among other things, the effort could put into reality principles such as the "responsibility to protect." While the responsibility to protect movement is focused on the worst crises, a concert for the promotion of human rights could play a much broader role in helping ensure that scarce resources are used wisely to advance the protection of human rights. A concert could also motivate like-minded stewards to take actions that they otherwise would not take on their own—not just in times of dire crisis like genocide, but also in everyday circumstances where people suffer violations of their rights.

The other source of inspiration is the insights, developed long ago, that like-minded actors will find it relatively easy to coordinate their efforts if they work in small groups. Collective action at the international level often fails because of the complexity of finding common ground when large numbers of countries are involved and interests do not easily align.[22] Today, human rights stewards don't much act as a group to protect human rights, in part because the existing mechanisms, such as UN-based treaty bodies, are particularly poorly suited for these steward states to find their common interest. The countries that are formally engaged in the international human rights system are as diverse as their interests and cultures—they are not and need not be solely democracies or Western. And although there is pervasive acceptance among some countries of the norms of the Universal Declaration of Human Rights, there is no common commitment to international law or an approach to apply the norms that the international legal system supports.[23] Collective action among large numbers of countries is further impeded by the bystander effect—a tendency that justifies inertia by diffusing responsibility in a group because each member of the group sits idle, assuming that someone else will solve the problem at hand.[24] Like people who witness a crime in a large group (and thus tend not to act), countries are often bystanders as well. Countries stood by during the hundred days in 1994 that it took for an estimated eight hundred thousand Rwandans to be murdered.[25] This tendency is amplified by the risk that governments free ride, shouldering less than their fair share of the burden of getting involved.[26] All these barriers to serious collective action are much easier to clear when groups are small and club-like.

Governments have been forming exclusive clubs for years—NATO, the Association of Southeast Asian Nations, the Organization for Economic Co-operation and Development, the Organization for Security and Co-operation in Europe, the European Union, and the G8. Those clubs have made all the kinds of decisions that would be needed for a club of human rights promoters to function effectively, such as choices concerning who joins, the coordination of policies, and decisions about allocating costs and other burdens such as those related to military intervention. In addition to these better-known clubs, there are also encouraging models such as the International Institute for Democracy and Electoral Assistance, which promotes democratic values including civil and political rights through a tight-knit membership of twenty-seven states.[27] A decision-making council of each country's local representatives (usually current or former public officials) produces policy recommendations, technical assistance plans, and more. Many clubs formed for other purposes are playing large roles in protecting human rights. The European Union and NATO create multilateral guidelines for collective triage, and set a code of conduct for which situations receive attention and in what priority. Similarly, the Development Co-operation Directorate of the Organization of Economic Co-operation and Development has formal guidelines for coordinating donor efforts and evaluating the impact of aid.[28] There are other clubs too.[29] The problem is that these existing clubs aren't very representative of the actual stewards today—some include states that have no aspiration for stewardship while others exclude stewards that are outside the organization's mandate.

Seen from the perspective of a human rights promoter, it seems obvious why working within a club of stewards is appealing: it will improve protections for human rights. Efforts to create other clubs have revealed that it is important for a club to generate tangible benefits that are at least partially exclusive to the club members. Such gains from cooperation create a durable incentive for club members to keep cooperating, and for effective clubs to expand and deepen.[30] In human rights, one such benefit of working in clubs is the extra leverage that stewards will gain through coordination of information and, where possible, policy for human rights. Using resources efficiently is especially critical for stewards because it generates leverage while reducing waste—and those "savings" give stewards more flexibility in how they use their power and other resources effectively. Another benefit is the moral authority that develops from becoming an effective humanitarian through action in concert with others rather than as a lone ranger—a charge made often against the

United States.[31] Moral authority doesn't follow automatically from making a club; rather, it must be earned through practice.[32] Working through a human rights club raises the prospects for stewards to develop greater authority, in part because a club promises more practical and conspicuous impact that reflects more than a single nation's norms.

## International Law and Reform

Triage is a political strategy based on harnessing the power of self-interest to yield the maximum improvement in the protection of human rights for some people. Clubs are not essential to triage, but they will make it easier for stewards to use their resources more efficiently and legitimately. One area where these countries, acting in concert, could have a large impact is in legal and institutional reforms. Already, as part II documented, the international legal system is clogged by the very governments that international human rights law most needs to hold accountable. Reform could target scarce resources more effectively, focusing the efforts of the system's many committees, agencies, and courts on the situations where they are most capable of producing judgments that can have actual authority and impact.[33] Yet reforms, as surveyed in chapter 7, have proved very difficult to implement.

Focused on triage and working in clubs, human rights stewards can help guide future international legal reforms for greater effect. The list of needed reforms is long—it includes changing existing practices inside the system, and redirecting scarce resources such as money, expertise, and attention to the parts of the system that work best. Applying the idea of triage requires focusing reform efforts on the parts of the legal system that can have the most leverage. Success probably will be greatest if those efforts begin by halting the production of more such laws, bureaucracy, and treaty bodies—an argument I made in chapter 7. Instead of expansion, what is needed is an investment in building more legitimacy, which will come by concentrating resources on ways to boost compliance with existing laws. Reform is a strategic process that is plagued by complexity and faces many enemies. Getting the countries that care most about successful reforms to work in concert can raise the odds of success.

## Getting Started

This book will disappoint anyone looking for a short list of the issues and victims that should get attention. Such lists require a major investment in human rights policy specialists, rooted in fact-based analysis and projections and a practical assessment of leverage. No single person has the expertise on all the relevant countries and issues to create those lists. My aspiration in this book is more practical: to identify steps in the process that will lead to those lists and the triage that will be needed to redirect resources to the highest-ranked countries and issues. That process must occur within the key steward countries so that it is anchored as well in national interest.

One step is for the steward countries to create high-level human rights administrators—high-profile "czars" or cabinet members with resources to coordinate and oversee a human rights steward's policies. Presently, most government-appointed human rights administrators, if they exist at all, have low-level status and visibility; they have little ability to coordinate between branches of government or government agencies, let alone with other governments. Stewardship requires more gravitas for making human rights decisions inside promoter governments.

Another step is to generate knowledge and research expertise—to encourage (and for stewards to fund directly) systematic research on human rights policy evaluation at top universities, think tanks, and research institutes. Human rights have never been a research priority for most governments, unlike other matters of national policy such as defense, trade, and finance. Yet if governments are to be more effective, they must learn how to triage. And triage requires knowledgeable projections about which policies and strategies are likely to minimize human suffering. Those projections are most likely to come from the growing community of scholars and researchers studying human rights in increasingly sophisticated ways, and in a growing number of disciplines. Research grants—like those that support defense-oriented social science—can develop knowledge in directly applicable ways to promote human rights.[34] Human rights czars will have little effect in government if they don't have a knowledgeable community of experts to draw from when framing policy options.

A third step is the translation of research into practical policy. That step is not straightforward because scholarly and policy communities are not well integrated. Fixing that problem requires topical experts inside government who work in tandem with external experts to evaluate real-world policy options, and thus, in turn, implement triage in a practical way. Political experts can play many roles, including the identification of situations and locations where research indicates that specific policies along with packages of intervention are most likely to alleviate human suffering. Doing that requires engaging experts from the main world regions who are knowledgeable about the relevant types of abuse, creating evolving lists of priorities and best practices based on systematic evidence, and integrating such expertise into the practical realities of politics. So far, not much of this is being done at all.

A final step is to open—and use existing—formal channels of communication with other human rights steward states on human rights promotion to coordinate and exchange information. A weak version of coordination would rely on informal discussions to share information about strategy and unofficially match up harmonious interests on human rights, not just in Europe (where much of this is already happening), but globally too. A deeper version would require a more formal setting—an exclusive club of steward states engaged in human rights promotion—to share information, set common standards, and coordinate the use of state power where possible. The Office for Democratic Institutions and Human Rights of the Organization for Security and Cooperation in Europe is an example of a forum where states have practiced the deeper version. One instance of how the member states of this organization have implemented their commitment to the human dimension of security—common standards of human rights and democracy—is in their efforts to assist and support NGO–government relations in the states that they monitor. In November 2009, the Office for Democratic Institutions and Human Rights hosted a roundtable event about NGO–government cooperation in Almaty, Kazakhstan.[35] More than eighty participants, including government officials, experts, and members of civil society, exchanged best practices, built action plans, and committed to follow-up on the implementation of those plans. The Organization for Security and Cooperation in Europe is a useful but imperfect model. Stewards outside the region are not members, and there are plenty of members (such as Kyrgyzstan and Russia) that are not human rights stewards. A legitimate and effective club for human rights requires membership from committed, proven stewards; it requires closing the doors to states that have not proven their commitment. Whether the exchange of information takes a weak or deep form, stewards must also become more comfortable talking with their publics—the ultimate source of national interest in most steward states—about the practical need to set priorities in human rights promotion.

These four steps could transform the process through which government stewards work to protect human rights and increase the returns on international promotion efforts to protect human rights.

## Anticipating Criticisms

Getting started with a stewardship strategy requires anticipating how important players in the human rights system will react. Those criticisms will be many, because the choices that are intrinsic to triage and the exclusivity of the process fundamentally contravene the universalist ideal that has organized most human rights law and activism for six decades. Five criticisms, in particular, will loom large.

First, a central criticism of human rights promotion that relies heavily on steward states is that those states are often guilty of abuses themselves and don't have any right to tell others what to do. The United States is frequently a target of this criticism, as it leaves its fingerprints around the world in ways that sometimes cause rather than alleviate suffering.[36] I am often reminded that the United States has not signed on to every human rights treaty or given jurisdiction to the ICC. And its government unquestionably has a history of committing human rights abuses, such as during the wars in Afghanistan and Iraq, among many other situations. Yet the United States is a recurrent shamer of other governments' human rights records and actively seeks to promote human rights around the globe.

In 2010, China released a public report shaming the United States. The report has its own critics, but it claims that the United States has "turned a blind eye to its own terrible human rights situation." Meanwhile, it seeks "to defame other nations' image and seek its own strategic interests," and exercises double standards on human rights, plus is malicious in its efforts to pursue hegemony under the pretext of human rights.[37] The report calls into question whether countries such as the United States have any right to lecture the world about human rights, much less flex their muscles.

The Chinese have a point. There is no excuse for human rights abuses committed by US troops and leaders in Afghanistan and Iraq, or anywhere else, including at home. But just because the United States must do more to prevent and punish citizens (including government agents) who commit human rights crimes does not mean it forfeits its ability to be a steward. If the criterion for human rights promotion is a perfect record, then no government on the planet would fulfill this standard; there would be no role for stewards, and many more people would suffer.

Governments do not need to embrace every aspect of the international human rights legal system to serve its principles. Refusing to join or expand a troubled legal system—another criticism often brought against the United States—may actually be an asset.[38] Stopping expansion of the existing system might help promote its reform, as I argued in chapter 7. What really matters is not that governments accept every international human rights treaty or participate in every procedure; instead it is that stewards work strategically to advance human rights with an eye to maximizing leverage.

A second criticism is that human rights promoters—whether states or NGOs—unfairly target the developing world. The West tells the rest what to do, and imposes norms, policies, and even laws.[39] And telling others what to do undermines any legitimacy behind the messages.

This criticism is important because illegitimate advocates can't effectively promote human rights. It's one reason why international legal strategies fail and why the use of state power can backfire. That is why localization is essential and why working in clubs can multiply the leverage of promoters. Human rights promotion will gain more traction if more governments get into the business of promoting human rights, mobilizing more power for human rights from beyond North America or Europe. Stewardship is a political choice that any state can make; nothing prevents states in other regions or with less than fully democratic political systems from choosing stewardship. The government of Qatar, for instance, has been a powerful steward in the Muslim world. It partially finances (and hosts) Al Jazeera—an independent broadcaster of news and current affairs television channel headquartered in Doha. Qatar also backs efforts in its region—most recently, in Libya and Syria—to protect civilians from atrocities committed by other Arab-led governments.[40]

The third criticism is that there's an unavoidable inequality to promoting human rights, especially through state power. Some governments have the resources to act more than others. The ones that have the resources pick and choose where to get involved. The ones that don't have the resources—the extremely impoverished least developed countries, for instance—don't have the ability to spread human rights around the world.

Nothing, however, says that a country must be super rich to be a steward. The governments of smaller economies can and do use their resources to promote human rights. Costa Rica is a small economy and a notable steward. It has a long history of activism in the United Nations and inter-American part of the international human rights legal system, hosts and participates in human rights research, conferences, and workshops, and promotes good human rights practices at home—receiving asylum seekers from many neighboring countries.[41] For smaller economies like Costa Rica, a stewardship strategy may be of particular value because state resources are especially scarce; triage and working in clubs will lead to greater efficiency in spending.

The fourth criticism is that a club approach is hopeless because the United States won't work in teams with other countries and tends toward isolationism. Polls suggest that isolationist sentiment in the United States is growing; the US public is less and less supportive of US missions abroad.[42] The United States has at times in its history gone through bouts of isolationism.[43] And the United States' approach to human rights differs from that of most other Western nations.[44] None of these details, though, make triage hopeless. The United States is not the only steward; triage can boost the effectiveness of human rights promotion efforts with or without US stewardship or participation in clubs. The United States may be different, but it is not, in fact, wholly isolationist when it comes

to human rights. It has a long history of active (though not always successful) efforts to promote human rights, including through the use of
its military, foreign aid, trade policy, and other forms of diplomacy. It
doesn't always act alone; it belongs to clubs on all kinds of other issues—
from security alliances like NATO to economic and social partnerships
like the Organisation of Economic Co-operation and Development. It sits
on the UN Human Rights Council despite reservations about the United
Nations' performance.[45] And it is engaged in dialogue on human rights
with other stewards. A non-UN club that helps coordinate human rights
policy among stewards, especially policies other than military intervention, is likely to have broad public support by Americans, given that a
large majority believes that promoting human rights is an important priority for US foreign policy.[46] And while clubs would help, they are not
central to a stewardship strategy—unilateral triage, if done in tandem
with careful localization, would be a vast improvement over current US
policy.

Fifth and finally, critics may continue the analogy of relating human
rights to health care and argue that triage comes too late in a crisis. Instead, prevention would be the best medicine. Triage, however, need not
be limited to crisis operations or reactive promotion. Human rights stewardship can prevent as well as help people recover from abuse, and triage
and localization can guide the strategy of resource allocation in both
instances. Yet this choice presents another trade-off between spending
scarce resources to prevent one crisis or heal another. Getting serious
about human rights prevention also requires getting serious about national interest, for public passions about human rights in the steward
countries are more likely aroused when abuses are already visible. Collective efforts to prevent human rights abuses will require more extensive
public campaigns within the steward states to focus attention on why
such preemptive investments are so important.

## Conclusion

International legal norms set high standards, and the machinery of the
international human rights legal system cannot stop all abuses. Nothing can do that. The efforts of steward states—especially if localized
and triaged—can help to support the international legal system's norms.
Making the whole system—international law as well as the actions of
stewards that support legal norms—work better requires a comprehensive strategy that deploys resources where they will be most effective.

Triage and localization allow states to focus their power more effectively. This strategy differs from the usual discourse about human rights

promotion, which revolves around duties and obligations to get involved. It starts with the interests of stewards in the promotion process; interests, along with a factual assessment of where human rights investments can gain leverage, are essential. The stewardship strategy discussed in this chapter can't create miracles; it won't do much immediately to stop the worst offenses, such as those that arise when government officials face insurrection and are willing to ignore almost any external incentive. Still, stewards can do a lot more than is done today if they better rationalize how resources for human rights promotion are spent and coordinated. The goal is not just to deliver larger, tangible benefits in the form of human rights protections; it is also to anchor those efforts of stewards on a stronger moral foundation.

I'm not prescribing the use of power for human rights but rather acknowledging that states already wield power in the name of human rights, and with the right strategy, they could do a lot more.

# Making More of Law and Power

During the twentieth century, the toll from human rights violations was greater than that of other crimes such as street violence that get more attention. Violations of human rights cost the lives of almost two hundred million people, and hundreds of millions were raped, tortured, and displaced.[1] What can be done to address this crisis? The answers lie in a careful rethinking of strategy. It requires choices, based on evidence, about how to allocate available resources more effectively. And it demands the ability to realize that in some settings, human rights promotion can't have much impact. The answers lead to a stewardship strategy where a few countries that care most about human rights play central roles in pushing to protect rights around the world. These stewards, I have argued, must localize their work and make hard triage choices if they are to be more effective.

I close by exploring whether a stewardship strategy is good news for international law. To date, most discussions of human rights promotion strategies are strongly rooted in the conviction that the process must be universal and the rights indivisible. As I explored in part II, universality is attractive because it involves everyone. But universality is also a liability. It opens the doors to fraud and defiance, and obscures the fact that allocating finite resources to alleviate suffering requires choices. Universality is an aspiration, not a strategy. A stewardship strategy is quite different from universal global legalism and likely to be controversial, especially among international human rights lawyers and advocates who have pushed for universalism and the indivisibility of rights.

A new approach is needed because the existing system isn't working well and it is poised to get even worse. The international human rights legal system and the bureaucracies that manage it are expanding in scope much faster than they can build the needed competence. Though many governments formally agree to bind themselves to international human rights law, in practice these laws are routinely broken. The legal system by itself doesn't have much enforcement or capacity-building power. Increasingly, international legal institutions are packed with human rights abusers whose interests lie more in show than in making the system actually work. With these foxes guarding the henhouse, parts of the human rights legal system have fallen into bureaucratic and political gridlock. Its legitimacy is waning, especially as the system is most impotent in the areas where most human rights abuses occur: in the states run by governments that don't want interference and accountability. Reformers have been working hard to improve the system, and a long list of additional reforms now exists. But in practice, meaningful reform has proved extremely difficult to implement.

One of the few areas of good news lies in the fact that steward states have proved willing to devote massive resources to the cause. They can do even more with their power to advance human rights—often by working around or outside the gridlocked formal human rights legal system. But the fact that state power has an impact creates still further troubles for the legitimacy of these human rights norms. Power-based promotion efforts seem ad hoc and even suspicious, untethered from international law, disconnected from on-the-ground realities, and out of touch with what many people being "helped" actually want or need.

This book has documented the tensions between the aspirations of global legalism and practical benefits of stewardship. On the one hand, international law plays the central role in defining human rights, and the universal norms of international law are profoundly appealing. On the other hand, much of the effort that actually advances human rights protections lies with particular countries, and the greatest promise for making those efforts even more effective rests with strategies such as triage and localization that require an even sharper turn away from global legalism. I'm optimistic that law and power can perform together better in tandem. But making that happen requires honesty about what works. Effectiveness requires framing which tools stewards use in which settings so that human rights are advanced while the process also builds legitimacy. It means knowing which parts of the legal system actually work and how to steer around the impotent elements. Luckily, much of what is needed for this clinical approach to assessing and promoting human rights is already in place. Systematic scholarly research, for example, is showing when and where promotion tools correspond with measurable improvements in the quality of human rights protections—not everywhere, nor for every group or every right.

This book is critical of the legal system, but it is not, and should not be read as, anti-international law. It is pragmatic. Indeed, the question of whether scholars and practitioners are "pro" or "anti" law is the wrong question. Being pragmatic means using legal tools when they are capable of supporting human rights promotion. It also means being realistic about where laws—and procedures—fall short. Many human rights problems don't fit the solutions available in the legal system. In those cases—which are numerous and perhaps even growing—it makes sense

to direct resources toward other promotion efforts that can have more effect, away from legal procedures that go nowhere, toward better-planned
use of stewards' power if possible.

This book has placed heavy emphasis on the opportunities for using
state power because that is the area with the greatest potential for more
impact. Given the structure of international politics, and the sunk costs
that have been spent on the international legal system, at best reforms in
the legal system will tinker at the margins. The legal system already has
realized its greatest achievement: it set standards that both value human
dignity and define our fundamental freedoms as people. It will never
implement those standards through the provision of its own incentives.
It could do a much better job of directing its own resources to focus on
those procedures and situations where the law matters most—indeed,
as chapter 11 explored, an explicit triage-driven strategy of reform can
improve legal institutions. But that strategy will be hard to implement,
even in the best of circumstances, because it requires doing the opposite
of what has driven most legal reforms to date—for example, reversing
the tide of universalism and stopping the expansion of open-door legal
obligations. A judicious use of state power can help make the legal system
more effective.

All of this raises essential questions. Are international law and state
power irreconcilably at odds? Must human rights advocates choose between law and power? Ideally the answers would be "no" since governments already use their power in an effort to support universal human
rights norms, even though their methods of diplomacy are far from universal or effective. I'm optimistic that law and power can work better in
tandem. Yet I'm also realistic that much of the practical improvement in
human rights, especially in the "hardest" cases, comes from the strategic
use of power to spread legal norms. And since that power is limited,
choices are unavoidable. Those choices require ignoring or even undermining some international legal procedures or obligations. Yet the international legal system itself is deeply divided over the role that state power
should play in implementing its norms.

A telling illustration of these hard-nosed choices lies in the debate playing out in the UN Human Rights Council. In 2008, that council passed
a resolution to condemn the use of state power, particularly "unilateral
coercive measures," including types of trade measures that can boost the
implementation of human rights norms. That resolution

urges all States to stop adopting or implementing unilateral coercive
measures not in accordance with international law, international humanitarian law, the Charter of the United Nations and the norms and
principles governing peaceful relations among States, in particular

those of a coercive nature with extraterritorial effects, which create
obstacles to trade relations among States, thus impeding the full realization of the rights set forth in the Universal Declaration of Human
Rights and other international human rights instruments, in particular
the right of individuals and peoples to development.[2]

The majority of the council's members at the time were in favor of this
resolution. They included Angola, Azerbaijan, Bahrain, Cuba, Djibouti,
Indonesia, Jordan, Nigeria, Pakistan, the Philippines, Qatar, the Russian
Federation, and Saudi Arabia—most of them states whose governments
don't actively promote human rights anywhere. To their dismay, many are
also the targets of promotion efforts by stewards. Eleven voted against the
resolution, most of them active human rights stewards: Canada, France,
Germany, Italy, Japan, the Netherlands, Slovakia, Slovenia, Switzerland,
Ukraine, and the United Kingdom.[3] This resolution underscores the resistance by many of the legal system's own members, including those that
hold positions of prominence and authority on human rights inside the
system, to any efforts outside the system to implement its norms through
power. In this context, relying on legal procedures alone won't do much
to advance human rights.

The tensions between law and power are real, but in practice they are
prone to massive over-statement. The international human rights system
is based on universal norms along with aspirations of fairness, equality,
and impartiality. But its operations are nearly always laden with power,
hierarchy, and partiality. Within the international legal system efforts to
apply legal principles are, in fact, not universal. Some states and kinds
of abuses get more attention and reproach than others. The system's
judges, administrators, and committee members are not evenhanded on
all crimes, or representative of the victims they are supposed to represent;
they come from certain classes of people, and demonstrate clear patterns
of favoritism and discrimination based on their (and their appointing
government's) political and cultural values. And the states operating inside this system of law regularly display their power—usually in their
own defense, but also often overseas to advance their own interests. The
heart of international law in practice is power, for it is states and people
that make, run, and react to the law. And it is precisely the struggle for
power inside the international legal system, pitting human rights stewards against human rights detractors, that is making the system falter so
badly on implementing global norms.

The real tension isn't between law and power; it is between aspira-
tional norms that seek to cover every person and right, and the practical
politics of decision making that require hierarchy and partiality. International law puts too many powerful participants on a level playing field.

It pits a growing group of governments that actively work to mire international law in gridlock and contention with a much smaller group of human rights stewards. State power by stewards can loosen the grip of gridlock.

In many ways, then, international law and state power are primed to work in tandem. Laws set standards for achievement. Steward states can use their power in an effort to implement certain international legal principles to promote and protect human rights in some places. Of course, they pick and choose which principles to endorse, but those endorsements are amplified by the gravitas of the legal system's collectively articulated values, if not by its own efforts to implement them. Law without power probably doesn't have much influence outside a narrow group of countries. State power without law leads to erratic and illegitimate efforts by stewards. Putting the two together—steered by a clear strategy of triage and active efforts by stewards to localize—can make the aspirations of human rights protection more of a reality.

# Notes

## Notes to Preface
1. Laboratory on International Law and Regulation, http://ilar.ucsd.edu/ (accessed April 9, 2012).

## Notes to Introduction
1. UN General Assembly, 3rd Sess., "217 A (III). Universal Declaration of Human Rights," A/RES/3/217A, December 10, 1948.

## Chapter 1. The Problem of Human Rights
1. "14 Students Sentenced for Tehran University Dorm Attacks," Radio Zamaneh, June 29, 2011.

2. Samson Desta, Reza Sayah, Mitra Mobasherat, and Saeed Ahmed, "Iranian Protesters Mostly Unfazed by Government Warnings," *CNN World*, June 17, 2009; Human Rights Watch, "Iran: Halt the Crackdown," June 19, 2009; Amnesty International, "Opposition Leaders Detained in Iran," June 19, 2009.

3. Amnesty International, *Iran: Election Contested, Repression Compounded* (London: Amnesty International Publications, 2009).

4. Amnesty International, "Nine at Risk of Execution over Iran Protests," February 2, 2010.

5. Erika de Wet, "The Prohibition of Torture as an International Norm of Jus Cogens and Its Implications for National and Customary Law," *European Journal of International Law* 15, no. 1 (2004): 97–121.

6. Sources include human rights NGOs, Amnesty International, and Freedom House as well as the US Department of State's Bureau of Democracy, Human Rights, and Labor. On data reliability, see Steven C. Poe et al., "How Are These Pictures Different? A Quantitative Comparison of the U.S. State Department and Amnesty International Human Rights Reports, 1976–1995," *Human Rights Quarterly* 23, no. 3 (2001): 650–77; Emilie M. Hafner-Burton and James Ron, "Seeing Double: Human Rights Impact through Qualitative and Quantitative Eyes," *World Politics* 61, no. 2 (April 2009): 360–401.

7. Dominic McGoldrick, *The Human Rights Committee: Its Role in the Development of the International Covenant on Civil and Political Rights* (Oxford: Oxford University Press, 1994), 20–22; David Harris, "The International Covenant on Civil and Political Rights and the United Kingdom: An Introduction," in *The International Covenant on Civil and Political Rights and United Kingdom Law*, ed. David Harris and Sarah Joseph (Oxford: Clarendon Press, 1995), 1–60; Eckart Klein, review of *The Law and Process of the U.N. Human Rights Committee*, by Kristen A. Young, *American Journal of International Law* 98, no. 4

(October 2004): 876; Thomas M. Franck, "Proportionality in International Law," *Law and Ethics of Human Rights* 4, no. 2 (2010): 230–42.

8. Author's calculations based on David L. Cingranelli and David L. Richards, "CIRI Human Rights Data Project," 2010, http://ciri.binghamton.edu/ (accessed April 9, 2012); Freedom House, 2010, http://www.freedomhouse.org/template.cfm?page=1 (accessed April 9, 2012).

9. Amnesty International, "Time for World Leaders to Ratify Disappearances Treaty," November 20, 2009; Human Rights Watch, "US: Ratify Women's Rights Treaty," July 15, 2010; Piero A. Tozzi, JD, "'Gay' Groups Lobby Treaty Body on Recognition of Yogyakarta Principles," *Catholic Family and Human Rights Institute* 12, no. 4 (January 8, 2009).

10. Ruth Benedict, "Recognition of Cultural Diversities in the Postwar World," *Annals of the American Academy of Political and Social Science* 228 (July 1943): 101–7; Alison Dundes Renteln, "Relativism and the Search for Human Rights," *American Anthropologist, New Series* 90, no. 1 (March 1988): 56–72; Sumner B. Twiss, "Comparative Ethics, a Common Morality, and Human Rights," *Journal of Religious Ethics* 33, no. 4 (December 2005): 649–57; John Tierney, "A New Debate on Female Circumcision," Tierney Lab, *New York Times*, November 30, 2007, http://tierneylab.blogs.nytimes.com/2007/11/30/a-new-debate-on-female-circumcision/ (accessed April 9, 2012); "The Burqa Debate: Are Women's Rights Really the Issue?" *Spiegel Online*, June 24, 2010, http://www.spiegel.de/international/europe/0,1518,702668,00.html (April 9, 2012).

11. Makau Mutua, "Human Rights in Africa: The Limited Promise of Liberalism," *African Studies Review* 51, no. 1 (2008): 23. For critiques of the international human rights legal system, see David Rieff, "The Precarious Triumph of Human Rights," *New York Times Magazine*, August 8, 1999, 36–41; David Kennedy, *The Dark Sides of Virtue: Reassessing International Humanitarianism* (Princeton, NJ: Princeton University Press, 2005); Eric Posner, *The Perils of Global Legalism* (Chicago: University of Chicago Press, 2009); Mahmoud Cherif Bassiouni and William A. Schabas, eds., *New Challenges for the UN Human Rights Machinery* (Cambridge, UK: Intersentia, 2011); Richard Thompson Ford, *Universal Rights Down to Earth* (New York: W. W. Norton and Company, 2011).

12. Jack Donnelly, *Universal Human Rights in Theory and Practice* (Ithaca, NY: Cornell University Press, 2003).

13. Ian Hurd, "Legitimacy and Authority in International Politics," *International Organization* 53, no. 2 (1999): 379–408; Tom R. Tyler and Yuen J. Huo, *Trust in the Law: Encouraging Public Cooperation with the Police and Courts* (New York: Russell Sage, 2002); Tom R. Tyler, *Why People Obey the Law* (Princeton, NJ: Princeton University Press, 2006); Mark A. L. Kleiman, *When Brute Force Fails: How to Have Less Crime and Less Punishment* (Princeton, NJ: Princeton University Press, 2009); Jutta Brunneé and Stephen J. Toope, *Legitimacy and Legality in International Law: An Interactional Account* (New York: Cambridge University Press, 2010).

14. Tom R. Tyler, "Procedural Fairness and Compliance with the Law," *Swiss Journal of Economics and Statistics* 133, no. 2 (1997): 219–40; Tom R. Tyler, "Psychological Perspectives on Legitimacy and Legitimation," *Annual Review of*

*Psychology* 57, no. 1 (2006): 375–400; Tom R. Tyler, "Psychology and Institutional Design," *Review of Law and Economics* 4, no. 3 (2008): 801–87.

15. Alyson Brysk calls them "global good Samaritans." Alison Brysk, *Global Good Samaritans: Human Rights as Foreign Policy* (Oxford: Oxford University Press, 2009).

16. Thomas Risse, Stephen Ropp, and Kathryn Sikkink, eds., *The Power of Human Rights: International Norms and Domestic Change* (Cambridge: Cambridge University Press, 1999).

17. Amitav Acharya, "How Ideas Spread: Whose Norms Matter? Norm Localization and Institutional Change in Asian Regionalism," *International Organization* 58 (2004): 239–75; Sally Engle Merry, *Human Rights and Gender Violence: Translating International Law into Local Justice* (Chicago: University of Chicago Press, 2006).

18. Emilie M. Hafner-Burton and James Ron, "Human Rights in the Global Underbelly" (working paper, University of California at San Diego, 2010).

19. UN General Assembly, 59th Sess., Agenda Items 45 and 55, "In Larger Freedom: Towards Development, Security, and Human Rights for All, Report of the Secretary-general, Addendum, Letter Dated 26 May 2005 from the Secretary-general to the President of the General Assembly," A/59/2005/Add.3, May 26, 2005.

20. Claudia Wallis et al., "Inside Abu Ghraib: Why Did They Do It?" *Time Magazine*, May 17, 2004.

21. Joachim J. Savelsberg, *Crime and Human Rights: Criminology of Genocide & Atrocities* (London: Sage Press, 2010), 9.

22. UN General Assembly, 3rd Sess., "217 A (III). Universal Declaration of Human Rights," A/RES/3/217A, December 10, 1948, Art. 1, Preamble, Art. 2.

23. These core human rights, often referred to simply as *jus cogens*, or peremptory norms, are defined by the Vienna Convention on the Law of Treaties as "a norm accepted and recognized by the international community of states as a whole as a norm from which no derogation is permitted and which can be modified only by a subsequent norm of general international law having the same character." United Nations, "Vienna Convention on the Law of Treaties," May 23, 1969, Art. 53.

24. Louis Henkin, "Idealism and Ideology: The Law of Human Rights," in *How Nations Behave* (New York: Columbia University Press, 1968), 228–39; Thomas Buergenthal, "The Normative and Institutional Evolution of International Human Rights," *Human Rights Quarterly* 19 (1997): 703–23; Ellen L. Lutz and Kathryn Sikkink, "International Human Rights Law and Practice in Latin America," *International Organization* 54 (2000): 633–59; Christine Min Wotipka and Kiyoteru Tsutsui, "Global Human Rights and State Sovereignty: Nation-States' Ratifications of International Human Rights Treaties, 1965–2001," *Sociological Forum* 23, no. 4 (2008): 724–54.

25. UN Office of the High Commissioner for Human Rights, http://www.ohchr.org (accessed April 9, 2012).

26. On global legalism, see Posner, *The Perils of Global Legalism*. On membership, see Ryan Goodman and Derek Jinks, "Measuring the Effects of Human

Rights Treaties," *European Journal of International Law* 14, no. 1 (2003): 171–83; Ryan Goodman and Derek Jinks, "How to Influence States: Socialization and International Human Rights Law," *Duke Law Journal* 54, no. 3 (December 2004): 621–703; UN International Human Rights Instruments, "Universal Ratification Improving the Operation of the Human Rights Treaty Bodies, Servicing of the Treaty Bodies," HRI/MC/1998/4, September 7, 1998; Harold Koh, "The Value of Process," *International Legal Theory* 10, no. 1 (Fall 2005): 27–38.

27. OAS Department of International Law, "Draft of Inter-American Convention against Racism and all Forms of Discrimination and Intolerance," Washington, DC, June 3, 2008; OAS Department of International Law, "Draft American Declaration on the Rights of Indigenous Peoples," Washington, DC, June 3, 2008.

28. UN General Assembly, 61st Sess., Agenda Item 68, "61/177. International Convention for the Protection of All Persons from Enforced Disappearance," A/RES/61/177, January 12, 2007.

29. Human Rights Council Briefing Meeting, Communications Procedure for the Convention on the Rights of the Child, Geneva, June 2008; UN General Assembly, Human Rights Council, 11th Sess., Agenda Item 3, "Promotion and Protection of All Human Rights, Civil, Political, Economic, Social, and Cultural Rights, including the Right to Development," A/HRC/11/13, April 22, 2009; UN General Assembly, Human Rights Council, 17th Sess., Agenda Item 5, Optional Protocol to the Convention on the Rights of the Child to Provide a Communications Procedure," A/HRC/17/L.8, June 9, 2011.

30. Beth A. Simmons, *Mobilizing for Human Rights: International Law in Domestic Politics* (New York: Cambridge University Press, 2009), 15, 122.

31. Benedetto Conforti, *International Law and the Role of Domestic Legal Systems* (Dordrecht, The Netherlands: Martinus Nijhoff Publishers, 1993); Anne-Marie Slaughter and William Burke-White, "The Future of International Law Is Domestic (or, the European Way of Law)," *Harvard International Law Journal* 47, no. 2 (2006): 327–52; Margaret E. McGuiness, "Exploring the Limits of International Human Rights Law," *Georgia Journal of International and Comparative Law* 34 (2006): 393–421.

32. Mark Fathi Massoud, "Do Victims of War Need International Law? Human Rights Education Programs in Authoritarian Sudan," *Law and Society Review* 45, no. 1 (2011): 1.

33. Shannon Speed, "Dangerous Discourses: Human Rights and Multiculturalism in Neoliberal Mexico," *PoLAR: Political and Legal Anthropology Review* 28, no. 1 (May 2005): 29–51; Winifred Tate, *Counting the Dead: The Culture and Politics of Human Rights Activism in Colombia* (Berkeley: University of California Press, 2007); Bettina Shell-Duncan, "From Health to Human Rights: Female Genital Cutting and the Politics of Intervention," *American Anthropologist* 110, no. 2 (June 2008): 225–36.

34. Emilie M. Hafner-Burton, "Sticks and Stones: Naming and Shaming the Human Rights Enforcement Problem," *International Organization* 62 (October 2008): 689–716; James C. Franklin, "Shame on You: The Impact of Human Rights Criticism on Political Repression in Latin America," *International Studies Quarterly* 52 (2008): 187–211.

35. Rieff, "The Precarious Triumph of Human Rights," 39.

36. Anne F. Bayefsky, "First Report of the International Law Association's Committee on International Human Rights Law and Practice," submitted to the Helsinki Conference, August 11–17, 1996, Introduction.

37. James Crawford, "The UN Human Rights Treaty System: A System in Crisis?" in *The Future of UN Human Rights Treaty Monitoring*, ed. Philip Alston and James Crawford (New York: Cambridge University Press, 2000), 1.

38. International Criminal Court, "The States Parties to the Rome Statute," http://www.icc-cpi.int/Menus/ASP/states+parties/ (accessed April 10, 2012).

39. "AU Votes against Cooperating with ICC Arrest Warrant for Bashir," France 24, July 3, 2009; Xan Rice, "Sudanese President Bashir Faces Darfur Arrest Warrant," *Guardian*, March 4, 2009.

40. Jack Goldsmith, "The Self-defeating International Criminal Court," *University of Chicago Law Review* 70, no. 1 (Winter 2003): 89–104; Stephen Rademaker, "Unwitting Party to Genocide," *Washington Post*, January 11, 2007; Stephen Rademaker, "Obama's Missteps on Libya Cement Gaddafi's Advantage," *Washington Post*, March 11, 2011; Mary Jo Anderson, "International Criminal Court: Justice or Menace?" *Crisis Magazine*, June 2, 2011.

41. Michael J. Gilligan, "Is Enforcement Necessary for Effectiveness? A Model of the International Criminal Regime," *International Organization* 60, no. 4 (2006): 935–67; Allison M. Danner and Beth A. Simmons, "Credible Commitments and the International Criminal Court," *International Organization* 64, no. 2 (2010): 225–56.

42. David G. Victor, *Global Warming Gridlock: Creating More Effective Strategies for Protecting the Planet* (New York: Cambridge University Press, 2011).

43. On the United States, see Kathryn Sikkink, *Mixed Signals: U.S. Human Rights Policy and Latin America* (Ithaca, NY: Cornell University Press, 2004); Christopher Bodeen, "China: U.S. Human Rights Hypocrisy," Associated Press, February 11, 2009. On other nations, see Manish Raiji, "Viewpoint—Human Rights Hypocrisy: Subverting the United Nations," *Michigan Daily*, May 14, 2001.

44. For other pragmatic views, see Rieff, "The Precarious Triumph of Human Rights," 36–41; David Kennedy, "The International Human Rights Movement: Part of the Problem?" *Harvard Human Rights Journal* 101 (2002): 101–25; Suzanne Katzenstein and Jack Snyder, "Expediency of the Angels," *National Interest* (March–April 2009): 1–8; Brunneé and Toope, *Legitimacy and Legality in International Law*.

45. For evidence, see chapters 5 and 6 in this book. For commentary, see Jeane J. Kirkpatrick, "UN Human Rights Panel Needs Some Entry Standards," *Daily Times*, May 15, 2003.

46. On the ICC, see Julian Ku and Jide Nzelibe, "Do International Criminal Tribunals Deter or Exacerbate Humanitarian Atrocities?" *Washington University Law Quarterly* 84 (2007): 777–833. On the African court, see George Mukundi Wachira, *African Court on Human and Peoples' Rights: Ten Years on and Still No Justice* (London: Minority Rights Group International, 2008). On the inter-American court, see James L. Cavallaro and Stephanie Erin Brewer, "Reevaluating Regional Human Rights Litigation in the Twenty-First Century: The Case of the Inter-American Court," *American Journal of International Law* 102, no. 4

(2009): 768–827. On the European court, see Chatham House, *European Court of Human Rights: A Court in Crisis?* (London: Royal Institute of International Affairs, 2009).

## Chapter 2. Contexts

1. There is a long history in criminology of locating the cause of crime in biology, biochemistry, mental disorders, or hormonal imbalances. Cesare Lombroso, *Criminal Man*, trans. Mary Gibson and Nicole Hahn Rafter (1876; repr., Durham, NC: Duke University Press, 2006); Saleem Shah and Loren Roth, "Biological and Psychological Factors in Criminality," in *Handbook of Criminology*, ed. Daniel Glaser (Chicago: Rand McNally, 1974), 101–73; Matthew B. Robinson and Kevin M. Beaver, *Why Crime? An Interdisciplinary Approach to Explaining Criminal Behavior* (Durham, NC: Carolina Academic Press, 2009). For a review, see Adrian Raine, "The Biological Basis for Crime," in *Crime*, ed. James Q. Wilson and Joan Petersilia (Oakland, CA: ICS Press, 2002), 43–74.

2. Gary S. Becker, "Crime and Punishment: An Economic Approach," *Journal of Political Economy* 76 (2001): 169–217.

3. Don C. Gibbons, *The Criminological Enterprise: Theories and Perspectives* (Upper Saddle River, NJ: Prentice Hall, 1979).

4. Edwin H. Sutherland and Donald R. Cressey, *Criminology*, 9th ed. (Philadelphia: J. B. Lippincott, 1974).

5. US Department of State, "Background Note: Somalia," May 17, 2011.

6. Human Rights Watch, "Somalia," in *World Report 2010* (New York: Human Rights Watch, 2010), 157–63.

7. Amnesty International, "Somalia" in *Amnesty International Report 2009* (London: Amnesty International Publications, 2009); US Department of State, "2009 Human Rights Reports: Somalia," March 11, 2010.

8. Karen Rasler, "War, Accommodation, and Violence in the United States, 1890–1970," *American Political Science Review* 80 (1986): 921–45.

9. American Civil Liberties Union, "Does the USA PATRIOT Act Diminish Civil Liberties?" http://aclu.procon.org/view.answers.php?questionID=000716 (accessed April 11, 2011).

10. Jane Mayer, "Outsourcing Torture: The Secret History of America's 'Extraordinary Rendition' Program," *New Yorker*, February 14, 2005, 106; Emilie M. Hafner-Burton and Jacob A. Shapiro, "Tortured Relations: Human Rights Abuses and Counterterrorism Cooperation," *PS: Political Science and Politics* 43 (2010): 415–19.

11. Michael Stohl, "War and Domestic Violence: The Case of the United States, 1890-1970," *Journal of Conflict Resolution* 19 (1975): 379–416; Robert D. McKinlay and Alvin S. Cohan, "Performance and Instability in Military and Nonmilitary Regimes," *American Political Science Review* 70 (1976): 850–64; Steven C. Poe and C. Neal Tate, "Repression of Human Rights to Personal Integrity in the 1980s: A Global Analysis," *American Political Science Review* 88 (1994): 853–900.

12. Cathy S. Widom and Michale G. Maxfield, *An Update on the "Cycle of Violence"* (Washington, DC: National Institute of Justice, February 2001).

13. Marvin E. Wolfgang and Franco Ferracuti, *The Subculture of Violence: Towards an Integrated Theory in Criminology* (Beverly Hills, CA: Sage, 1982); Daniel J. Goldhagen, *Hitler's Willing Executioners: Ordinary Germans and the Holocaust* (New York: Alfred A. Knopf, 1996).

14. Joachim J. Savelsberg, *Crime and Human Rights: Criminology of Genocide and Atrocities* (London: Sage, 2010).

15. Robert J. Sampson and John H. Laub, *Crime in the Making: Pathways and Turning Points through Life* (Cambridge, MA: Harvard University Press, 1993).

16. Rhoda E. Howard and Jack Donnelly, "Human Dignity, Human Rights, and Political Regimes," *American Political Science Review* 80, no. 3 (1986): 801–18.

17. R. J. Rummel, *Death by Government* (New Brunswick, NJ: Transaction Publishers, 1994).

18. Seth Mydans, "Monks in Myanmar Protest for Third Day," *New York Times*, September 21, 2007.

19. Amnesty International, "Myanmar" in *Amnesty International Report 2008* (London: Amnesty International Publications, 2008).

20. "Myanmar," *New York Times*, June 10, 2012.

21. Conway Henderson, "Conditions Affecting the Use of Political Repression," *Journal of Conflict Resolution* 35 (1991): 120–42.

22. Emilie M. Hafner-Burton, Susan D. Hyde, and Ryan S. Jablonski, "When Governments Use Election Violence to Stay in Power," *British Journal of Political Science* (2013).

23. Mark Warr and Mark Stafford, "The Influence of Peers: What They Think or What They Do?" *Criminology* 29, no. 4 (November 1991): 851–66; Eric Rasmusen and Richard McAdams, "Norms and the Law," in *Handbook of Law and Economics, Volume 1*, ed. A. Mitchell Polinsky and Steven Shavell (Oxford: North-Holland, 2007), 1575–618; Jaqueline B. Helfgott, *Criminal Behavior: Theories, Typologies, and Criminal Justice* (Thousand Oaks, CA: Sage Publications, 2008).

24. Raj K. Sah, "Social Osmosis and Patterns of Crime: A Dynamic Economic Analysis," *Journal of Political Economy* 99, no. 6 (December 1991): 1272–95.

25. Antony Anghie, *Imperialism, Sovereignty, and the Making of International Law* (New York: Cambridge University Press, 2005).

26. "Getting Away with Torture? Command Responsibility for the U.S. Abuse of Detainees," *Human Rights Watch* 17 no. 1 (April 24, 2005): 1–93; Yves Beigbeder, *Judging War Crimes and Torture: French Justice and International Criminal Tribunals and Commissions (1940–2005)* (Leiden, The Netherlands: Martinus Nijhoff Publishers, 2006).

27. UN Office of the High Commissioner for Human Rights, "Frequently Asked Questions on Economic, Social, and Cultural Rights, Fact Sheet No. 33," December 2008, 22, http://www.ohchr.org/Documents/Publications/FactSheet33en.pdf (accessed April 11, 2012); Makau Mutua, "Human Rights and Powerlessness: Pathologies of Choice and Substance," *Buffalo Law Review* 56 (2008): 1027–34.

28. Poe and Tate, "Repression of Human Rights to Personal Integrity in the 1980s"; Christian Davenport, "Constitutional Promises and Repressive Reality:

A Cross-national Time-Series Investigation of Why Political and Civil Liberties Are Suppressed," *Journal of Politics* 58, no. 3 (1996): 627–54; Sabine Zanger, "A Global Analysis of the Effect of Political Regime Changes on Life Integrity Violations, 1977–1993," *Journal of Peace Research* 37, no. 2 (2000): 213–33; Barbara Harff, "No Lessons Learned from the Holocaust: Assessing Risks of Genocide and Political Mass Murder since 1955," *American Political Science Review* 25, no. 1 (2003): 57–74.

29. Monty G. Marshall, Keith Jaggers, and Ted R. Gurr, "Polity IV Project: Political Regime Characteristics and Transitions, 1800–2008."

30. Christian Davenport and David A. Armstrong II, "Democracy and the Violation of Human Rights: A Statistical Analysis from 1976 to 1996," *American Journal of Political Science* 48, no. 3 (2004): 538–54.

31. Helen Fein, "More Murder in the Middle: Life Integrity Violations and Democracy in the World, 1987," *Human Rights Quarterly* 17, no. 1 (February 1995): 170–91.

32. Jack Snyder, *From Voting to Violence: Democratization and Nationalist Conflict* (New York: W. W. Norton and Company, April 2000).

33. Davenport and Armstrong II, "Democracy and the Violation of Human Rights." See also Sabine C. Carey, "The Dynamic Relationship between Protest and Repression," *Political Research Quarterly* 59, no. 1 (2006): 1–11.

34. Charles Tilly, *From Mobilization to Revolution* (Reading, MA: Addison-Wesley, 1978); Ted Gurr, "The Political Origins of State Violence and Terror: A Theoretical Analysis," in *Government Violence and Repression: An Agenda for Research*, ed. Michael Stohl and George Lopez (New York: Greenwood Press, 1986); George Lopez, "National Security Ideology as an Impetus to State Violence and State Terror," in *Government Violence and Repression: An Agenda for Research*, ed. Michael Stohl and George Lopez (New York: Greenwood Press, 1986); Hafner-Burton, Hyde, and Jablonski, "When Governments Use Election Violence to Stay in Power."

35. Ariel Zirulnick, "After Syria Crackdown, Calls for International Action against Assad," *Christian Science Monitor*, April 26, 2011.

36. "Middle-East Protests: Country by Country—Libya," BBC, updated November 23, 2011, http://www.bbc.co.uk/news/world-12482311 (accessed April 12, 2012); "Middle-East Protests: Country by Country—Bahrain," BBC, updated November 24, 2011, http://www.bbc.co.uk/news/world-12482295 (accessed April 12, 2012).

37. David Davis and Michael Ward, "They Dance Alone: Deaths and the Disappeared in Contemporary Chile," *Journal of Conflict Resolution* 34 (1990): 449–75; Christian Davenport, "Multi-Dimensional Threat Perception and State Repression: An Inquiry into Why States Apply Negative Sanctions," *American Journal of Political Science* 39, no. 3 (1995): 683–713; Ron Francisco, "Coercion and Protest: An Empirical Test in Two Democratic States," *American Journal of Political Science* 40, no. 4 (1996): 1179–204; Will H. Moore, "Repression and Dissent: Substitution, Context, and Timing," *American Journal of Political Science* 45, no. 3 (1998): 851–73.

38. Davenport, "Multi-Dimensional Threat Perception and State Repression."

39. Robert McNamara, quoted in Neil J. Mitchell and James M. McCormick, "Economic and Political Explanations of Human Rights Violations," *World Politics* 40, no. 6 (1988): 478.

40. Reinhard Heinisch, "The Economic Nature of Basic Human Rights: Economic Explanations of Cross-National Variations in Governmental Basic Human Rights Performance," *Peace & Change* 23, no. 3 (July 1998): 333–70; Pablo Fajnzylber, Daniel Lederman, and Norman Loayza, "What Causes Violent Crime?" *European Economic Review* 46 (2002): 1323–57; Paul Collier, "The Conflict Trap," in *The Bottom Billion: Why the Poorest Countries Are Failing and What Can Be Done about It* (Oxford: Oxford University Press, 2007), 17–37; Todd Landman and Marco Larizza, "Inequality and Human Rights: Who Controls What, When, and How," *International Studies Quarterly* 53 (2009): 715–36; James A. Piazza, "Poverty, Minority Economic Discrimination, and Domestic Terrorism," *Journal of Peace Research* 48, no. 3 (2011): 339–53.

41. Leo Carroll and Pamela I. Jackson, "Inequality, Opportunity, and Crime Rates in Central Cities," *Criminology* 21 (May 1983): 178, quoted in Ralph C. Allen, "Socioeconomic Conditions and Property Crime: A Comprehensive Review and Test of the Professional Literature," *American Journal of Economics and Sociology* 55, no. 3 (July 1996): 294.

42. John R. Lott, "A Transaction-Costs Explanation for Why the Poor Are More Likely to Commit Crime," *Journal of Legal Studies* 19 (1990): 243–45; Joseph Deutsch, Uriel Spiegel, and Joseph Templeman, "Crime and Economic Inequality: An Economic Approach," *Atlantic Economic Journal* 20, no. 4 (1992): 46–54.

43. Albert K. Cohen, *Delinquent Boys: The Culture of the Gang* (Glencoe, IL: Free Press, 1955); Savelsberg, *Crime and Human Rights.*

44. US Department of State, "2010 Human Rights Report: Sierra Leone," April 8, 2011.

45. Alberto Alesina and Roberto Perotti, "Income Distribution, Political Instability, and Investment," *European Economic Review* 40, no. 6 (1996): 1203–28.

46. Landman and Larizza, "Inequality and Human Rights."

47. *Doe v. Unocal Corp*, US Court of Appeals, 9th Cir., 248 F.3d 915, April 27, 2001; Anne F. Bayefsky, ed., *Human Rights and Refugees, Internally Displaced Persons, and Migrant Workers: Essays in Memory of Joan Fitzpatrick and Arthur Helton* (Leiden, The Netherlands: Koninklijke Brill NV, 2006).

48. Organization of African Unity, African Commission on Human and People's Rights, *Case No. ACHPR/COMM/A044/1*, May 27, 2002; Fons Coomans, "The Ogoni Case before the African Commission on Human and Peoples' Rights," *International and Comparative Law Quarterly* 52, no. 3 (July 2003): 749–60.

49. Jim Yong Kim, Joyce V. Millen, and John Gershman, eds., *Dying for Growth: Global Inequality and the Health of the Poor* (Monroe, ME: Common Courage Press, 2000); UN Economic and Social Council, Committee on Economic, Social, and Cultural Rights, 25th Sess., Agenda Item 5, "Substantive Issues Arising in the Implementation of the International Covenant on Economic, Social, and Cultural Rights: Poverty and the International Covenant on Economic, Social, and Cultural Rights," E/C.12/2001/10, May 10, 2001; Paul Farmer,

*Pathologies of Power: Health, Human Rights, and the New War on the Poor* (Berkeley: University of California Press, 2003); Natasha Sawh, "Negotiation on the Ground: Realizing Economic, Social, and Cultural Rights in South Africa, Nigeria, and Peru" (globalization working papers 09/2, McMaster University, Hamilton, Ontario, April 2009).

50. Alicia Ely Yamin, "The Future in the Mirror: Incorporating Strategies for the Defense and Promotion of Economic, Social, and Cultural Rights into the Mainstream Human Rights Agenda," *Human Rights Quarterly* 27 (2005): 1201.

51. Jeanine Anderson, *Tendiendo Puentes: Calidad de Atención Desde la Perspectiva de las Mujeres Rurales y los Proveedores de los Servicios de Salud* (Lima: Movimiento Manuela Ramos, 2001). In April 2009, the Legal Framework for Universal Healthcare—Law No. 29344—which legalized the right of every Peruvian to health insurance, was signed into force. Peru, Congress of the Republic, *Law No. 29344, Legal Framework for Universal Health Insurance*, April 9, 2009; Julio Castro, "Towards Universal Health Assurance In Peru," *Revista Peruana de Medicina Experimental y Salud Publica*, 26, no. 2 (2009): 232–35.

52. Terry Boswell and William Dixon, "Dependency and Rebellion: A Cross-national Analysis," *American Sociological Review* 55, no. 4 (1990): 540–59; Poe and Tate, "Repression of Human Rights to Personal Integrity in the 1980s"; Mitchell and McCormick, "Economic and Political Explanations of Human Rights Violations."

53. Kathryn Sikkink, "A Human Rights Approach to Sept. 11," Social Science Research Council, para 5.

54. Jack Levin and Jack McDevitt, *Hate Crimes: The Rising Tide of Bigotry and Bloodshed* (New York: Plenum Press, 1993); Barbara Perry, *In the Name of Hate: Understanding Hate Crimes* (New York: Routledge, 2001).

55. Helen Fein, *Genocide: A Sociological Perspective* (London: Sage, 1993); Mahmood Mamdani, *When Victims Become Killers: Colonialism, Nativism, and the Genocide in Rwanda* (Princeton, NJ: Princeton University Press, 2002); James Waller, *Becoming Evil: How Ordinary People Commit Genocide and Mass Killing* (Oxford: Oxford University Press, 2002); Josias Semujanga, *Origins of Rwandan Genocide* (Amherst, NY: Humanity Books, 2003); Eric D. Weitz, *A Century of Genocide: Utopias of Race and Nation* (Princeton, NJ: Princeton University Press, 2005); Saul Friedländer, *The Years of Extermination: Nazi Germany and the Jews, 1939–1945* (New York: Harper, 2007).

56. Philip Zimbardo, *The Lucifer Effect: Understanding How Good People Turn Evil* (New York: Random House, 2008).

57. Herbert C. Kelman and V. Lee Hamilton, "The My Lai Massacre: Crimes of Obedience and Sanctioned Massacres," in *Corporate and Governmental Deviance: Problems of Organizational Behavior in Contemporary Society*, ed. David M. Ermann and Richard L. Lundman (Oxford: Oxford University Press, 2002), 195–224.

58. "Rwanda: How the Genocide Happened," BBC, December 18, 2008.

59. Timothy Longman, "Identity Cards, Ethnic Self-perception, and Genocide in Rwanda," in *Documenting Individual Identity: The Development of State Practices in the Modern World*, ed. Jane Caplan and John Torpey (Princeton, NJ: Princeton University Press, 2001), 345–58; Philip Gourevitch, *We Wish to Inform*

*You That Tomorrow We Will Be Killed with Our Families: Stories from Rwanda* (New York: Picador, 1998); Samantha Power, *A Problem from Hell: America and the Age of Genocide* (New York: Perennial, 2003).

60. Ross L. Matsueda, "Differential Social Organization, Collective Action, and Crime," *Crime, Law, and Social Change* 46, nos. 1–2 (September 2006): 3–33; Emilie M. Hafner-Burton, Miles Kahler and Alexander H. Montgomery, "Network Analysis for International Relations," *International Organization* 63 (Spring 2009): 559–92.

61. Diane Vaughan, "The Dark Side of Organizations: Mistake, Misconduct, and Disaster," *Annual Review of Sociology* 25 (August 1999): 271–305; Diane Vaughan, "Criminology and the Sociology of Organizations," *Crime, Law, and Social Change* 37, no. 2 (March 2002): 117–36; James William Coleman, *The Criminal Elite: Understanding White-collar Crime* (New York: Worth, 2006).

## Chapter 3. Rationales

1. Albert Bandura, Bill Underwood, and Michael E. Fromson, "Disinhibition of Aggression through Diffusion of Responsibility and Dehumanization of Victims," *Journal of Research in Personality* 9 (1975): 253–69.

2. Roger Hopkins Burke, *An Introduction to Criminal Theory*, 3rd ed. (Cullompton, UK: Willan, 2001).

3. Eric R. Kraemer, "Holocaust Evils and Divine Limitations: A Reexamination," *Journal of Genocide Research* 4, no. 4 (2002): 569–80.

4. Alex Woolf, *Exploring Tough Issues: Why Do People Commit Crime?* (Chicago: Raintree, 2005); Nicole Hahn Rafter, *The Criminal Brain: Understanding Biological Theories of Crime* (New York: New York University Press, 2008); Charles King, "Can There Be a Political Science of the Holocaust?" *Perspectives on Politics* 10, no. 2 (2012): 323–41.

5. Erica Goode, "Insane or Just Evil? A Psychiatrist Takes a New Look at Hitler," *New York Times*, November 17, 1998.

6. Ervin Staub, " The Psychology of Perpetrators and Bystanders," *Political Psychology* 6 (1985): 61–86.

7. John Conroy, *Unspeakable Acts, Ordinary People: The Dynamics of Torture: An Examination of the Practice of Torture in Three Democracies* (New York: Alfred A. Knopf, 2000), 27.

8. Brian Mullen and C. Johnson, "Distinctiveness-Based Illusory Correlations and Stereotyping: A Meta-analytic Integration," *British Journal of Social Psychology* 29 (1990): 11–28; Brian Mullen, Rupert Brown, and Colleen Smith, "Ingroup Bias as a Function of Salience, Relevance, and Status: An Integration," *European Journal of Social Psychology* 22, no. 2 (March–April 1992): 103–22.

9. Philip Zimbardo, *The Lucifer Effect: Understanding How Good People Turn Evil* (New York: Random House, 2008).

10. Roy F. Baumeister, *Evil: Inside Human Violence and Cruelty* (New York: Henry Holt and Company, 1999).

11. Susan T. Fiske, Lasana T. Harris, and Amy J. C. Cuddy, "Why Ordinary People Torture Enemy Prisoners," *Science* 306 (November 2004): 1482–83. Also see Ervin Staub, "The Roots of Evil: Social Conditions, Culture, Personality, and Basic Human Needs," *Personality and Social Psychology Review* 3, no. 3 (August

1999): 179–92; Albert Bandura, "Moral Disengagement in the Perpetration of Inhumanities," *Personality and Social Psychology Review* 3, no. 3 (August 1999): 193–209; Leonard Berkowitz, "Evil Is More Than Banal: Situationism and the Concept of Evil," *Personality and Social Psychology Review* 3, no. 3 (August 1999): 246–53.

12. Robert J. Lifton, *The Nazi Doctors* (New York: Basic Books, 1986); Hannah Arendt, *Eichmann in Jerusalem: A Report on the Banality of Evil* (New York: Penguin Books, 1994).

13. Molly Harrower, "Rorschach Records of the Nazi War Criminals: An Experimental Study after Thirty Years," *Journal of Personality Assessment* 40 (1976): 341–51.

14. Mika Haritos-Fatouros, "The Official Torturer: A Learning Model for Obedience to the Authority of Violence," *Journal of Applied Social Psychology* 18, no. 13 (1988): 1113; Mika Haritos-Fatouros, *The Psychological Origins of Institutionalized Torture* (London: Routledge, 2003).

15. US Army Commission of Inquiry, quoted in Conroy, *Unspeakable Acts, Ordinary People,* 88.

16. Errol Morris, *Standard Operating Procedure,* Sony Pictures Classics, April 25, 2008.

17. Philip G. Zimbardo, Craig Haney, W. Curtis Banks, and David Jaffe, "The Psychology of Imprisonment: Privation, Power, and Pathology," in *Doing unto Others: Joining, Molding, Conforming, Helping, Loving,* ed. Zick Rubin (Englewood Cliffs, NJ: Prentice Hall, 1974).

18. Stanford prison experiment, http://www.prisonexp.org/ (accessed April 12, 2012).

19. Christopher R. Browning, *Ordinary Men: Police Battalion 101 and the Final Solution in Poland* (New York: HarperCollins, 1998).

20. Emma Brockes, "What Happens in War Happens," *Guardian,* January 3, 2009.

21. Randall Collins, *Violence: A Micro-Sociological Theory* (Princeton, NJ: Princeton University Press, 2008).

22. David J. Whittaker, *Terrorists and Terrorism in the Contemporary World* (London: Routledge, 2004); John Horgan, *Walking away from Terrorism: Accounts of Disengagement from Radical and Extremist Movements* (London: Routlegde, 2009).

23. Sagit Yehoshua, "The Social-Psychology of Non-radicalisation: How Not to Become a Terrorist and Why" (Atkin paper series, King's College London, January 2010).

24. Roy F. Baumeister, Arlene M. Stillwell, and Sara R. Wotman, "Victim and Perpetrator Accounts of Interpersonal Conflict: Autobiographical Narratives about Anger," *Journal of Personality and Social Psychology* 59 (1990): 994–1005.

25. For justifications based on arguments that victims deserved their ill treatment, see Jack Katz, *Seductions of Crime: Moral and Sensual Attractions in Doing Evil* (New York: Basic Books, 1988); Zimbardo, *The Lucifer Effect.* For justifications based on arguments that victims are somehow less human, see Peter

Suedfeld, *Psychology and Torture* (New York: Hemisphere Publishing Corporation, 1990).

26. Klaus Barbie, quoted in Janice T. Gibson, "Factors Contributing to the Creation of a Torturer," in *Psychology and Torture*, ed. Peter Suedfeld (New York: Hemisphere Publishing Corporation, 1990), 80.

27. Conroy, *Unspeakable Acts, Ordinary People*, 106.

28. Sean Thomas, "Will Comrade Duch Be the Last of the Khmer Rouge to Face Justice?" *First Post*, September 23, 2009.

29. Baumeister, *Evil*, 47; Arendt, *Eichmann in Jerusalem*.

30. Tom R. Tyler, *Why People Obey the Law* (Princeton, NJ: Princeton University Press, 2006), 161.

31. Robert C. Ellickson, *Order without Law: How Neighbors Settle Disputes* (Cambridge, MA: Harvard University Press, 1991).

32. Robert Agnew, *Why Do Criminals Offend? A General Theory of Crime and Delinquency* (Oxford: Oxford University Press, 2005).

33. Emilie M. Hafner-Burton and James Ron, "Seeing Double: Human Rights Impact through Qualitative and Quantitative Eyes," *World Politics* 61, no. 2 (April 2009): 360–401.

34. Zimbardo, Haney, Banks, and Jaffe, "The Psychology of Imprisonment"; Jeffrey H. Goldstein, Roger W. Davis, and Dennis Herman, "Escalation of Aggression: Experimental Studies," *Journal of Personality and Social Psychology* 31 (1975): 162–70; Staub, " The Psychology of Perpetrators and Bystanders"; Ervin Staub, *The Psychology of Good and Evil: Why Children, Adults, and Groups Help and Harm Others* (Cambridge: Cambridge University Press, 2003).

35. Ervin Staub, "The Psychology and Culture of Torture and Torturers," in *Psychology and Torture*, ed. Peter Suedfeld (New York: Hemisphere Publishing Corporation, 1990), 65.

36. Henry Victor Dicks, *Licensed Mass Murder: A Socio-psychological Study of Some SS Killers* (New York: Basic Books, 1972).

37. Judith Kelley, "Who Keeps International Commitments and Why? The International Criminal Court and Bilateral Nonsurrender Agreements," *American Political Science Review* 111, no. 3 (August 2007): 573–89.

38. Stanley Milgram, "Behavioral Study of Obedience," *Journal of Abnormal Social Psychology* 67, no. 4 (1963): 277–85; Stanley Milgram, "Some Conditions of Obedience and Disobedience to Authority," *Human Relations* 18, no. 1 (1965): 55–57; David M. Mantel, "The Potential for Violence in Germany," *Journal of Social Issues* 27, no. 4 (1971): 101–12; Mitri Shanab and Khawla Yahya, "A Behavioral Study of Obedience in Children," *Journal of Personality and Social Psychology* 35, no. 7 (1977): 530–36.

39. Zygmunt Bauman, *Modernity and the Holocaust* (Ithaca, NY: Cornell University Press, 1991); Baumeister, *Evil*.

40. Staub, *The Psychology of Good and Evil*.

41. Staub, "The Psychology and Culture of Torture and Torturers."

42. Amnesty International, "Deaths under Torture, 1975–77" (London: Amnesty International Publications, 1978), quoted in Wolfgang S. Heinz and Hugo Fruhling, *Determinants of Gross Human Rights Violations by State and*

*State-Sponsored Actors in Brazil, Uruguay, Chile, and Argentina* (Leiden, The Netherlands: Martinus Nijhoff Publishers, 1999), 290.

43. Joseph Goldstein, Burke Marshall, and Jack Schwartz, *The My Lai Massacre and Its Cover-up: Beyond the Reach of Law?* (New York: Free Press, 1976), 100.

44. Portia Walker, "Human Rights Group Suspects Revenge Killings in Libya," *USA Today*, August 29, 2011.

45. Quoted in Conroy, *Unspeakable Acts, Ordinary People*, 106–7.

46. Agnew, *Why Do Criminals Offend?*

47. Emilie M. Hafner Burton, "Sticks and Stones: Naming and Shaming the Human Rights Enforcement Problem," *International Organization* 62 (October 2008): 689–716; Andrew Guzman, *How International Law Works: A Rational Choice Theory* (New York: Oxford University Press, 2008).

48. Scott Decker, Richard Wright, and Scott Logie, "Perceptual Deterrence among Active Residential Burglars: A Research Note," *Criminology* 31, no. 1 (February 1993): 135–47; Neal Shover, *Great Pretenders: Pursuits and Careers of Persistent Thieves* (Boulder, CO: Westview Press, 1996); Bradley R. E. Wright, Avshalom Caspi, Terrie E. Moffitt, and Ray Paternoster, "Does the Perceived Risk of Punishment Deter Criminally Prone Individuals? Rational Choice, Self-Control, and Crime," *Journal of Research in Crime and Delinquency* 41, no. 2 (May 2004): 180–213; Shover, *Great Pretenders*. For a review of the literature, see Louis Kaplow and Steven Shavell, "Economic Analysis of Law," in *Handbook of Public Economics*, ed. Alan J. Auerbach and Martin S. Feldstein (New York: Elsevier, 2002), 1661–784; Steven D. Levitt and Thomas J. Miles, "Empirical Study of Criminal Punishment," in *Handbook of Law and Economics, Volume 1*, ed. A. Mitchell Polinsky and Steven Shavell, (Amsterdam: North-Holland, 2007), 455–96.

49. Kathryn Sikkink, *The Justice Cascade: How Human Rights Prosecutions Are Changing World Politics* (New York: W. W. Norton and Company, 2011).

50. Ross L. Matsueda, Derek A. Kreager, and David Huizinga, "Deterring Delinquents: A Rational Choice Model of Theft and Violence," *American Sociological Review* 71, no. 1 (2006): 95–122.

51. Allen E. Liska and Steven F. Messner, *Perspectives on Crime and Deviance*, 3rd ed. (Upper Saddle River, NJ: Prentice Hall, 1999).

52. Richard T. Wright and Scott H. Decker, *Burglars on the Job: Street Life and Residential Break-ins* (Boston: Northeastern University Press, 1994); Shover, *Great Pretenders*.

53. James Q. Wilson and Richard Herrnstein, *Crime and Human Nature* (New York: Simon and Schuster, 1985); Michael R. Gottfredson and Travis Hirschi, *A General Theory of Crime* (Stanford, CA: Stanford University Press, 1990); Daniel S. Nagin and Greg Pogarsky, "Integrating Celerity, Impulsivity, and Extralegal Sanction Threats into a Model of General Deterrence: Theory and Evidence," *Criminology* 39 (2001): 865–92.

54. Matthew Silberman, "Toward a Theory of Criminal Deterrence," *American Sociological Review* 41 (1976): 442–61; Gordon Trasler, "Conscience, Opportunity, Rational Choice, and Crime," in *Routine Activity and Rational Choice: Advances in Criminological Theory, Volume 5*, ed. Ronald V. Clarke and Marcus

Felson (New Brunswick, NJ: Transaction Press, 1993), 305–22; Raymond Paternoster and Sally Simpson, "Sanction Threats and Appeals to Morality: Testing a Rational Choice Model of Corporate Crime," *Law and Society Review* 30 (1996): 549–83.

55. Wright, Caspi, Moffitt, and Paternoster, "Does the Perceived Risk of Punishment Deter Criminally Prone Individuals?" 186, 207.

56. On policing, see Thomas B. Marvell and Carlisle E. Moody, "Specification Problems, Police Levels, and Crime Rates," *Criminology* 34, no. 4 (1996): 609–46; Steven D. Levitt, "Using Electoral Cycles in Police Hiring to Estimate the Effect of Police on Crime," *American Economic Review* 87, no. 3 (June 1997): 270–90; Rafael Di Tella and Ernesto Schargrodsky, "Do Police Reduce Crime? Estimates Using the Allocation of Police Forces after a Terrorist Attack," *American Economic Review* 94, no. 1 (March 2004): 115–33. On incarceration, see Thomas B. Marvell and Carlisle E. Moody, "Prison Population Growth and Crime Reduction," *Journal of Quantitative Criminology* 10, no. 2 (1994): 109–40; Steven D. Levitt, "The Effect of Prison Population Size on Crime Rates: Evidence from Prison Overcrowding Litigation," *Quarterly Journal of Economics* 111 (May 1995): 319–25.

57. Shover, *Great Pretenders*; Wright, Caspi, Moffitt, and Paternoster, "Does the Perceived Risk of Punishment Deter Criminally Prone Individuals?"

58. Bandura, Underwood, and Fromson, "Disinhibition of Aggression through Diffusion of Responsibility and Dehumanization of Victims"; Zimbardo, *The Lucifer Effect*.

## Notes to Part II

1. For example, consult the four Geneva Conventions on war including "Convention (I) for the Amelioration of the Condition of the Wounded and Sick in Armed Forces in the Field," Geneva, August 12, 1949, and "Convention (IV) Relative to the Protection of Civilian Persons in Time of War," Geneva, August 12, 1949. For a full list of international treaties and documents, see "International Committee of the Red Cross," http://www.icrc.org/ (accessed April 16, 2012).

2. UN General Assembly, 3rd Sess., "217 A (III). Universal Declaration of Human Rights," A/RES/3/217A, December 10, 1948.

3. Edmund Kagire, "Rwanda: Belgium Sentences Genocidaire to 30 Years," *New Times*, December 3, 2009.

4. International Coalition for the Responsibility to Protect, http://www.responsibilitytoprotect.org/ (accessed April 16, 2012).

## Chapter 4. The International Human Rights Legal System

1. Alexander Orakhelashvili, *Peremptory Norms in International Law* (Oxford: Oxford University Press, 2006).

2. Karen Alter and Sophie Meunier, "The Politics of International Regime Complexity," *Perspectives on Politics* 7, no. 1 (March 2009): 13–24.

3. United Nations, "Human Rights," http://www.un.org/rights/ (accessed April 16, 2012).

4. William A. Schabas, "On the Binding Nature of the Findings of the Treaty Bodies," in *New Challenges for the UN Human Rights Machinery*, ed. Mahmoud

Cherif Bassiouni and William A. Schabas (Cambridge, UK: Intersentia, 2011), 97–106.

5. United Nations, "Charter of the United Nations and Statute of the International Court of Justice," June 26, 1945.

6. Louis Henkin, *The Age of Rights* (New York: Columbia University Press, 1990); Vojin Dimitrijevic, "Customary Law as an Instrument for Protection of Human Rights" (ISPI working paper 7, 2006).

7. UN General Assembly, 21st Sess., Agenda Item 62, "Resolution 2200 (XXI). International Covenant on Economic, Social, and Cultural Rights, International Covenant on Civil and Political Rights and Optional Protocol to the International Covenant on Civil and Political Rights," A/RES/21/2200, December 16, 1966.

8. UN General Assembly, 21st Sess., Agenda Item 62, "Resolution 2200 (XXI). International Covenant on Economic, Social, and Cultural Rights, International Covenant on Civil and Political Rights and Optional Protocol to the International Covenant on Civil and Political Rights."

9. UN General Assembly, 21st Sess., Agenda Item 62, "Resolution 2200 (XXI). International Covenant on Economic, Social, and Cultural Rights, International Covenant on Civil and Political Rights and Optional Protocol to the International Covenant on Civil and Political Rights," Art. 28.

10. Alfred de Zayas, "Petitions before the United Nations Treaty Bodies: Focus on the Human Rights Committee's Optional Protocol Procedure," in *International Human Rights Monitoring Mechanisms, Essays in Honor of Jakob Th. Möller*, 2nd rev. ed. (Leiden, The Netherlands: Martinus Nijhoff Publishers, 2009), 37. See also Thomas M. Franck, "The Emerging Right to Democratic Governance," *American Society of International Law* 86, no. 1 (1992): 46–91.

11. Philip Alston, "The Purposes of Reporting," in *Manual on Human Rights Reporting under Six Major Human Rights Reporting Instruments*, HR/PUB/97/1 Rev.1. (Geneva: United Nations, 1997), 19–24.

12. Yogesh Tyagi, *The UN Human Rights Committee: Practice and Procedure* (New York: Cambridge University Press, 2011).

13. UN General Assembly, 21st Sess., Agenda item 62, "Resolution 2200 (XXI). International Covenant on Economic, Social, and Cultural Rights, International Covenant on Civil and Political Rights and Optional Protocol to the International Covenant on Civil and Political Rights," Art. 29; UN Office of the High Commissioner for Human Rights, "Human Rights Committee: Members," http://www2.ohchr.org/english/bodies/hrc/members.htm (accessed April 16, 2012).

14. UN Office of the High Commissioner for Human Rights, Human Rights Committee, 95th Sess., March 16, 2009 to April 3, 2009.

15. UN Human Rights Committee, 95th Sess., "Consideration of Reports Submitted by States Parties under Article 40 of the Covenant: Concluding Observations of the Human Rights Committee, Australia," CCPR/C/AUS/CO/5, May 7, 2009.

16. UN Office of the High Commissioner for Human Rights, "Civil and Political Rights: The Human Rights Committee, Fact Sheet No. 15 (Rev. 1)," May 2005.

17. UN Economic and Social Council, "Resolution 1985/17. Review of the Composition, Organization, and Administrative Arrangements of the Sessional

Working Group of Governmental Experts on the Implementation of the International Covenant on Economic, Social, and Cultural Rights," E/RES/1985/17, May 28, 1985; UN Office of the High Commissioner for Human Rights, "Committee on Social, Economic, and Cultural Rights: Members," http://www2.ohchr.org/english/bodies/cescr/members.htm (accessed April 16, 2012).

18. UN Economic and Social Council, "Resolution 1985/17."

19. UN Office of the High Commissioner for Human Rights, "Committee on Social, Economic, and Cultural Rights: Sessions," http://www2.ohchr.org/english/bodies/cescr/sessions.htm (accessed April 16, 2012); UN Committee on Economic, Social, and Cultural Rights, *Land and Housing Rights in Cambodia: Parallel Report 2009* (Land and Housing Working Group, Cambodia, April 2009).

20. The Convention on the Prevention and Punishment of the Crime of Genocide allows any member state to request relevant UN institutions, including the International Court of Justice, to take action to prevent or stop genocide. UN General Assembly, "Resolution 260 (III). Convention on the Prevention and Punishment of the Crime of Genocide," December 9, 1948.

21. UN General Assembly, 20th Sess., "Resolution 2106 (XX). International Convention on the Elimination of All Forms of Racial Discrimination," December 21, 1965.

22. UN General Assembly, 34th Sess., Agenda Item 75, "34/180. Convention on the Elimination of All Forms of Discrimination against Women," A/RES/34/180, December 18, 1979.

23. UN General Assembly, 39th Sess., Agenda Item 99, "39/46. Convention against Torture and Other Cruel, Inhuman, or Degrading Treatment or Punishment," A/RES/39/46, December 10, 1984.

24. UN General Assembly, 44th Sess., Agenda Item 108, "44/25. Convention on the Rights of the Child," A/RES/44/25, November 20, 1989.

25. UN General Assembly, 45th Sess., Agenda Item 12, "45/158. International Convention on the Protection of the Rights of All Migrant Workers and Members of Their Families," A/RES/45/158), December 18, 1990.

26. UN General Assembly, 61st Sess., Agenda Item 67b, "61/106. Convention on the Rights of Persons with Disabilities," A/RES/61/106, December 13, 2006.

27. UN General Assembly, 61st Sess., Agenda Item 68, "61/177. International Convention for the Protection of All Persons from Enforced Disappearance," A/RES/61/177, January 12, 2007.

28. These oversight bodies include the Committee on the Elimination of All Forms of Racial Discrimination, the Committee on the Elimination of Discrimination against Women, the Committee against Torture, the Committee on the Rights of the Child, the Committee on the Protection of the Rights of All Migrant Workers and Members of Their Families, and the Committee on Enforced Disappearances.

29. There are also ways to bring complaints outside the treaty body system—for example, by using the special procedures and the 1503 procedure of the Commission on Human Rights, and through the Commission on the Status of Women.

30. Article 21 of the Convention against Torture and Other Cruel, Inhuman, or Degrading Treatment or Punishment as well as Article 74 of the International Convention on the Protection of the Rights of All Migrant Workers and Members of Their Families allow the relevant committee to consider state-to-state complaints. Articles 11–13 of the International Convention on the Elimination of All Forms of Racial Discrimination, and Articles 41–43 of the International Covenant on Civil and Political Rights create a dispute resolution procedure between states. Article 29 of the International Convention on the Elimination of All Forms of Discrimination against Women as well as Articles 30 and 92 of the Convention against Torture and Other Cruel, Inhuman, or Degrading Treatment or Punishment provide for negotiation, or failing that, arbitration by the International Court of Justice. For further information, see UN Office of the High Commissioner for Human Rights, "Human Rights Bodies: Complaints Procedures," http://www2.ohchr.org/english/bodies/petitions/index.htm (accessed April 16, 2012).

31. The Convention against Torture and Other Cruel, Inhuman, or Degrading Treatment or Punishment and the Convention on the Elimination of All Forms of Discrimination against Women both allow for this procedure.

32. UN Office of the High Commissioner for Human Rights, "Confidential Inquiries under Article 20 of the Convention against Torture," http://www2.ohchr.org/english/bodies/cat/confidential_art20.htm (accessed April 16, 2012).

33. UN General Assembly, 44th Sess., "44/128. Second Optional Protocol to the International Covenant on Civil and Political Rights, Aiming at the Abolition of the Death Penalty," A/RES/44/128, December 15, 1989; UN General Assembly, 54th Sess., Agenda Item 166a, "54/263. Optional Protocols to the Convention on the Rights of the Child on the Involvement of Children in Armed Conflict and on the Sale of Children, Child Prostitution, and Child Pornography," A/RES/54/263, May 25, 2000.

34. UN Office of the High Commissioner for Human Rights, "Human Rights Committee: Monitoring Civil and Political Rights," http://www2.ohchr.org/english/bodies/hrc/index.htm (accessed April 16, 2012).

35. At the time of this writing, the optional protocol needed two more states to ratify it before it would come into force. UN General Assembly, 63rd Sess., Agenda Item 58, "Optional Protocol to the International Covenant on Economic, Social, and Cultural Rights," A/RES/63/117, December 10, 2008.

36. United Nations, "Office of the High Commissioner for Human Rights," 1993, http://www.ohchr.org/EN/Pages/WelcomePage.aspx (accessed April 16, 2012).

37. UN Office of High Commissioner for Human Rights, "2009 Report: Activities and Results," (UN Office of the High Commissioner for Human Rights: Geneva, April 2010), 80.

38. UN Office of the High Commissioner for Human Rights, "The Human Rights Council," http://www2.ohchr.org/english/bodies/hrcouncil/ (accessed April 16, 2012).

39. UN Office of the High Commissioner for Human Rights, "Special Rapporteur on Violence against Women, Its Causes and Consequences: Annual Reports" http://www2.ohchr.org/english/issues/women/rapporteur/annual.htm (accessed April 16, 2012).

40. Radhika Coomaraswamy, UN Economic and Social Council, Commission on Human Rights, 58th Sess., Item 12(a) of the Provisional Agenda, "Integration of the Human Rights of Women and the Gender Perspective, Report of the Special Rapporteur on Violence against Women, Its Causes and Consequences, Ms. Radhika Coomaraswamy, Submitted in Accordance with Commission on Human Rights Resolution 2001/49, Cultural Practices in the Family That Are Violent towards Women," E/CN.4/2002/83, January 31, 2002.

41. On violence against women, see Radhika Coomaraswamy, UN Economic and Social Council, Commission on Human Rights, 57th Sess., "Integration of the Human Rights of Women and the Gender Perspective, Violence against Women, Report of the Special Rapporteur on Violence against Women, Its Causes and Consequences, Ms. Radhika Coomaraswamy, Submitted in Accordance with Commission on Human Rights Resolution 2000/45, Violence against Women Perpetrated and/or Condoned by the State during Times of Armed Conflict (1997–2000)," E/CN.4/2001/73, January 23, 2001. On human trafficking, see Radhika Coomaraswamy, UN Economic and Social Council, Commission on Human Rights, 56th Sess., "Integration of the Human Rights of Women and the Gender Perspective: Violence against Women, Report of the Special Rapporteur on Violence against Women, Its Causes and Consequences, Ms. Radhika Coomaraswamy, on Trafficking in Women, Women's Migration, and Violence against Women, Submitted in Accordance with Commission on Human Rights Resolution 1997/44," E/CN.4/2000/68, February 29, 2000.

42. UN Office of the High Commissioner for Human Rights, "Universal Periodic Review," http://www.ohchr.org/en/hrbodies/upr/pages/uprmain.aspx (accessed April 16, 2012).

43. Harold H. Koh, "How Is International Human Rights Law Enforced?" *Indiana Law Journal* 74, no. 4 (1999): 1397–417.

44. Constitutional Court of Spain, First Chamber, Sentence 32/2003, February 13, 2003; Amnesty International, "Spain: Follow-up Information to the Concluding Observations of the Committee against Torture," EUR 41/003/2010, November 12, 2010.

45. United Nations, "International Criminal Tribunal for the Former Yugoslavia," 1993, http://www.icty.org/sid/3 (accessed April 17, 2012); United Nations, "International Criminal Tribunal for Rwanda," November 4, 1994, http://www.ictr.org/default.htm (accessed April 17, 2012); Christopher Rudolph, "Constructing an Atrocities Regime: The Politics of War Crimes Tribunals," *International Organization* 55, no. 3 (2001): 655–91.

46. Rome Statute of the International Criminal Court, Art. 5(1), July 17, 1998.

47. There is a relationship agreement between the ICC and United Nations that establishes the legal foundation for cooperation within each organization's mandate. The ICC has its own mandate, which supports the Charter of the United Nations.

48. International Criminal Court, "Situations and Cases," http://www.icc-cpi.int/Menus/ICC/Situations+and+Cases/ (accessed April 17, 2012).

49. Steven Greer, *The European Convention on Human Rights: Achievements, Problems, and Prospects* (New York: Cambridge University Press, 2006).

50. Council of Europe, "The European Court of Human Rights: Some Facts and Figures, 1959—2009," April 2009.

51. In 1994, the members of the Council of Europe made an additional protocol to the convention: Protocol 11. This law, which came into force in 1998,
reformed the process for judicial enforcement of the convention. Before, there
was a two-tier system in place, with a court and commission. Individual victims
who wanted to lodge a complaint only had access to the commission, which
wrote nonbinding reports. Now, individual victims have direct access to the court
(the commission no longer exists). Council of Europe, "Protocol No. 11 to the
Convention for the Protection of Human Rights and Fundamental Freedoms,
Restructuring the Control Machinery Established Thereby," Strasbourg, May 11,
1994; Council of Europe, "European Court of Human Rights: Questions and
Answers," http://www.echr.coe.int/NR/rdonlyres/37C26BF0-EE46-437E-B810
-EA900D18D49B/0/ENG_QR.pdf (accessed April 17, 2012).

52. Council of Europe, "50 Years of Activity, the European Court of Human
Rights: Some Facts and Figures," http://www.echr.coe.int/NR/rdonlyres/ACD46
A0F-615A-48B9-89D6-8480AFCC29FD/0/FactsAndFiguresENAvril2010.pdf
(accessed April 17, 2012).

53. European Court of Human Rights, *McKerr v. the United Kingdom,* Application No. 28883/95, Judgment Strasbourg, May 4, 2001.

54. European Court of Human Rights, *Cyprus v. Turkey,* Application No.
25781/94, Judgment Strasbourg, May 10, 2001.

55. Frank Hoffmeister, "Cyprus v. Turkey. App. No. 25781/94," *American Journal of International Law* 96, no. 2 (April 2002): 445–52.

56. Council of Europe, Committee of Ministers, 992nd Meeting of the Ministers' Deputies, "Interim Resolution CM/ResDH(2007)25 concerning the Judgment of the European Court of Human Rights of 10 May 2001," CM/ResDH
(2007)25, April 4, 2007.

57. These procedures are stipulated in Resolution (99) 50. Council of Europe,
Committee of Ministers, "Resolution (99) 50," May 7, 1999.

58. Council of Europe, Commissioner for Human Rights, "Country Monitoring," http://www.coe.int/t/commissioner/Activities/countryreports_en.asp (accessed
April 17, 2012).

59. Inter-American Commission on Human Rights, "Resolution No. 3/87,
Case 9647, United States," September 22, 1987, 46–49; Inter-American Court
of Human Rights, "Interpretation of the American Declaration of the Rights and
Duties of Man within the Framework of Article 64 of the American Convention
on Human Rights, Advisory Opinion OC-10/89," July 14, 1989, paras. 35–45;
Veronica Gomez, "Rafael Ferrer-Mazorra et al. (United States), Report N° 51/01,
Case 9903," *Human Rights Law Review* 2, no. 1 (2002): 117–26.

60. Articles of the American Convention also include the "right to reply,"
"rights of the family," "right to a name," "right to nationality," "right to property,"
"freedom of movement and residence," "right to participate in government,"
"right to equal protection," and "right to judicial protection."

61. The member states of the Inter-American Commission also adopted a
convention in 1985 specifically to address torture through the Inter-American
Convention to Prevent and Punish Torture. OAS General Assembly, 15th Reg.
Sess., "Inter-American Convention to Prevent and Punish Torture," September 12,
1985.

62. Reporting procedures are stipulated in Article 41 of the American Convention. Organization of American States, "B-32: American Convention on Human Rights, Pact of San Jose, Costa Rica," November 22, 1969.

63. Antônio Augusto Cançado Trindade, "Reporting in the Inter-American System of Human Rights Protection," in *The Future of UN Human Rights Treaty Monitoring*, ed. Philip Alston (New York: Cambridge University Press, 2000), 333–46.

64. James L. Cavallaro and Stephanie Erin Brewer, "Reevaluating Regional Human Rights Litigation in the Twenty-First Century: The Case of the Inter-American Court," *American Journal of International Law* 102, no. 4 (2008): 768–827.

65. Organization of American States, "B-32: American Convention on Human Rights, Pact of San Jose, Costa Rica."

66. Inter-American Court of Human Rights, *Case of Garrido and Baigorria v. Argentina*, Sentence of February 2, 1996 (Merits); Inter-American Court of Human Rights, *Case of Garrido and Baigorria v. Argentina*, Judgment of August 27, 1998, (Reparations and Costs); Inter-American Court of Human Rights, Order of the Inter-American Court of Human Rights of November 17, 2004, Case of Garrido and Baigorria v. Argentina, (Monitoring Compliance with Judgment); Inter-American Court of Human Rights, Order of the Inter-American Court of Human Rights of November 27, 2007, Case of Garrido and Baigorria v. Argentina, (Monitoring Compliance with Judgment).

67. Laurence Helfer and Anne-Marie Slaughter, "Why States Create International Tribunals: A Response to Professors Posner and Yoo," *California Law Review* 93 (2005): 899–956.

68. African Union, http://www.africa-union.org/ (accessed April 17, 2012).

69. The African charter stipulates a country reporting system in Article 62. Organization of African Unity, "African (Banjul) Charter on Human and People's Rights," CAB/LEG/67/3, June 27, 1981.

70. African Commission on Human and Peoples' Rights, http://www.achpr .org/ (accessed April 17, 2012).

71. Both the state submitting the case and the accused state must have ratified the charter.

72. Malcolm D. Evans and Rachel Murray, eds., *The African Charter on Human and Peoples' Rights: The System in Practice, 1986–2000* (New York: Cambridge University Press, 2002); Organization of African Unity, "The African Charter on Human and Peoples' Rights," June 1981.

73. Frans Viljoen and Lirette Louw, "State Compliance with the Recommendations of the African Commission on Human and Peoples' Rights, 1994–2004," *American Journal of International Law* 101, no. 1 (2007): 1–34.

74. Organization of African Unity, "Protocol to the African Charter on Human and Peoples' Rights on the Establishment of an African Court on Human and Peoples' Rights," 1998; African International Courts and Tribunals, "The African Court on Human and Peoples' Rights," 1998, http://www.aict-ctia.org/ courts_conti/achpr/achpr_home.html (accessed April 17, 2012).

75. African Union, "Protocol on the Statute of the African Court of Justice and Human Rights," 2008.

76. Claiming Human Rights, "The ECOWAS Court of Justice," http://www.claiminghumanrights.org/ecowas.html (accessed April 17, 2012).

77. Socio-economic Rights and Accountability Project, "ECOWAS Court to FG: Nigerians Have a Legal Right to Education," http://www.serap-nigeria.org/cover/ecowas-court-to-fg-nigerians-have-a-legal-right-to-education/ (accessed April 17, 2012); Davidson Iriekpen, "Nigeria: ECOWAS Court—Give Every Child Free Education," *This Day*, November 30, 2010.

78. Alex Bell, "SADC Court Says Zim Government Undermining Rule of Law," *Zimbabwean*, January 14, 2011.

79. Organisation of Islamic Cooperation, Nineteenth Islamic Conference of Foreign Ministers, "The Cairo Declaration on Human Rights in Islam," August 5, 1990.

80. UN Human Rights Council, 63rd Sess.,"Report of the Human Rights Council," A/63/53, September 1, 2008.

81. Asian Human Rights Commission, "Asian Human Rights Charter—A People's Charter," May 17, 1998.

82. Asian Human Rights Commission, http://www.ahrchk.net/index.php (accessed April 17, 2012).

83. Working Group for an ASEAN Human Rights Mechanism, http://www.aseanhrmech.org/ (accessed April 17, 2012).

84. Wade Cole, "Sovereignty Relinquished? Explaining Commitment to the International Human Rights Covenants, 1966–1999," *American Sociological Review* 70 (2005): 472–95; Jay Goodliffe and Darren Hawkins, "Explaining Commitment: States and the Convention against Torture," *Journal of Politics* 68, no. 2 (2006): 358–71; Emilie M. Hafner-Burton and Kiyoteru Tsutsui, "Justice Lost! The Failure of International Human Rights Law to Matter Where Needed Most," *Journal of Peace Research* 44, no. 4 (2007): 407–42; Martin Edwards et al., "Sins of Commission? Understanding Membership Patterns on the United Nations Human Rights Commission," *Political Research Quarterly* 61, no. 3 (September 2008): 390–402; James Vreeland, "Political Institutions and Human Rights."

85. Christof Heyns and Frans Viljoen, "The Impact of the United Nations Human Rights Treaties on the Domestic Level," *Human Rights Quarterly* 23, no. 3 (2001): 483–535.

86. Andrew Moravcsik, "The Origins of Human Rights Regimes: Democratic Delegation in Postwar Europe," *International Organization* 54, no. 2 (2000): 217–52; Todd Landman, "The Political Science of Human Rights," *British Journal of Political Science* 35, no. 3 (2005): 549–72; Emilie M. Hafner-Burton, Edward Mansfield, and Jon Pevehouse, "Human Rights Institutions, Sovereignty Costs, and Democratization" (working paper 8, University of California at San Diego, 2011); Jana von Stein, "Making Promises, Keeping Promises: Democracy, Ratification, and Compliance in International Human Rights Law" (working paper, University of Michigan, 2011).

87. Landman, "The Political Science of Human Rights"; Eric Neumayer, "Qualified Ratification: Explaining Reservations to International Human Rights Treaties," *Journal of Legal Studies* 36, no. 2 (2007): 397–430; Judith Kelley, "Who Keeps International Commitments and Why? The International Criminal Court and Bilateral Nonsurrender Agreements," *American Political Science Review* 101, no. 3 (2007): 573–89; Wade Cole, "Hard and Soft Commitments

to Human Rights Treaties, 1966–2000," *Sociological Forum* 24, no. 3 (2009): 563–88.

88. Cole, "Sovereignty Relinquished?"; Goodliffe and Hawkins, "Explaining Commitment; Eric Neumayer, "Death Penalty Abolition and the Ratification of the Second Optional Protocol," *International Journal of Human Rights* 12, no. 1 (2008): 3–21; Christine Wotipka and Francisco Ramirez, "World Society and Human Rights: An Event History Analysis on the Convention on the Elimination of All Forms of Discrimination against Women," in *The Global Diffusion of Markets and Democracy*, ed. Beth Simmons, Frank Dobbin, and Geoffrey Garrett (New York: Cambridge University Press, 2008), 303–43; Christine Wotipka and Kiyoteru Tsutsui, "Global Human Rights and State Sovereignty: Nation-States' Ratifications of International Human Rights Treaties, 1965–2001," *Sociological Forum* 23, no. 4 (2008): 724–54.

89. Oona A. Hathaway, "Do Human Rights Treaties Make a Difference?" *Yale Law Journal* 111 (2002): 1935–2042. Also, Emilie M. Hafner-Burton and Kiyoteru Tsutsui as well as Heather Smith-Cannoy made similar claims, but argued that insincere participation is likely to backfire where civil society organizations are able to hold governments locally accountable for their treaty violations. Emilie M. Hafner-Burton and Kiyoteru Tsutsui, "Human Rights in a Globalizing World: The Paradox of Empty Promises," *American Journal of Sociology* 110, no. 5 (2005): 1373–141; Heather Smith-Cannoy, *Insincere Commitments: Human Rights Treaties, Abusive States, and Citizen Activism* (Washington, DC: Georgetown University Press, 2012).

90. Heyns and Viljoen, "The Impact of the United Nations Human Rights Treaties on the Domestic Level."

91. Jay Goodliffe and Darren Hawkins, "A Funny Thing Happened on the Way to Rome: Explaining International Criminal Court Negotiations," *Journal of Politics* 71, no. 3 (July 2009): 977–97; Emilie M. Hafner-Burton, *Forced to Be Good: Why Trade Agreements Boost Human Rights* (Ithaca, NY: Cornell University Press, 2009).

92. Pamela Jordan, "Does Membership Have Its Privileges?" Entrance into the Council of Europe and Compliance with Human Rights Norms," *Human Rights Quarterly* 25 (2003): 660–88.

93. United Nations, "Member States," http://www.un.org/members/list.shtml (accessed April 18, 2012).

94. European Court of Human Rights, "General Information on the Court," http://www.echr.coe.int/ECHR/EN/Header/The+Court/Introduction/Information+documents/ (accessed April 18, 2012).

95. Organization of American States, "B-32: American Convention on Human Rights, Pact of San Jose, Costa Rica."

96. African Union, "List of Countries Which Have Signed, Ratified/Acceded to the African Charter on Human and People's Rights," January 28, 2009, http://www.africa-union.org (accessed April 18, 2012).

97. African Union, "List of Countries Which Have Signed, Ratified/Acceded to the Protocol to the African Charter on Human and Peoples' Rights on the Establishment of an African Court on Human and Peoples' Rights."

98. Karen Alter, *The New Terrain of International Law: Courts, Politics, Rights* (Princeton, NJ: Princeton University Press, 2013).

99. Emilie M. Hafner-Burton, "Sticks and Stones: Naming and Shaming the Human Rights Enforcement Problem," *International Organization* 62 (Fall 2008): 689–718.

100. Harold H. Koh, "Transnational Public Law Litigation," *Yale Law Journal* 100, no. 8 (June 1991): 2347–402; Laurence Helfer and Anne-Marie Slaughter, "Toward a Theory of Effective Supranational Adjudication," *Yale Law Journal* 107, no. 2 (November 1997): 273–391; William A. Schabas, *An Introduction to the International Criminal Court* (New York: Cambridge University Press, 2001); Michael J. Gilligan, "Is Enforcement Necessary for Effectiveness? A Model of the International Criminal Regime," *International Organization* 60, no. 4 (2006): 935–67.

101. Benedetto Conforti and Francesco Francioni, eds., *Enforcing International Human Rights in Domestic Courts* (The Hague, The Netherlands: Kluwer Law International, 1997); Murray Hunt, *Using Human Rights Law in English Courts* (Oxford, England: Hart Publishing, 1997); Kathryn Sikkink, *The Justice Cascade: How Human Rights Prosecutions Are Changing World Politics* (New York: W. W. Norton and Company, 2011).

102. Tonya Putnam and Jacob Shapiro, "Do Treaties Matter to Citizens' Willingness to Punish Foreign Rights Abusers?" (working paper, Princeton University, 2009). See also Hathaway, "Do Human Rights Treaties Make a Difference?"

103. Tom R. Tyler, "Procedural Fairness and Compliance with the Law," *Swiss Journal of Economics and Statistics* 133, no. 2 (1997): 219–40; Tom R. Tyler, "Psychology and Institutional Design," *Review of Law and Economics* 4, no. 3 (2008): 801–87.

104. Martha Finnemore, *National Interests in International Society* (Ithaca, NY: Cornell University Press, 1996); Koh, "How Is International Human Rights Law Enforced?"; Andrew P. Cortell and James W. Davis Jr., "Understanding the Domestic Impact of International Norms: A Research Agenda," *International Studies Review* 2, no. 1 (2000): 65–87. For an interactional account of international law, see Jutta Brunnée and Stephen J. Toope, *Legitimacy and Legality in International Law: An Interactional Account* (New York: Cambridge University Press, 2010).

105. Tom R. Tyler and Yuen J. Huo, *Trust in the Law: Encouraging Public Cooperation with the Police and Courts* (New York: Russell Sage Foundation, 2002).

106. Margaret E. Keck and Kathryn Sikkink, *Activists beyond Borders: Advocacy Networks in International Politics* (Ithaca, NY: Cornell University Press, 1998).

107. Jon C. Pevehouse, *Democracy from Above: Regional Organizations and Democratization* (Cambridge: Cambridge University Press, 2005).

108. Abram Chayes and Antonia Handler Chayes, *New Sovereignty: Compliance with International Regulatory Agreements* (Cambridge, MA: Harvard University Press, 1995); Steven R. Ratner, "Does International Law Matter in Preventing Ethnic Conflict?" *New York University Journal of International Law and Politics* 32 (2000): 591–698.

109. Thomas Risse, "Let's Argue! Communicative Action in World Politics," *International Organization* 53, no. 1 (Winter 2000): 1–39.

110. Chayes and Handler Chayes, *New Sovereignty*; Alston, "The Purposes of Reporting"; Ryan Goodman and Derek Jinks, "How to Influence States: Socialization and International Human Rights Law," *Duke Law Journal* 54, no. 3 (2004): 622–703.

111. Philip G. Zimbardo and Micheal R. Leippe, *The Psychology of Attitude Change and Social Influence* (New York: McGraw-Hill, 1991), 127–67.

112. Martha Finnemore and Kathryn Sikkink, "International Norm Dynamics and Political Change," *International Organization* 52, no. 4 (Fall 1998): 887–917; Jeffrey T. Checkel, "Norms, Institutions, and National Identity in Contemporary Europe," *International Studies Quarterly* 43 (1999): 83–114.

113. UN Office of the High Commissioner for Human Rights, "International Law," http://www2.ohchr.org/english/law/ (accessed April 18, 2012).

114. John W. Meyer and Brian Rowan, "Institutionalized Organizations: Formal Structure and Myth and Ceremony," *American Journal of Sociology* 83, no. 2 (1977): 340–63; Walter W. Powell and Paul J. DiMaggio, eds., *The New Institutionalism in Organizational Analysis* (Chicago: University of Chicago Press, 1991); Chayes and Handler Chayes, *New Sovereignty*; Thomas M. Franck, *Fairness in International Law and Institutions* (Oxford: Oxford University Press, 1995); Harold H. Koh, "Why Do Nations Obey International Law?" *Yale Law Journal* 106, no. 8 (1997): 2599–659; Goodman and Jinks, "How to Influence States: Socialization and International Human Rights Law."

115. Zimbardo and Leippe, *The Psychology of Attitude Change and Social Influence*.

## Chapter 5. Scholarly Perspectives

1. James Lebovic and Erik Voeten, "The Politics of Shame: The Condemnation of Country Human Rights Practices in the UNCHR," *International Studies Quarterly* 50, no. 4 (2006): 861–88. Their study covers the period 1977–2001, during which sixty-one countries were formally reproached.

2. Wade M. Cole, "Individuals v. States: An Analysis of Human Rights Committee Rulings, 1979–2007" (working paper, Montana State University, 2011).

3. Erik Voeten, "The Politics of International Judicial Appointments: Evidence from the European Court of Human Rights," *International Organization* 61 (2007): 669–701. His data cover votes on 709 issues with thirty-eight states by ninety-seven judges between 1960 and 2006.

4. For example, partisan affiliation affects US Supreme Court justices' decision making. See Melinda Gann Hall and Paul Brace, "Justices' Responses to Case Facts: An Interactive Model, *American Politics Quarterly* 24, no. 2 (1996): 236–61. See also Daniel R. Pinello, "Linking Party to Judicial Ideology in American Courts: A Meta-Analysis," *Justice System Journal* 20, no. 3 (1999): 219–54.

5. Sources include human rights NGOs, Amnesty International, and Freedom House as well as the US Department of State's Bureau of Democracy, Human Rights, and Labor. See chapter 1 for a fuller description.

6. Oona A. Hathaway, "Do Human Rights Treaties Make a Difference?" *Yale Law Journal* 111 (2002): 1935–2042. Other international human rights treaties, including the UN Convention against Torture and Other Cruel, Inhuman, or Degrading Treatment or Punishment, do not seem to have much relationship to

human rights protection in the most democratic countries. Beth A. Simmons, *Mobilizing for Human Rights: International Law in Domestic Politics* (New York: Cambridge University Press, 2009).

7. Eric Neumayer, "Do International Human Rights Treaties Improve Respect for Human Rights?" *Journal of Conflict Resolution* 49, no. 6 (2005): 925–53. Neumayer finds that in nondemocratic states, ratification alone actually corresponds to an increase in civil and political rights abuses.

8. Hathaway, "Do Human Rights Treaties Make a Difference?"

9. Tonya Putnam and Jacob Shapiro, "Do Treaties Matter to Citizens' Willingness to Punish Foreign Rights Abusers?" (working paper, Princeton University, 2009).

10. Todd Landman, *Protecting Human Rights: A Comparative Study* (Washington, DC: Georgetown University Press, 2005), 147.

11. Simmons, *Mobilizing for Human Rights*. See also Emilie M. Hafner-Burton and Kiyoteru Tsutsui, "Human Rights in a Globalizing World: The Paradox of Empty Promises," *American Journal of Sociology* 110, no. 5 (2005): 1373–411; Neumayer, "Do International Human Rights Treaties Improve Respect for Human Rights?"; Heather Smith-Cannoy, *Insincere Commitments: Human Rights Treaties, Abusive States, and Citizen Activism.* (Washington, DC: Georgetown University Press, 2012).

12. Linda Camp Keith, "The United Nations International Covenant on Civil and Political Rights: Does It Make a Difference in Human Rights Behavior?" *Journal of Peace Research* 36, no. 1 (1999): 95–118. She studied 178 countries from 1976 to 1993.

13. Emilie M. Hafner-Burton and Kiyoteru Tsutsui, "Justice Lost! The Failure of International Human Rights Law to Matter Where Needed Most," *Journal of Peace Research* 44, no. 4 (2007): 407–25.

14. Sources include human rights NGOs, Amnesty International, and Freedom House as well as the US Department of State's Bureau of Democracy, Human Rights, and Labor.

15. There are older data on violations of civil and political rights, which explains why those portions of this figure show a longer "time since ratification."

16. Hathaway, "Do Human Rights Treaties Make a Difference?" For a critique, see Ryan Goodman and Derek Jinks, "Measuring the Effects of Human Rights Treaties," *European Journal of International Law* 14, no. 1 (2003): 171–83.

17. Hafner-Burton and Tsutsui, "Justice Lost!"; Simmons, *Mobilizing for Human Rights*; James R. Vreeland, "Political Institutions and Human Rights: Why Dictatorships Enter into the United Nations Convention against Torture," *International Organization* 62, no. 1 (2008): 65–101.

18. Hathaway, "Do Human Rights Treaties Make a Difference?"; Hafner-Burton and Tsutsui, "Human Rights in a Globalizing World"; Vreeland, "Political Institutions and Human Rights"; Michael J. Gilligan and Nathaniel H. Nesbitt, "Do Norms Reduce Torture?" *Journal of Legal Studies* 38 (2009): 445–70.

19. Neumayer, "Do International Human Rights Treaties Improve Respect for Human Rights?"

20. Emilie M. Hafner-Burton, Laurence R. Helfer, and Christopher J. Fariss, "Emergency and Escape: Explaining Derogations from Human Rights Treaties," *International Organization* 65 (2011): 673–707.

21. Eric Neumayer, "Do Governments Mean Business When They Derogate? Human Rights Violations during Notified States of Emergency," *Review of International Organizations* (2012): 1–31.

22. Hafner-Burton and Tsutsui, "Justice Lost!"

23. Freedom House, "Worst of the Worst 2011: The World's Most Repressive Societies," http://www.freedomhouse.org/sites/default/files/WorstOfTheWorst 2011.pdf (accessed April 19, 2012).

24. Emilia J. Powell and Jeffrey K. Staton, "Domestic Judicial Institutions and Human Rights Treaty Violation," *International Studies Quarterly* 53, no. 1 (2009): 149–74.

25. Beth Stephens, "Translating Filártiga: A Comparative and International Law Analysis of Domestic Remedies for International Human Rights Violations," *Yale Journal of International Law* 27 (2002): 2–57; Kathryn Sikkink and Carrie Booth Walling, "The Impact of Human Rights Trials in Latin America," *Journal of Peace Research* 44, no. 4 (2007): 427–45.

26. Powell and Staton, "Domestic Judicial Institutions and Human Rights Treaty Violation."

27. Courtenay Conrad and Jacqueline H. R. DeMeritt, "Human Rights Advocacy and State Repression Substitutability" (APSA annual meeting paper, 2011). See also Courtenay Conrad and Emily H. Ritter, "Tenure, Treaties, and Torture: The Conflicting Domestic Effects of International Law," *Journal of Politics* (2012).

28. Michael Byers, "The Law and Politics of the Pinochet Case," *Duke Journal of Comparative and International Law* 10, no. 2 (Spring–Summer 2000): 415–41; Darren Hawkins, *International Human Rights and Authoritarian Rule in Chile* (Lincoln: University of Nebraska Press, 2002); Cesare P. R. Romano and André Nollkaemper, "The Arrest Warrant against the Liberian President, Charles Taylor," ASIL Insights, June 2003, American Society of International Law, http://www.asil.org/insigh110.cfm (accessed April 20, 2012); "Sierra Leone Trial: 80 Years Urged for Charles Taylor," BBC, May 3, 2012.

29. Michael Gilligan, "Is Enforcement Necessary for Effectiveness? A Model of the International Criminal Regime," *International Organization* 60, no. 4 (2006): 935–67; Karen Alter, *The New Terrain of International Law: Courts, Politics, Rights* (Princeton, NJ: Princeton University Press, 2013).

30. Judith Kelley, "Who Keeps International Commitments and Why? The International Criminal Court and Bilateral Nonsurrender Agreements," *American Political Science Review* 101, no. 3 (2007): 573–89.

31. Beth Simmons and Allison Danner, "Credible Commitments and the International Criminal Court," *International Organization* 64, no. 2 (2010): 225–56; Terrence Chapman and Stephen Chaudoin, "Ratification Patterns and the Limits of the International Criminal Court," *International Studies Quarterly* (2012).

32. Laurence R. Helfer and Erik Voeten, "Do European Court of Human Rights Judgments Promote Legal and Policy Change?" (working paper, Duke Law, 2011).

33. Courtney Hillebrecht, "The European Court of Human Rights, Domestic Politics, and the Ties That Bind: Explaining Compliance with International Human Rights Tribunals" (paper presented at International Studies Association annual meeting, New Orleans, 2010).

34. Darren Hawkins and Wade Jacoby, "Partial Compliance: A Comparison of the European and Inter-American Courts of Human Rights," *Journal of International Law and International Relations* 6, no. 1 (2010): 35–85.

35. Fernando Basch et al., "The Effectiveness of the Inter-American System of Human Rights Protection: A Quantitative Approach to Its Functioning and Compliance with Its Decisions," *Sur International Journal of Human Rights* 7, no. 12 (2010): 9–37; Hawkins and Jacoby, "Partial Compliance"; Jeffrey Staton and Alexia Romero, "Clarity and Compliance in the Inter-American Human Rights System" (paper presented at the International Political Science Association meeting, São Paolo, 2011).

36. Robert E. Robertson, "Measuring State Compliance with the Obligation to Devote the 'Maximum Available Resources' to Realizing Economic, Social, and Cultural Rights," *Human Rights Quarterly* 16, no. 4 (November 1994): 693–714.

37. Alicia Ely Yamin, "The Future in the Mirror: Incorporating Strategies for the Defense and Promotion of Economic, Social, and Cultural Rights into the Mainstream Human Rights Agenda," *Human Rights Quarterly* 27, no. 4 (2005): 1200–44; Raj C. Kumar, "National Human Rights Institutions and Economic, Social, and Cultural Rights: Toward the Institutionalization and Developmentalization of Human Rights," *Human Rights Quarterly* 28, no. 3 (August 2006): 755–79.

38. Mashood Baderin and Robert McCorquodale, eds., *Economic, Social, and Cultural Rights in Action* (Oxford: Oxford University Press, 2007); Malcolm Langford, ed., *Social Rights and Jurisprudence: Emerging Trends in Comparative and International Law* (New York: Cambridge University Press, 2008); Mark S. Kende, *Constitutional Rights in Two Worlds: South Africa and the United States* (New York: Cambridge University Press, 2009); ESCR-Net, "Caselaw Database," http://www.escr-net.org/caselaw/ (accessed April 20, 2012); Malcolm Langford, *Making It Stick: Compliance with Social Rights Judgments in Comparative Perspective* (forthcoming).

39. *Sentencia: SU-039/97*, "Derechos Fundamentales de Comunidad Indigena," http://www.corteconstitucional.gov.co/relatoria/1997/SU039-97.htm.

40. ESCR-Net, "Caselaw: Defensor del Pueblo, doctor Jaime Córdoba Triviño (en representación de varias personas integrantes del Grupo Etnico Indígena U'wa) c/ Ministerio del Medio Ambiente y Occidental de Colombia, Inc. s. Acción de tutela, Summary," http://www.escr-net.org/caselaw/caselaw_show.htm?doc_id=409667 (accessed April 20, 2012).

41. "Occidental Petroleum Abandons Oil Development on U'wa Land," *Environmental News Service*, May 3, 2002.

42. Yamin, "The Future in the Mirror."

43. Scott Burris, Ichiro Kawachi, and Austin Sarat, "Integrating Law and Social Epidemiology," *Journal of Law, Medicine, and Ethics* 30, no. 4 (December 2002): 510–21.

44. Leo Beletsky, Grace E. Macalino, and Scott Burris, "Attitudes of Police Officers towards Syringe Access, Occupational Needle-Sticks, and Drug Use: A Qualitative Study of One City Police Department in the United States," *In-*

*ternational Journal of Drug Policy* 16 (2005): 267–74; Leo Beletsky, Lauretta E. Grau, Edward White, Sarah Bowman, and Robert Heimer, "The Roles of Law, Client Race, and Program Visibility in Shaping Police Interference with the Operation of U.S. Syringe Exchange Programs," *Addiction* 106, no. 2 (2010): 357–65.

45. Lisa L. Martin, *Coercive Cooperation: Explaining Multilateral Economic Sanctions* (Princeton, NJ: Princeton University Press, 1992); Jonathan Mercer, *Reputation and International Politics* (Ithaca, NY: Cornell University Press, 1996).

46. Leonard J. Schoppa, "The Social Context in Coercive International Bargaining," *International Organization* 53 (1999): 307–42.

47. Laurence Helfer and Anne-Marie Slaughter, "Toward a Theory of Effective Supranational Adjudication," *Yale Law Journal* 107, no. 2 (November 1997): 273–391.

48. Kathryn Sikkink, *The Justice Cascade: How Human Rights Prosecutions Are Changing the World* (New York: W. W. Norton and Company, 2011).

49. Yonatan Lupu, "Best Evidence: The Role of Information in Domestic Judicial Enforcement of International Human Rights Agreements," *International Organization* (forthcoming 2013).

50. Steven Greer, *The European Convention on Human Rights: Achievements, Problems, and Prospects* (New York: Cambridge University Press, 2006).

51. Harold H. Koh, "How Is International Human Rights Law Enforced?" *Indiana Law Journal* 74, no. 4 (1999): 1409.

52. For exceptions, see Sikkink, *The Justice Cascade;* Simmons, *Mobilizing for Human Rights.*

53. Mark Fathi Massoud, "Do Victims of War Need International Law? Human Rights Education Programs in Authoritarian Sudan," *Law and Society Review* 45, no. 1 (2011): 1–32.

54. Emilie M. Hafner-Burton and James Ron, "Seeing Double: Human Rights Impact through Qualitative and Quantitative Eyes," *World Politics* 61, no. 2 (April 2009): 360–401; Emilie M. Hafner-Burton, "International Human Rights Regimes," *Annual Review of Political Science* 15 (2012): 265–86.

55. Hafner-Burton and Ron, "Seeing Double."

56. David L. Cingranelli and David L. Richards, "The Cingranelli-Richards (CIRI) Human Rights Dataset," 2010, http://www.humanrightsdata.org (accessed April 20, 2012); Susan Hyde and Nikolay Marinov, "Which Elections Can Be Lost?" August 4, 2011, http://hyde.research.yale.edu/nelda/Hyde_Marinov_NELDA.pdf (accessed April 20, 2012).

57. Keith E. Schnakenber and Christopher J. Fariss, "A Dynamic Ordinal Item Response Theory Model with Application to Human Rights Data" (working paper, University of California at San Diego, 2011).

58. Hafner-Burton, "International Human Rights Regimes."

59. Daniel Ho et al., "Matching as Nonparametric Preprocessing for Reducing Model Dependence in Parametric Causal Inference," *Political Analysis* 15, no. 3 (Summer 2007): 199–236; Kosuke Imai, Gary King, and Elizabeth Stuart, "Misunderstandings among Experimentalists and Observationalists about Causal

Inference," *Journal of the Royal Statistical Society*, series A171, part 2 (2008): 481–502.

## Chapter 6. Practitioner Perspectives

1. Christof Heyns and Frans Viljoen, "The Impact of the United Nations Human Rights Treaties on the Domestic Level," *Human Rights Quarterly* 23, no. 3 (August 2001): 483–535; Christof Heyns and Frans Viljoen, *The Impact of the United Nations Human Rights Treaties on the Domestic Level* (The Hague: Kluwer Law International, 2002).

2. In Africa, the researchers studied Egypt, Senegal, South Africa, and Zambia. In Asia, they studied India, Iran, Japan, and the Philippines. In eastern Europe, they studied the Czech Republic, Estonia, Romania, and Russia. In Latin America and the Caribbean, they studied Brazil, Colombia, Jamaica, and Mexico. Finally, in western Europe and other regions, they studied Australia, Canada, Finland, and Spain.

3. Heyns and Viljoen, "The Impact of the United Nations Human Rights Treaties on the Domestic Level," 485.

4. Martin Scheinin, "Domestic Implications of International Human Rights Treaties: Nordic and Baltic Experiences," in *The Future of UN Human Rights Treaty Monitoring*, ed. Philip Alston and James Crawford (New York: Cambridge University Press, 2000), 229–44.

5. John Dugard, "The Role of Human Rights Treaty Standards in Domestic Law: The Southern African Experience," in *The Future of UN Human Rights Treaty Monitoring*, ed. Philip Alston and James Crawford (New York: Cambridge University Press, 2000), 269–86

6. Yogesh Tyagi, *The UN Human Rights Committee: Practice and Procedure* (New York: Cambridge University Press, 2011).

7. Heyns and Viljoen, *The Impact of the United Nations Human Rights Treaties on the Domestic Level*; UNICEF, *Protecting the World's Children: Impact of the Convention on the Rights of the Child in Diverse Legal Systems* (Cambridge: Cambridge University Press, 2007).

8. On regional treaties, see Steven Greer, *The European Convention on Human Rights: Achievements, Problems, and Prospects* (New York: Cambridge University Press, 2006). For a discussion of the influence of foreign law on the US Supreme Court, see Justice Ruth Bader Ginsburg's comments in Adam Liptak, "Ginsburg Shares Views on Influence of Foreign Law on Her Court, and Vice Versa," *New York Times*, April 11, 2009. For an example of how international law has been applied in Canadian courts, see Tanya Basok and Emily Carasco, "Advancing the Rights of Non-citizens in Canada: A Human Rights Approach to Migrant Rights," *Human Rights Quarterly* 32, no. 2 (2010): 342–66.

9. Heyns and Viljoen, "The Impact of the United Nations Human Rights Treaties on the Domestic Level," 502.

10. *Baker v. Canada*, 2 S.C.R. 817, 1999; Elisabeth Eid, "Interaction between International and Domestic Human Rights Law: A Canadian Perspective" (paper presented at the International Centre for Criminal Law Reform and Criminal Justice Policy, October 2001).

11. James L. Cavallaro and Stephanie Erin Brewer, "Reevaluating Regional Human Rights Litigation in the Twenty-First Century: The Case of the Inter-American Court," *American Journal of International Law* 102, no. 4 (2008): 768–827.

12. Heyns and Viljoen, *The Impact of the United Nations Human Rights Treaties on the Domestic Level*.

13. Greer, *The European Convention on Human Rights*, 319.

14. Heyns and Viljoen, *The Impact of the United Nations Human Rights Treaties on the Domestic Level*.

15. Scheinin, "Domestic Implications of International Human Rights Treaties."

16. Tyagi, *The UN Human Rights Committee*. See also Center for Civil and Political Rights, "Latest NGO Reports on Follow-up to the Concluding Observations," http://www.ccprcentre.org/en/ngomenu-ngo-follow-up-reports (accessed April 21, 2012).

17. Andrew Clapham, "UN Human Rights Reporting Procedures: An NGO Perspective," in *The Future of UN Human Rights Treaty Monitoring*, ed. Philip Alston and James Crawford (New York: Cambridge University Press, 2000), 175–98.

18. Clapham, "UN Human Rights Reporting Procedures."

19. Though prisoners were released, not all had their charges annulled or were compensated for their ordeal. Amnesty International, "Government Persists in Retaining Unfair Trial Procedures," AMR 46/25/96, 1996.

20. Philip Alston, "Beyond 'Them' and 'Us': Putting Treaty Body Reform into Perspective," in *The Future of UN Human Rights Treaty Monitoring*, ed. Philip Alston and James Crawford (New York: Cambridge University Press, 2000), 507.

21. For an alternative view on overlapping requirements, see Laurence R. Helfer, "Forum Shopping for Human Rights," *University of Pennsylvania Law Review* 148 (1999): 285–400.

22. Heyns and Viljoen, "The Impact of the United Nations Human Rights Treaties on the Domestic Level," 489.

23. UN General Assembly, International Law Commission, 58th Sess., "Fragmentation of International Law: Difficulties Arising from the Diversification and Expansion of International Law, Report of the Study Group of the International Law Commission, Finalized by Martti Koskenniemi," A/CN.4/L.682, April 13, 2006; House of Lords, House of Commons, Joint Committee on Human Rights, 32nd Report, "Building a Human Rights Culture," November 7, 2006; "Human Rights Being Trampled Because of Ignorance: MNA," *Dawn.com*, January 10, 2012, http://www.dawn.com/2012/01/11/human-rights-being-trampled-because-of-ignorance-mna.html (accessed April 21, 2012).

24. Human Rights Resource Center, University of Minnesota, "The Human Rights Education Handbook: Effective Practices for Learning, Action, and Change," 2000.

25. UN Committee on the Rights of the Child, "Initial Reports of States Parties Due in 1992: Uganda," CRC/C/3/Add.40, June 17, 1996.

26. Chris Maina Peter, "Accessing Justice by All Means: Individual Communications before UN Treaty Bodies—A Case Study of CERD," in *New Challenges*

*for the UN Human Rights Machinery*, ed. Mahmoud Cherif Bassiouni and William A. Schabas (Cambridge, UK: Intersentia, 2011), 130.

27. Amrei Müller and Frauke Seidensticker, *The Role of National Human Rights Institutions in the United Nations Treaty Body Process* (Berlin: German Institute of Human Rights, December 2007).

28. In the Heyns and Viljoen study, Supreme Court judges in one Jamaican human rights case dealing with the legal system did not even have copies of the relevant treaties.

29. In Iran, the only treaty that people were aware of in the Heyns and Viljoen study was the treaty protecting children. The treaty protecting economic, social, and cultural rights in particular was hardly known in many places, including India, Japan, Mexico, and the Philippines. By and large, knowledge of other treaties, such as the treaty outlawing torture, was largely confined to the small number of people directly responsible for their implementation.

30. On discrimination against minorities, see Maina Peter, "Accessing Justice by All Means," 123–36.

31. Heyns and Viljoen, *The Impact of the United Nations Human Rights Treaties on the Domestic Level.*

32. Anne F. Bayefsky, "First Report of the International Law Association's Committee on International Human Rights Law and Practice" (paper presented to the Helsinki Conference, August 11–17, 1996); Alston, "Beyond 'Them' and 'Us.'

33. UN General Assembly, 3rd Sess., "217 A (III). Universal Declaration of Human Rights," A/RES/3/217A, December 10, 1948.

34. Abram Chayes and Antonia Handler Chayes, "On Compliance," *International Organization* 47, no. 2 (Spring 1993): 175–205; Thomas Risse and Stephen C. Ropp, "International Human Rights Norms and Domestic Change: Conclusions," in *The Power of Human Rights: International Norms and Domestic Change*, ed. Thomas Risse, Stephen C. Ropp, and Kathryn Sikkink (New York: Cambridge University Press, 1999); Ryan Goodman and Derek Jinks, "Measuring the Effects of Human Rights Treaties," *European Journal of International Law* 14, no. 1 (2003): 171–83.

35. Tom R. Tyler, "Psychological Perspectives on Legitimacy and Legitimation," *Annual Review of Psychology* 57, no. 1 (2006): 375–400.

36. Membership as of April 21, 2012. UN General Assembly, 21st Sess., Agenda Item 62, "Resolution 2200 (XXI). International Covenant on Economic, Social, and Cultural Rights, International Covenant on Civil and Political Rights and Optional Protocol to the International Covenant on Civil and Political Rights," A/RES/21/2200, December 16, 1966.

37. UN General Assembly, 21st Sess., Agenda Item 62, "Resolution 2200 (XXI). International Covenant on Economic, Social, and Cultural Rights, International Covenant on Civil and Political Rights, and Optional Protocol to the International Covenant on Civil and Political Rights."

38. David Axe, "Water and Wood Shortages Worsen," *IPS News*, June 27, 2008; "In Brief: Chad under Water," *IRIN*, August 27, 2010.

39. Center for Economic and Social Rights, Social Justice through Human Rights, "Iraq," http://www.cesr.org/section.php?id=23 (accessed April 21, 2012).

40. Dogu Ergil, "The Kurdish Question in Turkey," *Journal of Democracy* 11, no. 3 (July 2000): 122–35.

41. These countries are classified here as those that received a one or lower on the CIRI scale of protections against torture. For the scale and its description, see CIRI Human Rights Data Project, http://ciri.binghamton.edu/ (accessed April 21, 2012).

42. Ivan Shearer, "UN Enforcement of Human Rights: Making It More Effective," in Ralph Wilde et al., *"United Nations Reform through Practice: Report of the International Law Association Study Group on United Nations Reform,"* December 11, 2011, 23.

43. Council of Europe, "Protocol No. 11 to the Convention for the Protection of Human Rights and Fundamental Freedoms, Restructuring the Control Machinery Established Thereby," Strasbourg, 11.V.1994; Greer, *The European Convention on Human Rights*.

44. European Court of Human Rights, "Annual Report 2007," Registry of the European Court of Human Rights Strasbourg, 2008.

45. Dinah Shelton, "The Boundaries of Human Rights Jurisdiction in Europe," *Duke Journal of Comparative and International Law* 13 (2003): 95–153.

46. Organization of American States, Inter-American Commission on Human Rights, "B-32: American Convention on Human Rights 'Pact of San Jose, Costa Rica,' General Information of the Treaty," November 22, 1969, http://www.oas .org/juridico/english/sigs/b-32.html (accessed April 21, 2012).

47. Fernando Basch et al., "The Effectiveness of the Inter-American System of Human Rights Protection: A Quantitative Approach to Its Functioning and Compliance with Its Decisions," *Sur International Journal on Human Rights* 7. no. 2 (June 2010): 9, 18–21.

48. Darren Hawkins and Wade Jacoby, "Partial Compliance: A Comparison of the European and Inter-American Courts of Human Rights," *Journal of International Law and International Relations* 6, no. 1 (2010): 35–85. For further information, see chapter 5.

49. There currently are thirty African states subject to the tribunals in the Economic Community of West African States and the South African Development Community—the Community Court of Justice and the South African Development Community's Community Tribunal, respectively, which have the authority to render decisions on some human rights issues. For further information, see chapter 4.

50. Anne F. Bayefsky, "Implementing Human Rights Treaties: The Prognosis after Vienna," *Proceedings of the Annual Meeting of the American Society of International Law* 88 (April 1994): 435.

51. Klaus Hüfner, *How to File Complaints on Human Rights Violations: A Manual for Individuals and NGOs* (Bonn: German Commission for UNESCO, 2005).

52. UN General Assembly, 59th Sess., Agenda Items 45 and 55, "In Larger Freedom: Towards Development, Security, and Human Rights for All, Report of the Secretary-general, Addendum, Letter Dated 26 May 2005 from the Secretary-general to the President of the General Assembly," A/59/2005/Add.3, May 26, 2005; Human Rights Law Center, Expert Workshop on Reform of UN Human Rights

Treaty Monitoring Bodies, Senate Chamber, University of Nottingham, February 11–12, 2006.

53. Markus Schmidt, "Servicing and Financing Human Rights Supervisory Bodies," in *The Future of UN Human Rights Treaty Monitoring*, ed. Philip Alston and James Crawford (New York: Cambridge University Press, 2000), 481–98; Tyagi, *The UN Human Rights Committee.*

54. Elizabeth Evatt, "Ensuring Effective Supervisory Procedures: The Need for Resources," in *The Future of UN Human Rights Treaty Monitoring*, ed. Philip Alston and James Crawford (New York: Cambridge University Press, 2000), 461–79.

55. Clapham, "UN Human Rights Reporting Procedures; Gerison Lansdown, "The Reporting Process under the Convention on the Rights of the Child," in *The Future of UN Human Rights Treaty Monitoring*, ed. Philip Alston and James Crawford (New York: Cambridge University Press, 2000), 113–28.

56. Evatt, "Ensuring Effective Supervisory Procedures," 461–62.

57. Greer, *The European Convention on Human Rights*, 318.

58. Council of Europe, "Fact Sheet: Protocol 14, the Reform of the European Court of Human Rights," May 2010, http://www.echr.coe.int/NR/rdon lyres/57211BCC . . . /0/CPProtocole14EN.pdf (accessed April 21, 2012).

59. Rolv Ryssdal, "The Coming of Age of the European Convention on Human Rights," *European Human Rights Law Review* (1996): 22.

60. Cavallaro and Brewer, "Reevaluating Regional Human Rights Litigation in the Twenty-First Century," 781.

61. Jo M. Pasqualucci, *The Practice and Procedure of the Inter-American Court of Human Rights* (New York: Cambridge University Press, 2003).

62. Inter-American Court of Human Rights, "Informe a la Comisión de Asuntos Jurídicos y Políticos del Consejo Permanente de la Organizacíon de los Estados Americanos (OEA) en el Marco del Diálogo Sobre el Sistema Interamericano de Protección de los Derechos Humanos 32 (March 16, 2000)," quoted in Cavallaro and Brewer, "Reevaluating Regional Human Rights Litigation in the Twenty-First Century," 783.

63. Inter-American Court of Human Rights, "2006 Annual Report of the Inter-American Court of Human Rights," 2006.

64. Cavallaro and Brewer, "Reevaluating Regional Human Rights Litigation in the Twenty-First Century."

65. Scott Leckie, "The Committee on Economic, Social, and Cultural Rights: Catalyst for Change in a System Needing Reform," in *The Future of UN Human Rights Treaty Monitoring*, ed. Philip Alston and James Crawford (New York: Cambridge University Press, 2000), 129–44.

66. Clapham, "UN Human Rights Reporting Procedures," 175.

67. Tyagi, *The UN Human Rights Committee*, 633.

68. Anne Gallagher, "Making Human Rights Treaty Obligations a Reality: Working with New Actors and Partners," in *The Future of UN Human Rights Treaty Monitoring*, ed. Philip Alston and James Crawford (New York: Cambridge University Press, 2000), 225–26.

69. UN General Assembly, "Interim Report on Updated Study by Mr. Philip Alston on United Nations Human Rights Treaty Bodies."

70. UN General Assembly, 44th Sess., Agenda Item 109, "Effective Implementation of International Instruments on Human Rights, including Reporting Obligations under International Instruments on Human Rights, Note by Secretary-general," A/44/668, November 8, 1989.

71. Evatt, "Ensuring Effective Supervisory Procedures," 461–79.

72. The freedom of association, for example, appears in the UN Convention on the Rights of the Child, the International Convention on the Protection of the Rights of All Migrant Workers and Members of Their Families, and in several International Labor Organization (ILO) treaties. UN General Assembly, "Interim Report on Updated Study by Mr. Philip Alston on United Nations Human Rights Treaty Bodies."

73. Leckie, "The Committee on Economic, Social and Cultural Rights," 129–44; Henry J. Steiner, "Individual Claims in a World of Massive Violations: What Role for the Human Rights Committee," in *The Future of UN Human Rights Treaty Monitoring*, ed. Philip Alston and James Crawford (New York: Cambridge University Press, 2000), 15–53; Heyns and Viljoen, "The Impact of the United Nations Human Rights Treaties on the Domestic Level."

74. Felice D. Gaer, "Implementing Treaty Body Recommendations: Establishing Better Follow-up Procedures," in *New Challenges for the UN Human Rights Machinery*, ed. Mahmoud Cherif Bassiouni and William A. Schabas (Cambridge, UK: Intersentia, 2011), 112.

75. Heyns and Viljoen, *The Impact of the United Nations Human Rights Treaties on the Domestic Level*.

76. UN Economic and Social Council, 59th Sess., Item 18 of the Provisional Agenda, "Effective Functioning of the Human Rights Mechanism Treaty Bodies, Note by the OHCHR," E/CN.4/2003/126, February 26, 2003.

77. Penny Parker, "The State of the UN Human Rights Treaty Body System: An NGO Perspective," Minnesota Advocates for Human Rights, June 20, 2007.

78. Tyagi, *The UN Human Rights Committee*.

79. Penny Parker, "Minnesota Advocates for Human Rights Report: The State of the UN Human Rights Treaty Body System," June 20, 2007.

80. Leckie, "The Committee on Economic, Social, and Cultural Rights," 129–44.

81. Heyns and Viljoen, *The Impact of the United Nations Human Rights Treaties on the Domestic Level*.

82. Clapham, "UN Human Rights Reporting Procedures."

83. Bayefsky, "First Report of the International Law Association's Committee on International Human Rights Law and Practice."

84. Olivier de Frouville, "Building a Universal System for the Protection of Human Rights: The Way Forward," in *New Challenges for the UN Human Rights Machinery*, ed. Mahmoud Cherif Bassiouni and William A. Schabas (Cambridge, UK: Intersentia, 2011), 250–53.

85. Leckie, "The Committee on Economic, Social, and Cultural Rights," 131.

86. UN Economic and Social Council, 53rd Sess., Agenda Item 15, "Final Report of the Independent Expert on Enhancing the Long-term Effectiveness of the UN Human Rights Treaty System, by the Independent Expert, Mr. Philip Alston," E/CN.4/1997/74, March 27, 1996.

87. Bayefsky, "First Report of the International Law Association's Committee on International Human Rights Law and Practice"; Roland Bank, "International Efforts to Combat Torture and Inhuman Treatment: Have the New Mechanisms Improved Protection?" *European Journal of International Law* 8 (1997): 613–37; Leckie, "The Committee on Economic, Social, and Cultural Rights," 129–44; Anne F. Bayefsky, *The UN Human Rights Treaty System: Universality at the Crossroads* (Ardskley, NY: Transnational Publishers, 2001).

88. Gallagher, "Making Human Rights Treaty Obligations a Reality."

89. Human Rights Law Center, "Expert Workshop on Reform of United Nations Human Rights Treaty Monitoring Bodies."

90. UN Economic and Social Council, 53rd Sess., Agenda Item 15, "Final Report of the Independent Expert on Enhancing the Long-term Effectiveness of the UN Human Rights Treaty System, by the Independent Expert, Mr. Philip Alston," E/CN.4/1997/74, March 27, 1996.

91. Roland Bank, "Country-Oriented Procedures under the Convention against Torture: Towards a New Dynamism," in *The Future of UN Human Rights Treaty Monitoring*, ed. Philip Alston and James Crawford (New York: Cambridge University Press, 2000), 145–74.

92. Heyns and Viljoen, "The Impact of the United Nations Human Rights Treaties on the Domestic Level"; UN Economic and Social Council, 53rd Sess., Agenda Item 15, "Final Report of the Independent Expert on Enhancing the Long-term Effectiveness of the UN Human Rights Treaty System, by the Independent Expert, Mr. Philip Alston," E/CN.4/1997/74, March 27, 1996, 35.

93. Heyns and Viljoen, *The Impact of the United Nations Human Rights Treaties on the Domestic Level.*

94. Steiner, "Individual Claims in a World of Massive Violations," 15–53.

95. UN Human Rights Committee, 87th Sess., "Consideration of Reports Submitted by State Parties under Article 40 of the Covenant, Concluding Observations of the Human Rights Committee, United States of America," CCPR/C/USA/CO/3/Rev.1, December 18, 2006; Mark Tran, "UN Human Rights Council Urges U.S. to End Death Penalty," *Guardian*, November 5, 2010.

96. Heyns and Viljoen, "The Impact of the United Nations Human Rights Treaties on the Domestic Level."

97. Council of Europe, Commissioner for Human Rights, "Follow-up Report on the Hellenic Republic (2002–2005): Assessment of the Progress Made in Implementing the Recommendations of the Council of Europe Commissioner for Human Rights," CommDH(2006)13, March 29, 2006.

98. Inter-American Commission on Human Rights, http://www.cidh.oas.org/publi.eng.htm (accessed April 23, 2012).

99. Author's calculation based on resolutions available online. OAS General Assembly, "Declarations and Resolutions," http://www.oas.org/consejo/GENERAL%20ASSEMBLY/Resoluciones-Declaraciones.asp (accessed April 23, 2012).

100. African Commission on Human and People's Rights, "Status on Submission of State/Initial Periodic Reports to the African Commission," http://old.achpr.org/english/_info/statereport_considered_en.html (accessed April 23, 2012).

101. African Commission on Human and People's Rights, "Chapter Five: Fifth Annual Activity Report of the African Commission, 1991–1992."

102. African Commission on Human and People's Rights, "Status on Submission of State/Initial Periodic Reports to the African Commission."

103. Rachel Murray, "Report on the 1998 Sessions of the African Commission on Human and Peoples' Rights," *Human Rights Law Journal* 21, no. 374 (2000): 374–98.

104. Rachidatou Illa Maikassoua, African Commission of Human and People's Rights, "The Implementation of the African Charter on Human and Peoples' Rights by the States Parties," October 2011, 6.

105. Bayefsky, "First Report of the International Law Association's Committee on International Human Rights Law and Practice"; Bayefsky, *The UN Human Rights Treaty System.*

106. Office of the High Commissioner for Human Rights, "Human Rights Bodies: Complaints Procedures," http://www2.ohchr.org/english/bodies/petitions/index.htm#interstate (accessed April 23, 2012).

107. On the "keystone," see Levi Ruffinelli (Paraguay), Third Committee Records (1966), mtg. 1420, para. 45, quoted in Tyagi, *The UN Human Rights Committee,* 382. On the "crux," see Paolini (France), Third Committee Records (1966), mtg. 1420, para. 37, quoted in Tyagi, *The UN Human Rights Committee,* 382. On the "best," see O'Leary (Ireland), Third Committee Records (1966), mtg. 1420, mtg. 1427, para. 2, quoted in Tyagi, *The UN Human Rights Committee.*

108. Article 45 of the American Convention on Human Rights provides that only states that have accepted the competence of the inter-American commission are eligible to place or defend interstate complaints. For example, see Organization of American States, Inter-American Commission on Human Rights, Report No. 11/07, Interstate Case 01/06, Nicaragua v. Costa Rica, March 8, 2007. On Africa, see African Commission on Human and People's Rights, "Communication 227/99: D. R. Congo/Burundi, Rwanda and Uganda."

109. Tyagi, *The UN Human Rights Committee.*

110. Inter-American Court of Human Rights, "Rules of Procedure of the Inter-American Court of Human Rights," 2009, http://www.corteidh.or.cr/reglamento/regla_ing.pdf (accessed April 23, 2012).

111. The Human Rights Committee may consider individual communications if the accused state has ratified the First Optional Protocol to the International Covenant on Civil and Political Rights. The Committee on the Elimination of All Forms of Discrimination against Women may consider individual communications if the accused state has ratified the Optional Protocol. The Committee against Torture may consider individual communications if the accused state has made the necessary declaration under Article 22 of the treaty. The Committee on the Elimination of All Forms of Racial Discrimination may consider individual communications if the accused state has made the necessary declaration under Article 14. UN Office of the High Commissioner for Human Rights, "Human Rights Bodies: Complaints Procedures," http://www2.ohchr.org/english/bodies/petitions/index.htm (accessed April 23, 2012). A new Optional Protocol to the International Covenant on Economic, Social, and Cultural Rights allowing the committee to receive and consider individual complaints is open for signature. UN General Assembly, 63rd Sess., Agenda Item 58, "63/117 Optional Protocol to the International Covenant on Economic, Social, and Cultural Rights," A/RES/63/117, March 5, 2009.

112. Tyagi, *The UN Human Rights Committee.*

113. Parker, "Minnesota Advocates for Human Rights Report."

114. Heyns and Viljoen, "The Impact of the United Nations Human Rights Treaties on the Domestic Level."

115. Mark Fathi Massoud, "Do Victims of War Need International Law? Human Rights Education Programs in Authoritarian Sudan," *Law and Society Review* 45, no. 1 (2011): 1–32.

116. Heyns and Viljoen, *The Impact of the United Nations Human Rights Treaties on the Domestic Level.*

117. Tyagi, *The UN Human Rights Committee.*

118. Laurence R. Helfer, "Redesigning the European Court of Human Rights: Embeddedness as a Deep Structural Principle of the European Human Rights Regime," *European Journal of International Law* 19 (2008): 125.

119. Owen Bowcott, "UK Courts Following European Human Rights Rulings too Strictly, Warn Judges," *Guardian*, November 15, 2011.

120. Michael Pinto-Duschinsky, *Bringing Rights Back Home: Making Human Rights Compatible with Parliamentary Democracy in the UK* (London: Policy Exchange, 2011).

121. Greer, *The European Convention on Human Rights.*

122. Jamil Ddamulira Mujuzi, "Michelot Yogogombaye v. the Republic of Senegal: The African Court's First Decision," *Human Rights Law Review* 10, no. 2 (2010): 372–81.

123. Frans Viljoen and Lirette Louw, "State Compliance with the Recommendations of the African Commission on Human and Peoples' Rights, 1994–2004," *American Journal of International Law* 101, no. 1 (2007): 1–34.

124. Christof Heyns, "The African Regional Human Rights System: In Need of Reform?" *African Human Rights Law Journal* 1, no. 2 (2001): 155–74.

125. Eric Tistounet, "The Problem of Overlapping among Different Treaty Bodies," in *The Future of UN Human Rights Treaty Monitoring*, ed. Philip Alston and James Crawford (New York: Cambridge University Press, 2000), 383–401.

126. Rachael Lorna Johnstone, "Streamlining the Constructive Dialogue: Efficiency from States' Perspective," in *New Challenges for the UN Human Rights Machinery*, ed. Mahmoud Cherif Bassiouni and William A. Schabas (Cambridge, UK: Intersentia, 2011), 59–93.

127. Helfer, "Forum Shopping for Human Rights."

128. Tistounet, "The Problem of Overlapping among Different Treaty Bodies."

129. Tistounet, "The Problem of Overlapping among Different Treaty Bodies."

130. Laurence R. Helfer, "Overlegalizing Human Rights: International Relations Theory and the Commonwealth Caribbean Backlash against Human Rights Regimes," *Columbia Law Review* 102 (2002): 1832–911.

131. Mahmoud Cherif Bassiouni, "A Critical Introduction Assessment of the UN Human Rights Mechanisms," in *New Challenges for the UN Human Rights Machinery*, ed. Mahmoud Cherif Bassiouni and William A. Schabas (Cambridge, UK: Intersentia, 2011), 3.

132. Bassiouni, "A Critical Introduction Assessment of the UN Human Rights Mechanisms," 3.

133. UN Press Release, "Human Rights Committee Concludes Sixty-Fourth Session: Committee Adopts Recommendations on Reports of Iceland, Belgium, Armenia, the Libyan Arab Jamahiriya, Japan, and Austria," HR/CT/98/46, November 6, 1998.

134. Tyagi, *The UN Human Rights Committee*, 623. See also Murat Metin Hakki, "The Silver Anniversary of the UN Human Rights Committee: Anything to Celebrate?" *International Journal of Human Rights* 6, no. 3 (2002): 85–102.

135. The UN Committee against Torture has the most elaborate visit procedures. Article 9 of the Convention on the Prevention and Punishment of the Crime of Genocide gave the *International Court of Justice* jurisdiction over disputes.

136. Steiner, "Individual Claims in a World of Massive Violations," 37.

137. Wilde et al., "United Nations Reform through Practice."

138. Julian Ku and Jide Nzelibe, "Do International Criminal Tribunals Deter or Exacerbate Humanitarian Atrocities?" *Washington University Law Quarterly* 84 (2007): 1–49.

139. Renee Doplick, "Bassiouni 'Quite Doubtful' International Criminal Court Will Succeed: The Failures, Challenges, and Future of International Criminal Law," March 31, 2010, http://www.insidejustice.com/law/index.php/intl/2010/03/31/cherif_bassiouni_international_criminal (accessed April 24, 2012).

140. ICC Assembly of State Parties, 8th Sess., "Proposed Programme Budget for 2010 of the International Criminal Court," ICC-ASP/8/10, July 30, 2009.

141. Eric Posner and John C. Yoo, "Judicial Independence in International Tribunals," *California Law Review* 93, no. 1 (2005): 1–74. For an alternative view, see Laurence Helfer and Anne-Marie Slaughter, "Toward a Theory of Effective Supranational Adjudication," *Yale Law Journal* 107 (1997): 273–392.

142. Hawkins and Jacoby, "Partial Compliance."

143. Viljoen and Louw, "State Compliance with the Recommendations of the African Commission on Human and Peoples' Rights, 1994–2004."

144. Cavallaro and Brewer, "Reevaluating Regional Human Rights Litigation in the Twenty-First Century," 770. See also chapter 5.

145. Georg Ress, "The Effect of Decisions and Judgments of the European Court of Human Rights in the Domestic Legal Order," *Texas International Law Journal* 40, no. 3 (2005): 359–82.

146. Greer, *The European Convention on Human Rights*.

147. Martin Krygier and Adam Czarnota, eds., *The Rule of Law after Communism* (Dartmouth, UK: Aldershot, 1999); Peter Ulram and Fritz Plasser, "Political Culture in East-Central and Eastern Europe: Empirical Findings, 1990–2001," in *Political Culture in Post–Communist Europe: Attitudes in New Democracies*, ed. Detlef Pollack et al. (Burlington, VT: Ashgate Publishing Company, 2003), 31–46; Herman Schwartz, *The Struggle for Constitutional Justice in Post–Communist Europe* (Chicago: University of Chicago Press, 2000).

148. Greer, *The European Convention on Human Rights*.

149. Neil Hicks, "Legislative Reform in Turkey and European Human Rights Mechanisms," *Human Rights Review* 2 (2001): 83. Hicks also explains that Turkey has made progress on human rights—especially on legislation—since its military coup in 1980.

2

38 • Notes to Chapter 7

50. Lionel N. Brown and John Bell, *French Administrative Law*, 5th ed. (Oxford: Oxford University Press, 1998); Greer, *The European Convention on Human Rights*.

151. Hawkins and Jacoby, "Partial Compliance"; Helfer and Slaughter, "Toward a Theory of Effective Supranational Adjudication"; Rolv Ryssdal, "The Enforcement System Set Up under the European Convention on Human Rights," in *Compliance with Judgments of International Courts*, ed. Mielle K. Bulterman and Martin Kuijer (Leiden, The Netherlands: Martinus Nijhoff Publishers, 1997), 49–70; Cavallaro and Brewer, "Reevaluating Regional Human Rights Litigation in the Twenty-First Century," 787.

152. Victor Peskin, *International Justice in Rwanda and the Balkans* (New York: Cambridge University Press, 2008).

153. Xinyuan Dai, *International Institutions and National Policies* (New York: Cambridge University Press, 2007).

154. UN General Assembly, World Conference on Human Rights, "Report of the Regional Meeting for Asia of the World Conference on Human Rights," A/CONF.157/ASRM/8 A/CONF.157/PC/59, April 7, 1993, para. 8.

155. Joanne R. Bauer and Daniel A. Bell, eds., *The East Asian Challenge for Human Rights* (New York: Cambridge University Press, 1999), 3–23.

156. Sally Engle Merry, "Human Rights Law and the Demonization of Culture (and Anthropology along the Way)," *Polar: Political and Legal Anthropology Review* 26, no. 1 (2003): 24–25.

157. Sally Engle Merry, "Tensions between Global Law and Local Social Justice: CEDAW and the Problem of Rape in Fiji" (paper presented at Justice across Cultures Conference, Hassenfeld Conference Center, Brandeis University, March 2004).

158. Heyns and Viljoen, "The Impact of the United Nations Human Rights Treaties on the Domestic Level"; Makau Wa Mutua, "Savages, Victims, and Saviors: The Metaphors of Human Rights," *Harvard International Law Journal* 42, no. 1 (2001): 201–46; Antony Anghie, *Imperialism, Sovereignty and the Making of International Law* (Cambridge: Cambridge University Press, 2005).

## Chapter 7. System Reform
1. Philip Alston, ed., *The United Nations and Human Rights: A Critical Appraisal* (Oxford: Clarendon, 1992); Philip Alston and James Crawford, eds., *The Future of Human Rights Treaty Monitoring* (New York: Cambridge University Press, 2000); Anne F. Bayefsky, ed., *The UN Human Rights Treaty System in the 21st Century* (The Hague: Kluwer Law International, 2001); Andrew Hudson, "Dangerous Potential: Streamlining the United Nations Human Rights Committees," *Australian Journal of Human Rights* 15 (2002): 55–78; International Commission of Jurists, "Reforming the Human Rights System: A Chance for the UN to Fulfill Its Promise," 2005. On the European Union, see Steven Greer, *The European Convention on Human Rights: Achievements, Problems, and Prospects* (New York: Cambridge University Press, 2006); Laurence R. Helfer, "Redesigning the European Court of Human Rights: Embeddedness as a Deep Structural Principle of the European Human Rights Regime," *European Journal of International Law* 19 (2008): 125–59.

2. UN Office of the High Commissioner for Human Rights, "Dublin Statement on the Process of Strengthening the United Nations Human Rights Treaty Body System: Response by Non-governmental Organizations," November 2010; UN Office of the High Commissioner for Human Rights, "The Marrakech Statement on Strengthening the Relationship between NHRIs and the Human Rights Treaty Bodies System," June 10, 2010; UN Office of the High Commissioner for Human Rights, "The Poznan Statement on the Reforms of the United Nations Human Rights Treaty Body System" (paper presented at the International Seminar of Experts on the Reforms of the UN Human Rights Treaty Body System, Poznan, September 28–29, 2010); UN Office of the High Commissioner for Human Rights, "Seoul Statement on Strengthening the UN Human Rights Treaty Body System" (paper presented at the Civil Society Consultation on Treaty Body Strengthening, National Human Rights Commission of Korea and the Korea Foundation, Seoul, April 19–20, 2011).

3. UN Office of the High Commissioner for Human Rights, "Promoting Knowledge of the Treaty Body System, Strengthening the United Nations Human Rights Treaty Body System" (paper presented at the Dublin II Meeting, November 10–11, 2011), 9.

4. Greer, *The European Convention on Human Rights*; Commission on Legal Empowerment of the Poor and United Nations Development Programme, *Making the Law Work for Everyone, Volume 1* (New York: UN Development Programme, 2008).

5. Gary Haugen and Victor Boutros, "And Justice for All: Enforcing Human Rights for the World's Poor," *Foreign Affairs* (May–June 2010): 51–62.

6. Jessica I. Yeh, "Promoting Human Rights in China through Education: An Empirical Impact Evaluation of the Swedish Approach from a Student Perspective," *Asian-Pacific Law and Policy Journal* 10, no. 1 (2008): 114–67; Human Rights House Network, Belarus in Exile: Vilnius, "Electronic Human Rights Education for Lawyers," http://humanrightshouse.org/Members/Belarus/About_HRH_Belarus/Projects/ILIA/EHREL/index.html (accessed April 24, 2012).

7. UN Office of the High Commissioner for Human Rights, "The Treaty-Strengthening Process: Pretoria Statement on the Strengthening and Reform of the UN Human Rights Treaty System," June 20–21, 2011; Anne F. Bayefsky, *The UN Human Rights Treaty System: Universality at the Crossroads* (Ardsley, NY: Transnational Publishers, 2001); UN Office of the High Commissioner for Human Rights, "Report of the Informal Technical Consultation for States Parties on Treaty-Body Strengthening," Sion, Switzerland, May 12–13, 2011.

8. UN Economic and Social Council, 53rd Sess., Agenda Item 15, "Final Report of the Independent Expert on Enhancing the Long-term Effectiveness of the UN Human Rights Treaty System, by the Independent Expert, Mr. Philip Alston," E/CN.4/1997/74, March 27, 1997.

9. UN General Assembly, 44th Sess., Agenda Item 109, "Effective Implementation of International Instruments on Human Rights, including Reporting Obligations under International Instruments on Human Rights, Note by Secretary-general," A/44/668, November 8, 1989; UN General Assembly, "Interim Report on Updated Study by Mr. Philip Alston on United Nations Human Rights Treaty Bodies," A/CONF.157/PC/62/Add.11/Rev.1, April 22, 1993.

10. Anne F. Bayefsky, "Making the Human Rights Treaties Work," in *Human Rights: An Agenda for the Next Century*, ed. Louis Henkin and John Lawrence Hargrove (Washington, DC: American Society for International Law, 1994).

11. UN Office of the High Commissioner for Human Rights, "Seoul Statement on Strengthening the UN Human Rights Treaty Body System."

12. UN Economic and Social Council, 53rd Sess., Agenda Item 15, "Final Report of the Independent Expert on Enhancing the Long-term Effectiveness of the UN Human Rights Treaty System, by the Independent Expert, Mr. Philip Alston," para. 47.

13. US Department of State, "Human Rights Reports." For an analysis, see Steven Poe et al., "How Are These Pictures Different: Assessing the Biases in the U.S. State Department's Country Reports on Human Rights Practices," *Human Rights Quarterly* 23 (2001): 650–77.

14. For a critical view, see María Gabriela Egas, "The State Department's Human Rights Assessment: Only a U.S. Perspective," Council on Hemispheric Affairs, April 16, 2010.

15. US Department of State, "U.S. Treaty Reports," http://www.state.gov/j/drl/hr/treaties/index.htm (accessed April 24, 2012).

16. UK Foreign and Commonwealth Office, *Human Rights and Democracy: The 2010 FCO Report* (London: Crown Copyright, 2012).

17. Amnesty International, *Annual Report 2011* (London: Amnesty International Publications, 2011).

18. Freedom House, http://www.freedomhouse.org/ (accessed April 24, 2012).

19. Emilie M. Hafner-Burton, "Sticks and Stones: Naming and Shaming the Human Rights Enforcement Problem," *International Organization* 62 (October 2008): 689–716; James C. Franklin, "Shame on You: The Impact of Human Rights Criticism on Political Repression in Latin America," *International Studies Quarterly* 52 (2008): 187–211.

20. Anne F. Bayefsky, "First Report of the International Law Association's Committee on International Human Rights Law and Practice" (paper presented to the Helsinki Conference, August 11–17, 1996).

21. Penny Parker, "Minnesota Advocates for Human Rights Report: The State of the UN Human Rights Treaty Body System," June 20, 2007.

22. UN General Assembly, "Interim Report on Updated Study by Mr. Philip Alston on United Nations Human Rights Treaty Bodies."

23. UN General Assembly, Report of the Secretary-general, 59th Sess., Agenda Items 45 and 55, "In Larger Freedom: Towards Development, Security, and Human Rights for All, Report of the Secretary-general, Addendum," A/59/2005/Add.3, May 26, 2005, 23.

24. Thomas Buergenthal, "A Court and Two Consolidated Treaty Bodies," in *The UN Human Rights Treaty System in the 21st Century*, ed. Anne F. Bayefsky (The Hague: Kluwer Law International, 2000), 299–302; Rachael Lorna Johnstone, "Cynical Savings or Reasonable Reform? Reflections on a Single Unified UN Human Rights Treaty Body," *Human Rights Law Review* 7, no. 1 (2007): 173–200.

25. Nico Schrijver, "Paving the Way Towards . . . One Worldwide Human Rights Treaty!" *Netherlands Quarterly of Human Rights* 29, no. 3 (2011): 257–60.

26. UN Economic and Social Council, Commission on Human Rights, 52nd Sess., Item 9, "Further Promotion and Encouragement of Human Rights and Fundamental Freedoms, including the Question of the Programme and Methods of Work of the Commission on Human Rights, Alternative Approaches, and Ways and Means within the United Nations System for Improving the Effective Enjoyment of Human Rights and Fundamental Freedoms, National Institutions for the Promotion and Protection of Human Rights, Written Statement," E/CN.4/1996/53, February 5, 1996; UN International Human Rights Instruments, Fifth Inter-committee Meeting of the Human Rights Bodies, Eighteenth Meeting of Chairpersons of the Human Rights Treaty Bodies, "Concept Paper on the High Commissioner's Proposal for a Unified Standing Treaty Body," HRI/MC/2006/2, March 22, 2006.

27. Asian Center for Human Rights, "Report of the Asian Center for Human Rights: Strengthening the UN Treaty Bodies," June 16, 2004.

28. UN Economic and Social Council, 53rd Sess., Agenda Item 15, "Final Report of the Independent Expert on Enhancing the Long-term Effectiveness of the UN Human Rights Treaty System, by the Independent Expert, Mr. Philip Alston"; UN Economic and Social Council, 60th Sess., Item 18 of the Provisional Agenda, Note by the UN Office of the High Commissioner for Human Rights, "Effective Functioning of the Human Rights Mechanisms Treaty Bodies," E/CN.4/2004/98, February 26, 2004.

29. Ralph Wilde et al., "United Nations Reform through Practice: Report of the International Law Association Study Group on United Nations Reform," December 11, 2011, http://ssrn.com/abstract=1971008 (accessed April 25, 2012).

30. Human Rights Law Center, "Expert Workshop on Reform of United Nations Human Rights Treaty Monitoring Bodies," Senate Chamber, University of Nottingham, February 11–12, 2006. See also James Crawford, "The Human Rights Treaty System: A System in Crisis?" in *The Future of Human Rights Treaty Monitoring*, ed. Philip Alston and James Crawford (New York: Cambridge University Press, 2000), 1–14; Amnesty International, "United Nations: Proposals to Strengthen the Human Rights Treaty Bodies," September 2003.

31. Françoise J. Hampson, "An Overview of the Reform of the UN Human Rights Machinery," *Human Rights Law Review* 7, no. 1 (2007): 7–27.

32. Markus Schmidt, "Servicing and Financing Human Rights Supervisory Bodies," in *The Future of UN Human Rights Treaty Monitoring*, ed. Philip Alston and James Crawford (New York: Cambridge University Press, 2000), 481–500.

33. Thomas Buergenthal, "The Human Rights Committee," in *The United Nations and Human Rights: A Critical Appraisal, 2nd Edition*, ed. Philip Alston (Oxford: Oxford University Press, 1999).

34. Schmidt, "Servicing and Financing Human Rights Supervisory Bodies," 481–500.

35. Roland Bank, "Country-Oriented Procedures under the Convention against Torture: Towards a New Dynamism," in *The Future of UN Human Rights Treaty Monitoring*, ed. Philip Alston and James Crawford (New York: Cambridge University Press 2000), 145–74.

36. UN Office of the High Commissioner for Human Rights, "The Treaty Strengthening Process."

37. Andrew Clapham, "UN Human Rights Reporting Procedures: An NGO Perspective," in *The Future of UN Human Rights Treaty Monitoring*, ed. Philip Alston and James Crawford (New York: Cambridge University Press), 175–200.

38. Roland Bank, "International Efforts to Combat Torture and Inhuman Treatment: Have the New Mechanisms Improved Protection?" *European Journal of International Law* (1997): 613–37; Anne Gallagher, "Making Human Rights Treaty Obligations a Reality: Working with New Actors and Partners," in *The Future of UN Human Rights Treaty Monitoring*, ed. Philip Alston and James Crawford (New York: Cambridge University Press, 2000), 201–28.

39. UN Office of the High Commissioner for Human Rights, "Annual Meeting of Chairpersons of Human Rights Treaty Bodies and Inter-committee Meeting," http://www2.ohchr.org/english/bodies/icm-mc/index.htm (accessed April 25, 2012).

40. Elizabeth Evatt, "Ensuring Effective Supervisory Procedures: The Need for Resources," in *The Future of UN Human Rights Treaty Monitoring*, ed. Philip Alston and James Crawford, (New York: Cambridge University Press, 2000), 461–80; Scott Leckie, "The Committee on Economic, Social, and Cultural Rights: Catalyst for Change in a System Needing Reform," in *The Future of UN Human Rights Treaty Monitoring*, ed. Philip Alston and James Crawford, (New York: Cambridge University Press, 2000), 129–44.

41. Yogesh Tyagi, *The UN Human Rights Committee: Practice and Procedure* (New York: Cambridge University Press, 2011).

42. UN Office of the High Commissioner for Human Rights, "The Treaty Strengthening Process."

43. UN Office of the High Commissioner for Human Rights, "Marrakech Statement on Strengthening the Relationship between NHRIs and the Human Rights Treaty Body System," June 10, 2010.

44. UN General Assembly, Sixty-Fifth General Assembly Plenary, 76th Meeting, "General Assembly Suspends Libya from Human Rights Council," GA/11050, March 1, 2011.

45. UN General Assembly, 60th Sess., Agenda Items 46 and 120, "Resolution Adopted by the General Assembly," A/RES/60/251, April 3, 2006.

46. Human Rights Watch, "UN Human Rights Council: Competitive Vote Would Improve Membership," May 13, 2010.

47. Matthew Saltmarsh, "A Bloated U.N. Bureaucracy Causes Bewilderment," *New York Times*, January 5, 2011; Stefan Halper, "A Miasma of Corruption: The United Nations at 50," Cato Institute, Cato Policy Analysis No. 253, April 30, 1996.

48. Evatt, "Ensuring Effective Supervisory Procedures," 461–62.

49. Tyagi, *The UN Human Rights Committee*.

50. UN General Assembly, Human Rights Committee, 101st Sess., "Human Rights Committee Adopts Reports of Special Rapporteurs for Follow-up on Concluding Observations, Individual Communications," HR/CT/736, March 30, 2011.

51. UN Office of the High Commissioner for Human Rights, "Annual Meeting of Chairpersons of the Human Rights Treaty Bodies and the Inter-committee Meeting"; UN General Assembly, 58th Sess., Item 60 of Provisional Agenda,

"Status of Implementation of Actions Described in the Report of the Secretary-general Entitled 'Strengthening of the United Nations: An Agenda for Further Change,'" A/58/351, September 5, 2003; UN Office of the High Commissioner for Human Rights, "Search by Translation," http://www.ohchr.org/EN/UDHR/Pages/SearchByLang.aspx (accessed April 25, 2012).

52. House of Commons Library, "Protocol 11 and the New European Court of Human Rights," Research Paper 98/109, December 4, 1998.

53. Andrew Drzemczewski, "The European Human Rights Convention: Protocol No. 11 Entry Into Force and First Year of Application," Instituto de Investigaciones Juridicas; Philip Leach, "On Reform of the European Court of Human Rights," *European Human Rights Law Review* 6 (2009): 725–35.

54. Greer, *The European Convention on Human Rights*.

55. Steven Greer, "Reforming the European Convention on Human Rights: Towards Protocol 14," *Public Law* (1993): 663–73; Council of Europe, Steering Committee for Human Rights, "Interim Activity Report: Guaranteeing the Long-term Effectiveness of the European Court of Human Rights—Implementation of the Declaration Adopted by the Committee of Ministers at Its 112th Session," May 14–15, 2003; Council of Europe, Steering Committee for Human Rights, "Addendum II: Final Activity Report on the Protection of Human Rights during Armed Conflict as well as during Internal Disturbances and Tensions," CDDH(2003)026, November 26, 2003.

56. Council of Europe, "Fact Sheet, Protocol 14: The Reform of the European Court of Human Rights," May 15, 2010, 4, http://www.echr.coe.int/NR/rdonlyres/57211BCC . . . /0/CPProtocole14EN.pdf (accessed April 25, 2012).

57. Council of Europe, "Interlaken Process, Follow-up of the High-Level Conference on the Future of the European Court of Human Rights," http://www.coe.int/t/dghl/monitoring/execution/themes/interlaken/index_EN.asp (accessed April 25, 2012).

58. James L. Cavallaro and Stephanie Erin Brewer, "Reevaluating Regional Human Rights Litigation in the Twenty-First Century: The Case of the Inter-American Court," *American Journal of International Law* 102, no. 4 (2008): 768–827.

59. Center for Justice and International Law, "The Inter-American Court and Inter-American Commission Reform Their Rules of Procedure," December 18, 2009.

60. Nsongurua J. Udombana, "An African Human Rights Court and an African Union Court: A Needful Duality or a Needless Duplication?" *Brooklyn Journal of International Law* 28, no. 3 (2003): 811–70.

61. Assembly of the African Union, 5th Ordinary Sess., "Decision on the Merger of the African Court on Human and Peoples Rights and the Court of Justice of the African Union," Assembly/Au/6 (V), Assembly/Au/Dec.83 (V), July 4–5, 2005.

62. African Union, 42nd Ordinary Sess., "Interim Rules of the African Commission on Human and People's Rights," November 2008.

63. Simon M. Weldehaimanot, "Towards Speedy Trials: Reforming the Practice of Adjudicating Cases in the African Human Rights System," *University for Peace Law Review* 1, no. 14 (2010): 14–39.

64. Crawford, "The UN Human Rights Treaty System," 6.

65. Evatt, "Ensuring Effective Supervisory Procedures," 471, 474.

66. Cavallaro and Brewer, "Reevaluating Regional Human Rights Litigation in the Twenty-First Century."

67. UN International Human Rights Instruments, Nineteenth Meeting of the Chairpersons of the Human Rights Bodies, "Report of the Working Group on the Harmonization of Working Methods of Treaty Bodies," HRI/MC/2007/2, January 9, 2007. On the legal and procedural challenges to creating a unified body, see Michael Bowman, "Towards a Unified Treaty Body of Monitoring Compliance with UN Human Rights Conventions? Legal Mechanisms for Treaty Reform," *Human Rights Law Review* 7, no. 1 (2007): 225–49.

68. Hudson, "Dangerous Potential: Streamlining the United Nations Human Rights Committees;" Michael O'Flaherty and Claire O'Brien, "Reform of UN Human Rights Treaty Monitoring Bodies: A Critique of the Concept Paper on the High Commissioner's Proposal for a Unified Standing Treaty Body," *Human Rights Law Review* 7, no. 1 (2007): 141–72; UN International Human Rights Instruments, Nineteenth Meeting of the Chairpersons of the Human Rights Bodies, "Report of the Working Group on the Harmonization of Working Methods of Treaty Bodies."

69. Hampson, "An Overview of the Reform of the UN Human Rights Machinery," 12.

70. Tyagi, *The UN Human Rights Committee.*

71. UN Economic and Social Council, 53rd Sess., Agenda Item 15, "Final Report of the Independent Expert on Enhancing the Long-term Effectiveness of the UN Human Rights Treaty System, by the Independent Expert, Mr. Philip Alston."

72. Bayefsky, "First Report of the International Law Association's Committee on International Human Rights Law and Practice"; UN Economic and Social Council, "Report of the Secretary-general on the Consultations Conducted in Respect of the Report of the Independent Expert on Enhancing the Long-term Effectiveness of the United Nations Human Rights Treaty System," Addendum, E/CN.4/2000/98/Add.1, March 9, 2000.

73. Anti-Defamation League, "Israel at the UN: Progress amid a History of Bias," http://www.adl.org/international/Israel_un_human.asp?m_flipmode=8 (accessed April 25, 2012); UN Human Rights Council, 13th Sess., Agenda Item 7, "Resolution Adopted by the Human Rights Council, Human Rights in the Occupied Syrian Golan," A/HRC/RES/13/5, April 16, 2010; UN General Assembly, Human Rights Council, 3rd Special Sess., "Human Rights Violations Emanating from Israeli Military Incursions in the Occupied Palestinian Territory, including the Recent One in Northern Gaza and the Assault on Beit Hanoun," A/HRC/S-3/L.1, November 14, 2006; UN General Assembly, Human Rights Council, 13th Sess., Agenda Item 7, "The Grave Human Rights Violations by Israel in the Occupied Palestinian Territory, including East Jerusalem," A/HRC/13/L.29, March 19, 2010.

74. Lauren Vriens, "Troubles Plague UN's Human Rights Council," Council on Foreign Relations, May 13, 2009; Linda Mamoun, "A Conversation with Richard Falk," *Nation*, June 30, 2008.

75. Hampson, "An Overview of the Reform of the UN Human Rights Machinery," 10, 27.

76. Leckie, "The Committee on Economic, Social, and Cultural Rights," 130.

77. Christof Heyns and Frans Viljoen, "The Impact of the United Nations Human Rights Treaties on the Domestic Level," *Human Rights Quarterly* 23, no. 3 (2001): 483–535.

78. Josefine Volqvartz, "ICC under Fire for Uganda Probe," CNN, February 23, 2005, http://articles.cnn.com/2005-02-23/world/uganda.volqvartz_1_icc-ugan dan-government-peace-talks?_s=PM:WORLD (accessed April 25, 2012).

79. Helfer, "Redesigning the European Court of Human Rights."

80. Michael Ignatieff, "We're So Exceptional," *New York Review of Books*, April 5, 2012.

## Part III. A Stewardship Strategy

1. Michael Edwards and David Hulme, *Non-governmental Organizations—Performance and Accountability: Beyond the Magic Bullet* (London: Earthscan, 1996); Margaret E. Keck and Kathryn A. Sikkink, *Activists beyond Borders: Advocacy Networks in International Politics* (Ithaca, NY: Cornell University Press, 1998); Alison Brysk, *From Tribal Village to Global* (Stanford, CA: Stanford University Press, 2000); Claude E. Welch Jr., ed., *NGOs and Human Rights: Promise and Performance* (Philadelphia: University of Pennsylvania Press, 2000); Clifford Bob, *The Marketing of Rebellion: Insurgents, Media, and International Activism* (Cambridge: Cambridge University Press, 2005); Stephen Hopgood, *Keepers of the Flame: Understanding Amnesty International* (Ithaca, NY: Cornell University Press, 2006); Lisa Jordan and Peter Van Tuijl, *NGO Accountability: Politics, Principles, and Innovations* (London: Earthscan, 2006); Scott Calnan, *The Effectiveness of Domestic Human Rights NGOs* (Leiden, The Netherlands: Martinus Nijhoff, 2008); Daniel P. L. Chong, *Freedom from Poverty: NGOs and Human Rights Praxis* (Philadelphia: University of Pennsylvania Press, 2010); James Ron, *Spreading the Word: Rights-Based Organizations in the Global South* (unpublished manuscript, 2012).

## Chapter 8. The Status Quo

1. Alison Brysk, *Global Good Samaritans: Human Rights as Foreign Policy* (Oxford: Oxford University Press, 2009), 3. Her focus is on global middle-power stewards.

2. David Kennedy, *The Dark Sides of Virtue: Reassessing International Humanitarianism* (Princeton, NJ: Princeton University Press, 2004).

3. Human Rights Education Associates, "Crimes of War—Educator's Guide: Humanitarian Intervention," http://www.hrea.org/index.php?base_id=132#_ftn8 (accessed April 25, 2012).

4. Alex de Waal, "No Such Thing as Humanitarian Intervention," *Harvard International Review*, March 21, 2007.

5. John R. Bolton, "Wrong Turn in Somalia," *Foreign Affairs* 73, no. 1 (January–February 1994): 56–66; Chester A. Crocker, "The Lessons of Somalia: Not Everything Went Wrong," *Foreign Affairs* 74, no. 3 (May–June 1995): 2–8;

Walter Clarke and Jeffrey Herbst, "Somalia and the Future of Humanitarian Intervention," *Foreign Affairs* 75, no. 2 (March–April 1996): 70–85.

6. Virginia Page Fortna, *Does Peacekeeping Work? Shaping Belligerents' Choices after War* (Princeton, NJ: Princeton University Press, 2008).

7. Stephen J. Stedman, "The New Interventionists," *Foreign Affairs* 72, no. 1 (1992–93): 1–16.

8. Samantha Power, "Rwanda: 'Mostly in a Listening Mode,' " in *A Problem from Hell: America and the Age of Genocide* (New York: Basic Books, 2002), 241.

9. Michael Ignatieff, "The Seductiveness of Moral Disgust," *Social Research* 62, no. 1 (1995): 77–97.

10. Alan J. Kuperman, *The Limits of Humanitarian Intervention: Genocide in Rwanda* (Washington, DC: Brookings Institution Press, 2001); Fiona Terry, *Condemned to Repeat? The Paradox of Humanitarian Intervention* (Ithaca, NY: Cornell University Press, 2002); Timothy W. Crawford, *Pivotal Deterrence: Third-party Statecraft and the Pursuit of Peace* (Ithaca, NY: Cornell University Press, 2003); Robert W. Rauchhaus, "Principal-Agent Problems in Humanitarian Intervention: Moral Hazards, Adverse Selection, and the Commitment Dilemma," *International Studies Quarterly* 53, no. 4 (December 2009): 871–84.

11. Timothy W. Crawford and Alan J. Kuperman, eds., *Gambling on Humanitarian Intervention: Moral Hazard, Rebellion, and Civil War* (New York: Routledge, 2006); Alan J. Kuperman, "The Moral Hazard of Humanitarian Intervention: Lessons from the Balkans," *International Studies Quarterly* 52, no. 1 (April 2008): 49–80.

12. Dugi Gorani, quoted in Allan Little, "Moral Combat: NATO at War," BBC2, March 12, 2000, http://news.bbc.co.uk/hi/english/static/events/panorama/transcripts/transcript_12_03_00.txt (accessed April 25, 2012).

13. Independent International Commission on Kosovo, *The Kosovo Report: Conflict, International Response, Lessons Learned* (Oxford: Oxford University Press, 2000). For an analysis of intervention in the former Yugoslavia, see Michael Mandelbaum, "A Perfect Failure: NATO's War against Yugoslavia," *Foreign Affairs* 78, no. 5 (September–October 1999): 2-8; Javier Solana, "NATO's Success in Kosovo," *Foreign Affairs* 78, no. 6 (November–December 1999): 114–20; James B. Steinberg, "A Perfect Polemic: Blind to Reality on Kosovo," *Foreign Affairs* 78, no. 6 (November–December 1999): 128–33.

14. Jide Nzelibe, "Courting Genocide: The Unintended Effects of Humanitarian Intervention," *California Law Review* 97 (August 2009): 1173.

15. Alison De Forges, *Leave None to Tell the Story: Genocide in Rwanda* (New York: Human Rights Watch, March 1999); Power, "Rwanda."

16. Scott Straus, "Darfur and the Genocide Debate," *Foreign Affairs* 84, no. 1 (January–February 2005): 123–33; Alex de Waal, "Why Darfur Intervention is a Mistake," BBC, May 21, 2008.

17. Human Rights Watch, *Human Rights in Guatemala during President De Leon Carpio's First Year* (New York: Human Rights Watch, 1994); Dexter Boniface, "Is There a Democratic Norm in the Americas? An Analysis of the Organization of American States," *Global Governance* 8 (2002): 365–81.

18. Gary C. Hufbauer et al., *Economic Sanctions Reconsidered*, 3rd ed. (Washington, DC: Peterson Institute for International Economics, 2007).

19. The US Trade Act of 1984 introduced a number of conditions to receive US GSP benefits, including prohibitions against aiding and abetting terrorists as well as requirements to provide or take steps toward providing for internationally recognized workers' rights. Stephen L. Lande, *Trade and Tariff Act of 1984: Trade Policy in the Reagan Administration* (Lexington, MA: Lexington Books, 1986).

20. "Out, Out: Guatemala," *Economist*, June 5, 1993; Maxwell A. Cameron, "Latin American Autogolpes: Dangerous Undertows in the Third Wave of Democratisation," *Third World Quarterly* 19, no. 2 (1998): 219–39.

21. Tracy Wilkinson, "Guatemalan Leader Tightens Grip, Muzzles Press: Latin America, Troops Block Newspapers. Serrano Refuses to Back Down from Seizure of Absolute Power despite Opposition," *Los Angeles Times*, May 27, 1993.

22. Human Rights Watch, *Human Rights in Guatemala during President De Leon Carpio's First Year*.

23. Seth G. Jones, *The Rise of European Security Cooperation* (New York: Cambridge University Press, 2007).

24. US Labor Education in the Americas Project, "Worker Rights under the New Guatemalan Government," August 12, 2008; US Department of State, "1999 Country Reports on Human Rights Practices: Guatemala," February 23, 2000; Human Rights Watch, "Americas, Guatemala," in *Human Rights Watch World Report 2002* (New York: Human Rights Watch, 2002).

25. US Department of State, "2001 Country Reports on Human Rights Practices: Guatemala," March 4, 2002.

26. Ratification of the convention was incorporated into GSP eligibility requirements under the US Trade and Development Act of 2000. International Labor Organization, "Ratifications of the Fundamental Human Rights Conventions by Country," http://www.ilo.org/ilolex/english/docs/declworld.htm (accessed May 1, 2012); Office of the US Trade Representative, *African Growth and Opportunity Act: An Implementation Guide* (Hauppauge, NY: Nova Science Publishers, 2006); "African Growth and Opportunity Act," Title I of Trade and Development Act of 2000, Public Law No. 106-200, H.R. 434, 106th Cong., 1st Sess. (May 18, 2000).

27. International Labor Organization, "CEACR: Individual Observation concerning Convention No. 87, Freedom of Association and Protection of the Right to Organize, 1948 Mauritania (Ratification: 1961)," 1994; International Labor Organization, "ILCCR: Examination of Individual Case concerning Convention No. 87, Freedom of Association and Protection of the Right to Organize, 1948 Mauritania (Ratification: 1961)," 1993.

28. US House of Representatives, Committee on Ways and Means, 107th Cong., "Overview and Compilation of U.S. Trade Statutes," 2001; US President Bill Clinton, "Presidential Proclamation 6575: To Modify Duty-free Treatment under the Generalized System of Preferences and for Other Purposes," June 25, 1993.

29. L'Etat de Droit, "Mauritania: Key Events," http://www.etat.sciencespobordeaux.fr/_anglais/chronologie/mauritania.html (accessed May 1, 2012).

Mauritania, including the Continued Practice of Chattel Slaveryp. 142, 104th Cong., 2nd Sess. (July 1996).

248 • Notes to Chapter 8

30. US Congress, House, *Regarding the Human Rights Situation in Mauritania, including the Continued Practice of Chattel Slavery*, H.Con.Res. 142, 104th
Cong., 2nd Sess. (July 1996).

31. The Human Rights, Refugee, and Other Foreign Relations Provisions Act,
Public Law No. 104-319, 110 Stat. 3864 (October 19, 1996).

32. US Department of State, "1997 Country Reports on Human Rights Practices: Mauritania," January 30, 1998.

33. US Department of State, "1997 Country Reports on Human Rights Practices: Mauritania"; International Labor Organization, "Mauritania: Ratification
Status of Up-to-date Conventions," http://www.ilo.org/ilolex/cgi-lex/ratifgroupe
.pl?class=g03&country=Mauritania (accessed May 1, 2012).

34. US Department of State, "1998 Country Reports on Human Rights Practices: Mauritania," February 26, 1999; US Department of State, "2000 Country
Reports on Human Rights Practices: Mauritania," February 23, 2001.

35. "Mauritania: President Receives Chinese Trade Vice-Minister, US, IMF Officials," BBC Monitoring, Middle East, May 18, 1998.

36. "Office of the United States Trade Representative," *Federal Register* 64,
no. 130 (July 8, 1999): 36952–55. Benefits were officially restored on September 1, 1999. US Department of State, "1999 Country Reports on Human Rights
Practices: Mauritania," February 25, 2000; US House of Representatives, Committee on Ways and Means, 107th Cong., "Overview and Compilation of U.S.
Trade Statutes," 2001.

37. "Iraq Says Mauritania Severed Ties to Please US," Agence France Presse,
November 5, 1999; M. Lee, "Mauritania Becomes Third Arab Nation to Recognize Israel," Agence France Presse, October 28, 1999.

38. International Labor Organization, "Ratifications of the Fundamental
Human Rights Conventions by Country"; Office of the US Trade Representa-
tive, *African Growth and Opportunity Act: An Implementation Guide*; "African
Growth and Opportunity Act."

39. For a discussion of the legality of this approach, see Anthony E. Cassima-
tis, *Human Rights Related Trade Measures under International Law* (Leiden, The
Netherlands: Martinus Nijhoff Publishers, 2007).

40. For examples led by European governments, see Barbara Brandtner and
Allan Rosas, "Trade Preferences and Human Rights," in *The EU and Human
Rights*, ed. Philip Alston, Mara Bustelo, and James Heenan (New York: Oxford
University Press, 1999), 699–722; Hadewych Hazelzet, "Carrots or Sticks? EU
and U.S. Reactions to Human Rights Violations (1989–2000)" (PhD diss., Eu-
ropean University Institute, 2001); Elena Fierro, *The EU's Approach to Human
Rights Conditionality in Practice* (The Hague: Martinus Nijhoff Publishers,
2003); Lorand Bartels, *Human Rights Conditionality in the EU's International
Agreements* (Oxford: Oxford University Press, 2005); Emilie M. Hafner-Burton,
*Forced to Be Good: Why Trade Agreements Boost Human Rights* (Ithaca, NY:
Cornell University Press, 2009).

41. Ann Devroy, "Clinton Grants China MFN, Reversing Campaign Pledge,"
*Washington Post*, May 27, 1994.

42. Lisa L. Martin, *Coercive Cooperation: Explaining Multilateral Economic
Sanctions* (Princeton, NJ: Princeton University Press, 1993).

43. Deborah Brautigam and Adama Gaye, "Is Chinese Investment Good for Africa?" *Council on Foreign Relations*, February 20, 2007.

44. *An Overview of the Sudanese Sanctions Regulations*, Title 31, Part 538, US Code of Federal Regulations, July 25, 2008; European Commission, "European Union, Restrictive Measures (Sanctions) in Force," December 14, 2011.

45. Peter S. Goodman, "China Invests Heavily in Sudan's Oil Industry," *Washington Post*, December 23, 2004, A01; Adam Taylor, "China Just Invested $8 Billion in South Sudan," *Business Insider*, April 30, 2012, http://www.business insider.com/china-south-sudan-oil-2012-4 (accessed May 2, 2012).

46. Jonathan Mercer, "Emotional Beliefs," *International Organization* 64, no. 1 (2010): 1–31.

47. Johan Galtung, "On the Effects of International Economic Sanctions: With Examples from the Case of Rhodesia," *World Politics* 19, no. 3 (April 1967): 378–416.

48. Mark A. R. Kleiman, *When Brute Force Fails: How to Have Less Crime and Punishment* (Princeton, NJ: Princeton University Press, 2009). See also chapters 2 and 3.

49. US Department of State, "2004 Country Reports on Human Rights Practices: Oman," February 28, 2005.

50. US Congress, House, Trade Act of 2002, 107th Cong., 2nd Sess., July 26, 2002; Hafner-Burton, *Forced to Be Good*.

51. Mary Jane Bolle, "U.S.–Oman Free Trade Agreement," CRS Report for Congress, October 10, 2006.

52. "Response from the Sultanate of Oman to the House Ways and Means Trade Subcommittee Minority Staff," January 4, 2006, quoted in Bolle, "U.S.–Oman Free Trade Agreement."

53. "Letter from Ambassador Hunaina Al-Mughairy, Omani Ambassador to the United States, to the Minority Chief Counsel of the Trade Subcommittee, House Ways and Means Committee, Accompanying Response from the Sultanate of Oman to the House Ways and Means Trade Subcommittee Minority Staff," January 4, 2006, quoted in Bolle, "U.S.–Oman Free Trade Agreement."

54. Qaboos bin Sa'id, Sultan of Oman, Royal Decree 74/2006, Amending Some Provisions of the Labor Law, 2006; "Letter of Omani Ambassador Hunaina Al-Mughairy regarding Royal Decree 74/2006 Signed by Qaboos bin Sa'id, Sultan of Oman, July 12, 2006," quoted in Bolle, "U.S.–Oman Free Trade Agreement." For later labor law improvements, see Qaboos bin Sa'id, Sultan of Oman, Royal Decree No. 112/2006 Amending Some Provisions of the Labour Code, 2006; Qaboos bin Sa'id, Sultan of Oman, Royal Decree No. 63/2009 Amending Some Provisions of the Labour Code, 2009; Ministerial Decree No. 561/2009 Establishing the Rules for Non-implementation of the Legal Proceedings Contained in the Offences Set Out in the Labour Code, 2009; Qaboos bin Sa'id, Royal Decree No. 113 of 2011 Amending Certain Provisions of the Labour Law, 2011.

55. In spring 2006, the US Senate Finance Committee amended the trade agreement with a provision prohibiting any trade benefits for goods made "with slave labor . . . or with the benefits of human trafficking." The Finance Committee was responding to reports by the National Labor Committee that Jordan was using sweatshop labor in several production plants for merchandise being exported to

the United States, and that similar practices could take place in other countries that sign trade agreements, including Oman. "Letter from Maqbool Ali Sultan, Minister of Commerce and Industry of the Sultanate of Oman to USTR Robert Portman on May 8, 2006," quoted in Bolle, "U.S.–Oman Free Trade Agreement."

56. In 2008, the government created a human rights commission and passed a comprehensive law to combat trafficking in persons. US Department of State, "2008 Human Rights Report: Oman," February 25, 2009.

57. Hafner-Burton, *Forced to Be Good*.

58. Pamela Jordan, "Does Membership Have Its Privileges? Entrance into the Council of Europe and Compliance with Human Rights Norms," *Human Rights Quarterly* 25 (2003) 660–88.

59. Chris Rumford, "Human Rights and Democratization in Turkey in the Context of EU Candidature," *Journal of Contemporary European Studies* 9, no. 1 (2001): 93–105.

60. European Council, "Council Decision of 8 March 2001 on the Principles, Priorities, Intermediate Objectives, and Conditions Contained in the Accession Partnership with the Republic of Turkey," 2001/235/EC, March 24, 2001, 10. From 2000 to 2006, preaccession aid came from the following programs: Phare, SAPARD, IPSA, Phare Cross-Border Cooperation and Coordination, preaccession financial assistance for Turkey, and CARDS. In 2007, conditional funding was consolidated under the Instrument for Pre-accession Assistance. Europa, Summaries of EU Legislation, "Instrument for Pre-accession Assistance," http://europa .eu/legislation_summaries/agriculture/enlargement/e50020_en.htm (accessed May 2, 2012); William Hale, "Human Rights, the European Union, and the Turkish Accession Process," *Turkish Studies* 4, no. 1 (2003): 108.

61. European Council, "Council Decision of 8 March 2001 on the Principles, Priorities, Intermediate Objectives, and Conditions Contained in the Accession Partnership with the Republic of Turkey." The commission's exact requirement was to "remove any legal provisions forbidding the use by Turkish citizens of their mother tongue in TV/radio broadcasting."

62. Commission of the European Communities, "2001, Regular Report on Turkey's Progress towards Accession," SEC(2001) 1756, November 13, 2001, 19.

63. Commission of the European Communities, "2001, Regular Report on Turkey's Progress towards Accession," 24.

64. European Commission, "Turkey 2005 Progress Report," SEC (2005) 1426, November 9, 2005, 4; Commission of the European Communities, "Communication from the Commission to the Council and the European Parliament, Recommendation of the European Commission on Turkey's Progress towards Accession," Brussels, COM(2004) 656 final, October 6, 2004.

65. "The Eurozone Crisis Live: EU Summit Optimism Tested by Record Unemployment," *Guardian*, Business Blog, January 31, 2012, http://www.guardian .co.uk/business/2012/jan/31/eurozone-debt-crisis-summit-greece (accessed May 2, 2012).

66. European Council, "Council Decision of 18 February 2008 on the Principles, Priorities, and Conditions Contained in the Accession Partnership with the Republic of Turkey and Repealing Decision 2006/35/EC," 2008/157/EC, February 26, 2008; European Commission, Enlargement, "Turkey: Financial As-

sistance," http://ec.europa.eu/enlargement/candidate-countries/turkey/financial
-assistance/index_en.htm (accessed May 2, 2012).

67. European Commission, Enlargement, Project Fiche, "Call, Don't Be Silent!"
http://ec.europa.eu/enlargement/pdf/projects-in-focus/selected_project/turkey_
call-don-t-be-silent_en.pdf (accessed May 2, 2012).

68. Commission of the European Communities, "Communication from the
Commission to the European Parliament and the Council, Enlargement Strategy,
and Main Challenges, 2009–2010," COM(2009) 533 final, October 14, 2009.

69. Emilie M. Hafner-Burton, "Sticks and Stones: Naming and Shaming the
Human Rights Enforcement Problem," *International Organization* 62, no. 4
(2008): 689–716; Emilie M. Hafner-Burton, Susan D. Hyde, and Ryan S. Jablonski, "When Governments Use Election Violence to Stay in Power," *British Journal
of Political Science* (2013).

70. US Department of State, "2009 Human Rights Report: Oman," April 8,
2010.

71. US Department of State, "2010 Human Rights Report: Turkey," April 8,
2011. Certainly, ongoing human rights abuses are not the only problem keeping
Turkey out of the European Union. Nevertheless, the case illustrates the enormous potential to use rewards to protect human rights as well as the serious
limitations.

72. Esther Pan, "Turkey's EU Bid," Council on Foreign Relations, September
30, 2005.

73. Sahin Alpay, "How Badly does Turkey Want Membership in the European
Union?" *Today's Zaman*, April 12, 2010.

## Chapter 9. Nongovernmental Organizations

1. Makau Mutua, *Human Rights: A Political and Cultural Critique* (Philadelphia: University of Pennsylvania Press, 2002); Makau Mutua, "Standard Setting
in Human Rights: Critique and Prognosis," *Human Rights Quarterly* 29 (2007):
547–630; Makau Mutua, "Human Rights in Africa: The Limited Promise of Liberalism," *African Studies Review* 51, no. 1 (2008): 17–39; Mark Mazower, "The
End of Civilization and the Rise of Human Rights: The Mid-Twentieth-Century
Disjuncture," in *Human Rights in the Twentieth Century*, ed. Stefan-Ludwig
Hoffmann (New York: Cambridge University Press, 2011), 29–44. On "human
rights imperialism" and hegemony, see Peter Erlinder, "Human Rights or 'Human
Rights Imperialism'? Lessons from the War against Yugoslavia," *Guild Practi-
tioner* 57, no. 76 (2000): 76–92; Balakrishnan Rajagopal, *International Law
from Below: Development, Social Movements, and Third World Resistance* (New
York: Cambridge University Press, 2003); Antony Anghie, *Imperialism, Sovereignty, and the Making of International Law* (New York: Cambridge University
Press, 2005).

2. Daniel M. Goldstein, *Outlawed: Between Justice and Rights in a Bolivian
City* (Durham, NC: Duke University Press, 2012); Sally Engle Merry, "Trans-
national Human Rights and Local Activism: Mapping the Middle," *American
Anthropologist* 108, no. 1 (March 2006): 38–51; Amitav Acharya, "How Ideas
Spread: Whose Norms Matter? Norm Localization and Institutional Change in
Asian Regionalism," *International Organization* 58, no. 2 (Spring 2004): 245.

My use of the term localization is inspired by, but differs somewhat, from Acharya's, which holds that "the role of local actors is more crucial than that of outside actors." I make no such valuation.

3. Goldstein, *Outlawed*.

4. Gay J. McDougall, "A Decade in Human Rights Law: Decade of NGO Struggle," in "A Decade in Human Rights Law," *Human Rights Brief* 11, no. 3 (Spring 2004): 15.

5. Chidi Anselm Odinkalu, "Why More Africans Don't Use Human Rights Language," *Human Rights Dialogue: Carnegie Council on Ethics and International Affairs* 2, no. 1 (Winter 2000): 4.

6. James Ron, *Spreading the Word: Human Rights Organizations in the Global South*, Draft manuscript 2012.

7. Daniel A. Bell and Joseph H. Carens, "The Ethical Dilemmas of International Human Rights and Humanitarian NGOs: Reflections on a Dialogue between Practitioners and Theorists," *Human Rights Quarterly* 26, no. 2 (May 2004): 300–329. On how international NGOs accept, adapt, and contest norms, see Aaron P. Boesenecker and Leslie Vinjamuri, "Lost in Translation? Civil Society, Faith-Based Organizations, and the Negotiation of International Norms," *International Journal of Transitional Justice* 5, no. 3 (2011): 345–65.

8. Ron, *Spreading the Word*.

9. Goldstein, *Outlawed*.

10. Birgit Lindsnæs, Hans-Otto Sano, and Hatla Thelle, "Human Rights in Action: Supporting Human Rights Work in Authoritarian Countries," in *Ethics in Action: The Ethical Challenges of International Human Rights Nongovernmental Organizations*, ed. Daniel A. Bell and Jean-Marc Coicaud (New York: Cambridge University Press, 2007), 127.

11. Acharya, "How Ideas Spread"; Ron, *Spreading the Word*.

12. Eric Werker and Faisal Ahmed, "What Do Nongovernmental Organizations Do?" *Journal of Economic Perspectives* 22, no. 2 (2008): 73–92.

13. Ron, *Spreading the Word*.

14. Michael Edwards and David Hulme, *Non-governmental Organizations—Performance and Accountability: Beyond the Magic Bullet* (London: Earthscan, 1996); Lisa Jordan and Peter Van Tuijl, *NGO Accountability: Politics, Principles, and Innovations* (London: Earthscan, 2006).

15. Daniel C. Thomas, *The Helsinki Effect: International Norms, Human Rights, and the Demise of Communism* (Princeton, NJ: Princeton University Press, 2001); Jeri Laber, *The Courage of Strangers: Coming of Age with the Human Rights Movement* (New York: Public Affairs, 2005); Edward Cleary, *Mobilizing for Human Rights in Latin America* (Bloomfield, CT: Kumarian Press, 2007).

16. Kathryn Sikkink, "Human Rights, Principled Issue-Networks, and Sovereignty in Latin America," *International Organization* 47, no. 3 (Summer 1993): 411–41; Alison Brysk, "From Above and Below: Social Movements, the International System, and Human Rights in Argentina," *Comparative Political Studies* 26, no. 3 (October 1993): 259–85; Lisa Martin and Kathryn Sikkink, "U.S. Policy and Human Rights in Argentina and Guatemala, 1973–1980," in *Double-edged*

*Diplomacy: International Bargaining and Domestic Politics*, ed. Peter Evans, Harold Jacobson, and Robert Putnam (Berkeley: University of California Press, 1993), 330–62; Alison Brysk, *From Tribal Village to Global Village: Indian Rights and International Relations in Latin America* (Stanford, CA: Stanford University Press, 2000); Ron, *Spreading the Word.*

17. Bell and Carens, "The Ethical Dilemmas of International Human Rights and Humanitarian NGOs."

18. Brigitte I. Hamm, "A Human Rights Approach to Development," *Human Rights Quarterly* 23, no. 4 (2001): 1005–31; Paul J. Nelson and Ellen Dorsey, "At the Nexus of Human Rights and Development: New Methods and Strategies of Global NGOs," *World Development* 31, no. 12 (2003): 2013–26.

19. Ron, *Spreading the Word.*

20. Comadres, http://www.comadres.org/main_english.html (accessed May 4, 2012).

21. Women of Zimbabwe Arise! http://wozazimbabwe.org/ (accessed May 4, 2012).

22. Amnesty International USA, "Still Fighting Despite the Odds," http://www.amnestyusa.org/our-work/cases/zimbabwe-women-of-zimbabwe-arise?id=1361020 (accessed May 4, 2012).

23. "Commemorating the Zimbabwe People's Charter," Media Centre, January 25, 2012, http://www.mediacentrezim.com/index.php?option=com_content&view=article&id=167:commemorating-the-zimbabwe-people-charter&catid=3:feature (accessed May 4, 2012).

24. National Campaign on Dalit Human Rights, http://www.ncdhr.org.in/ (accessed May 4, 2012).

25. Margaret E. Keck and Kathryn Sikkink, *Activists beyond Borders: Advocacy Networks in International Politics* (Ithaca, NY: Cornell University Press, 1998).

26. Marysa Navarro, "The Personal Is Political: Las Madres de Plaza de Mayo," in *Power and Popular Protest: Latin American Social Movements*, ed. Susan Eckstein (Berkeley: University of California Press, 2001), 241–58.

27. Brysk, "From Above and Below."

28. Sikkink, "Human Rights, Principled Issue-Networks, and Sovereignty in Latin America."

29. Keck and Sikkink, *Activists beyond Borders.*

30. Roberta Cohen, "Human Rights Diplomacy: The Carter Administration and the Southern Cone," *Human Rights Quarterly,* 4, no. 2 (Summer 1982): 212–42.

31. Section 620B of the Foreign Assistance Act of 1961, 22 U.S.C. Sec. 2372n (Supp. II 1978); International Security Assistance Act of 1977, H.R. 6884, 95th Cong. (August 5, 1977), "Prohibits, Subject to Presidential Waiver, Military Assistance, and Training Foreign Military Sales Credits and Sales, and Deliveries of Military Equipment Financed by the U.S. Government to Argentina."

32. Navarro, "The Personal Is Political," in *Power and Popular Protest*, ed. Eckstein.

33. Brysk, "From Above and Below," 274.

34. David P. Forsythe, *Human Rights and U.S. Foreign Policy: Congress Reconsidered* (Gainesville: University Press of Florida, 1988), 107.

35. Sikkink, "Human Rights, Principled Issue-Networks, and Sovereignty in Latin America."

36. Acharya, "How Ideas Spread."

37. Jorge I. Dominguez, "The Secrets of Castro's Staying Power," *Foreign Affairs* 72, no. 2 (Spring 1993): 97–107; Omar Sanchez, "The Sanctions Malaise: The Case of Cuba," *International Journal* 58, no. 2 (Spring 2003): 347–72; Julia E. Sweig, "Fidel's Final Victory," *Foreign Affairs* 86, no. 1 (January–February 2007); Jorge G. Castaneda, "Morning in Latin America," *Foreign Affairs* (September–October 2008); Brookings Institution, "Cuban American Opinions concerning U.S. Policy toward Cuba and Recent U.S. Election, 2008 Cuba Poll Digest," 2008.

38. Peter Spiro, "NGOs and Human Rights: Channels of Power," in *Research Handbook on International Human Rights Law*, ed. Sarah Joseph and Adam McBeth (Cheltenham, UK: Edward Elgar, 2010), 115–38.

39. This comment was made at Ethics in Action: The Successes, Compromises, and Setbacks of Transnational Human Rights and Humanitarian NGOs conference, New York, February 2002. See also Bell and Carens, "The Ethical Dilemmas of International Human Rights and Humanitarian NGOs."

40. Frances A. Althaus, "Female Circumcision: Rite of Passage or Violation of Rights?" *International Family Planning Perspectives* 23, no. 3 (September 1997): 130–33.

41. World Health Organization, "Fact Sheet: Female Genital Mutilation," February 2010, http://www.who.int/mediacentre/factsheets/fs241/en/ (accessed May 4, 2012).

42. Virginia L. Barnes and Janice Boddy, *Aman: The Story of a Somali Girl* (Toronto: Knopf, 1994), 280.

43. Tostan: Community-Led Development, http://www.tostan.org (accessed May 4, 2012).

44. Celia Dugger, "Senegal Curbs a Bloody Rite for Girls and Women," *New York Times*, October 15, 2011.

45. Nafissatou J. Diop et al., "The TOSTAN Program: Evaluation of a Community-Based Education Program in Senegal," Population Council, August 2004, http://www.popcouncil.org/pdfs/frontiers/FR_FinalReports/Senegal_Tostan%20FGC.pdf (accessed May 7, 2012); Nafissatou Diop, Amadou Moreau, and Hélène Benga, "Evaluation of the Long-term Impact of the TOSTAN Programme on the Abandonment of FGM/C and Early Marriage: Results from a Qualitative Study in Senegal," Population Council, January 2008, http://www.popcouncil.org/pdfs/frontiers/FR_FinalReports/Senegal_TOSTAN_EarlyMarriage.pdf (accessed May 7, 2012); UNICEF, "Long-term Evaluation of the Tostan Programme in Senegal: Kolda, Thies, and Fatick Regions" (working paper, Section of Statistics and Monitoring, Division of Policy and Practice, 2008), http://www.childinfo.org/files/fgmc_tostan_eng.pdf (accessed May 7, 2012). See also Gerry Mackie and John LeJeune, "Social Dynamics of Abandonment of Harmful Practices: A New Look at the Theory," (working paper no. 2009-06, UNICEF Innocenti Research Centre, Special Series on Social Norms and Harmful Practices), May 2009.

46. Molly Melching, "A Powerful New Opportunity to End Female Genital Cutting in Senegal," *Huffington Post*, February 24, 2012, http://www.huffington-post.com/molly-melching/a-powerful-new-opportunit_b_475046.html (accessed May 7, 2012).

47. Nafissatou J. Diop et al., "Experience from a Community-Based Education Program in Burkina Faso: The Tostan Program," Population Council, September 2004, http://www.popcouncil.org/pdfs/frontiers/FR_FinalReports/BurkinaFaso_FGC.pdf (accessed May 7, 2012).

48. "Sierra Leone: Child and Maternal Mortality Worst in the World—UNICEF," *IRIN*, March 3, 2008.

49. Amnesty International, "Maternal Death Rate in Sierra Leone Is a 'Human Rights Emergency,' " September 21, 2009.

50. Amnesty International, "Thousands Unite to End Maternal Mortality in Sierra Leone," September 23, 2009.

51. Issa Davies, "Sierra Leone Announces Free Health Care for Mothers and Children," UNICEF, April 27, 2010.

52. John Mw Makumbe, "Is There a Civil Society in Africa?" *International Affairs* 74, no. 2 (April 1998): 305–19.

53. Harri Englund, *Prisoners of Freedom: Human Rights and the African Poor* (Berkeley: University of California Press, 2006).

54. Oliver Walton, "Conflict, Peacebuilding, and NGO Legitimacy: National NGOs in Sri Lanka," *Conflict, Security, and Development* 8, no. 1 (March 2008): 133–67.

55. Human Rights Watch, "Ethiopia," in *World Report 2011* (New York: Human Rights Watch, 2011): 121–26; African Rights Monitor, "Submission from African Rights Monitor to the Committee on the Elimination of All Forms of Discrimination against Women, July 2011, New York, Related to the Discussion of the Country Situation in Ethiopia and Its Performance in Upholding the Convention on the Elimination of All Forms of Discrimination against Women," July 2011.

56. Amnesty International, *Ethiopia: Briefing to the UN Committee on the Elimination of Discrimination against Women, 49th Session* (London: Amnesty International Publications, 2011).

57. US Department of State, "2010 Human Rights Reports: Ethiopia," April 8, 2011. Appeals for the reinstatement of blocked funds were denied in October 2011. Eden Sahle, "Ethiopia: Women Lawyers Denied Access to Foreign Funds," *Addis Fortune*, November 14, 2011.

58. For the Ethiopian government's position, see Government Communication Affairs Office, "Ethiopia's Response to the U.S. State Department Report on the Human Rights Situation in Ethiopia," 2009, http://www.aigaforum.com/ethiopia_esponse_to_us_state_dept_report_2009_part1.pdf (accessed May 7, 2012); Peter Heinlein, "Ethiopia Declines to Respond to U.S. Rights Charges," *Voice of America*, April 24, 2011.

59. "Zimbabwe: Mugabe Threatens to Ban NGOs Again," *IRIN*, July 29, 2009.

60. Clifford Bob, *The Marketing of Rebellion* (New York: Cambridge University Press, 2005).

61. Peter Uvin, *Aiding Violence: The Development Enterprise in Rwanda* (West Hartford, CT: Kumarian Press, 1998).

62. Obiora Chinedu Okafor, *Legitimizing Human Rights NGOs: Lessons from Nigeria* (Trenton, NJ: Africa World Press, Inc., 2006).

63. Ron, *Spreading the Word.*

64. Englund, *Prisoners of Freedom.*

65. Okafor, *Legitimizing Human Rights NGOs.*

66. Englund, *Prisoners of Freedom.*

67. Reza Afshari, "An Essay on Islamic Cultural Relativism in the Discourse of Human Rights," *Human Rights Quarterly* 16 (1994): 235–76; Fred Halliday, "Relativism and Universalism in Human Rights: The Case of the Islamic Middle East," *Political Studies* 43 (1995): 152–67; Abdullahi An-Na'im, Interview, "Problems of Dependency: Human Rights Organizations in the Arab World," *Middle East Report* 214 (Spring 2000): 20–23, 46–47.

68. "Egyptian Rights Group 'Cannot Protect Gays,'" BBC, February 11, 2002.

69. Okafor, *Legitimizing Human Rights NGOs.*

70. Doug McAdam, John D. McCarthy, and Mayer N. Zald, "Introduction: Opportunities, Mobilizing Structures, and Processes—Toward a Synthetic, Comparative Perspective on Social Movements," in *Comparative Perspectives on Social Movements: Political Opportunities, Mobilizing Structures, and Cultural Framings,* ed. Doug McAdam, John D. McCarthy, and Mayer N. Zald (Cambridge: Cambridge University Press, 1996), 1–20.

71. An-Na'im, Interview, "Problems of Dependency.

72. Grantmakers for Effective Organizations, "Evaluation in Philanthropy: Perspectives from the Field," 2009, http://www.geofunders.org/storage/documents/Evaluation_in_Philanthropy_--_GEO_COF.pdf (accessed May 8, 2012).

73. Hugo Slim, "By What Authority: The Legitimacy and Accountability of Non-governmental Organisations" (working paper, International Council on Human Rights Policy, January 2002).

74. Council on Foundations and European Foundation Center, "Principles of Accountability for International Philanthropy," April 2007.

75. Emilie M. Hafner-Burton and Mark A. Pollack, "Mainstreaming Gender in Global Governance," *European Journal of International Relations* 8, no. 3 (September 2002): 339–73.

76. Sidney Tarrow, *Power in Movement: Social Movements and Contentious Politics,* 2nd ed. (New York: Cambridge University Press, 1998).

77. Herbert Kitschelt, "Political Opportunity Structures and Political Protest: Anti-nuclear Movements in Four Democracies," *British Journal of Political Science* 16 (1986): 57–85.

78. Uvin, *Aiding Violence,* 171.

## Chapter 10. National Human Rights Institutions

1. UN Office of the High Commissioner for Human Rights, "National Human Rights Institutions: History, Principles, Roles, and Responsibilities" (Geneva: United Nations, 2010), 13.

2. Jeong-Woo Koo and Francisco O. Ramirez, "National Incorporation of Global Human Rights: Worldwide Expansion of National Human Rights Insti-

tutions, 1966–2004," *Social Forces* 87 (2009): 1321–54; International Coordinating Committee of National Institutions for the Promotion and Protection of Human Rights, "Directory of Institutions: Global," December 2010, available at http://nhri.ohchr.org/EN/Contact/NHRIs/Pages/default.aspx (accessed July 25, 2012).

3. Linda C. Reif, "The Shifting Boundaries of NHRI Definition in the International System," in *Human Rights, State Compliance, and Social Change: Assessing National Human Rights Institutions*, ed. Ryan Goodman and Thomas Pegram (New York: Cambridge University Press, 2012), 52–73.

4. Linda C. Reif, *The Ombudsman, Good Governance, and the International Human Rights System* (Leiden, The Netherlands: Martinus Nijhoff Publishers, 2004), 2. On Albania, see People's Advocate, http://www.avokatipopullit.gov.al/?lang=en (accessed May 8, 2012). On Bermuda, see Office of the Ombudsman for Bermuda, http://www.ombudsman.bm/ (accessed May 8, 2012).

5. On Slovenia, see Human Rights Ombudsman of the Republic of Slovenia, http://www.varuh-rs.si/index.php?L=6 (accessed May 8, 2012). On Georgia, see Public Defender of Georgia, http://www.ombudsman.ge (accessed May 8, 2012). On Peru, see Defensoría del Pueblo, http://www.defensoria.gob.pe/ (accessed May 8, 2012).

6. Peru, Ley Orgánica de la Defensoría del Pueblo, Ley No. 26520 (1995).

7. Catherine Conaghan, *Fujimori's Peru: Deception in the Public Sphere* (Pittsburgh: University of Pittsburgh Press, 2005).

8. Charles D. Kenney, "Horizontal Accountability: Concepts and Conflicts," in *Democratic Accountability in Latin America*, ed. Scott Mainwaring and Christopher Welna (New York: Oxford University Press, 2003), 55–76.

9. Thomas Pegram, "Weak Institutions, Rights Claims, and Pathways to Compliance: The Transformative Role of the Peruvian Human Rights Ombudsman" (working paper no. 78, Center for Research on Inequality, Human Security, and Ethnicity, May 2010), 6.

10. This data—compiled into a tool called the "defensometro"—was available online until March 2012, and is currently available by request only from the ombudsman.

11. Enrique Peruzzotti and Catalina Smulovitz, eds., *Enforcing the Rule of Law: Societal Accountability in the New Latin American Democracies* (Pittsburgh: University of Pittsburgh Press, 2006).

12. Defensoría del Pueblo, "Difusión y Promoción de Derechos," http://www.defensoria.gob.pe/difusion-promocion.php?vd=3973#vdo (accessed May 8, 2012).

13. Republic of Namibia, Constitution of Namibia, (1990). The following link for Namibia's ombusdman is not active as of May 2012: Office of the Ombudsman, http://www.ombudsman.org.na/ (accessed May 8, 2012). For information on the ombudsman, see Electoral Institute for the Sustainability of Democracy in Africa, "Namibia: Office of the Ombudsman," December 2009, http://www.eisa.org.za/WEP/namagency.htm (accessed May 8, 2012).

14. Reif, *The Ombudsman, Good Governance, and the International Human Rights System*.

15. John Walters, "The Protection and Promotion of Human Rights in Namibia: The Constitutional Mandate of the Ombudsman," University of Namibia,

http://www.unam.na/centres/hrdc/6_the_protection_and_promotion_of_human_rights_in_Namibia.pdf (accessed May 8, 2012).

16. Werner Menges, "Walters Is New Ombudsman," *Namibian*, June 21, 2004.

17. Walters, "The Protection and Promotion of Human Rights in Namibia: The Constitutional Mandate of the Ombudsman," 128; Rutgers School of Arts and Sciences, "Center for Women's Global Leadership," http://16dayscwgl.rutgers.edu/ (accessed July 25, 2012).

18. International Council on Human Rights Policy and Office of the High Commissioner of Human Rights, *Assessing the Effectiveness of National Human Rights Institutions* (Versoix, Switzerland: International Council on Human Rights Policy, 2005); Richard Carver and Alexey Korotaev, "Assessing the Effectiveness of National Human Rights Institutions" (report, UN Development Program Regional Center, Bratislava, October 2007); Julie Mertus, *Human Rights Matters: Local Politics and National Human Rights Institutions* (Stanford, CA: Stanford University Press, 2009); Goodman and Pegram, *Human Rights, State Compliance, and Social Change.*

19. Australian Agency for International Development, "Human Rights and Australia's Aid Program."

20. Canadian Human Rights Commission, http://www.chrc-ccdp.ca/default-eng.aspx (accessed May 8, 2012); Sonia Cardenas, "Transgovernmental Activism: Canada's Role in Promoting National Human Rights Commissions," *Human Rights Quarterly* 25, no. 3 (August 2003): 775–90; Alison Brysk, *Global Good Samaritans: Human Rights as Foreign Policy* (Oxford: Oxford University Press, 2009).

21. On NHRIs' role in promoting international human rights norms in domestic political systems, see Goodman and Pegram, *Human Rights, State Compliance, and Social Change.*

22. Ghana, Commission on Human Rights and Administrative Justice Act, Act 456 (1993); Constitution of the Republic of Ghana, 1992, Article 216.

23. International Council on Human Rights Policy, *Performance and Legitimacy: National Human Rights Institutions* (Versoix, Switzerland: International Council on Human Rights Policy, 2000).

24. For criticisms, see Behind the Mask, the Voice of Africa's LBGTI Community, "Ghana Chief Says She Will Not Fight for the Rights of the Homosexuals," http://www.mask.org.za/ghana-rights-chief-says-she-will-not-fight-for-the-rights-of-homosexuals/ (accessed May 8, 2012).

25. Henrietta Mensa Bonsu, "Democracy, Good Governance, and Accountability: The Role of the Independent Commissions of Ghana" (mimeo, Accra, 1999), 27.

26. Edudzi Ofori and Chelsea Paradis, "Prisoners' Rights in Ghana" (report prepared for the Journalists for Human Rights, August 12, 2006).

27. "CHRAJ Rescues Mother and Baby from Prison," *Ghanaian Times*, November 23, 2006. Journalists for Human Rights, "Guilty Until Proven Innocent," September 28, 2010.

28. "CHRAJ Is Keen to Stop Trokosi: Ms. Lamptey," Ghana News Agency, August 11, 2011.

29. Nirit Ben-Ari, "Liberating Girls from Trokosi," *Africa Recovery* 15, no. 4 (December 2001): 26.

30. Emile Short, "Powerful Persuasion: Combating Traditional Practices that Violate Human Rights", (Minneapolis, MN: The Center for Victims of Torture, 2007).

31. Short, *Powerful Persuasion*, 6; "CHRAJ Is Keen to Stop Trokosi."

32. The Criminal Code's Act 29 (1998) was amended with Section 314A; "CHRAJ Is Keen to Stop Trokosi."

33. International Council on Human Rights Policy, *Performance and Legitimacy*.

34. "CHRAJ Recommends Anane's Dismissal," Ghana News Agency, September 15, 2006; Anna Bossman, "The Anti-Corruption Mandate of Ghana's Commission on Human Rights," (UN Conference on Anti-corruption Measures, Good Governance, and Human Rights, Warsaw, November 2006).

35. "CHRAJ Wins Appeal against High Court about Corruption Scandal," Ghana to Ghana, March 24, 2011.

36. "M and J Scandal: Gov't Should Aid CHRAJ with Needed Resources," *Daily Graphic*, September 14, 2011.

37. Afghanistan Independent Human Rights Commission, http://www.aihrc. org.af/en/ (accessed May 8, 2012).

38. Afghanistan Independent Human Rights Commission, "Annual Report, January 1–December 31, 2009," 16.

39. Abdul Karim Azizi and Yeseul Christeena Song, "Human Rights Promotion: The Afghanistan Independent Human Rights Commission," in *Human Rights Education in Asia-Pacific, Volume 2* (Osaka: Hurights Osaka, 2011).

40. Afghanistan Independent Human Rights Commission, "1389–1392 (2010–2013) Strategic and Action Plan," March 2010.

41. Afghanistan Independent Human Rights Commission, "Annual Report, January 1–December 31, 2009," 25.

42. Afghanistan Independent Human Rights Commission, "Annual Report, January 1–December 31, 2009," 25, 27.

43. Trilochan Upreti and Lara Griffith, "UN Support to the Afghan Independent Human Rights Commission Project Final Evaluation," (New York: UN Development Program, August 12, 2008); Afghanistan Independent Human Rights Commission, "Women's Rights Unit," http://www.aihrc.org/2010_eng/ Eng_pages/Units/wr.aspx (accessed May 9, 2012).

44. Afghanistan Independent Human Rights Commission, "Annual Report, January 1–December 31, 2009." For critical appraisals, see Human Rights Watch, *Afghanistan: Reject Known Abusers as Police Chiefs: Time for President Karzai to Show He Is a Genuine Reformer* (New York: Human Rights Watch, 2006); Tonita Murray, "Police-Building in Afghanistan: A Case Study of Civil Security Reform," *International Peacekeeping*, 14, no. 1 (2007): 108–26.

45. Anne Smith, "The Unique Position of National Human Rights Institutions: A Mixed Blessing?" *Human Rights Quarterly* 28, no. 4 (November 2006): 904–46; Peter Rosenblum, "Tainted Origins and Uncertain Outcomes: Evaluating NHRIs," in *Human Rights, State Compliance, and Social Change*, ed. Ryan Goodman and Thomas Pegram (New York: Cambridge University Press, 2012), 297–323.

46. Alkarama, "Algeria: The National Institution for Human Rights (CNCP-PDH) in the Hot Seat," May 15, 2009, http://en.alkarama.org/index.php?option=com_content&view=article&id=248 (accessed May 9, 2012).

47. Sonia Cardenas and Andrew Flibbert, "National Human Rights Institutions in the Middle East," *Middle East Journal 59*, no. 3 (Summer 2005): 411–36.

48. Amnesty International, "Algeria," in *Annual Report 2011* (London: Amnesty International Publications, 2011); Algeria-Watch, "Algeria: Harassment against Those Who Struggle for Human Rights Must Stop!" April 25, 2012, http://algeria-watch.org/en/hr/repression/harassment_must_stop.htm (accessed May 9, 2012).

49. Human Rights Watch, *Time for Reckoning: Enforced Disappearances in Algeria* (New York: Human Rights Watch, February 2003).

50. On trust, see Fredrik Uggla, "Through Pressure or Persuasion? Explaining Compliance with the Resolutions of the Bolivian Defensor del Pueblo," in *Human Rights, State Compliance, and Social Change*, ed. Ryan Goodman and Thomas Pegram (New York: Cambridge University Press), 270–96.

51. "What Future Awaits the NHRI?" *Bahrain Monitor*, http://bahrainmonitor .org/in-news/s-031-32-01.html (accessed May 9, 2012).

52. Bahrain Youth Society for Human Rights, "Press Statement on the Establishment of the 'National Human Rights Institution' in Bahrain," May 9, 2010, http://byshr.org/?cat=83 (accessed May 9, 2012).

53. Department of State, "2010 Human Rights Report: Indonesia," April 8, 2011.

54. For legal framework of Komnas HAM, see Indonesia, Presidential Decree No. 50 of 1993, National Commission on Human Rights (1993); Komnas HAM's powers were updated through Law 39 of 1999 and Law 26 of 2000, Indonesia, House of Representatives, Law 39 of 1999 concerning Human Rights (1999); Indonesia, House of Representatives, Law 26 of 2000 Establishing the Ad Hoc Human Rights Court (2000). For more on Komnas HAM's successful protection of land rights, see International Council on Human Rights Policy, *Performance and Legitimacy*.

55. Northern Ireland Human Rights Commission, http://www.nihrc.org/ (accessed May 9, 2012); Julie Mertus, *Human Rights Matters*.

56. Lynn Wartchow, "Civil and Human Rights Violations in Northern Ireland: Effects and Shortcomings of the Good Friday Agreement in Guaranteeing Protections," *Northwestern Journal of International Human Rights* 3 (Spring 2003); Department of Foreign Affairs and Trade, "Anglo-Irish Relations: The Peace Process," http://www.dfa.ie/home/index.aspx?id=334 (accessed May 9, 2012).

57. C. Raj Kumar, "National Human Rights Institutions and Economic, Social, and Cultural Rights: Toward the Institutionalization and Developmentalization of Human Rights," *Human Rights Quarterly* 28 (2006): 755–79.

58. Human Rights Watch, "Protectors or Pretenders? Government Human Rights Protections in Africa," January 1, 2001.

59. Rosenblum, "Tainted Origins and Uncertain Outcomes."

60. UN General Assembly, 85th Plenary Meeting, "National Institutions for the Promotion and Protection of Human Rights" A/RES/48/134, December 20, 1993. For a discussion of the Paris Principles, see Goodman and Pegram, eds., *Human Rights, State Compliance, and Social Change*.

61. UN Development Program and UN Office of the High Commissioner for Human Rights, *UNDP–OHCHR Toolkit for Collaboration with National Human Rights Institutions* (Geneva: United Nations, 2010).

62. UN Office of the High Commissioner for Human Rights, *National Human Rights Institutions: History, Principles, Roles, and Responsibilities.*

63. UN Human Rights Council, "NGO Participation," http://www2.ohchr.org/english/bodies/hrcouncil/ngo.htm (accessed May 9, 2012); UN Human Rights Council, "NHRI Participation," http://www2.ohchr.org/english/bodies/hrcouncil/nhri.htm (accessed May 9, 2012).

64. International Coordinating Committee, National Institutions for the Promotion and Protection of Human Rights, "Chart of the Status of National Institutions," http://nhri.ohchr.org/EN/Documents/Chart%20of%20the%20Status%20of%20NIs%20(30%20May%202012).pdf (accessed May 9, 2012).

65. Amnesty International, "National Human Rights Institutions: Amnesty International's Recommendations on the Effective Protection and Promotion of Human Rights," October 2001.

66. International Coordinating Committee, National Institutions for the Protection and Promotion of Human Rights, "Report and Recommendations of the Session of the Sub-committee on Accreditation (SCA)," Geneva, May 23–27, 2011.

67. Amnesty International, "Nigerian President Signs Landmark Human Rights Bill," March 29, 2011.

68. International Coordinating Committee, National Institutions for the Promotion and Protection of Human Rights, "Chart of the Status of National Institutions"; International Coordinating Committee, National Institutions for the Protection and Promotion of Human Rights, "Report and Recommendations of the Session of the Sub-committee on Accreditation (SCA)," Geneva, October 11–15, 2010.

69. International Coordinating Committee, National Institutions for the Protection and Promotion of Human Rights, "Report and Recommendations of the Session of the Sub-committee on Accreditation (SCA).

70. Catherine Renshaw, Andrew Byrnes, and Andrea Durbach, "Testing the Mettle of National Human Rights Institutions: A Case Study of the Human Rights Commission of Malaysia," *Asian Journal of International Law* 1 (2011): 165–98.

71. Human Rights Watch, "Burma's Continuing Human Rights Challenges," November 3, 2011.

72. Amitav Acharya, "How Ideas Spread: Whose Norms Matter? Norm Localization and Institutional Change in Asian Regionalism," *International Organization* 58, no. 2 (Spring 2004): 239–75; Sally Engle Merry, *Human Rights and Gender Violence: Translating International Law into Local Justice* (Chicago: University of Chicago Press, 2006); Obiora Chinedu Okafor, *Legitimizing Human Rights NGOs: Lessons from Nigeria* (Trenton, NJ: Africa World Press, Inc., 2006).

73. David S. Meyer, "National Human Rights Institutions, Opportunities, and Activism," in *Human Rights, State Compliance, and Social Change*, ed. Ryan Goodman and Thomas Pegram (New York: Cambridge University Press, 2012), 324–34; Thomas Pegram, "National Human Rights Institutions in Latin America: Politics and Institutionalization," in *Human Rights, State Compliance, and*

*Social Change*, ed. Ryan Goodman and Thomas Pegram (New York: Cambridge University Press, 2012), 210–42.

74. Australian Human Rights Commission, "Social Justice Report 2005," 2005.

75. Australian Human Rights Commission, "Close the Gap: Campaign for Indigenous Health Equality," 2011; Australian Government, Department of Families, Housing, Community Services, and Indigenous Affairs, "Closing the Gap: National Partnership Agreements."

76. National Human Rights Commission, New Delhi, http://nhrc.nic.in/ (accessed May 9, 2012).

77. All-India Network of NGOs and Individuals Working with National and State Human Rights Institutions, "An NGO Report on the Compliance with the Paris Principles by the National Human Rights Commission of India," April 2011.

78. National Human Rights Commission, New Delhi, "NHRC, India Comments on AiNNI Report," 2011.

## Chapter 11. Triage

1. For one view on this issue, see Thomas Pogge, "Priorities of Global Justice," *Metaphilosophy* 32, nos. 1–2 (January 2001): 6–24.

2. Peter Singer, "Why We Must Ration Health Care," *New York Times*, July 15, 2009, 3.

3. Marc D. Basson, "Choosing among Candidates for Scarce Medical Resources," *Journal of Medicine and Resources* 4 (1979): 313–33.

4. Tom L. Beauchamp and James F. Childress, *Principles of Biomedical Ethics* (Oxford: Oxford University Press, 1994); Valerie G. A. Grossman, *Quick Reference to Triage* (Philadelphia: Lippincott Williams and Wilkins, 2003); Jonathan D. Moreno, *In the Wake of Terror: Medicine and Morality in a Time of Crisis* (Cambridge, MA: MIT Press, 2004); Anna-Karin Andersson, Monica Omberg, and Marianne Svedlund, "Triage in the Emergency Department: A Qualitative Study of the Factors Which Nurses Consider When Making Decisions," *Nursing in Critical Care* 11, no. 3 (May 2006): 136–45; Brian Dolan and Linda Holt, eds., *Accident and Emergency: Theory into Practice* (London: Bailierre Tindall Elsevier, 2008); Emilie M. Hafner-Burton and James Ron, *Human Rights in the Global Underbelly* (working paper, University of California at San Diego, 2010).

5. Jack Goldsmith and Eric Posner, "Human Rights," in *The Limits of International Law* (New York: Oxford University Press, 2005), 107–34.

6. "Obama Presses China on Human Rights," Associated Press, January 19, 2011; "UK's Brown to Raise Human Rights with China," Reuters, August 20, 2008.

7. Emilie M. Hafner-Burton, *Forced to Be Good: Why Trade Agreements Boost Human Rights* (Ithaca, NY: Cornell University Press, 2009).

8. The case was discussed at length, earlier, in chapter 8.

9. "Hillary Clinton in Phuket: ASEAN Urged to Be Open about Human Rights," *Phukett Gazette*, July 23 2009; Howard La Franchi, "Historic Myanmar Trip for Hillary Clinton, Enough Focus on Human Rights?" November 30, 2011; "Burma Releases Pro-democracy Leader Aung San Suu Kyi," BBC, November 13, 2010.

10. Robert A. Senser, "USTR's Initiative on Worker Rights," *Human Rights for Workers*, Blogspot, July 23, 2009, http://humanrightsforworkers.blogspot.com/2009/07/ustrs-initiative-on-worker-rights.html (accessed May 10, 2012); Hafner-Burton, *Forced to Be Good.*

11. "EU to Cut Sri Lanka Trade Benefits over Rights," *EU Business*, February 15, 2010.

12. European Union, Delegation of the European Union to Turkey, "Projects Supported," http://www.avrupa.info.tr/EUCSD,Dihag_Revised.html?pageindex=1 (accessed May 10, 2012).

13. "The Defense of Human Rights in Brazilian Foreign Policy Enters the Presidential Campaigns," INESC, July 2010.

14. James Ron, Howard Ramos, and Kathleen Rodgers, "Transnational Information Politics: NGO Human Rights Reporting, 1986–2000," *International Studies Quarterly* 49, no. 3 (2005): 557–87; Emilie M. Hafner-Burton, "Sticks and Stones: Naming and Shaming the Human Rights Enforcement Problem," *International Organization* 62 (Fall 2008): 689–716.

15. For an example in Israel, see James Ron, "Varying Methods of State Violence," *International Organization* 51, no. 2 (1997): 275–300.

16. UN General Assembly, 3rd Sess., "217 A (III). Universal Declaration of Human Rights," Article 21, A/RES/3/217A, December 10, 1948.

17. Hafner-Burton, "Sticks and Stones." This has happened repeatedly in Zimbabwe under President Mugabe, for example. Barry Bearak, "In Zimbabwe Jail: A Reporter's Ordeal," *New York Times*, April 27, 2008; Emilie M. Hafner-Burton, Susan D. Hyde, and Ryan S. Jablonski, "When Governments Use Election Violence to Stay in Power," *British Journal of Political Science* (2013).

18. Fareed Zakaria, "The Rise of Illiberal Democracy," *Foreign Affairs*, November–December 1997: 22–43; Emilie M. Hafner-Burton, Susan D. Hyde, and Ryan S. Jablonski, "Surviving Elections: Election Violence and Leader Tenure," December 14, 2011, http://papers.ssrn.com/sol3/papers.cfm?abstract_id=1975026 (accessed May 10, 2012); Hafner-Burton, Hyde, and Jablonski, "When Governments Use Election Violence to Stay in Power."

19. US Department of State, "2009 Human Rights Report: Cameroon," March 11, 2010.

20. European Commission, Development and Cooperation—EuropeAid, "European Instrument for Democracy and Human Rights (EIDHR)," http://ec.europa.eu/europeaid/how/finance/eidhr_en.htm (accessed May 10, 2012).

21. Liz Sidoti, "McCain Favors a 'League of Democracies,'" *Washington Post*, April 30, 2007; John McCain, "America Must Be a Good Role Model," *Financial Times*, March 18, 2008; Anne-Marie Slaughter and Jon Ikenberry, "Democracies Must Work in Concert," *Financial Times*, July 10, 2008; Robert Kagan, "The Case for a League of Democracies," *Financial Times*, May 13, 2008.

22. Olson Jr., *The Logic of Collective Action*; Arthur A. Stein, "Coordination and Collaboration: Regimes in an Anarchic World," *International Organization* 36, no. 2 (Spring 1982): 299–324; Barbara Koremenos, Charles Lipson, and Duncan Snidal, eds., *The Rational Design of International Institutions* (New York: IO Foundation, 2001).

23. Hafner-Burton, *Forced to Be Good.*

24. John M. Darley and Bibb Latané, "Bystander Intervention in Emergencies: Diffusion of Responsibility," *Journal of Personality and Social Psychology* 8 (1968): 377–83; John M. Darley and Bibb Latané, "Bystander 'Apathy,'" *American Scientist* 57 (1969): 244–68; "Police Arrest Man in PA. Subway Hammer Attack," Associated Press, September 10, 2008.

25. Michael Barnett, *Eyewitness to Genocide: The United Nations and Rwanda* (Ithaca, NY: Cornell University Press, 2002); "Rwanda: How the Genocide Happened," BBC, December 18, 2008.

26. Mancur Olson Jr., *The Logic of Collective Action: Public Goods and the Theory of Groups* (Cambridge, MA: Harvard University Press, 1965).

27. International Institute for Democracy and Electoral Assistance, http://www.idea.int/ (accessed May 10, 2012).

28. Organization for Economic Co-operation and Development, "Harmonising Donor Practices for Effective Aid Delivery," DAC Guidelines and Reference Series, 2003.

29. Alyson Brysk, *Global Good Samaritans: Human Rights as Foreign Policy* (Oxford: Oxford University Press, 2009).

30. For more on this logic, applied to another area where clubs could make a difference (global warming), see David G. Victor, *Global Warming Gridlocks: Creating More Effective Strategies for Protecting the Planet* (New York: Cambridge University Press, 2011).

31. Loch Johnson, *Seven Sins of American Foreign Policy* (New York: Pearson Longman, 2007).

32. Rodney Bruce Hall, "Moral Authority as a Power Resource," *International Organization* 51, no. 4 (August 1997): 591–622.

33. Professor Steven Greer has made this point about the European court. See Steven Greer, *The European Convention on Human Rights: Achievements, Problems, and Prospects* (New York: Cambridge University Press, 2006).

34. Minerva Initiative, http://minerva.dtic.mil/overview.html (accessed May 11, 2012).

35. Organization for Security and Cooperation in Europe, Office for Democratic Institutions and Human Rights, *Annual Report 2010* (Warsaw: OSCE, Office for Democratic Institutions and Human Rights, 2010).

36. Brysk, *Global Good Samaritans*, 232.

37. "China Hits Back with Report on U.S. Human Rights Record," English. news.cn, April 10, 2011, http://news.xinhuanet.com/english2010/china/2011-04/10/c_13822179.htm (accessed May 11, 2012).

38. Kenneth Roth, "The Charade of U.S. Ratification of International Human Rights Treaties," *Chicago Journal of International Law* 347, no. 1 (2000); Harold Koh, "Why America Should Ratify the Women's Treaty (CEDAW)," *Case Western Reserve of International Law* 34, no. 263 (2002); Amitahh Pal, "United States Should Join the International Criminal Court," *Progressive*, April 1, 2010.

39. Makau Mutua, *Human Rights: A Political and Cultural Critique* (Philadelphia: University of Pennsylvania Press, 2002); Balakrishnan Rajagopal, *International Law from Below: Development, Social Movements, and Third World Resistance* (New York: Cambridge University Press, 2003); Balakrishnan Rajagopal, "Counter-hegemonic International Law: Rethinking Human Rights

and Development as a Third World Strategy," *Third World Quarterly* 27, no. 5 (2006): 767–83; Antony Anghie, *Imperialism, Sovereignty, and the Making of International Law* (Cambridge: Cambridge University Press, 2005).

40. Vivian Salama, "Arabs Back Allied Offensive on Libya as Leader Qaddafi Remains Defiant," *Bloomberg*, March 20, 2011.

41. Alison Brysk, "The Little Country That Could: Costa Rica," in *Global Good Samaritans: Human Rights as Foreign Policy* (Oxford: Oxford University Press), 95–118.

42. Michael Bowman, "Polls Show U.S. Isolationist Sentiment Growing," Voice of America, December 4, 2009.

43. Jhon Dumbrell, "Varieties of Post–Cold War American Isolationism," *Government and Opposition* 34, no. 1 (1999): 24–43; Herbert London, "Recurring U.S. Isolationism and Its Implications," *Human Events*, July 17, 2011.

44. Michael Ignatieff, ed., *American Exceptionalism and Human Rights* (Princeton, NJ: Princeton University Press, 2006).

45. "Americans Strongly Support UN in Principle, despite Reservations about Performance," WorldPublicOpinion.org, May 9, 2007, http://worldpublic opinion.org/pipa/articles/brunitedstatescanadara/356.php?lb=btun&pnt=356& nid=&id= (accessed May 11, 2012).

46. "Human Rights, Promoting International Human Rights," WorldPublic Opinion.org, http://www.americans-world.org/digest/global_issues/human_rights/ PromotingHR.cfm (accessed May 11, 2012).

## Chapter 12. Making More of Law and Power

1. Joachim J. Savelsberg, *Crime and Human Rights: Criminology of Genocide and Atrocities* (Thousand Oaks, CA: Sage Press, 2010).

2. UN Human Rights Council, 9th Sess., "Human Rights and Unilateral Coercive Measures," A/HRC/RES/9/4, September 17, 2008, 2. See chapter 8; Emilie M. Hafner-Burton, *Forced to Be Good: How Trade Agreements Boost Human Rights* (Ithaca, NY: Cornell University Press, 2009).

3. There were two abstentions: Bosnia and Herzegovina and the Republic of Korea.

# Index

Note: Page numbers followed by "f" indicate figures.